DYNAMICS

OF

DEVELOPMENT

An International Development Reader

DYNAMICS
OF
DEVELOPMENT

An International Development Reader

Edited by

GOVE HAMBIDGE

Foreword by Teodoro Moscoso

Introduction by Paul G. Hoffman

FREDERICK A. PRAEGER, *Publishers*

New York

BOOKS THAT MATTER

Published in the United States of America in 1964
by Frederick A. Praeger, Inc., Publishers
111 Fourth Avenue, New York 3, N.Y.

Library of Congress Catalog Card Number: 64-16678

Printed in the United States of America

FOREWORD

TEODORO MOSCOSO

THE APPEARANCE as well as the contents of this book should provide evidence that international development has come of age—as an academic discipline, as a profession, and, most important, as an objective of the national policy of countries that have committed themselves to the strengthening and expansion of freedom.

When I began to experiment in development work in Puerto Rico, it was far from a recognized discipline. We called it *fomento*, which is generally translated as *development*. But the two words do not mean the same thing, and the difference in connotations may hold some lessons for us today.

Development is generally associated with a variety of social and economic objectives, many of which are reflected in the major headings of this book. These specific objectives were isolated and shaped as we gained experience, during the postwar period, with widely varying development problems in countries throughout the southern half of the world. We then began to study the different aspects of development—planning it, paying for it, training people to do it, and all the other subjects covered in this book—and progressively applied the lessons we were learning to the work we were doing in the emerging countries.

Fomento has an earthier ring. Its origin was the political decision of Governor Luis Muñoz Marin to make a massive attack on stagnation in Puerto Rico and to convert the island into a socially healthy and economically prosperous community. The work of *fomento* in the investment of public funds for social and economic infrastructure, in attracting private investment from the United States, and in a host of other fields was made possible by the Governor's success in protecting us "fomentarians" with the shield of his political leadership. The fomentarians were great debaters. We had many night-long arguments over developmental problems and were conversant with the latest literature in this new and exciting field of the social sciences, even though the literature did not help us too much in those days, since it trailed rather than preceded our experience. Our discussions never became dry, for the pervasive presence of the Governor—in person or merely through our awareness of his thinking—never allowed us to lose sight of the fact that development is an intensely political phenomenon.

It is the politician who must decide whether he wants to incur the wrath of the landowners and suffer the effects of capital flight. It is he who must decide how much consumption he will ask the people to forgo in order to increase investment. It is he who must brave the attacks of the young Turks in his own movement when he sits down to make deals with capitalists whose investments are needed for the development of the country. It is the political leader who must distinguish between sterile extremism and genuine nationalism, between arrogant moneymen and progressive investors (both domestic and foreign), between the pressures of groups and the aspirations of the nation, between the distortions of the moment and the shape of the future.

Looking over the panorama of development problems in the world today, we find that the most difficult issues are not technical (developmental, in the ordinary meaning of the word), but political. In some key countries, the reform-monger, to use Albert Hirschmann's phrase, cannot perform his craft unless and until the political leadership of his country has made the decisions and achieved the consensus through which his activities can become relevant and, hopefully, effective.

At the same time, the capital-exporting nations, international lending institutions, and private investors in industrialized countries have some homework of their own to do. Are their expectations of self-help and reform in the developing countries realistic? Is their diplomacy geared to the requirements of political, economic, and social development, or are vestiges of thinking of a dead past still tying their hands? Have they learned to make the distinction between the advice of those in the developing countries whose voices have a familiar ring, but who may no longer be in the mainstream of their country's life, and the advice of those who talk and act in unfamiliar, but not necessarily hostile, ways? Is enough being done to explore and develop new patterns of private investment likely to be more in tune with dominant political trends and thus, in the long run, more secure and mutually profitable?

In each developing nation, the urgent need is either for the perpetuation—the strengthening and refinement—or the resumption of political leadership to provide the shield behind which development can proceed. In our own and other industrial countries, the need is for a thorough and utterly candid review of our own present policies and attitudes, so as to attune them to the political realities and the likely future course of the nations whose development we are pledged to assist.

Only then will the men and women whose research, experience, and wisdom are reflected in the ensuing chapters be afforded the opportunity to perform their chosen task—to make this the decade of development.

Washington, D.C.
December, 1963

PERUSER'S GUIDE

A FEW EDITORIAL explanations may help to guide the peruser's journey through this book.

First, a warning: The reader should wear his historical spectacles. These thirty-two chapters were originally articles in the INTERNATIONAL DEVELOPMENT REVIEW. Except for editing to correct obvious faults—mainly errors in punctuation or spelling—the text has not been altered. Nor has it always been brought up to date (though the biographical notes at the end of the book have been). Many things have happened since the earliest of the articles was published in October, 1959, and even since the most recent, in March, 1963. Such changes as have occurred in situations and viewpoints do not affect the validity or interest of the material, but the reader should keep them in mind, especially in relation to details. Static *development* would be a contradiction in terms; the word itself connotes change. To facilitate historical placing, the date when each article was originally published in the REVIEW is noted at the end of its author's biography.

To avoid repetition, the usual footnote escape clause, to the effect that the author speaks for himself and not for his organization, has been omitted from this book even when it appeared in the REVIEW. The peruser will please take it for granted. SID is an association of individuals—organizations belong, but have no vote —and the REVIEW has encouraged the free expression of individual opinion insofar as this is possible in affairs so politically allergenic as are many aspects of international development. A major function of the REVIEW is that of public forum where critics may expose faults or air new proposals. Authors even in the same agency may contradict one another without necessarily perturbing the editor, though such contradictions might well perturb the agency head.

For the sake of intellectual neatness, the articles have been grouped under nine main headings; but since the contents keep running out of the bottom like juice out of a sieve, the peruser should consider the classifications as highly approximate. There is no pigeonholing in the REVIEW, which, on the contrary, encourages authors to transgress lines of academic discipline as much as possible, in the belief that interdisciplinary exploration and exchange is a prime need in today's world of oversegregated specialism.

There are minor inconsistencies in the format of the articles. Some are divided into sections by side heads, some by white space only, according to the author's choice. Similarly, references and footnotes in some cases are inserted in the text, in some relegated to the end of the chapter. More uniformity in these matters would have been tidier, perhaps, for book purposes, but to achieve it would have taken time needed for more substantive things.

Readers familiar with the REVIEW may demur at some of the exclusions and inclusions in the book. Choices had to be made, however, and among so much good and varied material they were difficult. To justify all of them completely would be impossible; too often it was a matter of *mas o meno*; and the editor will never fully make up his mind whether something left out should have been in and something in, out. Doubtless, psychiatrists have a name for this mental state. At any rate, the responsibility for selection was a shared one: Andrew Rice, the new editor of the REVIEW, deserves blame or praise equally with the old editor, who is editing the book. We think the choices are reasonably representative of the REVIEW during the three-and-a-half-year period covered; but I regret that among the good things that had to be omitted were such contributions as the following: Don Adams' "Pitfalls and Priorities," Dale Barnard's "The Heifer Project," Dr. Candau's "World War against Malaria," Bernard R. Carman's "VITA Provides Answers," Evan Clinchy's "The New Education," William O. Douglas' "Plowman's Wisdom," Lucia J. Dunham and Harold L. Stewart's "Geographic Pathology of Cancer," Cornelius J. Dwyer's "The Truth about Foreign Capital," Richard Evans' "Dilemma of a Vanishing Paradise," David Felix' "Agrarian Reform and Industrial Growth," Paul Hoffman's "Development Priorities," Lucyle Hook's "In Triumph Through Persepolis," Lady Jackson's "Africa in 1970," Tai Dong Kim's "The Capital Requirement," Cecilio Morales' "The Need for Clarification and Balance,"

C. V. Narasimhan's "New Approach to International Coopera-
tion," Kenneth L. Neff's "Education and the Forces of Change,"
James Patton's "More Agriculture in World Affairs," Hollis W.
Peter and Edwin R. Henry's "Measuring Successful Performance
Overseas," Paul R. Porter's "Multilateral Protection of Foreign
Investment," Henry Reuss, Harlan Cleveland, and Gordon Boyce's
"Peace Corps Trilogy," Warren Robbins' "African Art—Tradition
and Transition," Director-General Sen's "FAO Mediterranean
Project," Derek Singer's "Hard Lessons from the Congo," Robert
Solo's "Creative Technology and Economic Growth," Robert
Theobald's "The Challenge of Abundance," U Tun Thin's "Three
Long-Term Problems," and Abdalla Abdel Wahab's "Making
Technical Assistance More Fruitful."

So much for general considerations. Now for specific notes on
some of the articles, corresponding to the numbers that follow:

1. Eugene R. Black's "So Hopeful a Challenge" was the first
article in the first issue, and this sentence appeared below the title:
"A rare revelation of personal philosophy that expresses the essential credo of workers in international development and strikes the
keynote of this REVIEW."

2. Hugh L. Keenleyside's "Obstacles and Means in International Development" originated as the presidential address of the
retiring first President of SID at the society's second international
conference.

3. B. K. Nehru's "A Rational Approach to Foreign Assistance"
originated in his address at the second international conference of
SID. At the first conference, the year before (1959), he had made
a speech that appeared in the first issue of the REVIEW under the
title "Objectives of International Economic Assistance." The
speech attracted widespread attention and was subsequently
printed in the U.S.A. Congressional Record. In it, Mr. Nehru
questioned the use of identical methods to meet radically different
situations in different countries, arguing that more discrimination
would assure more certain results and a quicker end to the need
for aid. His advocacy of a rifle rather than shotgun approach to
foreign assistance has been influential in development policy.

4. Henry A. Wallace's "The Most Important Investment,"
which originally appeared in the REVIEW under the title "Mexico
is a Bridge," derives from remarks made by Mr. Wallace in introducing the Mexican Ambassador at the second international conference of SID.

5. Antonio Carrillo Flores' "Unsolved Financing Problems" originated as the Mexican Ambassador's address at the second SID international conference.

8. Mendon W. Smith's "Recipe for International Investment" is the author's condensation of a book-length manuscript that originated as a thesis for Rutgers University's Stonier Graduate School of Banking.

10. Víctor L. Urquidi's "Legislation for Economic Development in Latin America" appeared originally in *Latin America: Evolution or Explosion*, published by the Council on World Tensions and Dodd, Mead & Company, Inc. We are grateful to the Council and to Dodd, Mead for permission to reprint, both in the INTERNATIONAL DEVELOPMENT REVIEW and in DYNAMICS OF DEVELOPMENT.

13. Milton J. Esman's "Institution Building in National Development" originated as a contribution to an inter-university conference on institution building, held at the University of Pittsburgh's Graduate School of Public and International Affairs late in 1962.

19. F. F. Hill's "Education: Key Issues for Policy Makers" (20) Don Adam's "Pitfalls and Priorities in Education," and (21) Robert Brittain's "An Alternative Approach to Mass Education" originally appeared in the REVIEW as separate articles under a general heading, "Education: The Need for Constructive Ideas—Problems and Prospects for Developing Countries." Dr. Hill's contribution originated as a lecture at the 1962 Cornell University Summer School.

22. Abel Wolman's "New Directions for Public Health" originated in his address at the third international conference of SID.

23. Harald Frederiksen's "Mortality Rates and Economic Development" derives from the author's "Determinants and Consequences of Mortality Trends in Ceylon," published in *Public Health Reports*. Vol. 76, No. 8, U.S. Public Health Service.

24. Robert W. Hudgens' "Essentials of Land Reform" derives from the author's address at the Eighth National Conference on International Economic and Social Development, Washington, 1961.

28. Henry W. Fairchild and Shamsul Haq's "Cooperative vs. Commune" is a condensation (with later additions) of the authors' book-length *A New Rural Co-operative System for Comilla Thana: First Annual Report: Rural Co-operative Pilot Experiment*, published by the Pakistan Academy for Village Development, Comilla,

East Pakistan, in 1961. The prime mover in this experiment has been Akhter Hameed Khan.

29. Akhter Hameed Khan and A.K.M. Mohsen's "Mobilizing Village Leadership" was a preliminary, and at the time unpublished, report on the Kotwali public works project of the Pakistan Academy for Village Development, Comilla, East Pakistan. Subsequently the recommendations made in the article were accepted by the Government of Pakistan, and the public works project became an important feature of the national development program. At the request of the government, the Comilla Academy undertook the training of hundreds of civil servants to conduct the program throughout the province. As noted in his biographical note elsewhere in this book, Mr. Khan received the Magsaysay Award for Government Service in 1963.

32. Edward T. Hall's "What Underdeveloped Countries Do Not Want" was one of several articles that appeared in the Review under the general heading "What the Less Developed Countries Want." This was the subject discussed by Panel 4, one of the five discussion panels at the first international conference of SID. The moderator of Panel 4 was Arthur Goldschmidt, then director of the United Nations Bureau of Technical Assistance Operations.

GOVE HAMBIDGE

INTRODUCTION

PAUL G. HOFFMAN

IN THE EIGHTEENTH and nineteenth centuries, economic development was essentially an uncoordinated process that depended on the efforts of numerous private individuals and, to a considerable extent, on fortuitous circumstances.

The great generators of progress were the industrial captains—prudent, thrifty, hard-headed men who started small businesses and built them up step-by-step into great industrial concerns. The efforts of these scattered individuals multiplied a thousandfold led to the economic development of entire nations. Then, toward the end of the nineteenth century, a new catalyst appeared. Germany and Japan showed that state guidance in the initial stages of development could help a country overcome the disadvantages of a relatively late start and achieve rapid economic growth.

Today, we have embarked on economic development on an unprecedented scale. An attempt is being made to change, in a relatively short time, the lives and the futures of two-thirds of the world's population in over 100 countries—and *all* of these countries are late starters in development.

It is generally conceded that to promote a nation's economic development today requires a measure of over-all economic planning and some government leadership and control. At the same time, it is also generally conceded that, in the proper economic climate, relatively free enterprise provides an almost unmatched efficiency, flexibility, and swiftness of response to new situations and new demands. In most developing nations today, the torch of economic development is no longer carried solely by the businessman or the bureaucrat—it is carried by both, and their relations are increasingly marked by mutual cooperation and consideration. Thus, in the hundred-odd low-income nations, a new group of men and women is emerging, usually highly educated, very often underpaid, but always dedicated to the common goal of raising the standards of life of their people and of adding to the sum of human happiness.

It is difficult to characterize this group. It is too small and too heterogeneous to be called a "new class"; it has none of the exclusiveness of a "club"; it does not pretend to be an "elite"; it is not sufficiently well articulated to be a brotherhood or a fraternity; but it *does* exist. It is distinguished occasionally by the similar educational backgrounds and the circumstances of some of its members, but the true bond exists in the similarity of their aims and their work, of the problems they face, and more often than not of the expedients and solutions they arrive at—in short, in a strong community of interests.

This group has its compeers in the industrialized countries also —people who, realizing that development is our grand task and its successful achievement essential in the building of stable societies, are increasingly concerned with the economic relations of the rich and the poor nations. These people apply their heritage of skills and knowledge to the problems of the developing countries, more often than not in those countries themselves.

It was the realization of the emergence of such groups in all nations that led sixty men and women to found the Society for International Development in Washington, D. C., in October, 1957.

The main aim of the Society was to create bonds laterally across the oceans, the mountain ranges, and the national frontiers dividing these groups, to build bridges between the professions and disciplines concerned in development, to articulate a truly international society of men and women, all dedicated to the common aim of eliminating poverty and creating the material requisites of human happiness and an orderly world. Like many another great endeavor, the Society began with literally nothing except hope.

In its first two years, 1957 and 1958, SID could not afford to publish a journal. In the third year, it could publish only one issue; in the fourth, two issues; in the fifth, four issues, of which one was a membership directory. Not until the fifth year, 1962, could the Society print four regular issues at the proper quarterly intervals.

But in spite of this impecunious beginning, the Society has flourished.

As early as October, 1961, its journal, the INTERNATIONAL DEVELOPMENT REVIEW, could claim:

SID has grown into a sturdy youngster. Now in Bombay and Madras and Karachi and Manila and Ankara and Khartoum and Geneva and Ann Arbor and New York, professional people meet under the aegis of SID in large gatherings and small study groups and committees to talk shop, the shop being the world; to exchange ideas and information about international development; to probe its myriad problems. Hundreds of other persons, widely dispersed in some seventy countries [now ninety-four]—doctors, engineers, teachers, economists, big and little officials, experts in many branches of knowledge and fields of practice—feel that their membership in SID has not only practical value but also the less tangible value of establishing professional consanguinity.

In its REVIEW, the society carries the exchange of ideas and information a step further by enabling people who cannot come together to *talk* about each other's experiences, to *read* about them. To quote once more from its editorial comment in October, 1961: "Here and there, throughout the Americas, Europe, Asia, and Africa, the INTERNATIONAL DEVELOPMENT REVIEW wanders into offices and libraries and laboratories and homes and hotels and boardinghouses; and in its contents, a few thousand people find something to their liking, something that informs, illuminates, encourages, stimulates, inspires, according to the individual's need and bent. . . ." The REVIEW has been described as "the most unspecialized of specialized journals." It welcomes articles from all persons connected with the process of economic and social development. In its pages, readers will find discussions of abstract economic theory and of contemporary practices, and pertinent views on the human, technical, social, and psychological factors in development and on a host of related issues.

DYNAMICS OF DEVELOPMENT has been culled from the pages of various issues of the REVIEW and fully reflects their broad spectrum of ideas on the developmental process.

To both students and practitioners of economic development, the selected articles provide a rare insight into the political, the social, and the psychological, as well as the purely economic, complexities of the developmental problem. Finally, in these pages, readers are likely to find the best example of the kind of fare they can expect in future issues of the REVIEW. In my opinion, both SID and the REVIEW have come to stay and to make an ever-increasing contribution to the heightened tempo of development throughout the world. This is true *a fortiori* of DYNAMICS OF DEVELOPMENT, where some of its most stimulating ideas are to be found.

Washington, D.C.
January, 1964

CONTENTS

THREE. Planning and Administering Development

FOUR. Manpower for Development

FIVE. The Educational Challenge

SIX. Toward Better Health

SEVEN. Agriculture and Industry

EIGHT. Community Development

NINE. The Cultural Aspects of Development

ONE

WHAT IS INTERNATIONAL DEVELOPMENT?

1. SO HOPEFUL A CHALLENGE

EUGENE R. BLACK

THROUGHOUT most of history, most human beings have lived in material poverty, but they have tended to take poverty for granted, often as a matter of divine will. Even as the Age of Enlightenment unfolded, with its strong assertion that poverty is not predestined, the fact of mass poverty was not a fact of first importance. It might excite the humanitarian instincts of "enlightened" man, but, insofar as it did not affect him personally, it rarely commanded his undivided attention.

Today it is possible to say that the existence of mass poverty is one of the most significant facts, if not the most significant fact, affecting mankind's future. As more and more millions throughout the world throw off their acquiescence in a life of material poverty and embrace the idea that they can have at least some say over their own destiny, the existence of mass poverty becomes an ever more important focal point for turmoil and discontent. And the greater the turmoil and discontent, the shorter the time that civilization based on a respect for individual dignity and tolerance among nations and races can survive side-by-side with mass poverty.

What has elevated the fact of mass poverty to such unprecedented importance is the relentless pursuit of knowledge about the physical world which has accelerated so dramatically over the past few centuries. On the one hand, it is possible to say that we know now virtually all we need to know to make a poor society, if not rich, at least less poor. No further inventions are needed; we know now how to make worn-out land yield more and what are the social organizations a society must have to grow rich. At the same time, the spread of this knowledge is the root cause of a historical transformation that threatens to rob man of his freedom to pursue knowledge and put it to a constructive use.

3

It is hard to exaggerate the toll that the technology and the philosophy of the Age of Enlightenment have taken of the ancient civilizations. These ancient civilizations, while varying in a wealth of detail, shared certain common characteristics, of which acquiescence in a life of material poverty was most important. This acquiescence was possible because life was well-ordered, by and large, and the individual felt the warmth of belonging to a family group or to a village or tribe. If man was neither free nor rich in worldly goods, he had the compensation of security, an assigned place in the community in which he was taken for granted. If society was static, it was by modern standards stable and well-ordered.

Today, there is no point on earth where the stability and security of these ancient civilizations has not been undermined by the impact of the very ideas and technology that are so often cited as a poor society's greatest asset. As a result of the public-health expert, whose efforts to stamp out disease have resulted in dramatically lower death rates and consequent "population explosions"; as a result of commercial agriculture, which introduced the idea of a money economy where barter used to rule; as the result of lawyers, who have introduced into status-ridden societies a code of laws where contracts among individuals are placed above social status; as the result of engineers, who have built roads and railroads to connect remote areas with the outside world; as the result of generals, who have invaded with all the modern technical paraphernalia of war; as the result of traders, who have brought everything from trousers to radios and the jet airliner—as the result of all these intrusions, mass poverty has become an increasingly intolerable state of affairs in the minds of the half of the world's population that used to live in the shelter of the ancient civilizations.

Never before in history was it possible to assign to the existence of mass poverty such significance as it has today, but never before in history have societies been so intimately, if reluctantly, bound together by a common body of knowledge. "The world today," writes the British anthropologist Jaquetta Hawkes, "is in the net of a single civilization." And her profound observation was echoed by Prime Minister Nehru when he told his countrymen, "The old civilizations, with the many virtues they possess, have obviously proved inadequate. . . . Our problems [today] are the problems of civilization itself." And of course India's number one problem is poverty.

In the nineteenth century, it was possible even for educated men and women to look with composure on the beginning struggles of the poor societies to throw off their poverty. It was then possible to believe that somehow, however hesitantly and awkwardly, these poor societies would evolve in a way compatible with the continued free pursuit of knowledge and its constructive application in an environment of tolerance among nations and races.

Today, we are wiser, if sadder. We have seen, in fact, that, so far, the spread of technology and knowledge about the growth process into the poorer societies has destroyed more than it has created. It has destroyed the stabilities and the securities of the old order without, in most places, doing away with abject poverty. Far from leading to an orderly evolution, the existence of mass poverty amidst a wealth of knowledge about how to enrich society materially has given rise in the poor societies to such a turmoil of frustration and discontent as to threaten the foundations of world order.

And where poverty has been relieved somewhat, as it was in pre-war Japan and Russia and as may happen in post-war China, we have seen that the cost was the suppression of every form of freedom at home and the adoption of aggressive and intolerant policies abroad. We have witnessed and are witnessing leaders who, rather than accept a life of poverty for themselves, are willing to ride roughshod over the entrenched habits and customs of their people, reducing individuals to the status of ants and elevating the state to the status of a deity.

These are some of the hallmarks of life in the twentieth century. They constitute a challenge to the very worth of knowledge. More specifically, they challenge the very heart of nineteenth-century optimism, namely, that a war on mass poverty can be fought without reducing individuals to mere cogs in a bureaucratic machine.

Without being either optimistic or pessimistic, it can be said that such a war must be waged if man is to preserve his faith in the worth of knowledge. If mass poverty is not the root of all evil in our world, it is so much at the root of discontent in our times that it offers the one concrete problem on which we can focus our energies and test the worth of our knowledge. No other problem of comparable scope or importance exists.

Further, we can say that knowledge does provide the hope that such a war can be fought successfully. It is true that the people of the poor societies do not have to wait out the slow process of invention before relieving themselves of the worst pangs of poverty; the knowledge exists now about how to exploit nature to insulate man from mere animal survival. And it is known now how to organize and order this knowledge in ways that will not result in the individual's being swallowed up by the state.

The test comes in our ability to adapt what is known to the conditions that exist in the poor countries and in our willingness to persevere in the face of inevitable disappointments. This exacting and often frightening task today is being carried out by an ever-growing army of professionally trained men and women of all nations and nationalities. The courage of these men and women is beyond praise. Each is working in the sure knowledge that science and technology will continue to force fundamental changes on the whole structure of human society; each is accepting the responsibility for helping to decide whether these changes enrich civilization or impoverish it, indeed perhaps destroy the worth of the individual entirely. Each knows that, for good or evil, his special knowledge is a tremendous power in the world and that he can divorce himself from that power only by ceasing to practice his profession.

And the complexity of the professional challenge these men and women face has no equal today. It is easy to forget how special are the institutions and attitudes toward life and work which are necessary for modern economic growth. There must be a habit of saving and a willingness to invest savings productively. There must be institutions to make this possible. People must be willing to accept new things in their lives and to accord a measure of respect and reward to those innovators who devote their time and talents to enriching the individual's material lot. People must be willing to move around to new homes and new jobs and to enter into the productive process at some point. There must be a liberal supply of technical education, liberally spread among the population. Just to mention a few of the basic requirements is to illustrate how complex is the task of adapting modern technology and modern knowledge of the growth process to essentially pre-technical societies.

Finally, each of these professionally trained people has the handicap of an inevitably inadequate training. It is clearly illogical to train a man to practice in the most competitive technological market and then expect him to work miracles in the poor societies. Conventional professional training takes for granted too many of the necessary basic institutions and attitudes, the absence of which, more than anything else, keeps poor countries poor. To make use of his special knowledge in a poor country, the professionally trained man must acquire broader knowledge and deeper understanding than is needed to follow a conventional professional career. For the most part, he must acquire that knowledge and understanding on the job.

Yet what other challenge today so adequately and thoroughly tests the worth of knowledge? What other problem is so important and so worthy of the best brains? And what besides the existence of poverty offers the professional man or woman so hopeful a challenge? None, I would say, for the simple reason that never before in history was it possible to say, as we can say now, that the kind of poverty that destroys individual dignity and stifles individual creative effort is not necessary.

2. OBSTACLES AND MEANS
IN INTERNATIONAL DEVELOPMENT

HUGH L. KEENLEYSIDE

WHY should there be a Society for International Development? What is it that has moved so many people from so many parts of the world, with such diverse backgrounds in race, religion, nationality, economic status, and social viewpoint to join an organization with such a lofty but imprecise label? Why is international development necessary? What, in fact, does it mean? What can anyone or any group of private citizens do about it?

Every country in the world is underdeveloped. To put it another way, there is no government or people that has reached the ideal state in which full use is being made of all the beneficial possibilities that science and technology have now provided for the material benefit of human society.

Ignorance, superstition, prejudice, inertia, intolerance, and greed still make it difficult in even the most advanced communities for human wisdom and knowledge to produce the measure of economic and social progress that could otherwise be achieved.

But while we recognize that every country has much to learn, it is obviously true that there is an enormous difference between the economic and social conditions existing in the more technically advanced nations and those that are characteristic of the countries usually described as underdeveloped.

Underdevelopment can be defined in many ways: by the incidence of poverty, ignorance, or disease; by maldistribution of the national income; by administrative incompetence; by social disorganization. The most frequently used and perhaps the most convenient, if not the most accurate, criterion is that of per capita income. This, of course, is not a scientific touchstone. There are countries in which the per capita income is high, but in which, because of the way the money is concentrated and used, few economic and social benefits accrue to the people. The purchase by a head of state of fifty gold-plated Rolls Royces as gifts for his friends, or the expenditure of $25,000 on a single reception by a delegation to the United Nations General Assembly are not necessarily incompatible with gross degradation in the home countries of those responsible for such stupid waste and vulgar extravagance.

Nevertheless, the use of the per capita income index is broadly indicative of the state of material development of a country and its people. Today, the average income per capita in the United States is just over $2,000. But there are in the world 66 countries, with a total population of 1,500 millions, in which the per capita income—insofar as it can be measured in monetary terms—is less than $200 a year. These are the truly underdeveloped lands. And so it is that, despite all the accumulated knowledge and the material resources at least theoretically available to all governments and all peoples at this point in the history of human progress, the following facts are beyond dispute:

Over half the people in the world are illiterate, thus lowering efficiency, inhibiting social improvement, and providing fertile soil for the weeds of superstition, prejudice, and fanaticism. Literacy does not ensure progress, but its absence makes significant progress impossible. An ignorant people cannot be free.

Over half the people of the world are ill or physically unfit, though most of them could be cured and many of the most prevalent diseases could be permanently eradicated by the use of knowledge and techniques now readily available. Persons born in Sweden or New Zealand or Canada can expect to live, on the average, seventy years—the Biblical three-score and ten. But in over twenty countries, including some of the largest in the world, the life expectancy, even for women with their two to five years favorable differential, is under thirty-five. Considering the kind of life they lead, the people in such countries are perhaps fortunate that it is so short.

Most of the people in the world are hungry most of the time, yet by applying even present knowledge with intelligence and good will to the problems of production and distribution, reasonable standards of nutrition could be assured for all peoples. (How long this will continue to be true if the population of the world maintains its present rate of increase is a problem that will soon have to be faced. The womb is slower than the bomb but it may prove just as deadly. Suffocation rather than incineration may mark the end of the human story.)

Most of the people in the world cannot afford adequate cloth-ing, housing, and recreation. It is only a few years since the President of the wealthiest nation on earth said that one-third of all Americans were "ill-housed, ill-clothed, and ill-fed." Despite enormous progress in many parts of the United States, this is still partly true, although much more radical improvements in housing, clothing, food—and education—could easily have been effected if less had been spent on gambling, alcohol, and the ludicrous vulgarities of automotive transport. (The sacrifice by each adult of one cocktail a month would build 20,000 schools a year in Canada and the United States.) If this is the situation among the luxury-ridden residents of North America, what can be said of the condition of other peoples? Despite the great technological discoveries of the last fifty years, there are more poverty-stricken families and more suffering in the world today than in 1900.

And finally, a large proportion of humanity is still affected by injustice in one or more of its manifold forms—slavery, peonage, forced labor, political despotism, legal corruption, and the whole grim range of totalitarian practice, whether Nazi, Fascist, or Communist.

That such conditions as these are no longer unavoidable is evident to all who have studied the problem. The honest and intelligent application of available knowledge could in a short time, as history measures time, make a phenomenal change in the conditions under which the great majority of human beings now exist. Significant efforts in this direction have now been started. For the first time in human history, a conscious, organized, and world-wide attempt is being made to bring the benefits of scientific knowledge to all governments and all peoples. Of course, the wealthy countries are working at the task with all the energy of a well-stuffed and drowsy python—but a perceptible start has been made.

Before considering these programs, it would be useful to examine the handicaps from which the underdeveloped countries suffer and some of the obstacles that hamper their attempts at progress.

Some students of the international scene like to compare the condition of the underdeveloped areas of today with that of the western world prior to the Industrial Revolution. This comparison has a certain plausibility, in some parts of Latin America, for example, but for most of the world the analogy is grossly misleading.

By 1750, when the Industrial Revolution may be said to have begun, the European world was already in the possession of many of the material assets, most of the theoretical concepts, and, above all, of the habits of mind that were to make rapid economic and technical progress feasible. Intellectual curiosity, scientific experimentation, a general concern with new ideas, and a comparative willingness to accept their implications were widely characteristic of the age. Two hundred years ago the work of Averroes and Bacon, of Galileo and Harvey, of Leibniz and Newton had become part of the intellectual framework of the educated man. In England, by the middle of the eighteenth century, the Royal Society was already 100 years old. And this is one organization of which it cannot be said that it was born that way.

Prior to the Industrial Revolution, long periods of profitable commercial activity had resulted in major accumulations of capital which were accessible for industrial purposes in Western Europe. Labor was plentiful and highly mobile, migrating with little formality from place to place, from country to country, as opportunity beckoned. The Protestant religion, characteristic of the countries that moved most quickly and most effectively into the industrial era, provided an ethic suited to the new techniques. Profit had become a form of piety.

Perhaps most important of all, as at once a stimulant and a tool, the larger part of Western Europe was integrated in an exchange economy.

Thus the people of the major national states were ready, intellectually, spiritually, administratively, and commercially, for the tremendous explosion of material progress that occurred in Western Europe and North America during the next 200 years.

Contrast this with the situation in most of the so-called underdeveloped countries today.

It is true that in many of these countries there is a small element at the top that understands and has assimilated the intellectual and scientific thought of the outside world. But the members of this select group are largely divorced from their own people. They are either migrants—often temporary—from the more developed countries, or persons who have been trained abroad or formed by foreign influences. They are much more a part of the intellectual life of the cosmopolitan world than they are of their indigenous cultures. Indeed, they are often less understanding and less sympathetic in their relations with their less fortunate compatriots than are the more enlightened members of a developed community. Like the "self-made man" of the West, the industrialist who "rose from one suspender," they are sometimes notoriously uninterested in those who do not or cannot follow their example of inheriting or otherwise achieving positions of personal advantage. Very often, their major preoccupations seem to be directed toward the puerile satisfactions of conspicuous waste.

It is true that some of the currently underdeveloped countries have historical traditions of great cultural significance. In many aspects of art, literature, and thought, such countries as Egypt, India, Persia, and China have made exceptional contributions to human achievement.

But for the most part—though not, of course, entirely—these contributions were of an aesthetic or philosophical, rather than of a scientific or technical, character. In almost every case, the social institutions that accompanied them were not congenial to the promotion of economic development. Unbridled exploitation, caste stratification, concentration on war and the military arts, religious intolerance of scientific enquiry, unrestrained procreation, scorn of the commercial arts and of manual labor, historical accident—all these played their part in the ultimate submergence of a large part of the cultural heritage of the Middle East and Asia. The inquiring, critical, skeptical mind is not characteristic of the less developed areas.

The majority of the people in these areas are still living largely outside the social, economic, and intellectual fabric that marks the culture of the more advanced segments of the contemporary world. Over a billion people in the underdeveloped countries are illiterate, and even of those that possess the magic power of the written word, very few have access to materials that make any pretense of giving an objective or useful picture of modern society. This is not, of course, intended to suggest that literacy ensures virtue, or that the intellectual elite are always socially valuable. But the fact that a tool is badly used is no argument against the tool.

In a few of the underdeveloped areas, almost undiluted barbarism still prevails. There are parts of Africa, Asia, and even Latin America in which people are living in conditions that have changed little for many hundreds of years. Less than fifty years ago cannibalism was still a not uncommon practice in several regions of the world. In some parts of Africa, it is still the law that meat cannot be sold except with the hide attached—to ensure that the purchaser is not being given human flesh! Slavery, open or only formally hidden, is still known to persist in a number of countries. In fact, organized slave raiding—usually accompanied by murder, castration, and other barbarities—has only very recently been stopped, if indeed it has been wholly eradicated even now.

Apart from such extremes—which affect only limited areas—perhaps the most distinctive characteristic of an underdeveloped country is the fact that subsistence agriculture is the prevailing mode; normal production is for home consumption or for exchange, by barter, in narrowly restricted local markets. Such circumstances prevail in many districts in Asia, Africa, the Middle East, and Latin America, yet the development of an inclusive exchange economy is an essential part of any serious national program of economic development.

If we assume that continuing and increasing efforts will inevitably be made to bring the people of the underdeveloped areas from the darkness of their misery into the comparative daylight enjoyed by those of the economically more advanced countries, what are the major obstacles to such a program? Some of them can be quickly summarized.

Climate: In the early history of humanity, the major preoccupation was the struggle for food and the provision of shelter against the elements. It was for these reasons that the initial advances in civilization occurred in river valleys where a surplus of food could be most easily produced and in the tropics where dress and housing were of minor importance. Thus, the lower valleys of the Nile, of Mesopotamia, and of the great rivers of central and southern China became the earliest centers of human progress.

Hot river valleys facilitated early progress but at a certain stage of development became a handicap rather than an aid. Given adequate techniques for the production of food and shelter, human beings live more successfully in temperate than in tropical regions. Thus today, there are few of the underdeveloped countries outside the torrid zone, while there is no real example of a fully developed economy between the tropics of Capricorn and Cancer. Modern science is beginning to make tropical life more bearable, but climate is one of the handicaps that most underdeveloped countries must face.

Disease: One direct effect of climate, and of related conditions, is the fact that a large percentage of the people in the underdeveloped countries suffer frequently or continually from disease. Malaria, yaws, dysentery, bilharzia, trachoma, tuberculosis, and other parasitic and respiratory afflictions are normal aspects of life in the poor countries. The individual effects are a life of misery and the probability of a premature grave. Socially, illness reduces productive capacity and thus hardens the vicious circle of underconsumption, disease, and low production.

Limited resources: Although further and more reliable resource surveys may change the picture, it is generally accepted today that most of the underdeveloped countries are poorly endowed with useful resources, except, in some cases, for the production of food and, more recently, of oil. Much of this poverty is due to the destruction of forests and the impoverishment or erosion of soils through centuries of wasteful and unscientific use.

Colonial heritage: Most of the underdeveloped parts of the world were ruled for generations or centuries by foreign powers. This external control was not universally and exclusively detrimental. Some of the legacies of colonialism have been beneficial, as, for example, the administrative tradition left in Pakistan, India, Burma, and elsewhere by the departing British. Generally, however, colonial rule, even good colonial rule, meant economic exploitation and a period of stagnation in the development of the inherent qualities of the subject peoples. Of all fields of human activity, government is perhaps the most nearly perfect example of an area in which the Deweyan principle of learning by doing is universally true. On balance, the colonial relationship was ultimately harmful to both the rulers and the ruled.

Excess population: Kept within rational limits, a large population can be considered a national asset. But what are rational limits?

There is no single or universal answer to such a question. In any given case, it will depend on such factors as the form of social and economic organization of the community, the ratio of population to developed and potential resources, the present quality or character of the people themselves, and their relations with their neighbors and the world. Belgium or England today can support, in decency, a denser population than that of China.

But judged by any reasonable standard, it must be clear that there are now many parts of the world that are "overpopulated," no matter what the definition of that term. Most of this pressure is in the underdeveloped countries, and yet here the population is growing about twice as rapidly as in most industrial societies. The sudden flaring of population that has marked the last hundred years, and in particular the last few decades, is rapidly creating a situation that threatens to destroy the hopes of those who are working for the economic and social development of the less advanced areas. The population of the world has doubled in the last seventy years; it will double again in the next forty. In many areas, in spite of intensive effort, conditions are deteriorating instead of improving. It is now clear that, unless drastic measures are soon employed, grim disaster will menace humanity.

Adverse social traditions: It is broadly true that many of the social traditions and the religious beliefs of the people of the underdeveloped countries are hostile to those qualities, institutions, and activities that are favorable to economic progress. Simple examples are the scorn for manual labor and the denigration of the commercial classes. In religion, the emphasis on contemplation, the influence of the mystic, and the persistent search for contact with the spiritual world may be beneficial to the individual soul but contribute little to the development of an economically viable community.

Lack of capital: The rate of the economic progress of a country depends in large part on how much of its current income can be applied to the development of the infrastructure, the creation of real capital—roads, railways, factories.

In most of the underdeveloped countries, the rapid accumulation of this essential surplus on any significant scale is almost impossible. What capital is available normally falls into the hands of those who have little interest in using it for general economic and social development. Most of the population is living on or near the subsistence level and much of it is entirely outside the money economy.

Recent figures indicate that the *developed countries* of the West are adding to their productive investment at the rate of about 10 per cent of their annual income. This means that an average of about $90 per capita is going into the purchase of new plant and equipment, which in turn results in the creation of more wealth. In the *pre-industrial countries* of Asia and Africa, on the other hand, the total per capita *income* is only roughly $60 a year. In other words, the people of the West are *saving* more than the people of Asia and Africa are receiving for all purposes. It is not surprising that the gap between the haves and the have-nots is steadily opening. How wide that gap is can be gauged from the fact that the industrial nations of the free world, with only a third of its population and a fourth of its land area, produce 86 per cent of its manufactured goods. The two-thirds of the population of the free world who occupy 75 per cent of its land produce 14 per cent of its manufactures. The rich are still getting richer; the only luxury of the poor is procreation.

It is not inconceivable that the Marxian belief in the inevitable widening of the gap between rich and poor, having been proved false in western industrial society, may yet demonstrate an unexpected validity in the international scene.

Professor Blackett summarized this point in a recent presidential address to the British Association, when he said that the situation is complicated by the fact that "most new scientific and technical discoveries or developments tend to widen the gap still more, just because the already rich countries have the capital to make full use of them, but the poor countries have not." ("Technology and World Advancement," *Nature*, September 7, 1957.)

Many of the less developed countries are also handicapped, as has been indicated, by the fact that even when there is or might be a useful margin of savings, much of this surplus is likely to be used for unproductive purposes. Wasteful consumption drains off such resources in a manner that is often both morally harmful and economically disgraceful. It is not only in the crude forms of individual or class extravagance that the tendency toward unwise expenditure is displayed. Spectacular investment in public buildings, luxury hotels, or an uneconomic steel industry may all have the same effect on the national economy.

Perhaps the most harmful, as well as the grossest, example of unwise expenditure by governments of underdeveloped countries is the outlay of such governments on military establishments. In certain of the most backward countries—states in which a large part of the populace is living at an almost subhuman level—as much as 60 per cent of the national income is spent on military, naval, and air "defenses." In some cases, governments have recently spent enormous sums on military aircraft—while a large proportion of their children have no schools. Such prestige expenditures are not only negatively harmful; they introduce a whole wide range of positive evils, not the least of which is the strengthening of a privileged class of service personnel whose social ignorance is normally matched only by their political ambitions and their individual and group venality.

Incidentally, one of the serious dangers in contemporary society arises from the fact that in many of the less developed countries the only really efficient foreign aid that is being received—judged by both quantity and quality—is in the realm of military equipment and training. This fact carries a clear threat to democratic institutions. It may well result in establishing or confirming military dictatorships, because only the military will have derived effective benefit from the application of modern technology. A twentieth-century army in a medieval economy can hardly fail to produce an imbalance that will make democratic practices improbable. It is not customary to find a general or a field marshal who is economically sophisticated or socially perceptive.

Absence of an effective middle class: One of the most conspicuous characteristics of an underdeveloped country is the absence or the meager size of its middle class, and particularly of the entrepreneurial and managerial components of such a class. To the extent that a middle class does exist, it is usually confined almost exclusively to a comparatively small group of merchants, agents, teachers, moneylenders, and appointed officials. Such an embryonic middle class contains very few business enterprisers or effective industrial managers. When such persons are found, they are usually supplied or recruited from outside the national boundaries. Local personnel are not trained for such activities. For centuries they and their forebears have traded and sold and been appointed to office—they have had no tradition of management or manufacture. They have manipulated—they have not made.

The historical reasons for this fact are obvious. The larger part of the population in the poorer countries is found in the peasantry. Their lives are, in general, confined to the deadening routine of a comparatively isolated and unproductive husbandry. Bound by tradition, stagnant of thought, they have no knowledge of and no incentive toward construction or management. The usual small aristocratic class is equally burdened by history. Traditionally, its members despised economic pursuits. They could rule, kill, exploit, fornicate, gamble, waste, but it was beneath their dignity to manufacture. The histories of their countries illustrate the result.

Lack of skilled labor: Most of the underdeveloped countries suffer from a shortage of trained artisans and mechanics. On the other hand, there is usually a surplus of unskilled labor. In many cases, the size of this surplus is likely to be underestimated because of the various forms of hidden unemployment that are characteristic of the more primitive economies. Thus it is important, in studying possible development programs, to place emphasis, in the early stages of national industrialization, on labor-intensive projects. But manpower, in most of the underdeveloped countries, is a *potential* source of economic and social strength but a *present* burden.

Incompetent administration: Partly as a result of the lack of managerial skill, and even more as a result of the inadequacy of private resources of investment capital, there is an inevitable tendency in the underdeveloped countries for governments themselves to undertake a much larger role in the national programs of economic development than is customary elsewhere, except in the totalitarian states. Dr. Eugene Staley has explained the situation in these words: "Private enterprise fails to function effectively in most underdeveloped countries, not so much because it is repressed or interfered with as because it does not yet exist in the modern sense in which Americans automatically think of it." (*The Future of Underdeveloped Countries* [rev. ed.; New York: Frederick A. Praeger, 1961], p. 239.)

The emphasis on state aid and participation underlines the dangers that result from the shortage of competent administrative personnel in the civil services of the underdeveloped countries. The importance of this weakness (which exists in private business as well as in government) would be hard to exaggerate, and it is one of the most difficult of all problems with which to deal.

The usual accusations against the administrative practices of the underdeveloped countries are that their organizational arrangements are bad, their leadership and personnel inexperienced, inefficient, and corrupt. Of course, these characteristics are not universal among the poorer countries, nor are they unknown among the stronger and wealthier states. As Dr. Hans Singer has written: "Development requires good administration, yet good administration is itself a result of economic development. It is not, of course, a necessary result, for some highly developed countries have very bad administrations. The difference is that once development has been achieved, bad administration can be afforded as a luxury. . . ." ("Obstacles to Economic Development," *Social Research*, March, 1953.)

These do not by any means exhaust the list of obstacles to economic progress in the underdeveloped countries. They merely indicate, in a brief and partial manner, the nature of a few of the more significant problems.

There will be no attempt here even to list the full extent or variety of the efforts that have been, and are being, made to solve these problems. It will suffice for the present purpose to note a few of the steps that are being taken to meet the depressing and dangerous situation presented by the gross inequalities in the world today and the sad measure of human suffering that still remains in this age of scientific miracles and of gradually awakening social conscience.

It is, of course, axiomatic that the basic responsibility for raising the standards of life in the underdeveloped areas rests primarily on the governments and peoples of the countries concerned. No amount of external example, urging, or aid can ensure domestic reform and progress. Excessive foreign pressure, no matter how wise in substance or however well intentioned in motive, would be likely to arouse domestic opposition. Many of the countries most in need of progress have a history of colonial exploitation or some other form of external control, and they are extremely sensitive to any suggestion that might be interpreted as a movement toward a re-establishment of foreign influence. Every plan for economic or social progress in the underdeveloped world must take this sensitivity into account. In practice, this means that the initiative must be taken by the governments of the underdeveloped countries themselves.

This situation presents difficulties that are often glaringly apparent. Many governments simply do not know how to approach the search for a solution of their problems. They can see the results of their national illness but cannot identify its causes or prescribe its cure. Often, even when aid is available, they do not know what to ask for or how to present their requests.

But there are certain things that governments can and indeed must do if they are to make any real economic and social progress.

First of all, they must have the determination to act. Unless the members of a government of a poor country are deeply concerned with its problems, nothing will be done. History is replete with examples of governments that found it easier, more convenient, and sometimes more personally profitable to their members to accept the status quo rather than to plan and work and even suffer to promote beneficial change. Inertia and corruption are today the greatest obstacles to national progress, energy and integrity the two greatest needs.

Fortunately, it is more difficult than it used to be for a government to disregard the condition of its people. New methods of communication—the press, cinema, radio, television, transport—have spread far more widely than ever before the knowledge of how the more fortunate members of human society live. With this knowledge has come an increasingly widespread and an increasingly impatient demand for emulation and participation. Not many generations ago, most of the underprivileged peoples felt that they merely shared the common lot of all humanity. They believed that it was a law of nature or of God that human beings should live in misery and hasten to an early grave. Now almost everyone, everywhere, knows that this is not true. No longer can people anywhere be persuaded to accept the assurance of happiness in a hypothetical or improbable paradise as a compensation or reward for misery on earth. Only a very strong or a very stupid government can today disregard the rising discontent of its people. So even if conscience fails, the instinct of self-preservation is likely to drive most governments into resolute efforts to promote economic and social progress. In governmental affairs, necessity is the foster-mother of virtue.

One of the most significant tests of the determination of a government to improve the condition of its people will be the character of its reaction to the problem of population growth. Any government whose people are directly affected by their own and their neighbors' unbridled fertility, that fails to deal seriously with this subject, is inviting the disaster that its irresponsibility brings rapidly nearer. In such countries, the national birth rate may soon be recognized as an index of national responsibility.

The second step required of any government that is concerned with national development is the effort to mobilize its domestic and other resources of capital and skill. In certain countries, the local resources are of significant dimensions. But in general, the underdeveloped countries face a serious shortage of both technical knowledge and financial strength. In some cases, this is due to meager national endowment of material resources. In others, it is the result of exploitation by foreign or by domestic entrepreneurs who have expatriated their profits.

Governments that view their responsibilities seriously will not fail to take advantage of the development in recent years of national, regional, and world-wide programs of technical assistance. These programs have offered one means by which governments in need of scientific knowledge and operational skills can loosen these handicaps. Although Point Four, the Colombo Plan, and the United Nations programs of technical assistance operate on a scale that is still infinitesimal in comparison with the need, they do provide a means of closing some of the gaps in knowledge and technique that plague the underdeveloped areas.

The procurement of foreign investment capital is an even more difficult yet equally important problem. The days when foreign private enterprise could be relied upon to meet most of the immediate and profit-promising needs of the less developed countries have now passed. In some areas, regrettable experiences with unstable or irresponsible governments have destroyed confidence. (To what extent the foreign investors themselves provoked or contributed to this instability and irresponsibility by their own behavior is a subject for another occasion.) The growth of a vigorous and sometimes unenlightened nationalism in certain of the needy states has added to the problem. Above all, the fact that investment capital can earn such a high return in the booming domestic economies of the major capital-exporting powers themselves has reduced the attractive differential that once lured capital abroad. Nevertheless, as Eugene Black, President of the International Bank, said recently in San Francisco, "The opportunity to attract foreign private capital is there for those nations that have the will and courage to grasp it."

A number of nations have now revised their laws governing foreign investment to meet the conditions of the time. Without reopening their countries to the kind of exploitation that once was common, they have established rules that give reasonable assurance of freedom from nationalization, the use of foreign personnel, and the export of convertible funds to cover new purchases, interest, and sizable profits. Even in these countries, the foreign investors have been slow to respond. Yet if private capital will not accept this challenge, the pressure for loans and grants from and to governments will continue to rise. The reluctance of private capital is an invitation to state action.

The situation is still further complicated by the tremendous increase during the last few years in the cost of capital goods. In heavy industries (steel, oil processing, chemicals), an investment of approximately $20,000 to $25,000 per man employed is now considered normal. Even in secondary industrial enterprises, the investment is likely to run at about $5,000 to $7,000 per worker. "The high capital cost of industrialization," says Professor Blackett, "is the main reason why the 'take-off' is such a difficult operation for the pre-industrial countries. This is especially so at present because most production goods must be imported, thus making heavy demands on foreign exchange, which, except in a few oil- and mineral-producing countries, is chronically short."

Thus at the same time that private capital has been drawing back from the foreign field, the needs of the borrowing countries have suddenly and dramatically increased. Moreover, while many of the capital needs of the underdeveloped countries arise from schemes that are essential to any serious program of development, and that will ultimately result in a national profit, they are not, in the ordinary sense and in the short run, "bankable" projects. To meet needs on this scale, and of this specialized kind, unusual sources of funds must be discovered and tapped.

It is in an effort to meet such requirements that the capital-providing factor has been incorporated in the Point Four and Colombo Plan schemes. (The United Nations Technical Assistance Programs have no capital components. In the United Nations, technical assistance means just that and nothing more. The loans of the International Bank for Reconstruction and Development, on the other hand, are strictly commercial transactions.) The amount of money available for capital purposes through Point Four, the Colombo Plan, the International Finance Corporation, and other similar services is wholly inadequate to the needs of the poorer countries—even if these are estimated in the most astringent manner. Estimates of the amount that should be made available to the underdeveloped countries if any really significant and rapid progress is to be anticipated have been made by a number of national organizations, by experts employed by the United Nations, and by several commissions appointed by the government of the United States. These estimates run as high as $15 billion a year, and in no case in which the matter has been seriously studied has the estimate fallen below $1½ billion.

The United Nations Special Fund is now operating on a scale that will make possible a few selected projects of modest proportions each year. Except possibly as an example, however, it will make only a small contribution to the satisfaction of the urgent needs of the poorer countries. The size and flexibility of the loan policy of the International Development Association give promise of a rather more hopeful contribution, but even its eventual capitalization at $1 thousand million (after five years) will not be enough to make any really effective impression on the ultimate problem. No general plan for a comprehensive attack on the problem of world development (such as was recently proposed by India in the General Assembly) is even remotely in prospect. It is probable that nothing less than a transfer to sane and useful purposes of much of the current expenditure on military budgets, by both East and West, will make such an attack feasible. It is perhaps just conceivable that the beginnings of such a movement may result from the summit conference later this spring.

But so long as they are denied support of this kind, the governments of the underdeveloped countries have no alternative but to make even greater efforts to mobilize their domestic resources of capital, to use everything they can obtain from the technical and other aid programs that are available, and to take whatever steps are possible, through the maintenance of stable and honest administrations and through the enactment and enforcement of sensible foreign investment codes, to enlist resources of private capital from abroad.

The problems of economic and technical progress in the underdeveloped areas are complex, urgent, and grave. They are susceptible of no early or easy solution.

But they are not insoluble, and many of them could be eliminated in whole or in part by a serious and honest application of existing knowledge with the use of established techniques. The great problem here, as in all other human affairs, is humanity itself. Mankind has extended its power over almost every aspect of nature —except human nature. Selfishness, greed, inertia, prejudice, unkindness—these are the real handicaps under which all men suffer. If they could be overcome, a new world would indeed be born. But such a reformation is still a long way off. And the patience of that vast part of the human race that is still suffering unnecessarily from disease, hunger, and injustice will not long remain unbroken. For men and governments of good will it is then imperative, if progress is to be made, to use the tools that lie at hand, to summon whatever resources of wisdom, knowledge, energy, and benevolence may be available, and, on grounds of self-interest and principle alike, to unite in the great task of bringing help to those that suffer and hope to those in despair.

3. A RATIONAL APPROACH TO FOREIGN ASSISTANCE

B. K. NEHRU

In an article in the first issue of the INTERNATIONAL DEVELOPMENT REVIEW, "Objectives of International Assistance" (VI, No. 1 [October, 1959], 21) I urged that the "objective of any foreign aid program should be to enable the economy which is receiving the aid to become self-supporting in the shortest practicable time."

Perhaps it is not incorrect to say that there is now more general appreciation of this basic objective of foreign assistance—not just to win friends and influence people by piecemeal, patchwork programs, but to set country after country on the road to self-help, so that before long the development of all nations could proceed at a politically acceptable pace without aid from extraordinary forms of government-to-government assistance. Objectives such as "reduction in inequalities of incomes among nations" are difficult to define and have little relevance to the aspiration of people everywhere who are interested not so much in abstract notions of equality or inequality as in opportunities for themselves to develop with dignity and self-respect. Nor is it sufficient to define the goal of foreign assistance as "an increase in per capita incomes at X or Y per cent per annum" for all less developed countries. Such an objective, while useful as an indication of the minimum goals that must be achieved if social and political stability is to be preserved, fails to focus on the end of the road, which it is in the interest of aid-giving as well as aid-receiving countries to reach as soon as possible. While there has thus been increasing recognition of the need for a new approach to foreign aid, the implications of this approach are not yet generally appreciated and are reflected but little in the actual administration of foreign aid programs.

The remarks that follow spell out some of the implications of a rational approach to developmental assistance as I see them.

Planning for Economic Assistance

Basically, self-sustaining growth presupposes an increase in internal savings sufficient to match the investment required for reaching and maintaining the rate of growth considered politically acceptable and a sufficient diversification of the economic structure to permit a fair degree of resilience in a country's balance of payments. If the objective of external assistance is to lead the developing countries as quickly as possible to the stage of self-sustaining growth, the first step to take obviously is to get a clear picture of how, over the long term, resources should be invested in order to get the country in question to the take-off point, where exactly in each particular case the shortage of resources lies, and how it can best be met. In other words, there has to be a long-term program for economic development, which need not necessarily go into great detail but which must be able to satisfy the outside world that the resources (whether in manpower or in money) it is being asked to provide will be used for the highest developmental priorities and will not be frittered away.

Some countries are sophisticated enough to be able to draw up developmental plans of this kind themselves; most countries, however, are not so well placed. The first action required in the case of the latter is, therefore, the drawing up of a developmental program with the help of an outside authority, which must be international—for example, the International Bank or the United Nations.

In the case of countries that are capable of drawing up or have already drawn up plans of this kind, it is still necessary that the prospective lenders should be satisfied that what the country proposes to do is sensible. As each individual creditor country may find it difficult to provide the personnel with the necessary technical ability to examine the developmental plans, and as, in any case, such separate examination would present obvious procedural and political difficulties, this function too should be assigned to an international authority.

Such an examination should give a not-too-indefinite picture of how long and in which sectors the country concerned will need foreign aid. It will also give a fairly clear picture of what action the country concerned is itself required to take and what sacrifices that action will entail.

A long-term survey of resources and requirements of priorities and prospects such as that suggested may not be practicable immediately for all the less developed countries; and the degree of detail that can be incorporated in any such survey will naturally vary from case to case. But action is urgent, and there is no reason why it should be held up till comparable surveys for all the countries become possible.

Quantum and Sources of External Assistance

If the capital needs for external assistance of the developing world are thus realistically assessed, it would also help in putting the debate on foreign aid in the aid-giving countries in proper perspective. There can, of course, be no automatic assumption that the aid-giving countries will readily provide whatever sums are required to promote self-sustaining growth in the developing nations. But realistically assessed, the figure that is likely to emerge, although substantial, should not be unmanageable. The gross national products of the industrialized countries are about $900 billion per annum. The annual increase in the gross national product is about $36 billion. It is unlikely that the annual sums that can be usefully absorbed by the developing world, if the latter were to mobilize its own resources to the full, would be more than 1 per cent of the gross national product of the developed world or 25 per cent of the annual increase in their income; in fact it is likely to be considerably less. But whatever the approximate sum, it is important that public opinion in the aid-giving countries should be able to appreciate fully the sacrifices it is called upon to endorse and the concrete achievements for which these sacrifices are demanded.

The basic decision the developed countries must make—and it is much too late in the day either for them or for the developing countries to camouflage this issue any longer—is whether or not they are willing to forego a part of the increase in their annual consumption for the sake of the developing world. The moral, political, and commercial reasons that make such a decision desirable are well known, but the decision must be taken in principle before the techniques for the transference of capital are discussed. And without such a decision or commitment about the broad order of the effort required, foreign aid programs would remain mere residual legatees of public policy—the last to be in and the first to be out whenever the budget is unbalanced, or the balance of payments is adverse, or money and capital markets are tight. If nations are determined that the capital must be transferred, then new institutions must be created or old institutions so worked as to cause this transfer to take place; otherwise the underdeveloped world will remain forever dependent for obtaining the funds it needs on the accidental conjunction of at least two of three factors—a surplus in the balance of payments, and a surplus budget or excess liquidity in the money market.

The wealth that is transferred from the rich countries to the poor countries can belong either to (1) the investor or (2) the taxpayer. It is desirable that the compulsion required in the latter category of transfer should be kept to the minimum possible. This requires action, not only on the part of the underdeveloped countries, as is generally supposed, but also by the developed countries; for it is clear now beyond any doubt that no matter what the former may do, private capital, without public guidance (with the unique exception of oil), will flow almost wholly from one developed country to another instead of from the developed countries to the underdeveloped countries. The reasons for this are that the former offer greater safety and security and familiarity with conditions than the latter, and the profit differential (if any) is not high enough to counteract these advantages in an age in which venture has disappeared from "venture capital" because of the change in the character of its ownership. Investment in a skyscraper in New York attracts capital from London; investment in a power house in Khatmandu would not, though the social need for the latter is infinitely greater than for the former.

To reduce the disadvantages which the underdeveloped world has by its nature in the attraction of direct foreign investments, the developed world can do three things. It can (1) guarantee compensation in the event of expropriation; (2) guarantee convertibility of profits, dividends, and capital, if capital has to be repatriated; (3) enter into double-taxation agreements that will ensure that any tax incentives given by the receiving countries will not be frustrated by action on the part of the tax authorities of the country of origin of the investor.

The model for action on the first two is that adopted by the United States in its ICA programs. (The original model of requiring recipient countries to enter into elaborate treaty arrangements binding themselves to be of good behavior is not likely to work.) These ensure to the investor that in the event of expropriation or lack of convertibility, he will get his money from a U.S. Government agency, with the U.S. Government left to press its claim with the government of the country concerned. The model for the third is the Double Taxation Treaty between the U.S.A. and India (now before the Senate of the United States for ratification).

Even if all this is done, the fact remains that not more than a very small proportion of the funds available for private investment abroad will ever go to the developing countries, and the total amounts will be much smaller than the minimum required for the purpose. It is only after a country has reached the point of take-off, and as a consequence of the resultant stability and confidence in its competence, that these funds will begin to flow in any appreciable measure.

The second source of investors' money is the capital market. No underdeveloped country can at present float a public issue, basically because of the lack of confidence of prospective investors in its ability to fulfill its obligations, owing partly to lack of knowledge of its conditions, but mainly to the poverty of the countries seeking to take on these obligations. No developing country can hope to use this source of funds (which throws no burden on the taxpayer) unless the country in which the borrowing takes place assumes the risk of the borrowing country's defaulting on its obligations as a result of lack of foreign exchange. In other words, to make use of this source of finance it will be necessary for the government of the lending country to guarantee the convertibility of the repayment. This means a contingent liability on the taxpayer, which, however, is better from the point of view of the governments than having to raise taxes immediately. A program of this kind, if used with care, can result in large transfers of capital without burden on the taxpayer.

The bulk of the resources needed, however, will have to be transferred by way of public assistance, which can take the following three forms: (1) direct loans by one government to another, (2) loans from central banks in developed countries to governments or central banks in the underdeveloped countries, (3) loans through international institutions.

From the point of view of the underdeveloped countries, it does not make much difference which of these three techniques is adopted. The first and third have been adopted with varying measures of success, but the second is available for those governments that plead poverty while the central bank has vast accumulations of gold and foreign securities. The finance provided by the underdeveloped world of the British Empire to the United Kingdom during World War II was wholly on this basis.

Terms and Conditions of External Assistance

What is more important from the point of view of the underdeveloped world are the terms and conditions on which the money is made available to them; and here a great deal of confusion has been caused by applying the criteria suitable for internal financing to international lending. Loans from a lending institution to a producing concern are usually linked to the period of amortization of the project for which the loan is made. In the case of international lending, this criterion has no significance whatsoever, for the debt has to be paid, not from the earnings of the project financed, but from the earnings of the entire economy. To say, therefore, that loans for the purchase of trucks should be repaid in three years and for the purchase of a powerhouse in 15 years, though wholly meaningful in terms of intranational lending, becomes completely meaningless in terms of international lending. Neither the truck debt nor the powerhouse debt will be paid from the earnings of the trucks or the powerhouse; both will be paid from the exports of the economy, which bear only an indirect relation to the transport of goods or the generation of power. In this context, the rules of the Berne Union and the efforts of national export promotion organizations that tempt foreign purchasers with the use of the word "credit" are not only meaningless but positively harmful, because insofar as foreign countries fall prey to the temptation, they eat into their credit-worthiness at a very rapid rate.

The proper way to approach this problem is to regard each individual country as a *project* of which individual projects—powerhouses, trucks, and the rest—are merely component parts. What has to be assessed is, therefore, at what point of time the *project*—that is, the country—will break even and at what rate thereafter it will make a profit. Till the break-even point is reached, there can be no net repayment of debt. This does not mean that there should be no repayment of debt prior to the break-even point; but this can happen only if other loans are in the meantime forthcoming in a manner that enables them to be utilized for the repayment of existing obligations—that is, if they are made available in the form of freely utilizable money.

The most important point in regard to financing underdeveloped countries is, therefore, the period for which money is lent to them. Those countries that are nearer the take-off point should be able to begin to repay earlier than those that are much farther removed from this point. But while those in the latter category do not require large sums of money, those in the former do; and if all the money necessary to help these countries to achieve the point of takeoff is made available to them, the indebtedness will be so great that a very long period of time will be required to discharge it. There are three possible methods of handling this situation. One is to make loans repayable in foreign currency over a period of forty to fifty years. Another is to make them repayable in local currency, the conversion, if any, being subject to negotiation at such time as the country concerned begins to throw up a surplus in the balance of payments after making provision for the maintenance of the economy and its development at a satisfactory rate. The third is to make grants instead of loans; and this, if the parliaments of both the developed and the underdeveloped countries are sophisticated enough to take it, is probably the best approach. Genuine long-term loans, as defined here, or loans repayable in local currency come very near grants; but till such time as the concept of large-scale grants becomes generally acceptable, these devices can be used with advantage.

If the device of loans repayable in local currency is used, it must be clearly understood that the only sensible use to which counterpart funds can be put within the country in which they are held is for the funds to be made to vanish through some respectable process. The grievous error that counterpart funds represent real resources capable of use for economic development is unfortunately so widely held in political as well as administrative circles that it creates a constant source of friction and irritation capable of breeding major political misunderstanding. Education on the true nature of counterpart funds is therefore highly necessary. (For an excellent discussion of this problem, see E. Mason, "Foreign Money We Can't Spend," *Atlantic Monthly*, May, 1960.)

Project Approach versus Program Approach

The fashion set by the International Bank, that it would lend money only for identifiable, isolatable projects that normally themselves give an economic return, has been followed by the U.S.S.R. and then by the U.S. Government and threatens to become the fashion among other lending countries, as a result of the high prestige in which the International Bank is held. As long as there was no clear philosophy of the objectives of foreign aid, and when countries did not have well-worked-out programs of economic development, the test the International Bank applied, which was designed basically to ensure that the money made available was in fact spent for economic development, was as good a test as could have been devised. But if it is agreed that the *project* is the country and the country has a regular developmental program accepted by the lending countries as generally satisfactory, the project approach becomes a limiting factor in the use of funds and does not ensure that they are used to the best advantage. When the project approach is coupled with financing tied to purchases in particular countries, the use of resources becomes demonstrably uneconomic because, even in markets otherwise competitive, higher prices have sometimes to be paid for parts of equipment that can be more cheaply bought elsewhere. When the lending country is a high-cost country, the effect is to divert funds meant for foreign economic development to a subsidy for native industry. Moreover, the project approach has the effect of stifling the small private entrepreneur who is attempting to expand his business; for his schemes, which consist of the addition of bits and pieces of machinery to his existing equipment, never reach the dignity of a project. In the underdeveloped world, "projects" are usually the monopoly of governments or of big business.

Another and additional hindrance to the effective use of funds is the ideological conditions that are sometimes attached to a project loan, namely, that if it is for industrial activity, that activity must be in the private sector. There is no economic justification for this at all. In most underdeveloped countries, where the alternative is not between the private and public sectors, but between the state creating an industry and the industry not being created at all, the effect of such limitation is to deny economic development. If the objective is to bring pressure on underdeveloped countries to change the pattern of their thought, that objective is hardly likely to be achieved, particularly in democratic countries, because of the natural resentment against the adoption of policies under pressure from outside authorities. Refusal to finance a project because it may be inefficiently managed or uneconomic is understandable; refusal to finance it because of ideological objections to certain kinds of ownership is neither economically justifiable nor politically wise.

The correct approach, at least for countries that have a well-worked-out program for economic development—and it has been argued that unless there is such a program, major capital aid can hardly be required—is that of financing the requirements of the program in such a manner that enough flexibility is left to the country being aided to make it possible for it to squeeze the maximum economic benefit from the funds made available to it. This requires first the commitment of funds over a long period of time, or at least the assurance to the country concerned that the funds needed for the fulfillment of the agreed program will be made available as and when required up to the amounts agreed. Secondly, while the project approach need not be ruled out, provided that global purchases are permitted, a substantial sum of money must be made available for purchases of developmental goods (which may sometimes not conform to the usual definition of capital goods)—in such a way that the borrowing country may use the money so provided with full flexibility, it being understood, of course, that it will be used for purposes within the program. The need for "flexibility" in utilization of aid has been recognized by the International Bank in what have come to be known as "impact" loans—that is, loans in foreign exchange to cover not only the direct foreign-exchange cost of the projects or programs financed, but likewise the indirect foreign exchange requirements arising from the effectuation of the programs. What is required is a more general and explicit recognition of the sound principles underlying this kind of lending.

The Mechanism of Control

End-use supervision of a project ensures that the money has been spent for the purpose for which it has been borrowed. If the approach is changed to the financing of a program for economic development, what mechanism can be devised to ensure that the money has actually been used for the purpose of the program? As the country concerned will have much greater flexibility in the use of its resources, it will at the same time be able, if it is so minded or if its administration is inefficient, to waste it.

The answer to this lies in an annual review of performance of the country concerned. This is a much more delicate and difficult task than end-use supervision of a project. It is delicate because sovereign nations do not like to have their accounts examined by outsiders; it is difficult because if programs are sensibly administered they must undergo much greater changes than projects do even during the course of twelve months. It follows that the agency for satisfying the outside world that the money being lent is used for the purposes for which it was represented that it was wanted must be an international agency; it follows also that the individuals assigned to the task must be of great understanding and tact. That this can be done without creating too much friction has been shown by the annual missions of the International Monetary Fund and the International Bank. This procedure would become even more acceptable to the underdeveloped countries if the policy decisions of these institutions could be demonstrated to be truly international in the sense of being influenced equally by the thinking of the underdeveloped and the developed parts of the world.

The Obligations of the Borrowing Countries

In the ultimate analysis, the achievement of self-sustaining growth must turn largely on the efforts and sacrifices of the developing countries themselves. The availability of foreign assistance should not in any way impair the determination of the aid-receiving countries to put forth all the effort they can reasonably be called upon to make. For this purpose, the borrowing country must demonstrate to the outside world before it can legitimately ask for external assistance:

1. That it has made every effort to raise all the resources it possibly can from within the country; for example, that its taxes are as high as the country will stand and its internal borrowing programs are as resourceful as possible.
2. That it has taken steps to ensure that as much as possible of the foreign finance it needs comes from the private investor.
3. That its own capital is not permitted to escape abroad.
4. Above all, that its investment program is based on economic priorities and not on prestige and other non-economic criteria.

Every dollar that an underdeveloped country raises from its own resources represents a sacrifice in human terms infinitely greater than the dollar made available to it by the developed world. If an equality of sacrifice were to be aimed at, practically the entire burden of developing that part of the world that is not yet developed would be thrown on the richer countries. There is, however, no question of an equality of sacrifice, both because such a concept is impracticable and, even more importantly, because it would destroy the greatest asset required for economic or any other development, namely, self-confidence and self-respect. Furthermore, too much money being as evil as too little, it is desirable that the underdeveloped countries should attain their economic independence through a measure of sacrifice that should of course fall short of the point of a collapse of the social system. If economic independence is attained at this cost, it will, like political independence, have a much greater chance of being cherished and preserved than otherwise.

It is impossible to say in quantitative terms what fraction of the cost of any developmental program should be borne by the country concerned. This will naturally depend on a variety of factors, of which the most important will be the per capita income—the lower the income, the less the burden the country can bear. Generally speaking, however, countries with similar per capita incomes should be expected to bear similar proportions of their developmental costs.

The Argument in Brief

To summarize, the theory and practice of economic aid that might with advantage be developed by the world is somewhat as follows:

Each underdeveloped country should be looked upon as a *project*.

The objective for each should be to bring it to the point at which its further economic development can take place from its own resources.

A *project* report should be prepared for each country—either by the country alone or with the aid of an international agency; the results will vary and will indicate varying requirements of technical and capital assistance for varying periods of time.

The developed countries must decide as a matter of principle to lay aside a certain percentage, say 1 per cent, of their national income (as a basic rate), for the benefit of the underdeveloped countries; that is, they must ensure that capital flows out at this rate to the underdeveloped world whether through private or governmental channels.

There should be variations from the basic rate of 1 per cent in either direction, based on variations in the per capita income of the developed countries.

The capital may flow through bilateral agreements, through international agencies, and through direct foreign investment and capital markets.

This outflow of capital must be sharply distinguished from activities of export promotion and surplus disposal, which should be excluded from computation of the 1 per cent. Private investment, whether direct or through the capital markets, should not, however, be so excluded, because though it results in a return to the lending country which might sometimes be substantial, it does, when it flows out, reduce the rate of growth of consumption within the capital exporting country.

The program of aid for underdeveloped countries should be on a continuing basis without regard to the vicissitudes of budgets, or balance of payments, or capital markets.

The aid should be made available on the basis of either (1) grants, (2) loans for fifty years at a noncommercial rate of interest, or (3) loans repayable in local currency. In the case of the last, it should be ensured that counterpart funds are sterilized.

The borrowing country must ensure (1) that it is raising as much of the resources required as it possibly can, (2) that its program of economic development makes sense to the lending countries, whose agent for this purpose must be an international organization, and (3) that it is taking all possible measures to attract private investment.

The aid made available should be on an untied basis; foreign aid should not be made an instrument for the subsidization of high-cost home industry.

While some aid may be on a project basis, a substantial part of it should be on the basis of programs and should include assistance in the nature of "impact" loans, so as to permit of its most economic use. Where aid is on a project basis, there should be no ideological discrimination between the public and private sectors.

The borrowing countries must assure the lending countries that the aid being given is used for the purpose for which it was meant and that the other conditions of the program—for example, the raising of local resources—are being fully met.

This assurance can be given through reviews by the International Bank and the International Monetary Fund.

Action is urgent and should not be held up till a world-wide survey of all the countries of the world has been made.

4. THE MOST IMPORTANT INVESTMENT

HENRY A. WALLACE

THE most explosive force in the world is what I called in 1942 "The March of the Common Man." This march cannot be stopped. The only question is whether it proves constructive or destructive.

Mexico, the nearest and most friendly of our Latin American neighbors, is the one country above all Latin American countries to demonstrate in recent years the capacity to rule without dictators or revolutions. It was not always so. When I was a young man, there was a doggerel about the man who overthrew Díaz—

> Viva Madero
> *Poco trabajo*
> *Mucho dinero.*

For long years after Díaz was overthrown, the productivity of Mexico went up only slowly. The yield of corn per acre was ten bushels back in the days of Díaz and still ten bushels thirty years later. Mexico, the probable original home of corn, was oftentimes still an importer. A superficial observer would say that the philosophy of little work, much money, and low productivity was still triumphant as recently as 1946.

Today, all that has changed. Mexican agricultural output now increases 7 per cent a year (a faster rate than that of the United States), while population goes up only 3 per cent. Few countries have made such amazing strides as Mexico in the past twenty years. If I have had only a small part in this, I am very proud. When President Roosevelt sent me as his representative to the inauguration of President Manuel Ávila Camacho in 1940, I traveled with the incoming Mexican Secretary of Agriculture, and I visited corn growers and corn breeders. When I got back to Washington, Raymond Fosdick of the Rockefeller Foundation called on me. He wanted to set up a public health service in Mexico. I urged him most strongly to put his emphasis on agriculture, so as to make sure that food expanded as fast as people.

Fosdick appointed three outstanding agricultural scientists, who reported in 1941. I have the report and Fosdick's letter asking my suggestions. I urged him to follow up the work in such a way as to ensure continuity of agricultural research despite changes in administration. This the Rockefeller Foundation did. Truly magnificent work was done with the full cooperation of the Mexican government, regardless of the administration in power. The Rockefeller Foundation personnel furnished continuity of administration, and slowly but surely the genetic composition of the corn, wheat, and other crops improved.

Dr. J. G. Harrar started the work at Chapingo with one Mexican helper. Today, there are about 18 Rockefeller Foundation members of the staff and 100 Mexican associates. The work has expanded beyond corn and wheat to beans, sorghums, soy beans, poultry, truck crops, and livestock.

I like to think that the original contacts I made with Secretary of Agriculture Marte Gómez and President Camacho had something to do with the splendid cooperation that has always existed between the Mexican government and the Foundation.

The headquarters for this magnificent work is at Chapingo, where the agricultural school is located. Splendid as is the very great increase in production of wheat and corn, even more important in the long run may have been the down-to-earth, practical yet scientific training received by 450 Mexican boys who both studied at the agricultural school and engaged in experimental work. Of these 450, 83 have taken postgraduate training in the United States.

The Mexican yeast has served as leaven for similar work in Colombia, Chile, and, to a lesser extent, in several Central American countries. And now a somewhat similar type of work is being started in India. In all of this I cannot emphasize too strongly that the Mexicans found Dr. Harrar *simpático*, willing to move slowly on a foundation of mutual understanding and respect.

When I went to Mexico in 1940, there were less than 20 million people; today there are 34 million, and by 1980 there will be 60 million. This kind of growth is going on all over Latin America, but unfortunately the food output is not increasing as rapidly in most of the other countries as in Mexico. By 1980 the United

States and Canada will have about 255 million people as compared with 330 million for Latin America. One hundred fifty years from now, Latin America may be more productive than Anglo-Saxon America.

Mexico is a bridge between the *Anglo-Sajones* of the North and the *Latinos* of the South. It is fortunate that Mexico has such a proud heritage, such a glorious past rooted in the ancient Aztec, Tarascan, Mayan, and Toltec traditions, as well as Spanish.

The United States will always need and value Mexico's friendship. Early in 1941, I recommended to President Roosevelt settlement of the oil expropriation by Cárdenas on a basis that did not altogether please the oil people. The detailed valuation which Morris Cook finally worked out was a lot closer to true value than American property owners in Cuba are now getting. Over the past 110 years, many things have taken place to cause trouble between Mexico and the United States, but gradually we have learned to understand and help each other. President Manual Ávila Camacho was definitely our friend in World War II. American money invested in Mexico has increased productivity there.

Just the same, I am worried even about Mexico, a land which so many of us love because of first-hand contacts. The Rockefeller Foundation work has been splendid and the food supply has been increased. But 40 per cent of the Mexican people cannot read or write, and the per capita income is only one-seventh that of the United States. But there is far more to it than figures on population, education, and income.

We must get into the realm of the spirit really to understand relationships between nations. It is here where we of the United States often lag somewhat behind. It is as though our wealth tended to dull our perceptions. Any red-blooded American businessman with money to invest overseas boils when he reads what Castro has done. He boils again when he reads of students greeting President Eisenhower with signs saying "Long live Castro— go home Eisenhower." He says, "Why should I invest money in countries where they hate us and dispossess us or graft off of us when there is a new dictator?" Yes, the cry of Yankee imperialism hurts—for the very reason that loans and investments are continually being solicited from the *Norte Americanos*. If the loans are turned down, we are hard-hearted and anti-*Latino*. If they are granted, we become imperialists. Whatever we do, we are hated by a considerable percentage of the students. They think that too many *Norte Americanos* assume superior airs.

Let's dig into this situation that causes so much hatred of Yankees on the part of certain Latin intellectuals. In some ways, this feeling was expressed with the greatest restraint, insight, and understanding by the Puerto Rican, De Hostos, in 1899, when he made a prophecy for the twentieth century. Foreseeing the march of the common man, he pointed out the difficulty of the Anglo-Saxon peoples, saying that the new century would demonstrate that they understood the fight for liberty well for themselves, but poorly for others. He raised the question long before civil rights legislation as to whether legislation for true freedom could be devised solely for Anglo-Saxons. He spoke of the men of color being *deceptively* invited by both the British and the *Norte Americanos* to partake of liberty and then strangely predicted that the new arbiters of civilization, the Slavs, would take part in the struggle. De Hostos in 1899, a year after the Spanish-American War ended, was reaching out with his subconscious to show up the Anglo-Saxons of both hemispheres. Therefore, he brought in the Slavs. Or perhaps De Hostos was not expressing his subconscious dislike of the Anglo-Saxons. Perhaps he was speaking with genuine historical or prophetic insight. At any rate, he said correctly in 1899 that rivers of blood would run through the twentieth century and new currents through its leveled territories.

Personally I want to know the new currents of thought running through the intellectuals of Latin America today. What would De Hostos say today? Have the Anglo-Saxons learned anything from their experience of the past sixty years? Do they still have a blind spot relative to men of color? Do they still act as though they were the chosen race? Do Latin American students today really believe as De Hostos did in 1899 that the Slavs have demonstrated the *"major aptitud de pensamiento y tradición para empezar a resolver el problema moderno de la industria: propiedad para todos; producción y consumo para todos"*? Were the students of Buenos Aires and Montevideo just hell-raising for the fun of it? Were they stirred and financed by Communists? Or were they serious and expressing a long tradition relative to the Yankees? Why should the feelings against the United States be expressed most strongly in those Latin countries where the income is highest and the illiteracy lowest?

By asking these questions, I am merely saying that the problem of modern international development is far more than money and techniques, vitally important as they are. It is more than knowledge of population trends, monetary policy, and economic forces. As non-industrialized nations are brought into the modern scheme of things, the most important investment of all is the human heart. All of our international development efforts must be permeated with *simpaticismo*. In saying that, I do not advocate that the "have" nations, in their efforts to develop the "have-not" nations, should be suckers or sitting ducks. *Simpaticismo* is a two-way street. The very minimum requirement is that the *Norte Americanos* should spend more effort learning languages, customs, and history.

TWO

PAYING FOR DEVELOPMENT

5. *UNSOLVED FINANCING PROBLEMS*

ANTONIO CARRILLO FLORES

In presenting some reflections on problems I consider unsolved up to now in the field of long-term international financing for economic development, it is logical for me to use Mexico's experiences, points of view, and interests as my guide. But on many points, the problems we have faced are common to at least several other Latin American nations.

No one questions that in each country the promotion of economic development—a complex process implying investment, diversification, organization, technique, and effort—is the foremost responsibility of that country. Our peoples would never agree to relinquishing that responsibility. For while we must have economic progress as a condition for social advancement, we demand and defend the right to achieve it in ways consonant with our liberties and our way of life.

At the Bogota Conference in 1948, the nations of this hemisphere defined the scope of international economic cooperation in such a way as to eleminate the visionary ideas of those who would have alien efforts or resources undertake the larger share of promoting economic progress. It likewise eliminated the fear—not to be ignored because it is unjustified—of those who think that, through international economic cooperation, our peoples would find themselves under pressure to deviate from the social and economic policies they adopted in the rightful exercise of their sovereignty.

Public and private savings generated by Latin American economies are insufficient to maintain an adequate rhythm of capitalization, particularly in view of the high index of our demographic growth. This fact, the most important obstacle to healthy expansion, must be faced by each of our countries. It requires, in the first place, a search for more effective use of our savings. Our governments recognize the meaning and the value of private investments and well know how they are stimulated. Our democratic constitutions provide a framework of guarantees favorable to the creation and continual strengthening of a spirit of enterprise. For this reason, it is gratifying that the focus on foreign private investment in recent years has been in terms of equality with national investment, but no more than equality.

Until recently, there was resistance to something many of us consider important: that foreign capital go into true partnership with national capital, in a free association, without external pressure or interference. This is particularly important in the case of enterprises considered by our peoples as fundamental in their economic life, whether because of magnitude, or the resources the enterprises exploit, or the public services they undertake. Now, there is a more receptive attitude toward partnership, even in undertakings that hitherto had persistently refused such association. This is undoubtedly a sign of progress.

New organizations that are being created in countries in the process of development to better integrate and coordinate their economies—for example, the free-trade zone treaty signed during 1960 in Montevideo by seven Latin American countries. Mexico included—will open new fields, some of them unexpected, to private investment. This very fact makes it especially urgent that new enterprises, with capital from the great industrial nations, adapt themselves to the spirit of our times.

For one thing must always be remembered: The question of foreign private investment is not merely an economic problem; it is also, and to a large extent, political and emotional. Our countries want to grow, but they want to be certain that growth will not deprive them of sovereign control over their own resources, or create entities in their midst that might claim more rights than those granted by the laws of the nation in which they operate.

On the other hand, there is an ever stronger conviction that the task of raising the standard of living is so arduous and of such magnitude that it requires the contribution of outside resources looking for legitimate profit and willing to enter into partnership for economic progress, particularly in industrial development.

The search for a healthful balance between economic nationalism and equitable, stimulating treatment of foreign investment is one of the most important in the economic panorama of a world in the process of development.

One thing appears beyond doubt: There are no magic formulas that permit determining, in a general way, for all countries and for all time, where that equilibrium is. Each nation must establish its own equilibrium, consistent with its own sovereignty. Only the nation is competent to take into account all the complex historical, political, and economic factors that must be considered.

As to Mexico, its government's criterion was set forth by Secretary of the Treasury Antonio Ortiz Mena in his address in late 1959 before the Mexican Bankers Association.

"We cannot ignore," he said, "as regards Mexico and other countries in similar economic conditions, the necessity, if their development is to accelerate, of foreign investments and of accepting the very useful complementary assistance of such resources." And he added that foreign investments must contribute to increasing national income and, above all, to enhancing production where there are shortages; to stimulating diversification of foreign trade; to bringing into the country, and helping it assimilate, advanced techniques for the ever more rational exploitation of productive resources. But it must abstain from displacing local capital and frustrating its future development.

Many facts could be mentioned to give a picture of foreign capital in Mexico. Here is one: In 1958, payments made by Mexico for dividends exceeded by $33 million the total of new foreign private capital received. In 1959, according to data just published by our Central Bank, direct foreign investments increased 33 per cent over 1958, a fact that is indicative of the climate for such investments in our country. This made capital received slightly greater than that which left as dividend payments.

The reverse was true of long-term credits, whose income exceeded outgo by $100 million in 1958 and by $85 million in 1959. This is why our best efforts have always been directed toward strengthening the means of financial cooperation and why we are pleased with the signing of the document creating the Inter-American Development Bank.

This interest in no wise arises from a disregard of the importance of the World Bank and of the Export-Import Bank in our development. Both these institutions have made valuable contributions, which my country has repeatedly acknowledged. The loans obtained by Mexico from these banks, amounting in the past five years to $210 million, have, by complementing our domestic savings, permitted the strengthening of large segments of our economy, especially in the fields of transportation and the generation of electric power.

There is sometimes discussion as to which of two important ways of financing is the more adequate—direct private investment or intergovernmental credits. I do not believe there is or can be any contradiction between them. Both have a broad field of action in Latin American countries. Each has its advantages and disadvantages. Which one is used, therefore, depends on the needs and peculiarities both of the country where the investment is to take place and of the type of undertaking or enterprise to be established.

It is true that direct private investments can sometimes place at the disposal of interested countries a larger volume of resources than those reasonably to be expected from intergovernmental credits. It is true also that such direct private investments assume greater risks and that generally they do not become a direct obligation assumed by those countries. Further, by servicing through dividends, they are better adapted to the economic conditions, good or bad, of the debtor nations and consequently facilitate simpler adjustments in the balance of payments, whereas intergovernmental loans generally tend to give a certain rigidity to the commitments of the countries obtaining them. These loans, on the other hand, permit better control of their use and are sometimes less of a financial burden, particularly when they go into such enterprises as public services, which do not present special risks and where amortizing terms are sufficiently long. Furthermore, as President Lopez Mateos has said on various occasions, our experience is that governmental investment, particularly in public works, makes work for more people.

Whoever even superficially compares the present situation with that in the immediate past must recognize that great progress has been made in financing through development loans, not only in the number of governmental and intergovernmental institutions operating in this field, but in the efficacy with which they work. This, of course, has been possible because of the zeal of our countries in rehabilitating their credit after experiences that were bad for all, creditors as well as debtors, in the first thirty years of this century.

We are now convinced—and Mexico, for example, made this principle a standard rule in 1946, under our constitution—that foreign public credits must not be used except for works of genuine benefit, actually promoting an increase in national wealth and production.

This is why we have been able to fulfill our obligations in such an exemplary manner, and why we enjoy ever growing credit.

In our hemisphere, the pioneer credit agency undoubtedly was the Export-Import Bank, and it is only elementary justice to recognize the outstanding contribution of that institution to the economic progress of Latin American countries.

For over ten years now, the transactions of the World Bank, which coincided with the economic recovery of Western European countries, have broadened opportunities even more.

As is well known, the funds provided by the Export-Import Bank must, in accordance with its regulations, be spent in the United States. Those loaned by the International Bank may be spent in any of the markets of its member countries except that of the borrower. In this sense, the International Bank has greater flexibility.

We have found, on the other hand, that the Export-Import Bank exhibits more flexibility in another aspect. The Eximbank has now been willing to lend us sums for the importation of capital goods from the United States without always insisting that, on every occasion, the purchase be linked to a specific development project. Such was the case with the loan of $100 million made to Mexico in 1959.

The increase in funds which the Congress of the United States approved for the Export-Import Bank, as well as the capital increase of the International Bank and the International Monetary Fund, are positive steps in the right direction.

I particularly want to refer, because it is only just to do so, to the fact that the Export-Import Bank has shown an increased activity in recent years. In 1958, it authorized loans that added up to the greatest annual total handled by this institution in the Western Hemisphere in the twenty-five years of its existence. Furthermore, it is fair to recognize that in the past decade the Bank's transactions with Latin America constituted almost half of its total loans.

The International Finance Corporation, intended for strictly private transactions without government guarantee, though not yet in full operation owing to several obstacles I shall not attempt to examine here, is still a hope, particularly for industrial development.

Lastly, the International Development Association, under the auspices of the International Bank, and the Inter-American Development Bank created by our countries in San Salvador early in 1960, have rounded out an integrated system of diversified credit institutions, at the intergovernment level, which complement one another in providing our economy with the capital needed to assist in financing development.

Regarding the Inter-American Bank, it is interesting to recall my government's understanding of how this new institution's activities are to unfold. "The Inter-American Bank," said the head of our delegation, "must have as its prime objective making loans as solid, guaranteed, and fruitful as loans made by the best international finance organizations. Only this policy, in which all countries must cooperate by submitting projects with these characteristics, will enable the new institution in due time to have ample access to the financial resources of world markets that Latin America requires for its development."

Now that we have a complete framework of credit channels, the next step in importance is that all these organizations, conscious of serving a common end that is perhaps the most important in our time, endeavor to coordinate their tasks and functions with the utmost efficiency in an effort to fill the gaps that have existed up to now. I shall mention a few of special importance.

1. First is the financing in local currency of expenditures for large public works. Mexico has posed this question on various occasions: at Bogota in 1948, at Quintandina in 1954, and at Buenos Aires in 1957. On those occasions, we succeeded in having unanimous approval for agreements or recommendations recognizing that in certain cases and under adequate conditions, long-term financing should share not only expenditures in foreign currency, but also a portion of those in local currency. The reason is clear: The function of foreign investment, from the standpoint of the country receiving it, is to complement insufficient domestic savings. And when savings are insufficient, they are insufficient independently of the monetary unit in which they are expressed. If this principle is not accepted, the consequences will be that many of the most important works undertaken for the development of Latin American countries, but in which the expense in foreign currency is relatively small—for example, irrigation or highways—will prove to be very difficult to finance internationally. There is also the added difficulty that the problem becomes more

acute precisely for those countries which, since they have passed the initial stages of their process of development, now possess sufficient local facilities in building and machinery and also have adequate organization and technique.

From another point of view, undoubtedly any expenditure in local currency indirectly but necessarily creates the need for foreign exchange at a later date. This is why we have maintained and still maintain that even in cases in which, for instance, the Export-Import Bank makes loans, as in the past, for highway construction or irrigation works, it is in reality financing a good many unavoidable United States imports, even though a direct relation could not be established.

We fully understand the justification of a policy under which countries in the process of development are supposed to save their credit to take care of their foreign exchange commitments, particularly those originated by their large purchases of equipment and other capital goods. But we believe it must be acknowledged that under this policy many of our countries must enlarge the resources earmarked for their public works programs if they wish, as obviously all of them do, those public works to be financed under procedures that will not involve the danger of falling back into harmful inflationary practices. And foreign loans can in many cases be the most healthy way to enlarge those resources.

2. If a satisfactory answer to this problem were to be found through one of the existing organizations, it would be possible for many of our countries to intensify projects, such as building schools, slum clearance, and sanitation, of paramount importance to their present and especially their future well-being, but for which, up to now, no formula has been found to obtain the benefits of international financial cooperation.

3. Now I wish to take up another question linking financial cooperation with the problem that is undoubtedly the most serious facing the economies of countries in the process of development: instability in the prices of the raw materials that we export and that constitute the largest source of income for financing development.

There still ring in our ears the words of chiefs of state of several American nations, at various ceremonies and on several occasions, when the Mexican President visited South America and on the recent trip of President Eisenhower. It is unnecessary to insist once more on the importance of a problem that has been and is the constant preoccupation of our countries, and one that they have taken to all postwar international conferences. I shall only say that what now remains to be done is to work out concrete formulas for its solution.

A few months ago, Eugene R. Black, President of the International Bank for Reconstruction and Development, addressing its Board of Governors, said in reference to underdeveloped nations, "I still know nothing that can provide a real substitute for exports." And he added that

> the lesson has equally important implications for the industrialized countries. For these countries too, aid is no substitute for trade in their effort to meet the pressing current needs of the underdeveloped world. . . . Many trade restrictions today, particularly on agricultural products and industrial raw materials, already stand in obvious contradiction to the professed aim of the more advanced countries to aid the underdeveloped lands. And to these restrictions must be added the continuing problem of commodity surpluses and consequent fluctuations in the income of the primary producing countries. Nothing we may do here [referring to financial institutions] should relieve [the Bank's] member countries from the need for addressing themselves to these matters with new vigor and imagination.

And not only with vigor and imagination, but also, I might add, with a constant sense of reality, carefully within the bounds of what is possible. For countries in the process of development are convinced that, on such matters, nothing is to be gained by dreaming. They know that prices reflect the fundamental relation between production and consumption in the international markets, and consequently they cannot expect relative stability except to the extent that they are prepared to cooperate in re-establishing the balance every time supply exceeds demand.

We Mexicans have been pleased to see a more understanding policy on the part of the high authorities in the United States toward such efforts as those that have been and are being made as regards cotton, coffee, lead, and zinc, which are some of our most important export products. In the case of cotton, just the news of the decision of producers to coordinate their sales program sufficed to give strength to a market that had almost completely lost it. This clearly shows that it is not true, as some skeptics think, that nothing can be done, and it confirms our belief that of all the concrete steps suggested for attacking the world problem of primary products, none is so well founded, so just and simple, as that of prior consultation among producers.

As Eugene Black said in no uncertain terms, we do not believe financial aid is a good substitute for trade. We believe, however, that the execution of economic development programs in many instances would be protected from serious trouble, to which they are subjected by price fluctuations, if approval were given to the suggestion made by the Economic Commission for Latin America at the Inter-American Conference in Quintandina in November, 1954. This was to the effect that, in such cases as are justified, international financial institutions approve financing that has as a specific purpose providing a substitute, for a limited time, for income lost by abrupt market fluctuations.

4. Within the consensus we have had as to a large volume of investments producing a healthful acceleration of economic progress, there has been a difference of emphasis at times in our gathering regarding the relative function of public and private investment in the international field. Those differences are explainable, for it is natural that each country tends to generalize by rationalizing its own experience, even though unintentionally. Free enterprise converted the United States of America within a century into the greatest political and economic power ever known in history. Many of our nations, on the other hand, cannot forget that their growth, particularly evident in the past decades, would never have been possible had their governments failed to undertake extensive investments for highways, irrigation, sanitation, and electric power, which in turn opened up multiple and unsuspected opportunities to private effort and initiative. In great industrial nations, the private promoter often resents the state's engaging in ambitious investment programs. In our countries, what he frequently fears is that the government might drastically reduce expenditures.

While it would be unfair to deny that public undertakings have had access to international financial institutions, it is undeniable that for certain fields, particularly those connected with exploiting natural resources, there are still restrictions and limitations without clear justification. I believe much is to be gained by generalizing the criterion that loans are to be granted or rejected only because of the intrinsic soundness of the projects and not because of their public or private nature.

All of us, of course, recognize that in matters of international finance maturity will be reached when our countries again have direct access to private capital markets. As regards Mexico, there are clear symptoms that it is getting there after over twenty years of faithfully meeting its obligations. I think likewise as to other Latin American sister republics.

At the right moment, a great impulse could be given to this effort by granting tax exemption, for the benefit of individual investors, on bonds issued by our countries, either directly or through the Inter-American Development Bank. I believe such a measure as this, taken by the legislatures of our nations, would be not only a concrete demonstration of authentic inter-American friendship, but a transcendently constructive step forward.

Now I should like to reiterate what we Mexicans have said many times: International financing, important as it is, will never be more than a complementary factor in the task of promoting the well-being and happiness of our peoples. The fundamental task is ours. But as the President of Mexico said before the United Nations last October, we may and do expect that formulas for international economic cooperation will be kept under constant observation, so that with their assistance our work may be more fruitful. For indeed, we know it is only our own effort that can forge our well-being and our happiness.

6. COUNTRY-LEVEL COORDINATION OF LENDING

RAYMOND F. MIKESELL

In recent years, we have witnessed a mushroom growth in the number of public foreign lending institutions: national (mainly United States), international, and regional. To some extent, it may be argued that the proliferation of public lending institutions is based on the need for filling functional gaps in our kit of development therapies. Thus, for example, the World Bank can only make hard loans to member governments or to private entities guaranteed by member governments. Therefore, new institutions or subsidiaries of old ones must be created to make (1) soft loans to members and (2) hard loans to private firms not guaranteed by member governments. On the other hand, I suspect that some of this proliferation of aid institutions is due to the fact that it is easier to get legislatures in the capital exporting countries, like the United States, to appropriate funds for "new" programs than to provide more money for old ones. (Those who seek money from private foundations for projects either in the United States or abroad have the same experience; they must as a rule come up with something "new" if they are to be successful in getting support.)

Thus, the U.S. Congress authorized U.S. membership in, and appropriated subscriptions to, the International Development Association, the International Finance Corporation, and the Inter-American Development Bank, with little or no opposition, while the same Congress and its committees regularly pare down by at least 25 per cent the administration's requests for foreign aid under old programs. Likewise, the new Development Loan Fund has provided a useful vehicle for getting more funds for less developed countries out of Congress. Without going so far as to generalize this experience into a kind of Parkinsonian law of legislative appropriations, it appears likely that a further multiplication of aid agencies may prove to be the most expeditious means of obtaining funds for economic development.

While this multiplication of foreign assistance agencies has been going on, there has been a growing demand by students of our foreign aid programs for better coordination of foreign assistance activities, especially at the country level. Notwithstanding that each new agency has been justified on the ground that it was designed to fill a special need, the fact is that the functions and powers of these agencies overlap substantially. Indeed, some of them are department stores in their field rather than specialty shops. For example, the Development Loan Fund has made both hard and soft loans, both specific project and general-purpose or balance of payments loans, and loans to governments as well as to local and international business enterprises. Much the same thing may be said regarding the powers of the Inter-American Development Bank, which, in addition to its full complement of lending authority, also provides technical assistance on a grant basis.

Whatever the advantages of decentralization at the operating level, and given the fact that we are likely to have more and not fewer separate agencies providing advice and largesse of various kinds to the less developed countries, it seems clear that in the interests of both economic efficiency and the achievement of the hoped-for social and political goals of foreign assistance, some means of policy and operational coordination at the country level must be established. Such coordination is imperative if we are to influence the direction of the host country's economic progress along lines dictated by a comprehensive assessment of internal economic and political factors.

It is also clear that such coordination does not exist today. In fact, as Harlan Cleveland and others have pointed out, government officials in the host country, as well as officials of the various private and public aid institutions, have considerable difficulty in discovering and keeping track of what fifteen or twenty different agencies, all operating in the same country, are doing or seeking to do. Before we can discuss the mechanics of coordination at the country level, however, we must consider the possible alternative relationships between international lending institutions and the developing countries they serve.

Four Approaches to Development Financing

One approach is to consider the international lending institution solely as a source of development capital for financing projects that meet certain standards or criteria. Each request for a loan is considered on its own merits, taking into account both capacity to repay and the economic and technical feasibility of the project to be financed. Under this approach, the lending institution assumes no responsibility for the general progress of the borrower's economic development or for its financing. It need only assure itself that the individual project for which financing has been requested is economically sound and may be expected to make a contribution to the economic welfare of the borrowing country.

A *second approach* is for the public lending institution to make general-purpose development loans on the basis of the borrowing country's capacity to service additional indebtedness. Under this approach the borrowing country would be left to determine the specific projects that are to be financed by the loan, without any prior review or supervision on the part of the lender. It is sometimes argued that the net result of this second approach is very little different from that of the first, since in any case an international lending institution is likely to provide no more than a small fraction of the country's total investment. It is, after all, the total allocation of investment funds, and not merely the nature of the externally proposed projects, that is going to determine the country's economic growth and ability to service the loan.

There would be some justification for this position if lending institutions looked no further than the specific projects they were prepared to finance. Even if this were so, however, their review and advice concerning the feasibility of these projects and their relationship to other aspects of the development program would have considerable value. In practice, international lending institutions have not confined themselves in considering loan applications to a narrow investigation of the technical and economic feasibility or profitability of the particular projects to be financed. In fact, it is quite impossible to give adequate consideration to an application for a loan for a hydroelectric dam, a railroad, a highway, or an irrigation project without becoming involved in an investigation of various sectors of the economy and of the country's development plans and prospects. The very fact that a prospective lender requests an economic and engineering analysis of the proposed project as it relates to various aspects of the economy has considerable educational value.

The general-purpose loan approach may also, of course, involve a broad analysis of the economy and of the government's development program and policies. It may, in addition, be accompanied by undertakings on the part of the borrower as to the types of investment on which the funds will be spent, or more broadly, undertakings regarding the country's general development programs and policies, including monetary, exchange, and fiscal policies.

A *third approach* might combine the specific project approach with that of a long-term, continuous relationship with the borrowing country, in which the lending institution would undertake to provide financing for a series of specific projects that formed a part of the country's development program. Under this approach, the international lending institution might have a relationship to borrowing countries analogous to that of an investment banking firm to an industrial concern that it has helped to organize or reorganize. The investment bank in this case is responsible for providing, or helping to provide, the external financing required for the company and advises the firm regarding its plans for expansion. Similarly, an international lending institution might advise a country with respect to its development planning and programming, assist the government in choosing and formulating projects suitable for external financing at a rate consistent with the country's borrowing capacity, and undertake to provide a more or less steady flow of external financing in accordance with a long-range program.

A *fourth approach* would be for the international financing institution to undertake to provide sufficient financing to achieve a predetermined rate of economic growth or a target level of per capita output, on the basis of a broad plan covering a period of several years. This approach tends to place the responsibility for the target rate of economic growth largely on the financing institution, and assumes that growth in turn is very largely a function of the amount of capital available for investment.

It is possible to find examples of all four types of relationships between international lenders and borrowers during the postwar period. Moreover, so far as the World Bank and the Export-Import Bank are concerned, it is impossible to identify them completely with any one of these approaches. To a considerable degree, both the World Bank and the Export-Import Bank have favored the specific project approach to development financing. On the other hand, it would be very unfair to say that these institutions have not been concerned with the general economic progress of borrowing countries. The World Bank, for example, has provided various forms of technical assistance relating to the development programs of its members and has taken into consideration investment priorities and the relationship of the individual projects they finance to the broad course of the country's development. The Export-Import Bank has made a number of general-purpose development loans in which its relationship to the borrowing country is similar to that set forth in our second approach. Both institutions have maintained relationships with certain countries that constitute at least some of the elements of our third approach. On the other hand, neither the World Bank nor the Export-Import Bank has undertaken responsibility for the rate of economic growth or for providing external financing sufficient to achieve a target rate of growth for particular countries.

Perhaps the closest approach to a concrete example of the fourth type of relationship is represented by the Marshall Plan under the Economic Cooperation Administration inaugurated in 1948. Here, the United States government undertook to achieve the restoration of prewar levels of living on a self-sustaining basis for the countries of Western Europe. Programs were formulated on a joint basis for achieving predetermined goals within a four-year period, and the U.S. government provided the financing, on both a grant and a loan basis, that was considered necessary for carrying out the programs. Although this approach has not been applied to the economic development of poor countries, a number of proposals have been made that would embody the relationships and responsibilities of our fourth approach to developing countries.

The difference between the specific project approach and our fourth approach was illustrated in the course of a controversy between the United States and the Brazilian positions at the conference on an inter-American development institution held at the Pan American Union in Washington, D.C., January–April, 1959. (See *The New York Times*, March 22, 1959, p. 20.) The Brazilians argued for an institution that would have as its goal the raising of per capita real income in Latin America by a target amount within a stated period of time. The development institution would make available capital assistance to countries in accordance with the requirements for meeting predetermined growth goals. The U.S. proposal, on the other hand, was for an inter-American bank to make loans on a project basis, operating in much the same way as the World Bank and the Export-Import Bank. Although the U.S. position prevailed, it is conceivable that the Inter-American Development Bank, as it has been established, may operate in a manner analogous to our third approach.

The relationship between an international lending institution, or for that matter a coordinated program of assistance administered by several external aid institutions, should not necessarily be the same for every country. There are some countries, such as Mexico, for example, where development is proceeding fairly satisfactorily and the external needs for capital can be met by project loans, from time to time, from the World Bank or the Export-Import Bank or even from private lending institutions. Even in such cases, however, a certain amount of coordination between public lending institutions, including the International Monetary Fund, is desirable. General agreement should be reached regarding the country's future capacity to service additional loans and upon the general scale of investment priorities within the country. The latter would certainly require a periodic economic survey of the country undertaken by, or under the general supervision of, an agency designed to coordinate the activities of the various external public lending and other aid agencies at the country level. In addition, there should be a review of the country's own development plans and general development programming and sectoral studies. Indeed, it is difficult to make rational decisions on requests for project loans in the absence of studies that will provide some basis for establishing investment priorities. It seems desirable, therefore, that the various public lending agencies that might be called upon by the country for loans, including perhaps private lending groups as well, should make their decisions on more or less the same body of facts and analyses, and should consult with one another before final decisions on loan applications are made.

There are undoubtedly occasions where general-purpose or balance of payments loans are warranted along the lines of our *second* approach. The postwar loans for European reconstruction, both by the World Bank and the Export-Import Bank, were largely of this type. The countries of Western Europe were rebuilding a relatively high productivity economy and not building a new economic and social structure. The disadvantage of loans of this type is that the lending agency does not become deeply involved in the country's development program through the process of evaluating and supervising expenditures for specific projects. It may even be argued that general balance of payments support should be limited to the activities of the International Monetary Fund, whose charter authorizes the Fund to examine carefully and make recommendations on monetary, fiscal, and other economic policies that will affect the country's future external and internal stability. Nevertheless, we cannot rule out the possibility that longer-term general-purpose loans—the Monetary Fund is supposed to make short-term loans for currency stability —may be warranted in countries where development is proceeding satisfactorily, and where a deep involvement by external agencies in the development program of the borrowing country seems unnecessary. Here again, however, coordination on the part of the lending agencies is called for along the lines indicated.

Coordination at the country level is much more important, however, in the case of the vast majority of developing countries where a satisfactory rate of economic progress has not been achieved or the balance of payments is in chronic disequilibrium or both. In these cases, which I believe are in the majority, agreement among the various aid institutions, including technical assistance agencies as well as hard and soft loan institutions, as to the directions in which the economy should be moving in the light of economic, social, and political conditions, and as to how the desired goals in the various sectors of the economy might best be achieved, is of the utmost importance. Moreover, it is with these countries that a close and continuous relationship between the external assistance agencies and the country's development program and planning for its over-all financing is essential for steady growth and for the maintenance of external equilibrium. It is here that our *third* approach, which emphasizes project loans within the framework of this close and continuous relationship, appears to have the most relevance. Under our *third* approach, the external financing institution or institutions would undertake to provide, or assist in providing, all of the external financing from both private and public sources that the developing country could productively employ under reasonable standards of performance. But such an undertaking could not be assumed under present

conditions of uncoordinated activities on the part of our external
assistance agencies.

Limitations of Present Institutional Structure

One barrier to the effectuation of our *third* approach, under
present conditions, is that developing countries tend to borrow
from several institutions and rarely does a particular institution
assume a close and continuing relationship with an individual
country and its development program. No one institution has
sufficient resources to undertake to supply *all* of the external
capital that *all* of the developing countries could properly absorb
and service. Moreover, external public lending agencies have different standards for making loans, and a country's capacity to
service loans from one agency may be impaired by the assumption
of new obligations to another. Nor has a rational set of standards
and procedures been developed for determining the proportion
of a country's total external borrowing that should be financed
on a "hard" loan rather than on a "soft" loan basis. Finally, the
ability of developing countries to obtain large intermediate-term
financing from private foreign banks and foreign suppliers, backed
up by guarantees provided by the governments of the exporting
countries, has further complicated the problem of applying loan
criteria.

It is partly for these reasons that the World Bank has found it
difficult to help borrowing countries plan for a steady inflow of
capital; the Bank must take into account loans from other sources,
private and public, that will affect the country's debt-servicing
capacity. A similar problem will face the Inter-American Development Bank. It seems clear, therefore, that if a development
institution is to have a substantial degree of responsibility for
providing the financing "required" by a particular country, there
must either be an agreement between the government of the
country and the financing institution regarding the use of other
sources of external funds, or there must be a higher degree of
cooperation among public lending institutions than has been
established in the past. Otherwise, lending institutions will continue to operate very largely on a project-by-project basis without
assuming any responsibility for continuing financial requirements
of individual countries' development programs.

Moreover, as we have already seen, there exist both hard loan institutions and soft loan institutions, and institutions with both hard and soft loan windows; and thus far there seems to be little coordination in determining the conditions under which countries should receive one type of financing or the other or just what the capacity to service hard loans is for particular countries.

Another problem arises from the fact that with a few exceptions, the technical assistance agencies, such as the U.N. Economic Commission for Latin America, the ICA, or the U.N. Special Fund, are not operating in close cooperation with the lending agencies in helping countries to formulate development programs. In addition, of course, most lending agencies, with the important exception of the World Bank, are not equipped to provide the technical assistance and continuous cooperation with individual countries required by the (*third*) approach to development lending that we are suggesting.

Coordination through Regional Institutions

It is beyond the scope of this article to discuss the mechanics of achieving coordination of financial and technical assistance activities directed toward the promotion of common economic and social goals in individual developing countries. There are not only the problems of coordination among the various national, regional, and international agencies themselves, but, perhaps more importantly, there are the political problems involved in dealing with the officials of the host government.

One solution may be the employment of a regional organization, such as the new Inter-American Development Bank (IDB), as the coordinating agency. I believe that the best hope for a coordinated approach to Latin American development lies in the activities of the IDB. If this new institution is to be just another external assistance agency to which Latin American countries can apply for financing of individual projects, it will not make a major contribution to the solution of Latin America's external financing problems. In this event, the IDB may merely make some of the loans that would otherwise have been made by the Export-Import Bank or the World Bank, and little additional capital for Latin America may be forthcoming. The basic limitation on loans to Latin America in the past has not been a lack of resources on the part of existing institutions. Rather, it has been a shortage of loan applications that met the standards of existing lending institutions and the inability of at least some Latin American countries to meet the standards of credit-worthiness established by existing institutions. Both of these limitations might be greatly ameliorated by a coordination of the activities of various financial and technical assistance agencies at the country level. It would be highly desirable for the IDB to establish resident missions in each member country. Countries might be assisted in the preparation of a series of projects suitable for external financing, and the lending agencies might reach an agreement regarding the appropriate rate of flow of capital funds to the country in the light of its long-run capacity to service external indebtedness. Because the IDB is governed by Latin Americans, it is also in the best position to make recommendations to countries regarding their development policies.

Thus we may hope that the IDB will provide a model for coordination at the country level and a new approach to development assistance that might be applied in Asia, Africa, and the Middle East. This will, of course, require a further addition to the roster of external lending agencies, but as we said earlier, this is likely to happen in any case.

7. USE AND ABUSE OF LOCAL COUNTERPART FUNDS

H. W. SINGER

LOCAL currency funds are of different kinds and have different origins. Some of them are the result of surplus food sales, and these, broadly speaking, are in the legal ownership of the United States Government. Others, arising from aid transactions under the Mutual Security Act, are, broadly speaking, in the legal ownership of the receiving country. Different accounts are open to different uses and different procedures, depending on their origin and the nature of agreements that govern their use.

These distinctions, however, are of interest to lawyers more than to economists. The local counterpart funds all have in common the following economic characteristics: They are the counterpart of some preceding aid transaction, in the form either of money or of goods; their use or disposal can take place only by agreement between the two partners to the original aid transaction; and they are supposed to be either wholly or in major part for the benefit and economic development of the receiving country.

In what follows, attention will be concentrated on the funds that have arisen as a result of transfer of surplus food under U.S. Public Law 480. These are about half of the total funds and have had a definite tendency to increase in recent years. *Mutatis mutandis*, however, the argument would also apply to any other kind of counterpart fund.

Again broadly speaking, as a result of the rising volume of counterpart funds there is a problem of their "use" or "disposal." The question arises whether this is a real or an imaginary problem. Even an imaginary problem can, of course, have real effects if it is considered to be a real problem.

There is a widespread belief that counterpart funds offer a real opportunity for constructive action. The very legislative concept that these local funds are to be "used" for the benefit of the receiving country implies that here is something that *can* be used and can give real benefits. In its crudest form, the belief is that the use of counterpart funds provides a means of repeating, or doubling, the value of aid given. First you give aid by transferring money or surplus food; then you give further aid by using the arising local counterpart funds wisely. If you lend the counterpart funds rather than grant them to the receiving country, the process may go on more or less indefinitely as you re-lend the original funds. In this way, so it is believed, you can introduce a sort of multiplier into your foreign aid and make $1 worth of aid do the work of $2, $3, or $4.

In this crude form, such a belief would not be shared by persons with a degree of economic sophistication, but it is sufficiently plausible to the unsophisticated to make it worth-while pointing out that it can cut both ways. By the unsophisticated supporters of foreign aid it can be used as an argument in favor of aid, because of the imagined multiplier effects. By the unsophisticated opponents of foreign aid it can be used as an argument for cutting aid, since the local funds are imagined to be there to take the place of further aid appropriations.

In a somewhat less crude form, the belief in the "reality" of these local counterpart funds takes the form of using them as a contribution by the owning government—for instance, as contributions to international organizations or as the local cost contributions of governments to further aid programs or technical assistance operations. It should be noted at this point that such suggestions may be made either by those who believe in the reality of these funds or by those who, while not believing in the reality of the funds, propose to use their existence as a handle for promoting worthy causes.

A demonstration of the essentially unreal nature of these local funds should not, however, be taken as an argument against the worthy causes proposed; nor is the use of local funds as a handle to promote such causes necessarily to be considered unworthy. It seems justified to try to get worthy causes promoted by methods that rouse least resistance and give the greatest chance of success; beyond this, it can often legitimately be argued that unless used for the promotion of worthy causes the accumulation of local currency funds would give rise to continuous irritation, and by troubling relations between the aid-giving and the aid-receiving country, defeat one of the chief purposes of such aid.

Even so, it is important that the proponents of worthy causes should not deceive themselves. It is one thing to use the existence of counterpart funds for getting things done that would not otherwise get done—whether for rational or irrational reasons. It is quite another thing to imagine, for instance, that the acceptance of local currency funds as local cost payment of aid or technical assistance programs is genuine evidence of a matching local effort. Insofar as the purpose of insisting on local contributions by aid-receiving governments is precisely to provide evidence that the receiving government is attaching priority to the project and is willing to put in its own resources as evidence of such priority, the acceptance of the funds as a local cost equivalent does not clearly satisfy this basic purpose of a local cost contribution.

The belief that local currency funds represent real resources and that their subsequent use and possibly repeated re-use could multiply the effects of foreign aid is easily confused with similar statements about the multiple benefits of foreign aid. There certainly is a possible multiplying effect of foreign aid. One dollar's worth of foreign aid can conceivably do $2 or $4 worth of good in the receiving country. If, for example, the supply of surplus food makes it possible to mobilize otherwise unemployed manpower and other resources, or to break a vital bottleneck in the development of the country, it might legitimately be said that the availability of $1 worth of aid at the right time and used in the right way can increase the national income of the receiving country by a a high multiple of this sum. But this has nothing to do with the establishment and subsequent use of local currency funds; it has to do entirely with the nature and effectiveness of the original aid transaction.

Similarly, aid can certainly have multiple functions. It can add to available investment funds; it can help to mobilize domestic resources; it offsets inflationary pressure; it may secure continuity when export proceeds drop; it may be an instrument for adding socially desirable objectives to the development program of the receiving country. But again, these multiple benefits have nothing to do with the establishment and use of counterpart funds. The benefits are again entirely inherent in the original aid transaction and in the way in which it is incorporated in the general development plans and policies of the receiving country.

It is also true that there is perhaps need for a halfway house between straight grants and straight loans. The grant relationship is perhaps not ideal between two sovereign countries, while the loan relationship is perhaps not ideal between developed and underdeveloped countries. Hence, the recognized need for soft loans may often be imagined to be such a halfway house between grants and loans. But in fact, the establishment of local currency accounts is again irrelevant. Terms and conditions of soft loans may be arranged beforehand without involving local currency funds at all.

Likewise it is true that if the original injection of surplus food has been effectively used as the basis for an enlargement of development programs and an increase in capital formation, this will provide additional resources flowing from the newly formed capital, and these resources can be ploughed back into new development on a rising scale (since savings out of increments to income may easily be higher than savings out of the low present incomes). Indeed, it is one of the prime purposes of aid to lead to such "self-sustaining" growth. But here again, although there seems to be a superficial similarity, the accumulation and use of local counterpart funds is not relevant to this process. The process may happen without any local counterpart funds being accumulated; vice versa, the accumulation and use of counterpart funds provides no evidence whatsoever that this process is actually taking place.

The effectiveness of the aid originally given, say through a supply of surplus food, is determined by the quality of the planning and use of aid at the time the surplus food is injected into the economy of the receiving country. If the aid is effectively used *at that stage*, it helps to mobilize the domestic resources of the receiving country. The subsequent use of counterpart funds cannot add to the effectiveness of the use of the aid, or remedy any failures in such use at the time the aid is given. Hence, the belief that the use of aid is determined, not at the time of the original transaction, but subsequently at the time when the counterpart funds are assigned, may result in a situation where the boat is missed at the crucial time and the aid becomes ineffective.

The local counterpart funds may be used subsequent to the aid either for a project that is part of the development plans for the assisted country or for an additional project that the receiving country would not otherwise have undertaken. In the former case, the use of counterpart funds is an unnecessary formality, since the government could have printed the money. In the second case, the use of the funds is harmful, since it leads to inflation and causes submarginal projects to be executed at the expense of better ones.

This is the purist position, but a proviso should be added in both cases. In the former case, there may be legal or administrative reasons why the government cannot print money or otherwise obtain authority to pay for the local cost, even of a proper non-inflationary program. In such circumstances, the use of counterpart funds can avoid the legal difficulty. In the second case, it is of course possible that the additional project squeezed in by the use of counterpart funds is better than the project it displaces. It is also possible that the inflationary pressure generated by the additional projects helps to add to the total volume of investment. But these are clearly secondary possibilities. Essentially, the use of counterpart funds for these purposes is either unnecessary or harmful.

One particular case where the use of counterpart funds in new development projects becomes more meaningful must be mentioned. If the original food aid has not been effectively used to enlarge investment and promote development in the receiving country, the arrival of the surplus food will depress agricultural prices and may discourage the local farmers. In that case, the intended aid would have done more harm than good. The subsequent use of local counterpart funds for additional investment may then serve to re-employ the local resources that have been put out of action by the unintended harmful effect of the original aid, and it may serve to raise domestic food prices back to the level where they would have been if the aid had not arrived and had not backfired in the first place. This is a rather faint justification for the use of counterpart funds, since it applies only where the original aid was not properly organized and had harmful effects. Even in this case, of course, the compensating benefits of counterpart fund expenditures could also have been achieved by printing the money.

Provided the real (or rather unreal) nature of counterpart funds is clearly understood, they may be a useful device for keeping the aid-giving country and the aid-receiving country in contact with each other. Strictly speaking, of course, between two friendly and rational countries there should be no need to set up counterpart funds so that their subsequent disposal might provide an opportunity or pretext for continued contacts and discussions. Such discussions may be helpful, particularly if they lay the foundation for continued cooperation and possibly renewed acts of aid, and generally maintain that atmosphere of friendly cooperation which the aid relation is presumably intended to promote. But all this does not in any way substitute for the necessary contacts and cooperation at the time the aid is provided, since the effectiveness of the aid is determined at that earlier point and not when counterpart funds are used.

Moreover, if the function of counterpart funds is understood as merely to provide an occasion for subsequent contacts, this again may cut both ways. If the subsequent contacts are of an unfriendly nature and lead to mutual irritation, the benefits of the original aid act may be undone rather than followed up. There is nothing more irritating to sovereign governments than having to discuss with others the use of "their own money." These dangers can be avoided only when both sides are sophisticated enough to know what they are talking about when they discuss the "use" of counterpart funds.

Insofar as the counterpart funds are used for specific projects, as is often the case, rather than for general budgetary support, in fact the illusions of the project approach may be added to illusions about the real nature of counterpart funds. The project approach is itself basically illusory, since whatever the project label may be, in fact aid finances not the project that provides the label, but the marginal project in the total investment picture of the country, that is, the project that would be cut out if the foreign aid should not materialize. Like the use of counterpart funds, the project approach may be a useful device despite its basically fallacious nature, provided both sides are aware of the underlying illusion. When the "use" of counterpart funds for a specific development "project" is under discussion, the problems of escaping the double illusion involved become very difficult.

The preceding discussion has dealt with the use of local counterpart funds only insofar as these funds are used for the benefit, real or at any rate intended, of the aid-receiving country. That part of the counterpart funds that is used for local expenditures for which otherwise dollars would have to be used—such as expenses of U.S. embassies abroad—has not been considered in this note. Insofar as local counterpart funds are used for such purposes, that part of the food aid of which they are the counterpart obviously should not be treated as aid, but rather as trade.

In conclusion, if local counterparts are to be used at all, the important thing seems to be not to have any illusions about their nature and to try to give them a decent burial while using the occasion for such incidental advantages as the counterpart funds technique may offer.

8. RECIPE FOR INTERNATIONAL INVESTMENT

MENDON W. SMITH

GOVERNMENT-TO-GOVERNMENT grants and loans are an inadequate response to the problem of efficiently transferring capital from the United States to underdeveloped countries. They are politically ineffective at home and often economically ineffective abroad. We need a new approach that will be politically attractive in the United States—sufficiently attractive to lead to a really substantial increase in the outflow of capital—and that will create viable economic ties between the United States and the underdeveloped countries.

Development loans have some built-in disadvantages. The obvious one is the likelihood that they can never be paid back. The underdeveloped countries need equity capital, that is, permanent capital that will stay in the country. Very few capital investments are so productive that they will earn sufficient foreign exchange to pay back the full capital and interest cost in any reasonable number of years. Even if some individual projects might meet this test, the necessity of using foreign exchange to pay us back, instead of for other vitally needed imports, will cause considerable ill will. When the time comes, most of our "loans" will be forgiven, but we will not be thanked for our generosity. The necessity for asking for cancellation will gall our debtors.

Government loans and grants have another major and very practical drawback. They lack Congressional support. Every year it is the same story—bipartisan support by the executive and leaders of both parties, but strong grassroots objections. I happen to live in one of those areas where the "man-in-the-street" objections are violently strong. I do not believe that this feeling is going to change rapidly. "Gift, loan, grant," are all red flags to those who see nothing but a huge outflow of their dollars with nothing to show for it. These feelings are naturally reflected in the attitudes of the representatives who are elected from these areas. Unless the general political system of the United States is substantially changed, there will remain in Congress for many years a strong opposition to such programs.

If government grants and loans have such rough weather, can we solve the whole problem by leaving it to private enterprise? Private foreign investment offers several healthy alternatives to public loans and grants. Private investment is primarily equity investment. This is important. Equity investment does not have to be liquidated. There is no contractual obligation to pay interest and dividends. While it is essential that the investment be productive over a period, it is understood by both parties that in periods of economic strain no dividends need be paid, while in periods of prosperity there may be good dividends. It has been the custom, both at home and abroad, for private companies to retain and reinvest in the business substantial amounts of earnings. In this way, the initial investment is increased importantly with no strain on the economy or foreign exchange position of the under-developed country. Equity investment has important theoretical advantages over loans and grants.

In addition, it has important qualitative advantages over public loans and grants. A dollar of private equity investment is likely to be much more fruitful than a dollar of government money. This is clearly described by the National Planning Association in *The Political Economy of American Foreign Policy:*

Direct private investment of the latter kind is capable of building relationships between the industrial and the underdeveloped countries which are organic and continuous. It usually involves relations between people, not governments; relations which become integral parts of the economic and social fabric of the recipient country. It normally carries with it the technical knowledge which is as sorely needed in the underdeveloped areas as are capital funds. Such continuous and often cumulative transfers of capital and technology under private auspices are much more likely to result in durable capital assets and permanently absorbed technological innovations in the underdeveloped countries than are publicly financed investment and the intergovernmental technical assistance programs with their necessarily limited scope and short term character.

Direct, long term private investment fosters in various ways the growth within the underdeveloped countries of a constructive middle class and habits of private, decentralized decision-making and enterprise. . . . Both the cultural backgrounds of many of these countries and the nature of the internal difficulties and external threats which they now face are strongly conducive to centralization of initiative, decision-making and control in authoritarian governments. If liberal values compatible with those of the West, and indigenous institutions capable of realizing them, are ever to evolve in Asia, Africa and Latin America, it is necessary for alternative modes of choice and action to be increasingly available within these societies. By precept and example, as well as by actually involving growing numbers of local people in privately directed economic activities, private foreign investment can help to foster democratic patterns of decision and action in the underdeveloped countries.

This is an attractive siren song, and many have been tempted to leave it at that. It seems clear to me that it will not work. Private foreign investment that is not guided and intensified by government help will be too little and in the wrong place. The tendency of private investment is to seek the safest place with the greatest return, which may not at all coincide with the most desirable area from a political point of view.

The argument generally runs, (1) we must invest more abroad to save our political hides; (2) private sources will not come through fast enough; (3) we can't wait; so (4) public resources must be used via public agencies. Even more crudely, "If we do nothing, the private sector will let us down, so give me a couple of billion a year and I'll show you some real results." No one seems to have asked the question, "What would the private sector accomplish if it had the tangible encouragement of $1.5 or $2 billion a year to spur it on?" Yet isn't it grossly unfair to compare what a public agency with $2 billion a year could do with what the private sector might do without any money at all? That is a contest anybody would lose.

But report after report admits that the private sector cannot do the job in time, and since there is a terrible emergency, we must pour additional billions through additional public agencies. Granted that these billions must come for the time being from the public purse, is it necessary to have large public agencies to spend them? I think not. The real question is: "How can these billions—which we assume a kind Congress will provide—be invested in the most efficient and effective way? How can these billions be used to give a concrete example of our economic way of life to the underdeveloped countries?"

The question that is being answered by all of these serious

studies—the wrong question—is this: "Can private foreign investment compete in volume and in politically desirable areas with a $2-billion-a-year public program?" The answer, not unnaturally, is no, despite the often described superiority of private investment as a means of establishing viable international economic relationships. The questions that should have been asked are these: "Can $2 billion a year of public money be invested in politically desirable areas most effectively by using foreign subsidiaries of private domestic companies or by using a large public lending agency?" "Which method of channeling this capital will create the most enduring economic and political gains for us and for the recipient countries?" "Which program, the public or the private one, is most likely to achieve the rather substantial political success of prying an additional $2 billion a year out of a conservative Congress?" These are the pertinent questions that have not been asked.

How can public funds be effectively channeled through private corporations? Just what kind of partnership between the government and the private sector of the economy can we set up?

The concept of a mutual fund is intriguing to me. I would propose an International Development Corporation of the United States. This fund would receive capital, initially from the federal budget, perhaps later on from other sources, and would invest it in equity ownership of foreign business corporations. Such corporations would be operating subsidiaries of domestic corporations, and primary responsibility for control and operations would be in the parent company.

The International Development Corporation would be the bridge between public capital and private utilization of the capital. Its purpose would be to provide the incentive for private corporations to invest in economically strange but politically desirable areas. I visualize a relatively small research staff devoted to allocating investment funds to different areas and companies, much as the staff of a domestic mutual fund allocates its investment among different common stocks. Such experts would be thoroughly familiar with the investment needs and climate of each particular target area and would work with the foreign operating arms of our domestic companies in setting up steel, power, automotive, farm equipment, chemical, drug, petroleum, mining companies in various underdeveloped countries. Final investment decisions would be made by the board of directors of the IDC.

For example, the IDC directors might allocate $500 million of

their annual capital receipts to India. The India section of the
IDC research staff would then break down their annual allotment
into industry segments, based upon their own judgment, the flow
of applications they had on hand, and consultation with appropriate Indian planners. As a result, a Bethlehem Steel of India or
International Harvester of Bombay might be incorporated—or
expanded—in any given year. After full consideration of all the
facts, the probability of success, the character of the private investor, the desirability of the investment from the recipient country's
point of view, the board of directors would authorize the investment. Once made, the investment is on the books. If it prospers,
as it should, then in due course earnings and dividends may appear.
Other sections of the IDC staff would be preparing similar programs for other underdeveloped areas. Thus, the IDC would
quickly build up a valuable portfolio of foreign equity investments.

The IDC is the carrot, the incentive to pull an active interest
from the economic talent of our major private corporations. How
would the carrot entice? A fundamental and time-tested method
of making profits is to pyramid capital resources. Thus, a corporation might get a 10 per cent return on a $100 million investment;
if $70 million of the investment were borrowed funds on which
you paid 5 per cent, then the $30 million equity investment would
get a return of about 22 per cent. If the IDC put up half the
equity investment, but asked to get only a quarter of the equity
profits, then the multiplier would become even more favorable.
The terms for such an investment can be manipulated endlessly.
The greater the political risk, the more attractive the terms could
be made.

The equity ownership of these foreign business corporations
would not be limited to the IDC and U.S.A. domestic corporations. Wherever possible, investment by local interests should be
brought in. One of the major purposes of a foreign business corporation is to foster the growth of the local private economy, to
attract and marshal local capital resources, and to develop private
economic initiative. The foreign business corporation would be
controlled by a triumvirate made up of the IDC, U.S. domestic
interests, and foreign interests. The IDC would provide a good
portion of the capital on favorable terms; the U.S. domestic interests would provide the technical knowledge and managerial skills
and some capital; the foreign interests would provide local knowledge, local capital and, it would be hoped, local managerial skills.

The profits would be split, perhaps unequally, between the IDC and the private interests, domestic and foreign. But it is fully expected that there will be profits, and that some of them will be returned in the form of dividends. This is not an eleemosynary operation. Profits are expected—perhaps not in every year, but on the average. The equity capital, however, is permanent capital; there is no thought of repatriation and therefore no agonizing problems such as we are setting up with our soft loans—what to do with the soft currencies, or how to let the borrower gracefully default. If the flow of capital to the underdeveloped countries is of reasonable size, and if the economies do make some progress, there should be sufficient room in the balance of payments to allow moderate payment of dividends. Some dividend return is important. It is a concrete demonstration to Congress that this is an investment and not a give-away program.

Could an International Development Corporation designed to feed equity capital from the federal budget through foreign business corporations to the economies of the underdeveloped countries receive concrete Congressional support to the tune of $1.5 to $2 billion a year? A closely related consideration is whether current efforts to increase the government-to-government programs via the Development Loan Fund, the IDA, and the like can succeed in increasing their take by $1.5 to $2 billion a year over present levels?

Taking the negative first, I would guess that future efforts to increase substantially the funds allocated to foreign economic aid are not likely to be more successful than past efforts. Despite the intensity of the support of the "liberals" for important increases in foreign aid programs, there does not seem to be enough independent or moderate support to put the actual appropriations over. Every year, the foreign aid portion of the budget seems to be the most vulnerable. There are few signs that this conservative hostility to things foreign is losing ground. Even the rather substantial Democratic, presumably liberal, majorities that resulted from the 1958 elections did not alter the normal foreign aid difficulties at appropriation time. Nor is it likely that the competition for the federal dollar will markedly lessen with time.

Could a new approach emphasizing free enterprise allied with government capital succeed where current efforts may fail? No dogmatic answer is possible. I think, however, that it is possible to foresee a more hopeful political result. Current programs have almost no support in the conservative segment of the community.

I believe that there is an important section of conservative business opinion that could be attracted to a foreign investment program based upon a real and effective use of private enterprise. Such political power as this group represents, when combined with the power of the liberal groups who see the vital political necessities involved, might add up to a political bloc powerful enough to put through an increase in our foreign investment activities of really significant size.

The International Development Corporation would have substantial political assets that current loan programs do not have. First and foremost it would parade as an investment, not as a giveaway. It could point to expected, and, in due course, actual, dividend returns; its balance sheet would represent permanent investments, not a list of doubtful loans; it could point to some private capital accompanying each government dollar; it would be more in keeping with our experience and the development of our domestic economy, and the flag of private enterprise could be waved vigorously. Of course, the more rabid of our anti-business liberals might attack the IDC as a big-business graft, but I think that most of the liberal strength is sincere in its devotion to the cause of foreign economic development and would accept the IDC as the only way to rally sufficient political strength to put their foreign investment program across. In the area of predicting future political attitudes, no cast-iron, footnoted, irrefutable proofs can be offered. I do offer my guess that only through the union of liberal and conservative elements can a foreign investment program of adequate size be successfully pried out of the federal budget in the sixties.

Would such a public-private foreign investment program be acceptable to the underdeveloped countries? Capitalism is an unsavory word in many of the countries we want to help. Imperialism, capitalism, colonialism are all connected in the minds of the people and are rejected wholeheartedly. So goes the orthodox line. But while hostile attitudes do exist, I think one may legitimately question the assumption that they are immutable, or that a cogently offered, substantial program of private investment would be rejected out of hand.

In this murky world of value judgments—judgments on other people's attitudes—no proof is possible, but here are some comments.

Granting the predominantly socialist and Marxist background of the political elite in many of the underdeveloped countries, how can you fit private investment into a nationalized economy? Two responses are valid here. First, attitudes are changing. As economic growth begins to take hold, the very immensity of the task of rigidly controlling everything becomes apparent. It is much easier and more fruitful to encourage private initiative to get as much done for you as possible. The advantages of the "mixed" politico-economic structure become evident. This is all we need. Secondly, I offer here private enterprise with a difference. The participation of the U.S. Government through the IDC and of foreign interests in the management of the subsidiary firms operating in the underdeveloped countries would bridge the gap between the uncontrolled private capitalism of the colonial days and the controlled economies now being attempted.

There are two methods of creating capital—forced savings through taxation or inflation, or voluntary saving and investment through creating an attractive economic atmosphere for domestic and foreign investors. Any leader of an underdeveloped country is quickly made aware of these alternatives, regardless of his economic predilections. If private investment were offered in important quantity in return for reasonable attitudes toward private concerns, I suspect that most leaders would be interested.

Analyzing the current five-year plan in India, Professor Malenbaum concludes (in *East and West in India's Development,* [Washington, D.C.: National Planning Association, 1959]):

> Thus, on both private and public account, the current Indian Plan did give ample scope for foreign participation—by international institutions, by governments, or by private firms—in India's development effort. . . . Foreign countries anxious to assist in India's economic growth could find in the planned program a wide scope, both with respect to the amount and the type of assistance that could be used.

Here a concrete plan by a socialist-oriented government includes room for private enterprise.

Any successful international investment program must be acceptable to both parties. The underdeveloped countries have great need for capital, and we have large capital resources available for fruitful investment. But the relationship must be mutually advantageous. It seems to me that a program such as I have outlined could be adapted to the mixed economies now appearing in the underdeveloped countries. It is just as important that any program appear advantageous to us, both to Congress and to our major economic organizations. The second half of this social equation is where current programs have failed.

THREE

PLANNING AND ADMINISTERING DEVELOPMENT

9. MANPOWER PLANNING

JOHN F. HILLIARD

DURING the past thirty years, every country that has undertaken a significant program of economic and social development has found itself impeded by a shortage of trained manpower. Since conditions preceding a development program are usually characterized by severe unemployment, even of university graduates, the realization of the need for immediate and large-scale manpower planning in most countries has been slow in developing. Consequently, the early stages of development are usually characterized by large-scale unemployment on the one hand, and on the other, acute shortages in occupations essential to the development program.

The training of men and women in key fields is a lengthy process and requires the making of plans, taking of decisions, and investment of capital from two to six years before any large increase in trained manpower can be expected to appear. In the early years of development, when many difficult immediate problems are faced and the competition for all available resources is keen, there is an understandable tendency to put off taking action to prevent serious problems five years or more away. Yet a nation's people are the basic resource for development, as, indeed, they are the main reason for development. Machinery, capital, materials may be obtained from many sources, but manpower for the development of any nation can come basically from only one source—the men and women of that nation.

Nature of Manpower Planning

Since manpower planning is crucial to national development, its nature and requirements must be brought into clear focus. The very term "manpower" has never been formally defined in the sense in which it is widely used today. Manpower planning therefore may convey widely divergent ideas. Educators tend to regard it as a form of educational planning. Government administrators tend to see it as a staffing problem connected with the administrative service of state-administered industries. Some see it essentially as a problem of training engineers, finding jobs for the unemployed, counseling young people, and so on.

All of these are part of the process of manpower planning, but they are not the whole of it. Manpower planning means the total process by which proper development and wise utilization of the human resources of a nation is achieved in attaining the objective to which the nation has committed itself.

In this light, manpower planning includes identification of the human skills required for every major activity, and a determination of the magnitude and timing of such requirements. It involves the use of existing or the development of new institutions to produce the manpower required, at the right time, in the right quantity, and of the right quality. It requires careful integration of the various institutions so that, in the total of their functions, they produce the people with the skills and knowledge necessary to the nation's economic, technological, intellectual, and spiritual growth.

The practical implications of this concept of manpower planning are many.

First, it is essential that those doing manpower planning have an adequate understanding of the nation's goals and of the general strategy by which those goals are to be achieved.

Secondly, it requires careful and continuous study of the activities that create manpower requirements and of the institutions that develop manpower resources.

Thirdly, it requires the continuous projection of manpower resources and requirements four to eight years into the future—based upon an economy that is envisaged but not actually in being.

Fourthly, it requires the systematic taking of timely action to balance manpower requirements and resources, now and in the future, to assure that progress toward established goals is facilitated by the availability of trained personnel.

This type of comprehensive, integrated planning obviously cannot be done on a hit-or-miss basis, nor can it be improvised on the spur of the moment. It requires not only a penetrating understanding of the relationships between human skills and national progress, but the systematic application of technical tools that have been developed during the past three decades.

Development of Manpower Planning

No more than twenty-five years ago, very little of a scientific character was known about manpower as an economic resource. For example, in the United States of America, which has engaged in large-scale manpower research in recent years, it was not known with any degree of precision how many workers were in the labor force, how many were working, or how many were unemployed. Relatively little systematic knowledge existed about the jobs by which Americans earned their living, how they acquired their skills, or what motivated them to behave as they did as workers. There was not even a vocabulary with which to describe the basic features of employment skills and experience in a society that had been growing progressively more industrialized for over a hundred years. This was also roughly the position of the other principal industrial countries of the world.

Prior to the 1930's, the western world generally regarded manpower resources as something created automatically as a product of economic incentives, and accommodating itself to the vagaries of economic cycles and technological innovations. The U.S.S.R., which was undertaking its early five-year plans, looked upon manpower as an economic resource to be fed into the economy in a manner fundamentally no different from that of other resources. It was in the 1930's that both these concepts became obviously incorrect in certain basic ways. In the West, the great depression swept away the complacent assumption that manpower is an automatic product of economic motivation and that it will conform to that concept of economic law. In the Soviet Union, it became evident that the power to command was not sufficient to secure the human skill and motivation necessary for that vast country to hoist itself up from its earlier feudalism.

Something was wrong with both concepts. Manpower was more than "hands," more than the agent of a command. It was the one resource that could feel and think and act upon its own volition. It was the one resource that could not be left in the ground or stockpiled in semifinished form. It was the resource that demanded economic progress, but whose skills and attitudes were the ultimate determinants of the rate and direction of progress.

Failure of the concepts of manpower in both East and West brought on a vast program of research in manpower and employment.

Because of the great differences of economic and social systems, research in different countries took different forms, but, in all, it reflected a fundamental change in outlook regarding the nature of manpower and of the mainsprings of its development and utilization. The first task was to create adequate tools of analysis. Among its products were dictionaries of occupations, industrial classification systems, labor market analysis techniques, occupational and employment forecasting, aptitude testing and employment counseling. Countless inquiries were launched into the economic, psychological, and sociological aspects of manpower and employment. The field of human resources became suddenly, in the great depression, one of the world's most fruitful areas of research. (In the U.S.S.R., because of its highly integrated society and economic institutions, this research was primarily empirical and "applications engineering" in the manpower field.)

This new-found knowledge developed immediate uses in industry, in schools and colleges, and in community development. For the first time, it became possible to analyze and describe in a systematic way the skills and processes by which a national labor force is developed and utilized to supply the complex economic and social requirements of a nation.

Application of this knowledge was greatly accelerated by the occurrence of World War II. By the end of the first two years of the war, it had become increasingly clear that the ultimate determinant of the war would be manpower, both highly trained armed forces and equally highly trained and efficiently utilized civilian labor forces. Consequently, the war not only precipitated large-scale application of the manpower research of the 1930's, but accelerated such research in all major combatant countries. A fair appraisal of the war in the perspective of nearly two decades would account for its outcome through many factors, but the skill, motivation, and management of manpower would rank high among them. Even the atomic bomb, which brought the war in the East to an abrupt close, was dramatic testimony to the utilization of trained scientific manpower.

The end of the war found many of the world's advanced economies in ruins. Others required great change and modification to meet the needs of peace and reconstruction. Again these requirements forced a vast retraining and readjustment of manpower—tens of millions of soldiers to be brought back into civilian employment, hundreds of millions of war workers to be either retrained or reoriented for the pursuits of peace. And again the pressure of reconstruction forced a continuation of research in and planning of manpower resources by the industrially advanced countries.

At the same time, the industrially underdeveloped countries surged forward in what has been aptly called "the revolution of rising expectations." In the years since the war, a great many nations have been born into political independence. More will follow. These have instantly confronted the tremendous problems of providing the skills for the management of their national affairs; in addition, nearly all are committed to rasing the standard of life of their people through economic developments that, in many instances, amount to deliberately created national emergencies. And all are encountering the old problem: Economic and social progress requires large numbers of highly developed human skills, involving lengthy periods of training and effective only when managed with skill and wisdom.

Contemporary Experience in Manpower Planning

That the solution of this problem is central to national development is attested by the efforts directed toward solving it in the industrially most advanced countries. In the United States of America and in the Soviet Union, for example, the development of high-talent manpower is regarded as a major function of government. For the past eight years in the U.S.A., the coordination and direction of manpower policies and programs has been vested in the Executive Office of the President, with specific responsibilities and functions assigned to the several executive departments and agencies. Committees of the Congress regularly inquire into various problems of manpower training and utilization as a basis for framing appropriate legislation. Scientific and engineering societies have joined together to establish an Engineering Manpower Commission and a Scientific Manpower Commission. Continuous research is directed toward all aspects of manpower development and utilization.

Similar activities have been undertaken since the war by most of the countries of Western Europe. In addition, recognizing their independence in the fields of science, technology, and teaching, they established a high-level committee on Scientific and Technical Personnel in the Organization for European Economic Cooperation, to pool resources in meeting critical manpower problems.

In 1956, the Republic of India confronted growing manpower shortages in various technical fields so severe as to threaten the success of the second and third five-year plans. To meet this problem, the government established a cabinet committee on manpower under the chairmanship of the Prime Minister. To provide staff services for the cabinet committee and see to the effectuation of its decisions, a manpower directorate was created at a top level in the Ministry of Home Affairs; a manpower divison was established in the Planning Commission to conduct studies of manpower resources and requirements, both short- and long-term; a manpower officer was appointed in each central ministry, in each zonal council, and in each state government. As a result, sweeping changes have taken place in allocation of funds for various types of educational activities; targets for the training of key personnel have been enlarged, in some instances as much as 100 per cent; and programs for improving utilization of trained personnel have been launched.

Since that time, a large number of newly developing countries have launched studies of their manpower resources and requirements, and many have undertaken action programs to meet their trained manpower needs. Some of these countries are Nigeria, Ghana, Uganda, and Tanganyika in Africa; Lebanon, Jordan, and Iran in the Middle East; Brazil and Argentina in South America; and Italy, Greece, and Turkey in Europe.

A survey of manpower planning and administration in the countries of the world shows great diversity in form and detail, but on certain fundamentals they agree. To be fully successful, manpower planning and administration require the following:

1. Development of an adequate appreciation at top levels of government of the manpower problems created by rapid economic development, and a sense of urgency in doing something about them.

2. Development of an adequate organizational structure within the government for dealing effectively with these problems on a continuing basis.

3. Formulation of a comprehensive, integrated manpower program geared to both short- and long-term needs of national development.

4. Securing top policy level understanding of and the support for the program.

5. Vigorous effectuation of the program, with periodic review, evaluation, and extension.

Laying the Base for Plans and Programs

There is in every country a substantial degree of manpower planning going on. In many, however, this planning is short-range, narrow in scope, and fragmented among many ministries and agencies. There is no general design or strategic plan geared to the evolving pattern of requirements in both short and long terms. Manpower planning is frequently regarded as an adjunct to each development project rather than as a major aspect of national development itself. Measures for joint planning and coordination are ill-defined or insufficiently used.

In dealing with these various problems, it is profitable to examine briefly the fundamentals mentioned above.

Creating Awareness of the Problems

This must, of course, be achieved through a variety of measures. Many countries have found, however, that an intelligent national interest and awareness can be created most quickly by one or a series of addresses by national leaders highlighting the importance of manpower—of people—in the various aspects of development. Such addresses are well received, since they have great human and social interest, drawing attention to development as not just factories, dams, and power stations, but also as the opening of new and challenging opportunities for people—and for their sons and daughters.

Such statements may profitably be supplemented in both popular and technical terms by encouraging the publication of papers and interviews by appropriate government officers, industrial leaders, and university professors.

Organizational Structure

Proposals for new organizational structures frequently arouse apprehension among those countries charged with the function concerned. Fortunately, the types of manpower organization generally found to be most satisfactory require no substantial reorganization of existing agencies, but rather providing the organizational elements needed to bring them into closer and more effective cooperation. Moreover, this new structure provides them with the opportunity to participate in framing policy, developing comprehensive programs, and fitting their own activities more meaningfully into the development program as a whole.

The basic elements of organization are: (1) a policy committee at the ministerial level to review major policy and program proposals, to take decisions, and to evaluate progress periodically; (2) a planning and executive division in an appropriate ministry to serve the policy committee and to provide coordination and leadership in program planning and execution; (3) one or more responsible officers in each ministry or major agency to stimulate intelligent manpower planning and to provide liaison with the central manpower planning division; (4) adequate arrangements for continuous consultation with leaders in important fields, such as education, industry, and labor.

No feasible alternative has been found to central direction and control of manpower planning. By the same token, there is no feasible alternative to decentralized development and execution of manpower plans. Experience has shown that this process not only produces the best results qualitatively, but is the only way that sufficient resources can be made available to attack the problem on a broad front.

Program Development

A comprehensive integrated manpower program is very unlikely to be developed preceding an organizational arrangement along the general lines described above. Once this type of organization is established, however, the pooling of all existing knowledge and judgment makes relatively easy the task of determining the content of the program. (This does not imply that execution of the program will necessarily be easy.)

The elements of a manpower program usually may be roughly divided into three categories—development of manpower information required for further administrative decision and action; execution of manpower projects on which sufficient data and policy guidance exists to permit immediate action; and further study of manpower projects on which additional data or guidance are required.

Within these categories, every aspect of manpower must be considered. The experience of most countries, however, is that the greatest weight of attention should be focused upon those groups of skills that in the aggregate are most basic to development and that require the longest periods of training.

These groups usually are (1) engineers, (2) scientists, in both physical and social sciences, (3) teachers at all levels, (4) health and medical personnel, (5) administrators for the public service, (6) industrial managers, (7) agricultural personnel, and (8) skilled craftsmen.

An appendix at the end of this article suggests the types of considerations that must go into comprehensive manpower planning.

Since manpower requirements for the short term must be met for the most part from those already trained, any satisfactory program must emphasize improvement of their motivation and utilization.

There are wide variations in the efficiency with which such highly trained men as engineers are utilized, between countries, between industries, and, frequently, between departments of the same enterprise. Well-informed manpower authorities estimate that probably every country could, through carefully devised programs, improve its trained manpower utilization by at least 20 per cent.

Policy-Level Understanding and Support

Manpower problems of major significance can be solved only by committing substantial resources for which competition is usually keen. Not infrequently this involves taking decisions that are objected to by important groups such as university faculties, industrial managers, or labor unions. Consequently, it is imperative that such program proposals be firmly decided at a level sufficiently high so that they will not be challenged successfully or subverted by noncompliance. Otherwise, manpower planning becomes a process of solving only small problems that in the aggregate are not crucial to the development program. It is for this reason that an active committee at the ministerial level is needed. Even so, on matters of great importance or controversy, the head of the government should be fully informed and consulted.

Implementation and Review

Effectuation of the manpower program does not mean it should be carried out on a "crash" basis. On the other hand, it should not be an exercise in slow motion. Timeliness is an indispensable ingredient of success in planning for rapidly changing economic conditions. Moreover, the coordinated effectuation of the program is important, with all the relevant governmental and private institutions playing their appropriate parts. It is this balance and harmony of effort that is most required for success.

Evaluation of progress in a manpower program is not easy. It requires a relentless insistence upon facts and demonstrable judgments, rather than ambiguities and "weather reporting," which are so often put up as progress reports. Generally, it is advisable to develop a synthesized progress report on a quarterly basis, but in no event less than twice a year. This report should be submitted to the policy committee together with proposals for program changes or extensions.

Training of Manpower Staff

As has been indicated, very significant manpower activities of various kinds are under way in virtually every country. Often these are directed by highly competent officers of the various ministries and agencies concerned with manpower. Among the fields in which well-trained manpower technicians are usually found are manpower and population statistics, employment service operation, labor market reporting, vocational training, industrial and occupational classification.

An over-all approach to manpower planning as defined in this paper, however, will involve some additional training of those directing these various activities, as well as further recruitment and training of technical staff in the various manpower activities. Manpower officers appointed in the ministries and agencies could profit from training in the principles of manpower planning and administration. This training need not precede the establishment of a manpower organization and program; in fact, it would be preferable to conduct it as an ongoing part of program development and execution.

The training staff. Obviously the officers directing manpower activities must assume the major responsibility for further study and for conducting training for subordinate and technical staff. In addition, a considerable number of university faculty members are highly qualified in the conceptual approach to manpower planning, as well as in such technical subjects as economics, statistics, personnel administration, and training. These can be utilized to excellent advantage on a part-time basis.

Materials. Fortunately, during the past fifteen years, a tremendous amount of literature has been published on manpower planning and mobilization for national emergencies or economic development. This literature describes the actual experience and technical developments in manpower administration in countries ranging from the most advanced industrially to those just undertaking development programs. Moreover, each country's own experience is a valuable guide if it is carefully studied.

Training methods. Basically, the training method for directors of manpower activities and manpower officers of the ministries should be a continuing series of weekly seminars under the leadership of those most competent in various manpower fields. These seminars should consist of study of selected materials, followed by a two- or three-hour discussion led by a competent discussion leader. Summary notes on these discussions should be reproduced for distribution to the technical staff and to other officers interested in manpower matters. Training of the technical staff should be undertaken on an increased scale by those now responsible for this function. Additional training in various specialties with the cooperation of university faculty members can usually be arranged. The possibility of short foreign-study tours for carefully selected manpower officers and for promising technical staff members should be explored.

In Conclusion

Manpower planning for national development is fundamentally similar to planning for the intelligent utilization of other resources. Although it presents certain unique problems, the development of human resources lends itself to the application of tested principles and practices through effective organizational arrangements. Application of these principles and practices at the right time is indispensable to the achievement of national goals.

APPENDIX. ELEMENTS OF AN ASSESSMENT OF MANPOWER RESOURCES AND REQUIREMENTS FOR ECONOMIC DEVELOPMENT

   (I) Population characteristics: (A) Age, (B) Sex, (C) Education, (D) Health, (E) Geographical distribution.
  (II) Labor force characteristics:
        (A) Composition by (1) Size, (2) Sex, (3) Age.

(B) Industrial distribution by (1) Agriculture, by major types; (2) Non-agricultural activities, by major types; (3) Region or state.

(C) Occupation skills, principally (1) Technological manpower (scientists and engineers); (2) Teachers at all levels; (3) Health personnel; (4) Administrative personnel (government); (5) Executives, managers, and technical support personnel (industry, private and public); (6) Agricultural personnel (highly trained); (7) Social scientists (highly trained); (8) Craftsmen and skilled industrial workers.

(D) Quality and motivation: (1) Aptitudes as demonstrated in existing industrial enterprises; (2) Social and geographical mobility; (3) Motivation toward change and economic improvement; (4) Literacy and educational achievement pattern.

(III) Employment and unemployment:

(A) Trend in employment by major activities;

(B) Manpower shortages, if any;

(C) Unemployment and underemployment: (1) Agriculture; (2) Non-agricultural activities; (3) By special classes of personnel or by geographical areas.

(IV) Growth factors at work in the economy:

(A) Programmed expansion goals for planned economic growth (1) By industry (including agriculture), (2) By time table.

(B) Current and prospective trend in "unplanned" economic growth from (1) Domestic, private capital investment; (2) Foreign capital investment.

(C) Major basic resource assets and limitations.

(V) Trained manpower producing institutions:

(A) Educational system: (1) Elementary and secondary; (2) Vocational and technical; (3) College and postgraduate; (4) Estimates of quality at each level; (5) Numbers and distribution of students; (6) Foreign training by numbers, fields, and country; (7) Employment experience and expectations of products of each level of education.

(B) Government, industry, and professional associations: (1) In-service training and development of government administrative and technical personnel; (2) In-service training and development of executive, managerial, and technical personnel in industry; (3) Efficiency of systems of recruiting, training, and utilizing trained personnel—government and industry; (4) Effectiveness of collateral institutions, such as management associations and professional societies.

(VI) Organization, objectives, and activities of the labor movement:
- (A) Major units, numbers and orientation;
- (B) Activities conducted by each in fields of union organization, worker education, and development of responsible unions;
- (C) Management attitudes toward labor organizations and collective bargaining;
- (D) Industrial relations experience in major sectors of economy and outlook for future.

(VII) Organization of government for manpower planning and administration: (A) Basic governmental organization for planning and conducting economic development; (B) Awareness of the manpower problem and sense of urgency in solving it; (C) Extent and kinds of arrangements for building manpower plans into economic development programs; (D) Extent and kinds of organizations to conduct manpower resources-requirements studies and to help manage manpower resources; (E) Extent and quality of cooperating nongovernmental and quasi-governmental organizations available to contribute to manpower planning.

(VIII) Evaluation of manpower resources and requirements for anticipated economic growth by
- (A) Present adequacy of resources;
- (B) Estimated requirements by time periods;
- (C) Resources and facilities for meeting requirements within lead time available;
- (D) Measures required to meet requirements and to adjust imbalances in resources and requirements.

(IX) Inter-country comparisons:
- (A) Comparison of basic resources characteristics of countries in regional grouping by soil, water, climate, minerals, power, transportation, industry, agriculture, and manpower;
- (B) Comparison of attitudes toward and explicitness of plans for economic development;
- (C) Construction of a "comparison grid" to show basic similarities and differences;
- (D) Identification of human resource (or other) development programs in which regional cooperation is practical and mutually advantageous.

10. LEGISLATION FOR ECONOMIC DEVELOPMENT IN LATIN AMERICA

VÍCTOR L. URQUIDI

At any given moment in the process of trying to establish a clearly defined development policy and, if possible, a coherent program or plan, there is a body of existing legislation that has to be taken into account. Its origin may sometimes be obscure (this is frequently the case with tax legislation), or it may be the result of some short-term emergency. Most tax laws have been written to enable the government to obtain revenues, without sufficient regard to their economic effects. A good deal of legislation affecting foreign exchange transactions has been of the emergency type and frequently self-defeating. Legislation on foreign investments, though often related to exchange control, has had primarily a political content. Social security, enacted to pursue a definite welfare purpose, has rarely been devised to serve also, through its accumulation of savings, as an instrument in financing economic development. Labor legislation has in some cases run ahead of economic reality and failed to achieve its aims.

On the other hand, existing legislation may represent a survival of nineteenth-century economic liberalism or even of the pre-independence economic framework, or a contradictory mixture of both. Nineteenth-century freedom of enterprise as established in most constitutions, together with the enactment of laws granting an individual or a corporation exclusive rights to produce, import, or transport something (in other words, creating a private legal monopoly), is a combination that is difficult to understand, but is found in some countries. Whatever its particular merits, it is certainly not a good legal basis for economic development.

Minimum wages, land reform, and the income tax have not gained a strong foothold in countries where the social structure has produced governments content with short-term objectives or believing that the free working of market forces produces the best results.

The absence of suitable banking and financial legislation (and even of a central bank) can be explained only in terms of an inapplicable and unrealistic economic ideology. The same can be said for the lack of agragrian legislation, or the piecemeal approach to industrial development that prevails in many countries.

If a Latin American country should succeed in appraising its development problems and in firmly adopting some sort of rational long-range program, one of the first steps to be taken should be to revise critically all economic legislation, beginning with constitutional provisions, in order to determine its compatibility with a development policy or a program. Many basic legal concepts would have to come under review, since, fundamentally, a development program is usually devised to achieve a desired allocation of investment, specific targets in the growth of productive capacity and output, and a redistribution of income and wealth in favor of the underprivileged. Legislation for development thus involves an individual's right to dispose of property and income and his right to pursue an economic activity or enterprise of his own choice.

To effectuate a development policy, the main areas of necessary legislation—and the implicit need for reviewing and revising existing legislation—can perhaps usefully be identified by taking as a vantage point that of the economist concerned specifically with development as a whole. The following discussion will attempt to indicate legislative needs in terms of the economic objectives to be pursued.

A Development General Staff ✳

The first requirement is for a government to establish a clearly defined and adequately staffed technical body fully responsible for analyzing, on a continuous and full-time basis, the long-term trends and structural changes in the economy, and for preparing short-, medium-, and long-range projections of the economy as a whole and of its sectors, to serve as a general framework for development policy decisions. Such a body should not only have authority to obtain the best available information from all public and private sources (and this may involve overcoming some legal taboos), but should also be treated by the executive as its economic development general staff.

Policy decisions should obviously be taken by the executive at the ministerial or cabinet level, preferably through a council or committee composed of the principal ministers or secretaries concerned with development and including the head of the central bank, the development corporation, and any other agency of similar importance.

The actual formulation of the public investment program and its financing should be made by each government department and every significant autonomous agency, under the guidance and supervision of a programming committee composed of representatives of the budget office (or treasury), the development projections staff, the central bank, and the development corporation. Similar committees, involving representatives of specified ministries (agriculture, industry, etc.) can be set up to review the investment plans or programs of the main private sectors. Suitable subcommittees, advisory groups (in which private sector representatives ought to take part), and working groups should function when necessary.

Final adoption of the over-all investment and financial program should be made by the ministerial committee on the basis of proposals and recommendations submitted by the development projections staff and the programming committees. Implementation of the program should be supervised by the same committees, with a view to making recommendations to the executive for further action or for modifications, as should appear necessary. Presentation of the development program or plan as a whole to the legislative branch, where appropriate, should be made by the executive through the minister of the treasury in connection with authorization of the budget.

The above mechanisms could be regarded as a minimum in government organization for development. It is important to realize, however, that what is involved is not the setting up of a few more official bodies to deal with new functions, but a complete centralization of the strategy and general formulation of the development program and its financing under the highest authority, while its detailed formulation and its operations should be decentralized and, where suitable, regionalized. Thus, unless some traditional legislation is modified to make room for the central development programming function over and above ordinary ministerial or departmental functions, and unless legal and constitutional relations between federal or central and state or provincial governments are changed to fit the concept of centralized general programming with regionalized execution, it is doubtful that much could be accomplished in the effort to intensify economic and social development as envisaged by the Alliance for Progress.

Now, even assuming that the organizational problem is not ideally solved, the main areas of development legislation that should be reviewed in any case may be stated as follows:

Investment Inducements ✳

To achieve a higher ratio of investment-to-product requires the adoption of a general investment target based on an expected relationship between the growth in investment and the growth of output. Aggregate required investment has to be allocated by activity and divided in each one between the public and the private sector. Hence, some basic decisions are necessary (whatever the projections and the desired goals) regarding the extent and type of public investment in each activity (agriculture, industry, power, transport, etc.), the proportion of public to total investment, and the allocation of financial resources. But given the decisions on public investment, and assuming that the necessary legislation is enacted authorizing the state to undertake investment in fields not previously considered appropriate (e.g., electric power, steel, chemicals), and that the financial resources are similarly assured, there remains then the critical question of creating conditions conducive to the growth of private investment in accordance with the targets set up. It is not enough for a government to proclaim the need for private investment. A whole series of legal provisions and administrative policies should, as a consistent whole, attempt to induce the desired volume of private investment.

In manufacturing and mining, as well as utilities, aside from questions of general political atmosphere or the state of short-term economic uncertainty, the problem revolves around the adequacy of tax incentives, rates of taxation on profits, labor legislation, social security contributions, tariff protection and import controls, equitable treatment of foreign private capital, utility rates, and, in some cases, special legislation regulating the integration and expansion of an industry through both publicly owned and privately owned plants. It is obvious that failings in any one type of measure, the adoption of contradictory legislation, or the application of mutually inconsistent operational policies will result in delays in private industrial investment and a falling short of desired targets.

Unfortunately, tariffs and import controls are too often handled by Latin American governments under particular pressures, instead of under broad policy lines. Tax-exemption laws have operated on a first-come first-served basis, instead of as part of an industrial development plan. Certain incentive features of tax laws, such as special or accelerated depreciation allowances, have hardly been made use of or have been offered but sparingly. Taxation of profits is often inequitable to the small and medium-sized business, or among equal-size enterprises that are variously affected by inadequate or inefficient tax administration measures. Foreign capital especially has been subjected to ambiguous policies—being wanted and at the same time not wanted—and in most countries in Latin America, it would prefer to know where it stood as to permissible fields of investment, extent of local capital participation required, treatment of exchange transfer of profit, and security of investment.

Investment in the expansion of the power and transport sectors, apart from direct public investment, is determined in large part by rate regulation, and here again, the policy and the legislation are not always consistent with the development programs. Most frequently, the holding down of rates as a subsidy to the consumer or a stimulant to business has resulted in a serious lag in investment and thus is a negative contribution to development, compounded by the deteriorating financial position of state-owned power and transport enterprises. The fuel sector has posed special problems of its own, connected with the predominance of foreign investment in petroleum in some countries and the reluctance or refusal to accept foreign capital in others. It is for each country to enact the legislation that suits its own decision on the subject, once an appraisal of its needs and prospects has been carried out nationally.

The Agricultural Sector

To promote agricultural development, there is a limit to what public investment can do directly in most Latin American countries, beyond providing public irrigation and river regulation schemes, roads, experiment stations, power, and long-term credit facilities for permanent improvements. But agricultural output and investment in private hands are extremely dependent on government policies on farm prices, taxation, foreign trade, rural wages, marketing and storage services, and so on. Again, a set of mutually consistent types of measures is needed to encourage the long-range improvements that alone can raise farm productivity, help to solve problems of domestic foodstuffs and raw materials supply, and also alleviate balance of payments pressures.

The basic question Latin America faces today, however, is that of land reform, understood not in the limited sense of redistribution of large holdings among the rural population, but of redistribution plus fuller and better use of land, improved farm methods and higher productivity, and retention of earnings in the hands of the rural mass itself, which is a vast potential market for manufacturing growth. Indeed, agrarian reform is increasingly accepted as an essential requisite for agricultural development, since the land-tenure structure prevailing in most Latin American countries favors the use of a fraction of the available farmland and tends to keep peasant incomes at the subsistence level.

With the exception of Mexico, Bolivia, Cuba (in its own way), and, recently and limitedly, Venezuela and Colombia, the agrarian economy is essentially an area of free enterprise, free acquisition and accumulation of land, unfettered use or non-use of land, and gross social injustice. Agrarian legislation today, however, must not stop at the breaking up of large estates, whether through expropriation, purchase, or taxation, but should envisage the organization and productive improvement of agriculture at all levels and the raising of the skill and culture of the peasant and the farm laborer, all of which will require the establishment of agriculture credit media, cooperative marketing organizations, suitable price policies, and so forth.

Human Resources

It is becoming fashionable to speak of improvements in the quality and skills of manpower, through education and training, as a form of investment. The projection of manpower needs, hinging on economic projections in general, requires gazing much further into the future than a ten-year program of public and private investment. This is because, at any given moment, the bulk of the employed labor force is adult and beyond the influence of an educational reform apart from special adult education programs and industrial training or retraining schemes. It is therefore difficult to translate the manpower needs of, say twenty years hence, which can only be vaguely determined, into the educational and training programs of today, except in gross quantitative terms

—raising school attendance generally and making secondary education universal—and on the assumption that an orientation away from purely academic and toward technical trades and careers and scientific pursuits is clearly desirable.

Yet this alone would require in most Latin American countries a thorough reappraisal of the educational systems, of industrial legislation, parts of labor and employment legislation, the social security regimes, and the general welfare policies affecting the ability of families to keep their children in school. As the recent Santiago Conference on Education and Development showed, these problems are far from being understood by economists and much less by educators. Educational planning, hardly existent in Latin America in the true sense of the term, is not even conceived as a key part of general economic development programs. Hence, the latter are not covering one of the most potentially productive types of investment for development.

Patterns of Consumption

Obviously, a development policy should aim at raising consumption, which is the ultimate purpose of an economic system. The often-stated dilemma between higher consumption and larger investment is in practice a false one in Latin America, since it is not generally borne out by experience. Nevertheless, a development program must envisage measures to adapt the pattern of consumption to structural needs and to balance of payment requirements.

Granted that in Latin America it will be considered desirable to allow freedom of consumers' choice within broad limits and also to maintain a largely free (partly regulated) price system, certain forms of consumption can be encouraged and others discouraged as a means of facilitating investment and development generally. One of the means of bolstering private consumption lies in the provision of free or subsidized educational, health, sanitation, and welfare services, as well as housing, to the lower income groups. If financed largely out of taxation and social security contributions (and provided the tax system is progressive), such programs are redistributive and should enable the urban and rural mass to grow into a stronger market force favoring industrial and agricultural expansion.

If this should be one of the objectives, there are important implications for tax policy. There will be a need to reform the tax structure, particularly through the adoption and extension of full progressive personal income taxation, the establishment of taxes on capital gains and possibly on net wealth, the alleviation of indirect taxes, including local taxes, on basic commodities, and the creation of special purchase taxes on goods and services consumed by the higher income groups. The aim should be to discourage luxury consumption (including imports) and divert resources, through taxation, to the implementation of governmental, educational, and other social programs. The important problem in this field is, of course, not to set rates of taxation that would discourage saving or reduce investment incentives.

The insistence on tax reform under the Alliance for Progress is quite justified. The Latin American tax structure and its administration are inadequate to exert a desirable influence on the pattern of consumption, furnish governments with sufficient current revenues, or, through appropriate provisions, encourage enough investment. With some exceptions, and aside from some recent reforms in a few countries—or even including these reforms—tax legislation continues to be a composite of piecemeal measures that are unsuitable in their effects, unjust, and inefficiently administered.

Stimulating Savings

Taxation is essentially related also to the whole question of the desirable use and flow of savings in a development program, as a counterpart to the investment objectives. A great deal of attention is usually paid to the effects of taxation and other measures on personal and business savings, but not enough to their importance in the formation of public savings, that is, in creating a surplus of current income over current expenditure in the public sector. Even when the "public sector" is sufficiently well defined in Latin America to include, besides government, the autonomous agencies, social security funds, state enterprises, and sundry commissions, boards, and institutes, it is rarely possible to have an adequate integrated financial statement covering all sources of income and expenditure and indicating clearly the amount of savings (as defined above) generated in each of the divisions and entities of the sector.

Usually in Latin America, the public sector as a whole runs a capital investment deficit (as would be expected under a development program), requiring the transfer to it of savings from the private sector or from other countries (external loans, etc.). In some cases, however, the public sector runs a current deficit, which means that the private and external sectors have to finance, out of their surplus, part of the public sector's consumption expenditures. This situation, insofar as domestic financing is concerned, is usually associated with inflationary expansion through central bank operations ("printing of currency"). It should therefore be an immediate aim of financial policy to avoid a current account deficit in the public sector.

To avoid such a deficit will require both reduction of less urgent central government expenditures (for instance, on military equipment, and certain subsidies) and, generally, increases in revenues. It will also involve economies in current expenditures of autonomous agencies and government enterprises and, where applicable, increases in their current income through adjustment of rates, prices, etc., in order to generate sufficient net earnings. It will in many cases be necessary to raise the rate of contributions to social security funds in order to maintain the latter's liquidity and provide the public sector with resources that may temporarily finance investments of the central government or of public corporations.

But, even more important, the effort should go further in the direction of creating a current surplus in the public sector that could be used to finance a considerable part of public investment. Such a surplus exists in many Latin American countries, but it is either not large enough or has been dwindling because of such factors as the rise in current expenditures, the inelasticity of the tax systems, and the fixing of utility rates.

For a well-ordered development program in which the public sector is to carry a large share of total investment, say one-third to one-half, it is essential that savings generated in the public sector should cover at least one-half to two-thirds of the required financing, since external funds cannot usually be obtained to finance more than about one-third of the public investment projects, and the domestic capital market and the banking system cannot, without inflationary consequences, absorb internal government debt issues beyond narrow limits.

In fact, the key to much of the foreign borrowing required for public investment projects lies in the need to increase domestic public financial resources to the point where a sizable public saving becomes available. Thus, tax reform and improvement in the finances of government entities and corporations is vitally important. If tax reform should have desirable distributive effects, as well as resulting in considerable revenue, and be devised so as to stimulate private investment, it may become one of the most powerful tools of economic development in Latin America. If the necessary measures are taken, also, to integrate the finances of the whole of the public sector, to increase net earnings of government autonomous agencies, and allow transferability of savings within the public sector to meet priority investment needs, a significant step will have been taken toward the adoption of a financial plan consistent with a development program as a whole. Much remains to be done in these respects.

To obtain a higher rate of over-all investment also requires, for the private sector, a better use of private savings. Most private savings normally consist of retained earnings and depreciation allowances of business enterprises, and it is assumed also that a considerable proportion of private gross investment, in manufacturing, power, transport, distribution, and the like, is financed in Latin America out of business savings. Nevertheless, there is need for both greater fluidity in the use of savings through financed intermediaries (such as investment banks) and through the securities market. An increase in such savings could be achieved also with the help of better business practices and of fiscal incentives.

There is need too for making the securities market more accessible to the small individual saver and for a greater choice of forms of financial investment suited to the savings structure. With one or two exceptions, the banking systems in Latin America are not yet sufficiently integrated, or tailored to assets that could serve as effective alternatives to the traditionally liquid foreign exchange or bullion holdings or the traditionally secure real estate holdings and short-term commercial and speculative claims. In short, the banking and financial systems are not yet making a substantial contribution to economic development.

Function of Foreign Capital

The role of external borrowing (and direct foreign investment) in Latin America's economic development is essentially to release domestic resources that can then be diverted to forms of expenditure not amenable to foreign or international financing. Provided a development program is being carried out that implies a higher rate of investment and a more efficient over-all effort, external financing will permit growth and capital formation to take place without sacrificing basic consumption. External aid is also a necessary supplement to current foreign exchange earnings and enables the developing country to generate an import surplus—in other words, to increase the available amount of goods and services beyond the limits of current output.

It is, therefore, necessary that the best possible use be made both of current foreign exchange earnings and of capital borrowings (including direct foreign investment). Current earnings need to be economized to provide for essential imports over unessential purchases, and to make it possible to limit borrowing to the maximum compatible with the future exchange-earning capacity out of which debt service is to be met. This is also the reason, from a balance of payments point of view, why external credit should be used judiciously.

The implications of these principles are important, for although much use has been made in Latin America of foreign capital in recent years, and different forms of exchange rationing have been adopted, it is doubtful that most governments have been able to formulate and carry out a general plan for the use of external financing. This does not necessarily mean control of transactions, but basically the execution of a consistent policy, particularly within the public sector. The sometimes indiscriminate resort to foreign short-term credit for medium- and long-term development projects, and the uncontrolled accumulation of current account indebtedness, with the consequent immediate burden on payments possibilities, are witness to the absence of an integrated financial policy of the sort that should match the general development effort. It thus appears that this, too, is an area where there is need for a careful reappraisal of existing legislation and regulation covering foreign exchange transactions, the use of external credit, and the exchange operations of direct foreign investment.

Legislation is obviously but an instrument with which to carry out policy, and it may be changed accordingly. If legislation relating to economic matters is inadequate, the fault—aside from judicial blocks—must lie with the policy itself, with the definition of the ends and the means. It may also occur that the legislative process is inappropriate, or that those who write the laws—rarely economic experts—are not fully competent. But essentially, the right policy decisions must be the determining factor. Latin America faces a huge challenge, and it is to be hoped that comprehensive development programs and policies will increasingly be undertaken and that the necessary revision and adoption of legislation will take place with the same sense of urgency.

11. TRANSPLANTING ADMINISTRATIVE TECHNIQUES

HENRY C. BUSH

WHILE professors of international relations continue to teach the "trinity" of international politics, international organization, and international law, practitioners of and recruiters for foreign policy work find more and more that what they need is experts in specific economic and administrative techniques. The extent of technical assistance is astonishing. For example, some 44,000 people from other countries study American methods at any given moment in the U.S.A., and 33 per cent are from the Far East— more than from any other region.[1] Some 15,000 U.S. engineers and technologists are working abroad at any given moment.[2] So complex have American efforts become that one section of only one functional division of the U.S. International Cooperation Administration finds it necessary to schedule training programs in seventeen different subfields of public administration alone.[3] In most non-Communist countries of Asia, where once the only foreigners one met were ruling colonials and stray missionaries, today ex-county assessors advising on tax records, U.N. experts on water systems, Colombo Plan teachers of English, and other such interesting specialists are familiar to every student of the Asian area who travels extensively in Asian countries. Further, the trend is toward increased efforts; Africa is clearly the next area of major involvement.

How effective are we? So far, in the eleven years of major U.S. efforts in technical assistance, nothing much has been done to evaluate what we do. Administrators and technicians abroad are caught up in the processing of projects; whether they are U.S., U.N., or other organizations' specialists in "overseasmanship,"

EDITOR'S NOTE: Notes corresponding to reference numbers in the text will be found at the end of the chapter.

108

their focus is on their current projects and on the process of getting approval and appropriations for planned projects, not on how well or how badly past projects did. Their wisdom includes many— sometimes conflicting—rules of thumb on how not to make a nuisance of yourself abroad. Cultural anthropologists, for example, are now found on the staffs of foreign missions and in the "orientation" sections of U.S. departments, and they are expert in telling us how not to misbehave abroad. The shortcoming is their one-culture-one-vote assumption. If head-shrinking or a taboo against cutting more than one stalk of rice at a time is *à la mode*, well, then, they tell us, that is the norm in those parts, and we should leave it that way. The difficulty is that "getting with" a culture is not going to change it; it is going to change the man sent there to change it. They tell us little or nothing about how to do what we want to do: bootstrap pre-industrial Asia into the mid-twentieth century. Change, not acculturation, is the business we are in.

Other U.S. advice to the U.S. on how to do it seems to run to fits of moral indignation that a man wants somewhat more money to work in central Kalimantan than in San Francisco, that Americans drive cars in lands where telephones and taxis are close to non-existent, and that Americans after a hot day battling language barriers, inertia, corruption, beggary, intestinal amoebae, prickly heat, and a general absence of trained clerical help, want occasionally to have a drink with other Americans. None of this helps much. The problem remains how to do it. The problem is to evaluate what we do in order to identify and concentrate our efforts upon effective techniques and abandon useless or nearly useless ones.

This is a report on the relevance and transferability of American systems of public administration to East Asian under-developed countries, based on experience in Indonesia and with Indonesians. It is a report on what transfers, what does not transfer, and why.

The Data

Indonesian local government officials were brought to the U.S.A., given concentrated background on U.S. local and state governments and administration, given the background of this background—that is, the major political, social, and economic institutions, taboos, and trends in the U.S.A. were described in order to put U.S. administrative imperatives and practices in focus—and interviewed informally, repeatedly, and at length to determine their duties at home, their professional interests, and their professional needs as they conceived them. Then they were "interned" for intervals varying from one to six weeks per internship with their U.S. counterparts, administrative supervisors in well-run U.S. local and state governments. After each such internship, each Indonesian official wrote a report.

Progress through internship sequences was from small and uncomplex administrative systems in small governmental units to large and complex systems in large units. Progress was "backstopped" and evaluated by tutorials and informal comparative sessions. On no internship were more than three or four Indonesian officials sent at the same time; wherever possible—some 85 per cent of the time—they were interned in pairs. This was done to prevent the U.S. officials from slipping into lectures. Each such program continued for about 11 months: about 6 months of core university instruction, 4½ months of internships, 2 weeks of final evaluation. After 2½ years of such work—30 Indonesian officials observed all the way through such programs, another 15 observed halfway through; 350 such on-the-job learning situations; 330 such reports—the reports were evaluated.

The Indonesian Background

It is necessary to describe Indonesian local government.

The nation is divided into provinces. Provinces, with some exceptions, are divided into residencies. Residencies subdivide into regencies, the regencies into districts, districts into subdistricts. Below the subdistrict is the village—a communal entity, largely self-subsistent, not unlike the Asian village in India, in China prior to 1949, in Korea, and in Southeast Asian countries generally.

Local government through this hierarchy extending from the central Ministry of Home Affairs down to the village head man (with the exception *only* of the village head man) is not government by the locality as it is known in the U.S.A.; it is government of the locality by central Ministry-of-Home-Affairs-appointed officials. The governor of a province is appointed. The residents, regents, district officers, assistant district officers (subdistrict officers), all are centrally appointed, centrally paid, centrally promoted or demoted, centrally transferrable, centrally controlled. Money, the lifeblood of autonomy, is centrally controlled: taxes are collected and remitted upstairs to the national government; local units' budgets are submitted upstairs for approval, reduction, or increase; and subsidies are allocated down this hierarchy by the national government for operations. Financial inspection is performed by central government officials. This pattern of central control is very East Asian. It is also very colonial; in fact, it is the pattern in Indonesia by means of which the Dutch once ruled the land and effectively controlled regions and subregions in which no Dutch official ever actually resided.

Services to the localities, compared to the American patterns of local government, are remarkably centralized in the hands of national ministries. In the U.S.A., police work, for example—except for anti-counterfeiting work, countering subversion, and other such quantitatively minor functions—is everywhere local; in Indonesia it is national, performed by what, in all but formal designation, is a ministry of police. To take another example, education in Indonesia above the level of elementary school is in the hands of the Ministry of Education. It, not local parents, teachers, and officials, decides and specifies curricula, enrollments, texts. And this too is typically East Asian.

Local Officialdom's Attitudes: The Gentry State

Indonesia as a whole has been moving only recently, only slowly, and preponderantly only in the cities from typical monsoon-Asia pre-industrial bureaucracy. The administrative or public service needs of localities, until recently, were regarded as largely static. The local administrator's skills were not specialized, nor was his authority specific, but general and all-encompassing. He was the emanation, so to speak, of the prince of old—speaking and acting with implied sacral authority of the regional rajah and, during 300 years of Dutch rule ending only 14 years ago, of the Dutch throne. He was gentry. He was not a public servant doing specific tasks, but an all-wise solon. He rarely referred to legislation or to administrative rulings of boards of appeal and almost never to the public's needs or demands for the sources of his authority to govern; he *was* government. By the power of his example, people were supposed to see how to behave, and that was enough. He did not serve; rather, he taught people their place. In cases of disputes not involving demands, needs, or claims against government, but between claimants each alleging equal traditional authority on his side of the dispute, the official referred preponderantly to various bodies of fixed custom: to *adat* (the unwritten custom of pre-literate local subcultures), to ancient Islamic law, to fixed or almost static penal codes.[4]

Before World War II, this system worked tolerably well *because* it inhibited social changes and therefore required little adaptation by the bureaucracy—that is, little administrative change. Administrators did not change often, either. They served long apprenticeships. They almost always served most of a lifetime in their native region. They rose in rank only after long years of executive experience. Many came from families of local government officials and indeed had begun to learn their future role even in childhood. Students of the Asian area will recognize these characteristics as being very Thai, very reminiscent of the Indian Civil Service, and very like the officialdom of old Mandarin China.

This iron rod of hierarchic control from the top was of course weakened by the Japanese invasion during World War II, the struggle for independence against the Dutch after World War II, the "second rising" of the Dutch, the Communist-led insurrection of 1948, Moslem dissident groups in some provinces, and, in 1957–59, small-scale rebellion in parts of Sumatra and Sulawesi. (Armed Moslem groups who want to establish an orthodox Moslem state in Indonesia are still a threat in the Bandung area and in northern and central Sulawesi; and the "outer islands rebellion" is still a major security problem in central Sumatra and likewise in Sulawesi.) Central control of local government was weakened by the opening of the hierarchy at the top by the removal of the Dutch; the successful revolution allowed many excellent men to move upward in the hierarchy and thus weakened it at the lower levels.

Further, rebellions create heroes, and in Indonesia, as in other countries recently emerged from colonialism to independence by revolution, the principal reward for valor in revolution was a place on the public payroll. There are few other rewards, and a government job is prized. Just as having been thrown into jail by the British was a primary requirement for entry into the Indian Civil Service after Indian independence, so having fought Japanese and Dutchmen was and still is a top qualification for entry into government service in Indonesia. Valor in battle is not a particularly useful skill at a desk, yet to this day, it is close to impossible to flunk a hero from a national training academy in Indonesia. This does not improve the civil service on the lowest and most local levels on which such ex-heroes serve.

The Local Government Revolution

But a last stage remains: the "local government revolution." When first an Asian colony wins its independence, its leading cliques of leaders divide what spoils there are. They do this by expropriation, by seizure of formerly Dutch, British, French, or other properties, by traffic in import licenses to dispossess or partly disposses ethnically unacceptable minorities (particularly from commerce), and by other such devices. Economic and ethnic nationalism are everywhere the modes of the first post-revolutionary period.[5]

This does not improve economic output and earnings, but disorganizes and decreases them somewhat. Soon there are balance of payments difficulties, troubles borrowing money abroad, and black market operations that depreciate the blocked currency. Also, there is at this stage nothing more—in fact there is less, the whole having begun to shrink—to distribute. The revolution is over, and the brave new world shows distressing signs of being even shabbier than before the revolution. Leaders have run out of Dutchmen (or Frenchmen or British) to dispossess.

Alternatives are now several. A country's leaders may find new scapegoats, permitting new cliques, new elites to promise heaven on earth and still come into power. They may, like Egypt recently, or Iraq, create new furor and new contents by dispossessing remnant royalty. They may invent—or actually feel—a grievance against the now ex-colonials, as the Indonesian leaders today make much of the issue of the useless plateau of West Irian.

Still another source of spoils and of power in this stage of post-revolutionary developments is to use democratic politics to take over that last remnant of colonialism, the old ex-colonial bureaucracy itself. The old officialdom continues to run local and regional affairs exactly as in colonial days. It is a natural target. By parliamentary majority it may be restricted—its retirement age, for example, may be lowered; sweeping grants of autonomy may be given to localities; offices may be created or made elective; and so on.

In sum, the new political elite do just what, in the U.S.A., the leaders of the Jacksonian revolution did to those very British rulers of early post-Revolutionary America, the Federalists—vote them out. They vote in what we call "spoils politics." This local government revolution is now on in Indonesia. It has been on since early in 1957.[6]

It is important to point out that spoliation or attempts at spoliation of the "iron rod" of traditional central hierarchic control of the local governments is only one of the new democratic political parties' efforts; they also seek to politicize the ministries of national government. It is important also to point out that the "local government revolution" and parallel, similarly motivated, politicization produces major reactions other than those dealt with here. In some Asian countries, the armed forces step in as arbiter and close down or severely limit political party activity—for example, in Pakistan and in Thailand recently and in Indonesia to a degree since late in 1957;[7] Egypt is a recent non-Asian example. In such Asian countries, as Mary Matossian has recently shown, there is likely also to be a major attempt, usually by whomever is outstandingly the symbol of national unity and outstandingly the charismatic leader, to invent and propagate some ideological rationalization to justify restraining the political parties. In Indonesia at this moment, it is "guided democracy" and "return to the Constitution of 1945 and the spirit of the Revolution." Where one of the major parties in the "local government revolution" is a Communist party (as in Indonesia), the need is particularly urgent to somehow justify, by ideological invention, suppressing party activity.

Criteria of Success or Failure

So much for the Indonesian (and East Asian) political and administrative context. To turn from it and return to the evaluation of U.S.-based training of Indonesian officialdom:

The trainees evaluated were staff officers of governors, residents, regents, regents' staff officers, district officers, and subdistrict officers. They came from urban jurisdictions and from paddyland jurisdictions. They came from the "gentry" status of Indonesia's senior officialdom. They came also from the very ungentrylike battle to preserve local government from political spoliation.[8]

Each such U.S.-based trainee, as has been said, completed an internship sequence in which he worked with U.S. counterparts in local governments, observing and discussing administrative systems. We who devised and ran this system of training were not pushing any particular administrative systems; we offered what we have in local governments known to be well run. The object was to maximize each Indonesian official's choice among administrative systems close to his needs, and thus, we hoped, to maximize prospects that he would find systems adaptable to his job, his needs.

From each trainee we had about twelve reports. If a trainee (a) indicated in his reports or in the follow-up tutorial sessions specific aspects or parts of local government administrative systems that he thought were useful and possibly adaptable, or (b) if he reported on them in such comprehensive detail that we were convinced that he comprehended them and had focused on them exceptionally sharply, and if he did (a) or (b) an average of one out of every two reports or evaluative sessions, then we on our part counted him a "success." If he indicated either possibilities of adaptation or complete comprehension of the U.S. administrative systems an average of one out of every three or four we labeled him "some progress"—comparable to a C or C-minus student. If less than that, or if for other reasons we were unable to put him in these learning-choosing internship situations, we labeled him our "failure." So much for criteria.

Findings I: Successes, Partial Successes, Failures

How many do we fail with? How many have we succeeded with?

Year	1956–57	1957–58	Average, both years
Successes, per cent	41	80	63
Some transfer, per cent	25	20	22
Failures, per cent	33	0	14

Striking differences between the 1956–57 and 1957–58 groups were not due to changes in the program, but very probably to major changes in recruitment by Indonesia. The 1958–59 trainees are in the first internships of their internship sequences at the time of writing, and their work must be evaluated later, but preliminary judgments of their "success" or "failure" suggest that they tend to scale somewhere between the 1956–57 and 1957–58 groups.

The point is that American public administration is transferrable. It is not culture-bound. A record of 63 per cent successes and 36 per cent partial or total failures may be expensive, but it is not hopeless.

Findings II: What Transferred

Running a country is complex, and there are subfields or divisions of labor within public administration: personnel, finance, records-keeping, coordinating work such as that of an executive secretary, public relations, police administration, planning, public works, and others. There are also various units of local government —townships, counties, cities, states, regional authorities. The units vary in scale—small cities of 20,000, medium-sized ones of 150,-000–200,000, and great colossi like St. Louis or Detroit. We deal in these programs with particular substantive subfields; we have to because of our staff and resources. We use units of government to illustrate these subfields of public administration in terms of certain scales of size and of certain degrees of clusters of urban or rural problems. For example, we expose most of our trainees to American budgeting operations. We expose them to the budget and finance officer or controller and through him and his staff to budgeting operations in small cities, in medium-sized cities, in rural and in complex semi-urban counties, and in large state governments where the scale of expenditures may run, as does Michigan's, as much as $1,000,000 a year.

The fields of public administration in which we have trained and interned Indonesian officials are finance, records systems and interoffice and intergovernmental coordination, personnel, legislative reference work, public relations, public works administration, police administration, and headquarters-field supervision. I add reporting, but we do not intern anyone at that; we have them report on each internship situation.

Each field of public administration breaks down into further divisions of labor in the total process of running the country. For example, personnel administration involves recruitment, examinations and interviewing, job classification, performance records, wage and salary and fringe benefits administration, disciplinary actions, in-service training, and retirement or pension problems; finance includes tax assessments, tax and other money collection, budgeting, appropriations control or allocation, auditing, and costing of planned (possible, but not yet existing) government operations. These are administrative operations, and they are organizable. The political operations of creating, maintaining, or simulating consensus are something else.

What do Indonesian officials respond to and say may be useful and in part adaptable? What do they not respond to?

They respond remarkably to certain subfields of organization and management—records systems and interoffice coordinative techniques. This we think is very promising. They respond very favorably to certain subfields of personnel administration—examinations and testing, wage controls, performance records, and central personnel agency controls of lesser departments and of lesser units of government. This we have doubts about, for reasons given just below. They respond to certain subfields of financial administration—budgeting, appropriations control, financial records systems, tax collection methods, and auditing. This we think is very promising of desirable changes abroad, for reasons given below.

In some subfields of public administration, we have found that we can transfer nothing.

Public relations work leaves them cold. They observe it, but wonder why we bother. In Indonesia, as in most of underdeveloped Asia, there are protocol officers but no publics. The only useful job analogue for protocol work would be court etiquette. Public relations and the idea of explaining government in advance of trying to effect it will come about in Indonesia, and in the rest of underdeveloped Asia, only when small publics demand it.

In *public works administration*, nothing transfers. Public works in America is so mechanized, so fast-moving, so closely timed to maximize output of labor and of large expensive equipment, and so dependent upon private contractors that it is completely un-Asian (certainly completely un-Indonesian). Public works construction and maintenance in Indonesia is a make-work, scrounge-materials operation to which, in the U.S.A., only a depression welfare organization's simulation of some work (say the old WPA's) would come close. Anyone who has seen Indonesian, or for that matter Indian or Chinese, road gangs knows the order of things: first corral the laborers, then string them out along the road to look for rocks for underfilling, and while that is going on—and it will go on for some time—try to scrounge some cement or tar for surfacing. The tar and materials are scarce and are the problem; the labor is abundant and will not cost much and will not run away. In fact, the repair of the road is incidental to the object of somehow using (somewhat) the gangs of laborers whose rice bowls need never be really filled, but must never be completely emptied. Other construction work is the same; for example, recent cost estimates by staff economists of the International Cooperation Administration in Indonesia indicate that major excavation works can be done for less by the most primitive of hand methods than by the use of earth-moving machinery.

In *police administration*, we can transfer nothing. A cop is apparently a cop the world round, and aside from American police communications gear, there seems to be nothing we have in the way of techniques that they do not already know about. In certain subfields of criminal investigation and criminal dossier-keeping methods, the Indonesians seemed to be ahead of American local police.

In *municipal, county, and state planning*—other than our highly accurate pre-costing techniques—we can transfer nothing. It is doubtful that we know how we do it ourselves, and planning problems are frequently so complex, so slow-moving, and so loaded with local and intergovernmental political implications that they are not explainable and generalizable, except to persons deep in the network of local-regional political, economic, and administrative conditions.

Lastly, in *headquarters-field relationships and control*, we can transfer nothing. This never comes through to the foreign observer. We do not know why; probably because it varies so from line agency to line agency and because the substantive operations of the agency observed obscure the system of supervision, central records, and control.

So much for what we cannot do. We cannot learn much about why we cannot transfer these. What we can do, that which does transfer, we know something about.

RECORDS SYSTEMS AND INTEROFFICE COORDINATION. Records systems in Indonesia, and underdeveloped countries in East Asia generally, are conspicuous by their absence where they should exist and by their abundance and disorder at odd unexpected levels of the various governmental hierarchies. An astonishing amount of top- and middle-level communication is oral. For example, in Indonesian urban areas, there is a considerable inflow of farm migrants, of landless laborers, and of drifters from other small towns. These people, as Bert F. Hoselitz and others have pointed out, are a large part of the welfare problem, the police problem, and the political problem in the towns and cities. Yet there is no system of registering them, keeping tabs on them, taxing them. In the absence of this, when the press of bicycle-taxi operators, able-bodied beggars, floating sidewalk vendors selling little of value, squatters at canal edges and on vacant lots, and pickpockets approaches the intolerable, the police or army make a raid, round up a few thousand, and either move them back to their original villages or work them in labor camps. This is the hard way, and registry records could make much of the problem easier.

Another example: In a country such as Indonesia, in which most people are peasants, disputes about land ownership and land servitudes are common. One would expect an accurate system of land records, but none exists except in occasional rare advanced jurisdictions. If, for example, a person wants to sell a piece of land, he and the buyer must bring their record of sale to the local government official for certification, but the local government official makes no record of the change; he merely, so to speak, notarizes it. The implications and difficulties of this state of things are obvious: If the government requires a piece of land for its own use or if it wishes to zone or rezone parts of a city, it must decide in a vacuum what it will do, because it does not know what it has or what it will cost to do what it wants. There are no records.

Another example: Most existing records are not cross-indexed; unless an inquirer happens to have a bit of information in the same terms as those of the keeper of the records, he can get nothing out of the records systems except by tedious searching through every possibly relevant item. In economic statistics, the inadequacy and inaccuracy of records on such basic items as incomes, tax revenues, and populations has been noted by the FAO, ECAFE, and U.S. staff economists.

So much for the state of records-keeping. The point of this report is that Indonesian officials respond to Americans' highly accurate systems of recording and coordinating communications and data. Not to our fast mechanical and electronic counters and sorters, not to punch-card equipment, for these are beyond their means and they know it. But to all non-mechanized systems. Just show them, say, an office of licenses and permits, or a city clerk's complaint and follow-up system, or a county's records of land ownership, and they are all notebooks, all interest, all questions about work flow, forms, who follows up on whose request, why window envelopes are used, and so on. Similarly in the complex of functions that we call interoffice coordination. From a county clerk or city manager of a tiny city of, say, 19,000, to the Office of Management Supervision of the Bureau of the Budget of the State of New York, they are interested in how to coordinate separate offices and lesser units, how to standardize information from them and to them, how to enforce compliance, and how to inspect them. This is obviously a promising field for transfer of administrative technique, and one in which our systems of running things are multinational and exportable.

PERSONNEL ADMINISTRATION. Personnel work, a highly developed —some say overdeveloped—art in the U.S.A., attracts Indonesian officials. They are not interested in our elaborate recruitment methods; they have a surplus of applicants hungry for jobs. They are not interested in our retirement systems; they have more generous ones. They are not interested in our techniques for decentralizing personnel work and developing personnel services at the level of the department; they want control upstairs in a central personnel agency. They are not responding to our elaborate methods known as job classification, for they do not have our degree of specialization or our rate of job or work change; their straight rank system is adequate for their needs, they insist. (It should be noted, however, that the trainees described are local government officials. The author's first impressions are that central ministry personnel are interested in the possibilities of job classification in Indonesia.) They are much interested in the techniques of central personnel agency supervision—especially control of examinations and of admission of the applicant to the bureaucracy. They are much interested in performance records—another aspect of central personnel agency control of promotions and of disciplinary actions.

We think these aspects of personnel administration appeal to the Indonesian professionals' vested interests in the bureaucracy. The "local government revolution" described earlier is the bureaucracy versus the political parties, the latter claiming to be the democratic agents of the people. In certain senses, the bureaucracy, and especially the senior men in the middle and upper positions in it, is the last major remnant of colonialism. In certain senses, the struggle for access to and control of local governments is the bureaucracy versus social change—which the parties demand and promise, and which they would probably initiate, albeit chaotically.

Much could be transferred and adapted from American personnel practices that would be exceedingly useful in Indonesia. (For example, at the moment of writing, Ministry of Home Affairs professional local government officials are in conference to develop a system to make it possible to transfer the local government professionals to temporary duty in the hierarchies of the newly elected officials without sacrificing their personal equities—rank, retirement claims, etc.—to the party politics of their bosses-to-be.)

On the other hand, we must be under no illusion that any minor changes, however widespread, in administrative systems can deny or turn back the "local government revolution"; it is part of a major social movement. We suspect that the Indonesians will seek to invoke American personnel systems and practices, especially the rocklike stability that overcentralized personnel control seems to induce in a bureaucracy—a system from which American personnel men and public administrators are shifting toward departmental autonomy in personnel matters—to protect their personal stakes. One can hear them invoking the American system against change and arguing that this works, this is made in America. In sum, personnel administration is a fairly promising field from which to borrow administrative techniques transferable and adaptable to East Asia, but there is a tendency to borrow some of our mistakes in our earlier battles against the politicization of local government. Indonesia could become like Turkey, where to make quite minor changes in officials' salaries or duties, one has to fight a law through the national legislature.

FINANCIAL ADMINISTRATION. In this field the Indonesians are not interested in large-scale credit operations (bonding, borrowing); there is little in citizens' savings to borrow locally in their land. But they are attracted to our systems of tax collections, our systems of penalties for tax delinquencies, our tax records systems. They take enthusiastically, too, to American local government systems of budget preparation and to techniques of control and allocation of appropriated funds. Their resources are sucked upward to the center in irregular amounts (no one very certain about the prospects in advance of tax collections) and then trickle downward in subsidies—no one upstairs certain that appropriated or allocated funds will not be diverted and trickle away at the lower levels, no one downstairs certain that upstairs they understand what he feels he must have to operate.

Auditing in Indonesia varies; in an occasional part of Java, it seems to be a systematic technique, yet in most jurisdictions it is little more than a combination of general field trips to investigate "end use" ("Where is that bridge we sent you the money for?") and really, in considerable part, to audit the operating subordinates' moral character—an imprecise business indeed! In anticipation of such inexact auditing with moral overtones, many small items are vastly overreceipted, overcertified, and overadministered, to the waste of fantastic amounts of time by busy men at high levels. This is the general picture in Indonesia.

The encouraging picture from our evaluations of Indonesian officials in U.S.-based training is that in any American financial system, from a county budget control clerk's desk to a state's department of administration (always controlling by means of the budget, despite the general name), when the Indonesians were shown an operation, they stuck with it, comprehended it remarkably rapidly, and showed interest in adapting parts of it. They particularly respond to systems of financial control and financial supervision of lesser units of government—for example, Michigan's or New Jersey's supervision of the financial behavior of towns, villages, small cities, school boards, and counties. Our local government financial systems are a promising field from which to borrow techniques adaptable in East Asia.

Findings III: Implication for Selection of Trainees

Specialists do better than generalists, and we do better with them. We "succeeded" with 77 per cent of all specialists. We "succeeded" with only 56 per cent of the generalists.

Senior officials do better than junior officials.[9] Contrary to much of the lore in the field—which has it that the older bureaucrats of Asia are set in their ways, colonial-practice-minded, hopelessly status-oriented, and that we should concentrate our efforts upon the young incoming civil servants—the more they knew when they came to us the more they acquired while with us. We "succeeded" with 77 per cent of all senior officials; we "succeeded" with only some 40 per cent of all junior officials.[10]

Indonesian officials from urban jurisdictions do better than officials from rural jurisdictions. (A note on overlap of factors is necessary: The senior officials are not especially urban—50 per cent were urban, 50 per cent rural; but the specialists were especially senior—40 per cent of the specialists, only 25 per cent of the generalists, were senior men.)

What does this mean respecting selection? It means we should concentrate upon senior men; they learn more while here, and this advantage is increased, because when they return they are in higher positions and more likely to be able to make changes or innovations. It means we should concentrate our recruitment-selection efforts on their large towns and their cities, because we cannot do as much for the paddyland executive. It means we should concentrate on those working in particular areas of administrative problems; we should prefer—insofar as our preference is influential in what is and must remain their selection process—the man who is in charge of something (for example, budgeting or a line operation) to the general administrator who is in charge of everything (for example, the rural district officer who is "papa" within his district and in on everything).

Attitude Shifts

I have not said anything about attitude shifts. Obviously it is easy, given a year, reasonable sympathy, money, and control of a small group, to make friends for the U.S.A. Obviously, also, this is minor and there are much less expensive ways to shift attitudes. One shift in the Indonesians' attitudes bore on public administration. It was obvious to us from their reports and conversations that as the result of exposure again and again to American local official-dom, elected and professional, the Indonesians became much less suspicious of and many quite friendly to the idea of local autonomy per se. As has been said, this is very much an issue in Indonesia.

What Is Needed

So much for our findings thus far, after two and one-half years' work. What is needed is painstaking evaluations, in comparative terms, of the many efforts by this country. To mention some primary source material that the scholars of Asian area studies, public administration, and international relations have not begun to use:

1. The International Cooperation Administration must have roomsful of "debriefing" tapes recording the conclusions of technicians just returned from two-year tours of duty abroad.

2. Some thirty U.S. universities are doing—and perhaps as many as sixty have done—contract work training foreign officials in the U.S.A. and/or abroad; there must be reports on this in their files.

3. Public Administration Service and other consultants have

long been working abroad on administrative systems design in many underdeveloped countries; PAS has men with experience in as many as five countries; they can be interviewed.

4. There is a vast flow of reports by ICA participants—trainees sent to the U.S.A., most of them individually, for special training.

5. Colombo Plan and U.N. technicians working in underdeveloped Asia write reports to their host countries and to their employing organizations.

In sum, the raw material exists to supplement historical studies and individual studies in Asia. It is time to get to work and push toward comparative local government and comparative public administration.

NOTES

1. "The Exchange Population," *Institute of International Education Bulletin*, November, 1958.

2. "U.S. Technologists Abroad," *Engineering and Scientific Manpower*, December 5, 1958.

3. Participant Training in Public Administration: Summary of Programs Available, July, 1959–July, 1960, Training Branch, Public Administration Division, International Cooperation Administration (Washington, D.C.: January, 1959, mimeographed).

4. See description of "Agraria" by Fred W. Riggs in "Agraria and Industria—Toward a Typology of Comparative Administration," in William J. Siffin, ed., *Toward the Comparative Study of Public Administration* (Bloomington: Indiana University Press, 1957), pp. 23–110. See also Professor Riggs' forthcoming work on "Transitia," the administrative implications of social and economic changes in societies moving recently from agrarian status toward industrialization (Brussels: International Institute of Administrative Sciences, 1960 or 1961). The author is indebted to Professor Riggs for pre-publication data on his model of transitional Asian societies. See also James N. Mosel, "Thai Administrative Behavior," in Siffin, *op. cit.*, pp. 278–324; Robert Redfield, *Peasant Society and Culture* (Chicago: University of Chicago Press, 1956); Karl A. Wittfogel, "Oriental Society in Transition," *Far Eastern Quarterly*, XIV (August, 1955); and Bert F. Hoselitz, "Agrarian Societies in Transition," *Annals* of the American Academy of Political and Social Science, 305 (May, 1956).

5. See, for example, Frank H. Golay, "Commercial Policy and Economic Nationalism," *Quarterly Journal of Economics*, November, 1958.

6. Law No. 1, 1957, Republic of Indonesia, authorized sweeping politicization of local government officialdom at the province, mid-province (or *kabupaten*), and district–to–villages or federated villages levels. Since then elections have taken place at the province level in all provinces in Java, in some in Sumatra, in some in Kalimantan; and they are scheduled to take place at that level in the Moluccas and in the Nusa Tenggara jurisdictions. Elections

at the mid-province level have taken place in some provinces in Java. Elections have apparently not yet taken place anywhere on the third and lowest level of legislated autonomy. Where elections have taken place, elected political executives and their politically appointed staffs occupy a hierarchy of local offices parallel to that of the centrally appointed and centrally controlled and directed local government officialdom. Actual transfers of money and functions are begun in some jurisdictions, duplicated by both hierarchies of local officials in others, indefinitely deferred in still others. In some parts of Sumatra and in all of Sulawesi, even initial elections are indefinitely deferred because the "outer islands rebellion" has deferred all politicking for office.

For the effects and bitterness and administrative anomalies created in local governments by these Jacksonian politics, see Report of the Secretary General, March 20, 1958 (Djakarta: Ministry of Home Affairs, mimeographed); Assistant District Officer Mintarum, "Annual Report of Governmental Activities of Kabupaten Malang" (Djakarta: Public Administration Division Cooperation Administration, USOM to Indonesia, 1958, mimeographed); issues of *Swatantra* (Local Government) monthly (Djakarta: Ministry of Home Affairs), particularly January, 1958, issue; "Soempono Djojowandono," ("Democracy in the Period of Development in Indonesia"), paper, Seminar on Democracy, conference of the Political Scientists of Indonesia, December 19, 1958, at Jogjakarta (Jogjakarta: Gadja Mada University, 1958, mimeographed); and Millidge P. Walker, "Daerah Government: A Study of Administration and Politics at the Sub-National Level in Indonesia" (Berkeley: University of California, June, 1960, doctoral dissertation).

7. Law No. 74, 1957, Republic of Indonesia, passed in order to deal with problems of the "outer islands' rebellion," authorized a state of martial law throughout all of Indonesia and authorized regional boards to deal with matters of "military governmental administration." On these boards, the military commander is chairman, the elected official is supposed to be vice chairman, the appointed governor and resident are "official advisors," and the police are represented. Reports and limited observations by the author in Java early in 1959 indicate that, in practice, the centrally appointed local government officialdom, the military authorities, and the police cooperate closely, and the locally elected officialdom is largely ignored.

8. The creation of a political hierarchy in local government parallel to, but not delegated the work of, the centrally appointed local government officialdom is resented and resisted by the latter. From their point of view, it has meant principally: (1) Diversion of part of their operating subsidies. The elected officials are given the prerogatives of office—buildings, cars, telephones, et cetera; these cost money; money is scarce; part comes out of what the professionals used to get. (2) Creation of more work, for the elected officials and their staffs seek to show what they can do in the narrow field in which they are, as yet, permitted to operate. They must, for back of them are electorates expecting results. But any additional activities in government create ripples of additional demand for social plant, additional pressures upon existing local government resources, and also additional burdens of coordinative work for the professionals. (3) Fear of loss of status and even of retirement equities —for were the elected officials given full power over local governments, the professionals would rapidly be abolished. (4) The irritant of political subversion within the professional hierarchy. The professionals are anti-political, but

they cannot be sure that their recently added subordinates are. Instances are reported in which young men, having qualified for the very lowest rungs of the ladders of rank in the professional hierarchy, and having also established political connections with major parties, have been advanced rapidly up to the professional hierarchy out of all proportion to their job experience or merit. Similarly, the professional hierarchy has tended to become politicized somewhat at the very top levels—the levels of heads of operating sections within the national ministry. (Based on the author's interviews with senior and middle-rank local government officials, both professional and elected, of the Ministry of Home Affairs, in Java and South Sulawesi, during March and April, 1959.)

9. By accident of selection, over which we had no control, the distinction was very clear in all three groups of trainees. Fifteen or more years' service and rank of *patih* or *bupatih* was senior; less than ten years' service and rank of *wedanah* or less was junior.

10. Incidentally, the lore that you cannot teach much to older officials is being disproved by evaluations of American in-service training programs. See, for example, Robert J. Mowitz, "Benefits from Management Training," *Public Administration Review*, Autumn, 1958.

12. TRAINING ADMINISTRATORS FOR DEVELOPING COUNTRIES

CLARENCE E. THURBER

EDUCATIONAL and administrative organizations in the United States of America are making a major effort to help train administrators from the underdeveloped countries. The importance of such an effort is obvious, for the tasks of government in these societies are crucial. In exploring some of the training problems, reviewing work under way, and suggesting desirable directions in this article, the author assumes that public administration, as a branch of knowledge, is closely related to cultural and political norms. It follows that most countries will have to develop their own "branches" of the field. Moreover, neither the U.S.A. nor other Western countries have the resources to train more than a small proportion of the administrators needed. We might do well, therefore, to give greater attention to the training of teachers and scholars from such countries as a kind of capital investment in the field and its growth abroad.

Foreign Trainees in Public Administration

About 900 trainees in public administration were brought to the U.S.A. during 1960. The International Cooperation Administration sponsored a total of 853 public administration participants (its term for trainees) in the fiscal year ending June 30, 1960. A majority of these were short-term assignments lasting from one to six months. For full-time instruction, the number of trainees from all other sources probably did not exceed 50. The United Nations had a total of five public administration fellows in its regular technical assistance program and a larger but unspecified number under the expanded program. The Ford Foundation, through its Overseas Development Program, sponsored about 20 fellows in the field during 1959–60.

Out of the total, only 380 foreign students studied public administration in U.S. universities. This was less than 1 per cent of the 44,486 foreign students, and about 5 per cent of the students in the social sciences. The vast majority of these foreign students came from the underdeveloped areas—200 from the Far East and South and Southeast Asia, not including Pakistan.

Significant numbers of trainees come from individual countries only when there are special projects or programs in public administration sponsored by one or more of the technical assistance agencies. The five leading countries in 1960 in terms of numbers of students in administration in the U.S.A. were Indonesia, 35; Korea, 33; India, 32; the Philippines, 25; Thailand, 25. All participated in projects supported by the United Nations, the International Cooporation Administration, or the Ford Foundation. The Colombo Plan has also provided assistance in the field, but its fellows have received training primarily in Australia and Canada.

The 380 students studying a full academic year at a college or university represent the group that is likely to get a fundamental exposure to the ideas and concepts, as well as the techniques and methods, of the field. It is from this group that it might be possible to recruit and train the corps of teacher-scholars in administration that may be assumed to be the seed corn for the future growth of the discipline in the underdeveloped countries. The possibility of recruiting teachers from the group of able practitioners also needs careful consideration.

Problems of Adjustment

The foreign trainee in the U.S.A. is subject to cultural shock just as is the American abroad. Moreover, he is likely to view American administration through his own cultural glasses, fitted at home. Means are therefore needed to assist the foreign trainee in his personal problems of adjustment and to help him appreciate American administration in its own political and cultural setting. (A good deal of research and writing has been done on the first of these, summarized by Simon Lesser and Hollis Peter in "Training Foreign Nationals in the United States," *Some Applications of Behavioral Research*, UNESCO, 1957.)

If we assume a reasonably successful personal adjustment, there are equally difficult intellectual and professional problems.

The trainee in administration needs a special introduction to the historical, political, and governmental situation in which American administration arose and is practiced today. The typical foreign trainee or student in administration has little knowledge or appreciation of, for example, American political history, federalism, or the presidential system of government. Graduate work usually assumes such knowledge. Trainees also need exposure to actual administrative operations.

Trainees and students from underdeveloped countries are frequently products of the "rote learning" system of education. Moreover, status relationships are such that a teacher or a superior officer in an organization is rarely questioned on points of fact or value. Thus "empirical thinking," or training in problem-solving methods, is not likely to be a part of the intellectual equipment of the foreign trainee. He will need special assistance if he is to acquire aptitude in these ways of thinking, which seem so natural to most Americans.

Trainees also need help in acquiring information and knowledge that will be especially useful in meeting administrative problems in the home country. Since the curriculum in most schools of administration and departments of political science is designed primarily for an American audience, this need poses a special problem for the scope and content of the discipline. The need for special attention here is particularly acute in relation to the writing of special papers and dissertations.

Although the practice of selecting persons of some standing and experience may reduce the need for assistance in placement on return home, the trainee and student in administration has need for continuation of professional contacts, if his training is to be of maximum value. Special efforts to maintain and build on the interest and competence established through training appear to be needed.

Response of U.S. Universities to the Problem

Contrary to some earlier practice, universities are now disposed to insist on high standards of selection and performance on the part of foreign students. This may be a response to the rising enrollment of American students. But it is also a judgment, based on experience, that anything else is self-defeating. The foreign students themselves are the first to resent the attitudes, apparently widespread in some of their home countries, that American education is inferior, and that their degrees, to use Clifford Wharton's phrase, are "underdeveloped Master's" or "Oriental Ph.D." degrees. Instead of a double standard of performance, there is a renewed effort to assist the foreign student in ways that will help him to compete on an equal basis. This is having effects all down the line, but especially in respect to (1) English language competence, (2) greater depth in orientation and post-training evaluation sessions, and (3) renewed efforts to help the foreign student think through the relevance of U.S. training to the home situation.

Special Arrangements in the Field of Public Administration

Departments of political science and schools of public administration have responded to the needs of foreign students and foreign trainees in three principal ways:

1. Special counseling arrangements for foreign students are frequently made, with advisers appointed in departments or schools, if the number of students is sufficient to make such an arrangement necessary. This is most often the case when the university is participating in a special project, such as an inter-university contract, bringing considerable numbers of foreign students to the campus. As an outgrowth of this arrangement, informal seminars for foreign students may be established, which serve a useful purpose in rounding out knowledge of American government and politics, views of Americans on social and cultural issues, and the peculiarities of the U.S. academic system.

2. Short courses, workshops, and institutes are frequently arranged at the request of the ICA or other technical assistance agency when a number of trainees need special training within a short period of time on such topics as personnel administration, organization and methods, or budgeting. They may be as short as two or three days or as long as three weeks. A great deal of ground can be covered when preparations for intensive work have been made in advance and when the participants are fully competent in English. The author attended one such short course in the spring of 1960, on the financing of economic development, in which the participants were from a number of underdeveloped countries. There were obvious problems in communication. This was a "traveling" short course, in which the students visited a dozen or more cities within a space of three weeks. Traveling in a group, and having a definitely prepared schedule at each stop,

was an infinitely more effective way to use consultants and guest speakers than to send individuals out on their own. The group members also had the advantage of consulting with one another, and checking on impressions, between stops.

An example of a longer-term session was the twelve-week Institute in Economic, Social, and Industrial Development held at the School of Public and International Affairs of the University of Pittsburgh, also in the spring of 1960. This institute was serious business and not only provided an opportunity for a much broader and deeper examination of many problems in the field, but also encouraged better communication. Courses of such length may strike a reasonable compromise in terms of the needs of the short-term visitors.

3. Numerous special programs are organized by universities for special audiences. Three of them, described here, exemplify some of the experience and problems with foreign students in public administration.

THE NEW YORK UNIVERSITY–UNITED NATIONS PROGRAM. This was a one-year course, developed cooperatively by the United Nations and New York University, leading to the degree of Master of Public Administration. It was primarily the conception of the Public Administration Division of the U.N. Trainees were primarily United Nations fellows, although others were admitted to the course as well. Preference in the award of fellowships was given to those who had three to five years' experience in administration in their own countries.

Teaching materials were developed in a central seminar for both teaching and research-training purposes. Administrative systems and operations in the U.S.A., Europe, and the underdeveloped countries were examined. An attempt was made to discover the effect of different cultures on administrative practices. In addition, fellows studied various administrative specialties at NYU. An effort was also made to tap the rich resources of the City of New York for direct observation and analysis of administrative problems.

With the retirement of Mr. van Mook, the seminar leader and former U.N. official, the program has now been completed. Those who participated in it, and others, believed that it made a very useful contribution to training.

THE PAKISTAN PROJECT, UNIVERSITY OF SOUTHERN CALIFORNIA. This was instituted in 1957 under a three-year contract with the International Cooperation Administration. It is a six-month executive development course for mid-career officials in the Pakistan Superior Civil Services. The project was designed to demonstrate American and comparative experience in development, and to improve the competence of the Pakistanis in general administration. There have been five six-month courses, each attended by an average of twenty Pakistani officials.

Each course is divided into three phases—group work, on-the-job assignments, and a field-trip laboratory in national government. Group work consists of group discussions and team exercises, analyzing administrative problems, the appropriate use of methods, and practice in problem-solving exercises. This leads to a series of team reports comparing an area of administration observed during the on-the-job association, in which the Pakistani associates are placed in appropriate governmental jurisdictions, in the Los Angeles area, chosen primarily on the grounds of effective administrative practice. The laboratory in national government lasts about six weeks, during which visits are made to such agencies as the Immigration and Naturalization Service, El Paso; the Tennessee Valley Authority; executive and Congressional offices in Washington; the Port of New York Authority; the United Nations; and, weather permitting, the St. Lawrence Seaway.

A final phase of the program was to have been carried out by USC faculty on annual trips to Pakistan, as a means of keeping the Pakistani "alumni" up to date, but it has not been possible to activate this part of the program.

THE PUBLIC SERVICE FELLOWSHIPS IN ECONOMIC DEVELOPMENT OF LITTAUER SCHOOL, HARVARD UNIVERSITY. Established in 1957, this is an academic-year program leading to the degree of Master of Public Administration for fellows who have served at least five years in administrative capacities in underdeveloped countries. Usually, ten to twelve fellowships are awarded each year. The seminars and lectures that make up the instructional part of the program are open to Americans and others, but the program was designed to meet the needs of underdeveloped countries for advanced training in the administration of economic planning. Harvard's experience in providing a group of advisers, beginning in 1953, to the National Planning Board of Pakistan was the immediate antecedent of this program. Dr. Edward S. Mason, Director of the program, was the senior adviser in Pakistan.

Three or four courses make up the core of the program, the first two of which are invariably, and the others frequently, taken by the fellows. The first is a full-year lecture course on economic development; the second, a year-long seminar on problems of economic and political development; the third, a seminar on comparative administration and economic development; and the last, a lecture course on public finance in the developing countries.

The public service fellows are required to write an essay on a problem of economic development associated with a country not their own. During the spring of the year, they take field trips to various organizations in the United States, worked out to meet individual needs and requirements. These frequently include visits to the TVA, government agencies in Washington—ICA, for example, and the various development banks—and visits to land-grant colleges. Fellows also take advantage of international travel to visit agencies of interest, such as FAO in Rome, the American University in Beirut, and community development projects in India.

Special Training in Inter-University Contracts

Training in American universities as part of Inter-University Contracts deserves special attention. Frequently, through this means, groups of students or professors or both are brought to this country and given training programs including some or all of the features in the projects already described. These contract groups are especially important from the point of view of this article, because, more often than not, they are directly associated with the development of an indigenous educational or training institution in public administration, or business and public administration.

Some fourteen substantial training programs in public administration have been mounted in ten foreign countries through Inter-University Contracts, most of them financed by ICA. Even in such programs, however, it is a question whether sufficient attention is being given to the Ph.D.-level training of foreign faculty members, to their need for research-training attuned to the needs of their own country, and to providing continuing contacts with Western scholars and practitioners.

One aspect of the participation of U.S. universities in Inter-University Contracts has direct relevance to the training of foreign administrators here. This is the breadth of experience that has accrued to American faculty members in the affairs of underdeveloped countries. The exposure to the underdeveloped countries that the contracts, and other similar international experiences, have afforded, while not always as long and intensive as might be hoped, has been an important factor in preparing the U.S. faculty member for dealing more adequately with the problems of foreign students on the home campus. These experiences have also stimulated research interests that have made an important contribution to the growth of the field.

Common Characteristics of Programs

Certain common characteristics of the programs described here may be considered as major trends in the university training of foreign administrators in the United States:

1. Special programs have been established for the training of experienced administrators, usually those who have had at least five years in administration in their home countries. The emphasis is not only on training at the graduate as opposed to the undergraduate level, but on the selection of trainees who are more mature and experienced than those normally found in U.S. graduate schools. Such programs are almost invariably of an interdisciplinary nature, usually involving cooperation between faculties of administration and economics, and frequently of anthropology and sociology as well. Considerable emphasis is given to methods of problem formulation and problem solving.

2. Observation and study tours of American organizations are a necessary part of the training process, representing the quickest and most effective means for getting a "feel" for American practice. Observation and study of other foreign organizations, important in the field of international development, is of equal importance. In both cases, arrangements stop short of administrative internships.

3. Considerably higher priority is attached to the training of practicing government servants from the underdeveloped countries than to the training of teacher-scholars, though the latter has been a consideration in some inter-university contracts and in some of the fellowships awarded by the United Nations and the Ford Foundation. The normal maximum period of training, however, is one year, and the most frequently awarded degree is that of Master in Public Administration.

Thus, it is apparent that some, but by no means all, of the pressing needs of foreign students and trainees in public administration are being met by arrangements now in effect in some universities. Except for the special counseling arrangements noted, the field relies largely on general arrangements for assisting in social and cultural adjustment, and in language training, provided by the university. There is little special instruction for foreign students in public administration of relevant aspects of American history and government, or in the framework of social, economic, and political institutions in which American administrators operate. Informal observation and study tours are relatively brief and necessarily lack depth. The few real attempts at follow-up after the trainees return home indicate that this might be a promising area for future work. Many of these comments indicate shortcomings that are normal consequences of short-term assignments, or even of training for a full year.

Comparatively little priority has been accorded to the development of training programs to meet the special needs of foreign teacher-scholars in public administration, lasting two, three, or more years. Still to be developed are programs of research-training on problems of administration in developing societies, opportunities for data collection and field research in the home country or a related, less developed country, and supervision of field research by "returned alumni" and by U.S. faculty members serving in the field. The contribution that indigenous teacher-scholars trained under such arrangements might make to the future development of public administration is apparent. One reason why they have not been further explored and developed may be a result of the separation of efforts to train foreign administrators from efforts to develop new theory.

International Content in Public Administration

It is obvious that the ability of the field of public administration to offer effective training to foreign administrators is ultimately dependent upon its scope and content. The introduction of international content in the field is, however, a very recent development. The first seminar dealing primarily with an international subject matter at the Littauer School at Harvard was introduced in 1940–41. In most departments and schools, courses bearing on international aspects of administration were a post-World War II development.

Most of the current developments of interest can be grouped

under the broad heading of comparative government or administration. There is space to mention a few only. The Committee on Comparative Politics of the Social Science Research Council has broken new ground by developing a new framework for the comparative (and functional) analysis of the political processes—including administration—of the developing areas. The first major published work of the committee, *The Politics of the Developing Areas*, is a landmark in this field. This is just one example of the many new ideas and concepts currently subject to discussion and testing. Others are being spawned in new seminars on comparative administration and development that are a distinguishing feature of the current growth of the field, including those at Harvard under Professor Fainsod; at Yale under Professors Sharp, Kaufman, and Fesler; at Cornell under Professor Bent; at Oregon under Professors Wengert and Mikesell; at Indiana, under Professors Calwell and Riggs, among others. The Indiana group produced one of the early volumes in the field, *Toward the Comparative Study of Administration*. Also indicative of the growing work in this field is the special June, 1960, issue of the *Administrative Sciences Review* on the theme of comparative administration.

Research programs at the Maxwell School, Syracuse University, have taken a slightly different direction, as marked by the well-known work of Dean Cleveland and associates, and by the recent publication of the important volume on *The Overseas Americans*. Also, a number of faculty members at the Maxwell School will be associated during the next five years with colleagues at Syracuse in the fields of business administration, engineering, and education in a program of research on the theme of cross-cultural operations. This signifies the special involvement of Americans in "institution-building" in overseas programs.

At the University of Southern California, Dr. Richard Gable conducts an annual seminar on problems of technical assistance.

A new approach termed "development administration" is being discussed as possibly comprehending both western and non-western elements in the administrative process. A group headed by Dr. Edward Weidner at Michigan State University is currently engaged in research in this field. Certain implications are already being drawn from the concept for the training of foreign administrators. A report prepared by Professor Irving Swerdlow on the curriculum of the new Pakistan Administrative Staff College, with which Syracuse is associated, recommends training that will underline

(1) the importance to public administrators of an understanding of economic forces and relationships, and (2) the comparative politics and administration of development programs. Finally, according to Swerdlow, "there is the requirement that public administrators learn to stimulate and encourage a spirit of innovation and creativity, and to gear procedures and regulations to change and development. . . . This is merely the recognition of the need for a special kind of creativity in public administrators which will need to be encouraged and stimulated as much as the widened creativity in technological innovations necessary for economic development."

It is not surprising, perhaps, that a discussion of recent trends in thought and investigation in comparative administration would turn again to the requirements of training foreign administrators. It would seem important to stress the relationship of research to training in this field, and of the potential for collaboration in research between Americans and foreign nationals so trained. New trends of thought have also had ramifications in the organization of universities.

Institutional Implications

The growth of interest in U.S. universities in overseas development and administration has required the establishment of some new organizational arrangements. Although the training of foreign administrators is only one part of this interest, the ability of the universities to provide effective training is being strengthened. Notable examples are the School of Public and International Affairs at the University of Pittsburgh, the School of International Service at American University, and the Institute of International Studies and Overseas Operations at the University of Oregon. At Michigan State University, the process has gone even further, and an experiment in "university-wide involvement" in international affairs is going forward. Under the coordination of a central dean, assistant deans of international studies are being appointed in several of the colleges and professional schools, including agriculture, business, and public administration, and the liberal arts college. At other universities, some of the same objectives are sought through the modification of established forms. Public administrators are playing prominent parts in these developments. Perhaps more to the point is the fact that these arrangements are bringing the field of public administration into closer contact and communication with other public service fields in which numerous groups of foreign students and trainees are being trained. These include engineering, education, agriculture, and public health. A relationship of this kind has always been needed with respect to training for administration at home, but the urgency of assisting the underdeveloped countries has apparently opened up new possibilities.

Conclusions

The training of foreign administrators in the United States can be advanced most fundamentally by American universities that have both an interest and competence in "development." Such universities are making special efforts to meet the social and cultural and the intellectual and professional needs of the foreign group. Moreover, they are associated with the advancement of the field, and with its organization, in ways that have an obvious bearing on the relevance and on the scale of the contribution of the field to overseas development. It remains to be seen whether the special efforts made to date have set a pattern that others can learn from and build on, or whether the widespread experimentation that has marked the past decade needs to be broadened and accelerated.

The research trends in the field seem to be pointing toward a much needed theory of the role of administration in development. There are two traditional perspectives from which to view this role —that of the underdeveloped countries themselves, and that of the United States and other western countries as they contribute to development. Perhaps equally important is the construction of a framework in which the mutual contributions and interactions of each can be more effectively related. This, the perspective of the developing community of free nations is an appropriate framework for further work in "development administration."

One interpretation of the institutional and organizational changes in the field is that they are part of a broader need to redefine the role of the American university in world affairs. An aspect of this need is of special concern to public administration. How can the American members of the profession best participate with their colleagues in the less developed countries to establish and promote indigenous research, educational, and training institutions? How can cooperative relationships be developed and maintained over a long period of time?

Looked at in either context, the healthy growth of the field, and the extent to which it can further develop its potential for service to society, is dependent to a remarkable extent on the growth and maintenance of these colleague relationships across cultures. That is why the training of foreign teacher-scholars of administration is important and, in the author's opinion, deserving of higher priority in the training of foreign administrators in the United States.

13. INSTITUTION BUILDING IN NATIONAL DEVELOPMENT

MILTON J. ESMAN

THE literature on development in the past decade has passed through several phases and accented several themes. The earliest phase and the still dominant theme focuses on economic resources —savings, capital accumulation, and the allocation of investment. A subordinate theme, but one which has grown in emphasis, deals with the enhancement of human resources—improving health and developing vocational, professional, entrepreneurial, and administrative skills. The study of education as investment attempts to reduce this latter concept to terms convenient for economic analysis. In American public programming, the Marshall Plan emphasized the formation of capital; Point Four, the enhancement of human skills. Throughout this period, however, there has been a growing recognition of the development process as far-reaching culture change, as a societal transformation which affects fundamentally and often simultaneously every important aspect of community and individual behavior. This latter view of development comprehends political, social, and ideological, as well as economic, variables interacting in complex patterns.

In this broader context of modernization, institutional development is one factor that may merit considerably more attention than it has previously received. References to institution building or institutional development as a factor in modernization can be found scattered in writings and speeches over the past several years.[1] It has now been incorporated into the philosophy of the Agency for International Development, the current administrative incarnation of the United States aid program.[2]

Yet the concept has nowhere been carefully defined or systemati-

EDITOR'S NOTE: Notes corresponding to reference numbers in the text will be found at the end of the chapter.

cally investigated. It is our hunch that this process may be a very significant element in modernization, as fundamental perhaps as the accumulation of capital or the development of individual skills. It is worth exploring systematically, both for the discovery of new knowledge relating to modernization and to provide operating guides for administrators from the emerging countries and their advisors serving in international technical assistance programs.

The Concept of Institution

The term "institution" has different meanings both in technical social science literature and in common usage. In economics and in sociology, "institution" often denotes the incorporation of values or norms into conventions and patterns of social behavior that are sanctioned and enforced by formal and informal authority. Thus, contract, marriage, and private property may be regarded as institutions.

"Institution" may also be used in a broader sense to denote a complex social system which incorporates values and discharges services to the community.[3] One thus speaks of a university as an educational institution, a prison as a penal institution, a bank as a financial institution, a symphony orchestra as a cultural institution. This commonly accepted use of the term as a complex social system is the point of departure of this inquiry into institution building.[4]

Institutions, as used in this context, may perform economic, social, political, or administrative functions either in the governmental or in the private sector. This inquiry, however, focuses on institutions that are more clearly associated with public authority. In most developing countries, this includes the vast majority of institutions of all types, for these societies tend to lack traditions of voluntary association or of large-scale private economic activity beyond the scope of the extended family.

The context of this exploration is basic culture change, which affects both societal structure and process. Modernization implies the acceptance of values and norms that are consistent with modern science, their gradual diffusion throughout the society, their assimilation into patterns of behavior, and the emergence and distribution of new functions required to effectuate new social purposes.

Modernization is also accompanied by increasing functional

specialization. While single institutions in peasant societies perform a wide range of functions for their members—the extended family, church, royal court, or tribal headquarters—modern industrial societies are characterized by a complex, interacting network of differentiated and highly specialized institutions. In the spectrum of peasant-industrialized societies, there appears to be a close correlation between modernization, functional specialization, and interdependence. Modernizing functions are identified with every sector of community concern, including security, agriculture, public works, industry, health, and education, and include such activities as programming, finance, logistics, manpower, production, and distribution.

Modernization tends to be fostered by new elites whose efforts may encounter intense and prolonged opposition from entrenched traditional elites and apathy or resistance from other groups that continue to respect traditional norms and behavior patterns. Because it is a far-reaching and fundamental process, modernizing change is never evenly distributed throughout the society. In its early stages, the process is usually concentrated in a limited number of functional units. These entities are vehicles through which the modernizers attempt to promote specific social change. Because they are sponsored or protected by a modernizing elite, or are tolerated by a traditional elite that has lost its nerve or recognizes the social necessity of a new function, or because a balance of power or a power vacuum permits them to operate, these institutions become centers of change, incorporating internally and diffusing through the society new values, behavior patterns, and services. Their activities may be constrained and ultimately aborted, but if they survive, these new institutions tend to interact and reinforce one another, broadening and deepening their impact on the society.

Modernizing functions cannot be self-executing, nor can they be performed by atomized individuals, however skilled and dedicated. In order to be effective, skilled individuals must be recruited into viable structures which incorporate (institutionalize) the modernizing values and the specialized functions that promote and sustain development. These individuals become associated in ordered and predictable patterns that characterize a social system or structure.

The embodiment of a modernizing function in a specific, specialized, viable social structure is identified as institutional development. Such an institution must have the capacity not only to perform its function—to provide a major modernizing service—but also to sustain itself in a competitive, often hostile, and not wholly predictable environment. Institutions must therefore satisfy the tests both of functional efficiency and of survival power, and the balancing of these two values is one of the major preoccupations and dilemmas of institution builders. This concept includes both newly created bodies and previously established entities that have not been responding to the needs of a changing society and require fundamental restructuring and redirection.

Research into the process of institutional development can be highly significant to students of culture change for the information and insights it may convey about a key ingredient in modernization. Establishing and sustaining viable institutions should be a critical concern of modern political leaders, planners, and administrators in the developing countries, since this is a major element in their operating strategy. Foreign assistance personnel should evaluate their performance less by their success in the transfer of specific skills from one individual to another than by the creation and strengthening of institutions that can perform and sustain modernizing functions.[5]

Significant Elements in Institution Building

In a doctoral seminar at the University of Pittsburgh Graduate School of Public and International Affairs, an attempt was made roughly to conceptualize the institution-building process. Literature in sociology and organization theory were explored for useful insights and bench marks. Efforts were made to locate previous empirical studies of institution building in a modernizing or other context. The results were quite sparse. The most relevant theoretical insights were derived from Philip Selznick's inquiry into *Leadership and Administration*.[6]

A group of significant elements or variables was then identified. These were grouped into six major sections, each focusing on a basic process in institutional development. Their relevance was tested by several case studies, drawn from documentary sources, of successful and unsuccessful efforts at institution building. These included the Nigerian Produce Marketing Boards, the Convention Peoples Party of Ghana, the United States National Resources Planning Board, and the Indian Damodar Valley Corporation.

The original pattern of variables was modified and refined by this comparative inquiry. The result was a provisional guide to case writers, outlining the first rough approximation of factors that seem significant for the description, analysis, and understanding of institutional development. This guide attempts to combine elements essential both to effective internal structure and environmental relationships. The major headings of the guide set forth below suggest the scope and content of the specific variables that are omitted from this note because of space limitations:[7]

I. *Establishment, Adaptation, and Communication of Institutional Values and Purposes.* This group of variables focuses on the formulation and enunciation of the values and purposes of the institution; on the evolution of a doctrine that communicates these values and purposes; on the normative effect of doctrine on the behavior of persons associated with the institution; and on its utility in promoting and protecting institutional interests.

II. *Recruitment, Behavior, and Succession of Leadership.* This section deals with the composition and behavior of top leadership, a critical element in all social systems.

III. *Internal Structure.* This section focuses on the internal distribution of roles and energy and on the staffing function. Institutions that fail to deal adequately with these problems usually are unable to mobilize the strength to manage their program commitments in a competitive environment.

IV. *Mobilization and Allocation of Resources.* Developmental institutions are likely to be competing for scarce resources. The problems of resource mobilization may vitally affect programming decisions. Program choices, in turn, may directly condition ability to mobilize resources. These interrelationships are essential to the analysis of institutional development.

V. *Interaction with Environment.* Institutions function in a social environment and in relation to complementary and competing institutions which they are attempting to influence in the direction of change. At the same time, the environment may be imposing constraints or providing opportunities for institutional development and for the diffusion of modernizing values and services. How to influence and adapt to a changing and not entirely predictable environment is a major element in institution building.

VI. *Program Performance.* Institutions are essentially instruments for providing modernizing services within their societies, but they must also meet internal claims. The means by which these objectives are reconciled, the criteria applied in evaluating all elements of institutional performance, and the effects of evaluation on subsequent performance are included in this section.

Problems in Empirical Research

Verifying the relevance of these elements and establishing and testing hypotheses concerning interrelationships among them will require extensive empirical research. This research will have to be done in the field and probably in the form of intensive case studies. If possible, these studies should be conducted within a common conceptual framework so that results may be compared and generalizing inferences drawn from the variety of empirical evidence produced by the case studies. Throughout this process, the initial rough conceptualization of institution building will be subject to continuing modification.[8] From comparative case data, it may be possible to draw generalizing inferences for understanding and for action. As in the development of all new knowledge, one begins with hunches, applies them to empirical data, and reorders the original hunches into stable propositions based on empirical evidence.

Proceeding with this research enterprise, therefore, one faces a series of significant and as yet unresolved tactical problems:

1. *How can the large variety of institutional types be reduced to an ordered pattern for purposes of systematic research planning and analysis?*

The functional purpose of institutions may profoundly affect their behavior, each type requiring a specific analytic approach. There are many functional types of institutions and many possible methods of classifying them. One might attempt to classify them by the type of activity performed, by the economic or social sector they serve, or by a combination of both. There are many institutions serving each major sector, each of which may be related to one or more functional types. Thus, in the agricultural sector, there may be separate institutions dealing with production, marketing, education, and credit. There are inevitable combinations and overlappings in any system of classification. Thus, a rural bank is both an agricultural and a financial institution, an agricultural college is both an educational and an agricultural agency. Because institutions may exhibit distinctive behavior based upon common functional or environmental characteristics, a continuing concern of this research enterprise must be the development of a useful, empirically based classification.

2. *What is the dimension of an institution within the complex of governmental and quasi-governmental structures?* What criteria are helpful in distinguishing institutions from subinstitutions or from an institutional complex?

One may identify, for many nations, four levels of aggregation:

a. The national ministry combining several related programs in the same sector (e.g., Ministry of Education)

b. The major service or bureau performing a specific function or managing a single program (e.g., Bureau of Teacher Training)

c. The operating facility performing a specific service at a single location (e.g., Teacher Training College)

d. The unit or section of the operating facility (e.g., Tests and Measurements Section).[9]

There are, of course, numerous variations of this oversimplified model, and any attempt at rigid definition of this heterogeneous universe could readily degenerate into casuistry. A more precise working definition may have to await the accumulation of research data. Among the criteria that might be relevant, however, are functional specificity of program, operating autonomy of management, and corporate identity of staff.

Using these rough criteria—and applying a rule of reason—one should eliminate national ministries or departments for want of functional specificity and, in many cases, of strong corporate identity. A unit or section of an operating facility tends to have little operating autonomy, to depend on the entity of which it is a constituent for support and even survival.

The other two categories, the operating facilities and especially the major bureaus or services, seem best to qualify as institutions under the criteria suggested above. Thus, using U.S. examples, the Forest Service (of the U.S. Department of Agriculture) and the Internal Revenue Service (of the Treasury Department) certainly qualify under our concept of institution. So might the Beltsville Research Center (of the Agriculture Research Service of the U.S. Department of Agriculture) and the Children's Bureau (of the Social Security Administration of the Department of Health, Education and Welfare). Though much depends on the conventions by which institutions are aggregated for control purposes in different governments, the criteria already selected should assist in the selection and designation of entities as institutions for purposes of research.

3. *Whatever classification and definition are tentatively adopted, there remains the problem of an effective research strategy.*

Shall one begin with a single class of institutions—development banks, teacher training centers, police agencies—and study their comparative experience in different environments? If so, should one attempt to identify those institutions that are critical to modernization and concentrate on them? Or should one attempt the analysis of a cluster of interacting institutions in a single environment, selecting a single country and analyzing the development of a series or network of interacting modernizing institutions within the same ecological framework? Or should the first effort spread the net widely over a variety of experience, including different classes of institutions in different environments? This would provide a wide range of raw data that might suggest some of the more generic problems in institution building and strengthen the initial conceptual base from which more specific, specialized approaches could subsequently be undertaken.

Given the limited resources in qualified, interested, and available researchers and in finances, it is unlikely that these three strategies could be pursued simultaneously. Which one seems most feasible operationally and most likely to yield useful insights and knowledge?

4. *In construing the institution-building process, two major problems must be treated and treated simultaneously in a research enterprise. The first involves the strategy and tactics of building viable institutions; the second, the measurement and evaluation of their modernizing influence and consequences. Both elements must be incorporated into the conceptualization and the empirical case studies; theoretically, at least, these two elements may come into serious conflict.*

If each institution must be guided by a survival strategy in order to cope with a competitive environment, the process of building a sound and enduring structure may confront its leadership with choices that imply compromise or even the abandonment of its original social purposes.[10] An institution may manage to survive and to grow in strength, but what price survival? The capacity to survive and even to prosper is an essential measure of institutional success; the tactics of management in a competitive and often hostile environment are important data in the evaluation of institutional success or failure.

But mere survival, even growth and material prosperity, is not a sufficient measure of institutional performance. Development or modernization through the performance of significant public services is the social purpose associated with institution building in this study. How can one measure and evaluate this modernizing influence? There appear to be two broad possibilities:

a. One can attempt to measure the success of the institution in incorporating modernizing values and behavior *internally in the system*—in its doctrine, organizational design, staff incentives and rewards, performance criteria, etc. This procedure can test the modernizing character of the institution as a microcosm. It should be possible to accomplish this through careful research using a modernizing continuum.[11] This would not, however, test the modernizing impact of the institution on its wider environment, which is the more significant measure of performance.

b. One can attempt to measure the influence of the institution as a change agent *on its surrounding environment*. This assumes, of course, that the institution does not merely adapt to an existing environment, but that its program and its performance have a dynamic (modernizing) impact on the individuals and groups with which it comes into contact, on complementary institutions with which it transacts business, and ultimately on the entire community. It is no simple matter to devise or to apply an instrument to identify and measure this impact. Distinct criteria and perhaps even a separate testing instrument may have to be produced for each class of institutions and perhaps for each experience in institution building. Though one might question the possibility of precisely measuring or evaluating the modernizing influence of an institution on its environment, the effort seems warranted, since this is the basic social purpose underlying this inquiry.

5. *A complicating factor in such an evaluation would be the time horizon. Over what period of time should the performance of an institution be described and evaluated?*

Assuming that the bulk of the empirical evidence concerning institutional development was derived from case histories, what time periods should be covered? Can the life cycle of an institution be extrapolated from comparative experience so that critical periods can be identified for intensive investigation without risking the omission of important data and events that might not fall into these predetermined periods? Are significant events or decisional choices unique and specific over time for each institution? Or can they be classified and flagged in advance of specific inquiry so that research efforts may focus on predetermined periods and events? While economizing time and enhancing the comparability of evidence, this might fatally exclude significant information. The time perspective will be a difficult problem to solve in this research enterprise and may not be amenable to a standard solution.

A Cooperative Research Enterprise

The organization of a research activity to cover a subject of this scope will involve a series of practical decisions and arrangements beyond the few topics already mentioned. The conduct of field research for the collection of data will require considerable negotiation with governments and individual institutions which may be suspicious of such academic inquiry; access to data may be quite difficult in many situations. An inquiry of this scope is probably beyond the capacity of a single university department or professional school. This suggests a consortium of interested universities in the U.S.A., associated through a coordinating project headquarters, to stimulate the critical review of the institution-building concept, to sponsor and facilitate specific research arrangements, to diffuse research findings, and to develop operating guides based on empirical evidence. The consortium should associate with kindred institutions and scholars overseas, especially in the emerging countries, for joint research and systematic exchange of data and findings.

To outline the organization of a major research enterprise in this field is beyond the scope of this paper. Its major purpose is to reduce to print, for sharing with interested scholars and practitioners, the initial explorations that are being made into a phenomenon which may have important implications for those interested in the development and modernization of the emerging nations.

NOTES

The author acknowledges the valuable assistance of Mr. Hans C. Blaise in developing the concepts reported in this article.

1. Harlan Cleveland et. al., *The Overseas Americans* (New York: McGraw-Hill, 1960), pp. 157–62, 165–67, 182–84; Herbert Emmerich,

"Administrative Roadblocks to Coordinated Development," prepared for the U.N. expert working-group on Social Aspects of Economic Development in Latin America, U.N. Documents Distribution Section, 1961.

2. U.S. Department of State, *An Act for International Development (fiscal year 1962)*. A *Summary Presentation*, June, 1961, pp. 69-72.

3. "Institutions are generalized patterns of norms which define categories of prescribed, permitted, and prohibited behavior in social relationships for people in interaction with each other as members of their society and its various subsystems and groups." Talcott Parsons, *Structure and Process in Modern Societies* (Glencoe, Ill.: The Free Press, 1960), p. 177. But note also Arnold Rose's introductory essay on "The Comparative Study of Institutions" in the volume he edited on *The Institutions of Advanced Societies* (Minneapolis: University of Minnesota Press, 1958), pp. 30-32, for a definition of institution as "group" or "people in organized interaction." This latter definition is fully compatible with that used in this paper.

4. We use "institution" rather than the frequently used term "organization" because of the emphasis on internal structure usually associated with the term "organization." "Institution" seems more suitably to convey ideas of social purpose and of continuous adaption and interaction with the ecology which is indispensable to the utility of this concept in relation to the development or modernization of societies.

In Chapter 2, "Some Ingredients of a General Theory of Formal Organization," in *Structure and Process in Modern Societies, op. cit.*, Talcott Parsons attempts to expand the conventional view of "organization" to compromise an "institutional level" which "mediates" between the "managerial level" and the "community." He sometimes uses the term "institutional organization" to denote this higher-level function. We prefer to include all these levels, so far as they are structurally inter-connected, in the single concept, "institution."

5. This point is made repeatedly by Harlan Cleveland in *The Overseas Americans, op. cit.*, and other publications.

6. Evanston, Ill., 1957. Other useful sources were Rose, *op. cit.*; Parsons, *Structure and Process in Modern Societies, op. cit., The Social System* (Glencoe, Ill.: The Free Press); Robert K. Merton, *Social Theory and Social Structure* (rev. ed.; Glencoe, Ill.: The Free Press); James G. March and Herbert A. Simon, *Organizations* (New York: John Wiley and Sons, 1958). Among French social scientists, a recent and relevant treatment of *institutions organismes* appears in François Perroux' foreword to Elias Gannage's *Economie du Developpement* (Paris, 1962). A relevant study from recent experiences in a developing area is José Abueva's *Focus on the Barrio* (Manila, 1959), an administrative history of the Philippine community development program.

7. Case writers were advised not to follow these elements in sequence, either in data gathering, analysis, or writing, but only to be sensitive to these factors as an analytic system relevant to their research. The systematic analysis of cases according to these variables is envisaged as a subsequent procedure.

8. On the basis of the rough conceptualization outlined above, a field study is being performed by Mr. Hans C. Blaise, a doctoral candidate at the Graduate School of Public and International Affairs, University of Pittsburgh. He is studying the Kompong Kantuot Rural Teacher Training Center in Cambodia.

9. Some entities like national banks, planning boards, and political parties are clearly discrete institutions for the purpose of this research. The problem of definition and selection arises with units that are structurally related to larger or constituent establishments.

10. See Philip Selznick's study of the *TVA and the Grass Roots* (Berkeley: University of California Press, 1949), for an illustration of this problem.

11. One such scheme has been developed by Parsons, Shils, and Olds in Part II, "Values, Motives and Systems of Action," in Talcott Parsons and Edward A. Shils (ed.), *Toward a General Theory of Action* (Cambridge, Mass.: Harvard University Press, 1951), pp. 76ff.

14. *LET'S THINK SMALL FOR DEVELOPMENT*

MALCOLM D. RIVKIN

ARCHITECT Daniel Burnham made homiletic history with his plea for turn-of-the-century Chicagoans to "Make no little plans. They have no magic to stir men's blood." Burnham had just completed a magnificent classic scheme for the future of the city. His plan's power did capture the imagination of Chicago, so much so that over the course of the years a part of the grand design was effectuated. The outer drive, the fine series of lakefront parks, and the few monumental buildings that dot them are all elements of Burnham's masterpiece. Chicago is much the happier for Daniel Burnham and his big plan, though its vastness proved too heady for his devoted followers to see realized in entirety.

Burnham's remark has caught others besides city planners, whose spirits it bolsters in the face of traffic congestion and urban blight. Universities preface their expansion programs with "Make no little plans." Businessmen in search of capital for new ventures are fond of exhorting prospects with Daniel Burnham. He is so often cited in after-dinner speeches that the making of big plans is becoming a cliché.

The phrase sticks in American memories and aspirations. It has done so because the making of big plans—the conception of vast imaginative ideas and enterprises—is so much a part of American style. From the conquest of the West to the challenging of outer space, ours has been a society to find room for the new, different, and impossible; and therein lies much of its greatness.

By no means all the imaginative schemes in America's history have reached fruition, and few turn out exactly as viewed in the minds of their initial beholders. Compromise is often necessary and failure common. A plan can be only a start. Hundreds of successfully completed details, often dull and tedious, must follow the original shaft of brilliance. Steps toward a goal must be chosen and measured, lest the goal stand as mere pious hope. This process of working out details can modify an original bold scheme and is as much built into the system (though taken more for granted) as the freedom to conceive great ideas itself. Yet enough evidence still remains to uphold the belief that if men or institutions think big enough and work hard enough their hoped-for ends will be achieved.

Should Underdeveloped Countries "Think Big"?

Although the propensity toward the "grand vision" seems to have paid off in the U.S.A. and now in booming postwar Europe, one can seriously question whether it is profitable for newly developing countries at this stage in their histories.

Material and human resources of these countries vary so widely that any generalization on their abilities to achieve modernization is suspect. Thus, I proceed with some trepidation, knowing full well of significant exceptions, to offer the following hypothesis:

The leaders of many developing countries are thinking and planning on a scale too grand for human and organizational capacities to absorb. In this course they are abetted and encouraged by the West, which still looks at the growth process through its own prejudices. Much of the frustration of development is inherent in this "immodest" approach. Pervading as it does so many significant elements of the development process—from national economic planning, to the founding of new universities, to legislation for social reform, even to private entrepreneurial activity—an aim for the spectacular, without commensurate ability to adopt steady, reasoned, step-by-step procedures leading toward the goals, is cause for grave concern.

A fear of failure to measure up to the challenges of the modern world may play a part in this leap-before-you-look approach to development. These nations have so much catching up to do that they can feel unable to afford years to educate a responsible generation of chiefs and Indians for government and industry. Time is too short for experimentation, for small, gradual probing steps, for an economic and social system suited to their conditions and traditions to *evolve*.

But unlike the process of political independence, which can be accomplished violently and in a short time, the process of economic and social independence is not a product of quick emotional strivings. No great nation and no great institution has yet become so after only a few years of frenetic effort.

This is no objection to grand goals per se. If their immediate realization is unrealistic, they can at least serve as guides to what might be. But what are really crucial are shorter-range "operational" projects that can be handled within current limits of personnel and resources and on which people can be weaned before they tackle bigger issues. The courage to "think small," to experiment, and to pay heed to details, is what the process of development most needs.

Paralysis is a not uncommon response to ambitious objectives which national circumstances make impossible of achievement. It leads to a dangerous dissipation of energies that could be turned to productive purpose. For four years, this was the case with Turkey's regional planning agency. Finally, a breakthrough was made to productive effort that held some promise of aiding the nation's development. How this breakthrough occurred may offer interesting lessons in the process of thinking small.

Regional Planning in Turkey

A Department of Regional Planning was established in the Turkish Ministry of Public Works in 1956 and transferred to the new Ministry of Reconstruction in 1958. Pressure to create this governmental function came from influential architects, engineers, university professors, and journalists, some of whom held important government posts. As serious students of their society, they were aware of significant problems not subject to consistent public policy.

Turkey's population had grown rapidly since the war. Poverty on the land combined with the lure of urban work opportunities to generate a large migration from rural areas to Istanbul, Ankara, and Izmir. Public services in these metropolises were strained. Land speculation was excessive and land controls ineffective. Great tracts of illegal "mushroom" housing were covering the urban fringes. Social problems as well as the inability of many migrants to find jobs were important concerns. Meanwhile, large areas of the nation outside the heavily populated cities had extensive natural resources still untapped and offered potential for new industrial and agricultural settlement as possible alternatives to accelerated metropolitan growth.

There was an administrative problem, too. Many different government agencies had charge of phases of infrastructure and industrial development. Their decisions seemed uncoordinated and prey to political pressure. Factories went up without roads and other services. Infrastructure was underutilized in some areas and lacking in others.

These were the large issues that interested the small but influential circle of intellectuals. Some of them had studied abroad and were familiar with TVA and successful area planning in The Netherlands and other European nations. They read and absorbed Western literature on the subject. Since Turkish government was centralized, with most decision-making power in Ankara, a regional planning agency located somewhere within the national government seemed the most promising mechanism to deal with the problems.

Although the group's enthusiasm resulted in formation of such an agency, it was an office without specific legal responsibilities and restricted to a small budget. Only two men had actually been trained in planning overseas. They formed the nucleus of a small staff.

Despite its lack of power, personnel, and experience, the bureau set for itself several wide-ranging objectives: to prepare development plans for many areas of Turkey; to produce policies governing control of land in Istanbul, Ankara, and other large urban regions; to do something about diverting or stopping the flow of rural migrants to big cities; to foster coordination of investments in time and space among the many agencies responsible for public works, housing, and industry. These objectives reflected the range of problems that led to the bureau's creation.

During the first four years, several studies were attempted, mostly data-gathering on national economic and population trends using secondary sources. All were dropped when they became too big, too amorphous, or just beyond the ability of personnel to handle. Morale suffered. The bureau's leadership, who tried to comment on regional issues without data or analytic studies, began to feel government decision-makers were not interested in what they had to say. Their efforts had failed and they seriously questioned whether regional planning of any kind could be accomplished in Turkey.

Yet enough interest persisted, both before and after the 1960 revolution, for the Turkish Government to request outside technical assistance for the Ankara bureau and its new field station in Istanbul. The comments that follow (and which are limited to the situation in Ankara) reflect the author's own experience with the agency.

A New Approach

Quite soon after the resident advisor program began in 1960, the consultants realized that Regional Planning's objectives were far too high for what could reasonably be accomplished in many years. There had been little or no attempt to adapt these objectives to what might be achieved with the resources in hand. The dozen-odd staff members came from a wide variety of fields and lacked experience in simple data-gathering techniques. Rather rigid, formal higher education left them unprepared for experimental or analytic work even within their own specialties. Each had been assigned tasks unrelated to the work of others. Along with the low volume of production and intensity of effort, a foundation for cooperative endeavor or "agency spirit" was lacking. No one was satisfied with performance. It then became a question of what, if anything, could be accomplished on a practical basis.

For five months this question was discussed and debated among the agency's directors and the foreign technicians. Finally, the following principles of agreement were reached. Listed in this fashion they seem quite elementary. Yet at the time they represented a real breakthrough in the frustration cycle.

1. The staff, such as it was, must be welded into a unit. Each person should have a specific task related to those of others in the bureau.

2. Any project undertaken from then on should have two functions: as a training vehicle for the staff to learn planning and as a means of producing recommendations to decision-making agencies on current issues of high concern.

3. Since this was a regional planning agency, it should develop experience in planning for a region. Thus, instead of pursuing the so-far fruitless studies of national trends and characteristics, all efforts should focus on the study of a single area.

4. Since the exact content of regional planning remained unspecified by legislation, the agency should adopt an appropriate "operational" definition to guide its efforts. Regional Planning was within a ministry dealing with urban land use and facilities. Thus,

the department should be concerned with land use on a regional scale and with those aspects of a region's resources and human activity that bore on the use of land. Any studies of a region should focus on such problems. Any recommendations for future action should come with the clear objective of fostering more effective use of land.

All of these principles stemmed from the one overweening necessity: to concentrate the agency on a specific job with specific goals that could be realized in a relatively short time period.

The next task was the selection of the first region for study. The Turkish authorities handled this important choice with ease. Zonguldak was to be the place—a province bordering the Black Sea about 150 miles from Ankara. Only 1 per cent (8,000 square kilometers) of Turkey's land area, Zonguldak had all the coal mines and the one steel mill. Construction of a second mill under DLF sponsorship was imminent. Some additional industry existed in the region, which also held major forestry preserves. Population, about 60 per cent rural, was approximately half a million. Zonguldak's small cities were growing at rapid rates. A number of government investment projects, in infrastructure and industry both, were taking place in the province.

Zonguldak was clearly a strategic location, an area of great significance to the Turkish economy, where decision-making agencies might be willing to see any creditable work done in regional planning.

Thus, four years after its founding and five months after the resident consulting program began, Regional Planning's concerns shifted from broad, general, and paralyzing objectives to work in a single small but important area.

Stage 1

Stage 1 was to be a reporting exercise, a gathering of specific facts, in essence an endeavor as completely opposite from the concern with broad general goals as two efforts could be. A six-month deadline was set for the fact-finding mission. Each staff member received a specific assignment under the project director. Data were to be gathered on industrial activity and location, agricultural activity and land use, population characteristics and change, housing, transportation, water, power, education, and health. Base maps of the region, its topography and land use, were to be collected or made.

Most sector agencies charged with national programs in these matters were headquartered in Ankara. Each tended to operate independently of the others, a fact of life that produced Turkey's internal coordination difficulties. Yet these agencies were the richest source of data and ultimately would be the decision-makers to entertain Regional Planning's recommendations. Their help and confidence were needed. As staff members visited these operations, merely in quest of data, Regional Planning's presence became known. In almost every case, the reception was good and help forthcoming. Carefully, no attempt was made to challenge or supersede their authority.

The men and women of Regional Planning varied in their responses to this fact-gathering mission and the brief field trips to the region that funds allowed. Some approached the work avidly. Others shied away. Data began coming in; a few people began attempting to relate their activity to each other; morale was higher; but Regional Planning was not yet a functioning team.

The data produced serious problems. There were inconsistencies and wide gaps. Many essential studies were beyond the staff. Yet these difficulties, too, represented a step forward. For they were tangible difficulties that resulted from an actual "coming to grips" with a region's characteristics and the means of recording them.

In June, 1961, a presentation of findings to the ministry and officials of all relevant central and provincial agencies was scheduled. To permit clear understanding of the material, architects transferred the most representable data to graphic panels, where facts were shown in the most simplified visual manner. This picture of Zonguldak's resources and activities was the first time any such comprehensive effort had been attempted by a Turkish agency. Little analysis was offered. Gaps and inconsistencies were frankly admitted. Yet the effect on those present was enormous.

They became aware of relationships between activities on an area basis which affected the very nature of these activities. Population growth in urban centers and the resultant demand for space and services were directly traced to economic growth in the mines and mills and increasing shortage of land in rural areas. Defects in the transportation system presented bottlenecks to further industrial growth. As rural sections became overpopulated, a danger of mass emigration from the region appeared. The idea of examining such issues together rather than separately and focusing attention on a defined land area with concern for its future development were new concepts for most of those in attendance.

It is important to note that the bureau did not attempt to gain acceptance of recommendations at this stage. Its objective was to gain further support and achieve a favorable climate among decision-making agencies. None felt threatened. The work looked promising. Officials outside the ministry offered help where possible. The ministry itself responded by adding more staff positions.

At the end of Stage 1, Regional Planning was still a small operation with unclear responsibilities. But it had started to do a job and could finally command some interest.

Stage 2

One of the most powerful groups to show interest was the State Planning Organization. Before October, 1960, Turkey had no mechanism to perform national economic planning. The revolutionary government, aware of Turkey's serious economic and social problems, therefore decided to create a body within the Prime Ministry for this purpose. SPO's functions included approval of all investment projects over a certain level of expenditure and preparation of annual and five-year national development plans. Cabinet approval was necessary for any plans produced, but SPO had a good deal of power and funds, plus some very high-quality personnel. Above all, it had the ear of top government and military decision-makers.

The significance of SPO to Regional Planning was its status as a powerful organization with the goal of development. Regional Planning could conceivably help it identify needs and projects in strategic areas, and SPO support could be a major assist to the growth and influence of Regional Planning. SPO became particularly interested in the Zonguldak project as a test of how cooperation might be achieved. At the end of Stage 1, SPO agreed to provide assistance by its staff and foreign economists for further effort in the region. In itself, this meant the work of Regional Planning would now be considered in the highest levels of government.

During the summer of 1961, important changes occurred in Regional Planning's staff, giving it an even better base for Stage 2. A new director took over, and several promising new technicians were hired, bringing agency strength to about twenty-five.

The director was a leader, able to win loyalty and respect from his staff and from outside officials with whom he dealt. He had just returned from a year at an American university that followed upon previous planning experience in Turkey. Somehow, he was able to blend the two cultures and experiences and look for ways of applying planning principles to his own nation. He searched for harmony between viewpoints. As a pragmatist, well aware of his department's limitations, he was concerned with how to sell the idea of regional planning by making best use of the tools available. He was committed to experiment and exploration.

Most of the half-dozen new staff members were recent university graduates, again with a variety of backgrounds. They, too, were willing to explore. Over the past months they had heard that Regional Planning was "doing something" and were thus attracted to the agency. Already the image was beginning to change.

In February, 1962, a second presentation took place. Only the audience was the same. For the material now attempted to show how the region's characteristics, its potential and problems, made coordinated development policy desirable. It went a step further to indicate some of the programs various agencies might consider.

For example, location of new industries was proposed where the resource of labor potential warranted. These industries would be related to the iron and steel complex, the population growth to occur as a result of planned expansion of the mills, or the forestry resource. Alternative population projections for the region as a whole and for the urban and rural areas were made, depending on alternative levels of economic activity.

Other proposals included priorities for construction of elements in the transport system that would key in with economic growth; agricultural improvement programs in the most promising areas; projects for increased utilities needed to absorb growth now planned or possible; reservation of specific areas of land in the urban centers for industry and housing. Some recommendations represented ideas currently held by the sector agencies. Others were new and resulted from application of planning principles to problems that had been treated earlier in isolation.

The main administrative recommendation was that several sector agencies, SPO, and Regional Planning begin to pool efforts in a formal organization to guide future development in Zonguldak. This recommendation proved too big a step for the decision-makers to take. Yet the favorable reaction to the presentation, from political leaders as well as civil servants, was even higher than to the one six months before.

Over the next months, Regional Planning was asked to consult on several decisions regarding the area. Agencies that in earlier days could see little value in this small operation of the Reconstruction Ministry began to revise their own programs in light of the Zonguldak study. Highway priorities were changed. A water resource program for the area directly affected by the new steel mill was initiated. The bureau's population projections became the base for electric power demand studies. The new steel mill cooperated on pioneer research to examine its social and psychological impact on the immediate community. Regional Planning's work became the chief determinant of town plans for the main industrial centers. SPO requested and received a rough five-year capital works program for the region to be included in its forthcoming national plan.

Thus, although its proposal for an intergovernmental Zonguldak commission was rejected, Regional Planning continued to follow events in the region. With its experience and now-open door to powerful interests, the bureau could at the very least help guide future decision on land use and economic development.

The ministry responded by providing a 40 per cent increase in staff and a markedly increased budget. Meanwhile, SPO requested that the bureau begin work on a new development program for southern Turkey. Added foreign assistance was also promised.

To say the agency was successful would be premature. It had met one set of tests but still greater ones were in the offing. In lieu of formal responsibilities, it had opened a number of informal channels to centers of power and influenced decisions in one strategic area of the nation. For its influence to increase or even continue, the agency would have to turn out a much greater amount of production of even higher quality than before. About all one could say in the fall of 1962 was that Regional Planning had survived to perform useful activity.

But survival itself ranked as a major achievement in light of prospects two years earlier. The agency and the idea it represented now had an opportunity to grow which would not have materialized had the original set of broad objectives held sway.

Survival was largely the result of adopting a more pragmatic approach, geared to resources of staff and budget and directed at clarifying limited issues of current importance to the nation.

Regional Planning produced no migration policies or sweeping metropolitan land-use controls. Even the Zonguldak project was not a complete and comprehensive plan. Such efforts would be many years away.

But the work did involve application of planning principles to regional issues. Leadership materialized. Morale and capability of personnel improved. Awareness of a step-by-step process, of a time of experimentation in which ideas from a developed society would be adapted to, not adopted by, a society in transition, began to characterize the agency's approach.

The Courage to "Think Small"

This discussion of regional planning for Turkey indicates how one long-held set of bold ideas was leading a program on a path of self-destruction. Only by showing the courage to "think small" were the Turkish authorities and their foreign advisors able to pull out something of value.

The will and ability to think small cannot be imposed upon developing countries from the outside. So long as pressures for accelerated growth exist in context of a society with imperfect political and social institutions, deeply sincere individuals will want to rush into the modern world. It takes maturity, and often hard experience, to realize the many tiny, essential steps between the conception of a new idea and its realization.

Western advisors are in a particularly advantageous position to help. Many are sent to work on projects whose job specifications call for establishment of bold new agencies, drafting of sweeping administrative or social reforms. But the main avenue for help may not lie in blue-sky thinking called for in job descriptions. It may be in working with counterparts to break down concepts into detailed operating programs making maximum use of few funds, faulty facilities, and untrained people. Of necessity, these programs —to operate at all—may represent a more modest level of activity than the expert anticipated.

Often there will be resistance. The modest is also the unglamorous. Details are onerous. The advisor may find himself in the position, not of a catalyst for brilliant thoughts, but of a gadfly to produce sound ones. This is a difficult position to fill and one requiring far greater willingness to "learn" the country and its potential than mere attendance at orientation briefings. For the foreign advisor may find himself obliged to interpret this potential to his associates in ways that they may not initially be prepared to accept. Weakness must be admitted and dissected before it becomes strength. This is hard, although less frustrating than trying to implement big plans with tiny tools. Yet it is necessary if self-sustaining and growing success of a function or program is to be achieved.

I doubt that developing nations need more lessons in the art of thinking big. They desperately need guidance, however, in the science of thinking small.

FOUR

MANPOWER
FOR
DEVELOPMENT

15. THE TECHNICAL ASSISTANCE EXPERT

ANNE WINSLOW

UPWARDS of 40,000 individuals are carrying out technical assistance activities in underdeveloped countries under bilateral or multilateral programs and many thousands more under private auspices. France alone reports some 25,000 officials and experts working in the field in its various technical assistance programs. It is estimated that this total figure may double or triple within ten years. "There is no professional enterprise on which individuals can embark at this epoch of history fraught with more complexity, more untested problems, and more costly consequences of error than operations associated with the revolutionary changes now under way in the newly independent and emerging countries."[1] Yet "every day that passes, new recruits to international operations are entering the fold no better prepared for their tasks than those who first ventured upon these uncharted operations a decade and more ago."[2]

Such were the concerns that led the Società Italiana per l'Organizzazione Internazionale and the Carnegie Endowment for International Peace to convene a conference in Rome, February 12–16, 1962, on recruitment, selection, and training of technical assistance personnel. The conference brought together ninety-eight persons from all parts of the world—officials of governments and of the United Nations and specialized agencies, representatives of business and of training institutes, and consultants with special competence in the subjects under discussion. The primary objective was to afford an opportunity to exchange views and experiences, to survey the existing situation, and to indicate problem areas in which research was needed.

This report does not purport to be a literal rendering of the

EDITOR'S NOTE: Notes corresponding to reference numbers in the text will be found at the end of the chapter.

167

discussions during the conference. It derives from the discussions and from materials available to the conference and is intended to reflect the nature of the concerns expressed and the general areas of emphasis.

Where Are We?

The practice of technical assistance is strangely reminiscent of Gertrude Stein. A well is a well is a well. An expert is an expert is an expert. Only recently has there begun to dawn the painful realization that a well is not a well, and that an expert is not an expert, in any meaningful sense. The intricate process of effecting social change, of translating into workable terms knowledge and experience from one culture to another, of communicating across boundaries is not an occupation for amateurs. Yet the empirical research needed to lay the foundations for professional activity has not been carried out.

We do not even know the number of experts that may be needed in five years' time, although we can make a guess by projecting the rate of past increases into the future. We can assume, judging by present trends, a growing need for high-level, broad-gauge economic planners, institution builders, engineers, teachers of teachers, and highly specialized specialists, but again this is only an assumption. The number and type of foreign experts needed in the underdeveloped countries cannot be determined unless development plans have been formulated and local manpower resources assessed. This is no easy task in a fluid situation where the very success of one program may affect demands in another area: If infant mortality is lowered, the need for schools increases. Knowledge regarding the availability of experts is dependent upon reliable forecasts in the industrialized countries of their own needs and, hence, of their ability to provide personnel. Again, this poses problems.

The nature and number of technicians needed depend on a variety of economic factors not easily ascertained and upon "often unforeseeable political decisions (economic development plans, creation of an atomic energy administration, European common markets, etc.)."[3] But a serious, concerted effort must be made by host countries, technical assistance agencies, and recruitment bodies to arrive at some reasonably valid and realistic estimates—both short-term and long-term—if suitable training programs are to be developed.

Our ignorance regarding the personal qualities needed by instigators of social change is even greater. The preparation of laundry lists of desirable qualities has become a favorite occupation, but, alas, all that emerges is an ideal man who does not exist. We do not know how to create him, and we might not recognize him if we saw him. "He must be cultured and cross-cultured. He must be disciplined and interdisciplined. He must be well stocked with empathy and antifreeze. He should be a model himself, and he should know about model-building, institution-building, stadium-building, and body-building."[4]

Here we need research in the field. We need some effective criteria for evaluating success and failure, and some method of distinguishing the personal failure of an expert from the failure of a project for reasons beyond the expert's control. We need to know whether certain types of individuals do better in one culture or another and to what extent experience in one culture is transferrable to others. How can desirable tests be devised that are not culture-bound? What modifications is it possible to make in an adult's outlook and approach? How can latent qualities be brought out?

"No sane person would attempt to put a space ship in orbit without elaborate supporting educational and research activities. Yet this is precisely what we have attempted in the more subtle and complex areas of overseas operations."[5]

Recruitment and Selection

"The problem of scarcity of human skills and of highly qualified specialists is as important as the scarcity of physical capital formation which has been the focus of more attention in many developing areas."[6] Yet the reservoir of available technical assistance experts is shrinking rapidly. At the same time, needs for experts are multiplying and are changing in character. As development proceeds and as training programs build up a stratum of technicians, the demand for high-level and specially qualified personnel grows. Many of the industrialized countries are undergoing a period of economic expansion that is creating new demands for precisely this type of manpower. Terms and conditions of service at home are far more appealing than abroad. A recent survey of some agencies in the United Kingdom revealed the fact that two-thirds of the available posts for overseas personnel remained unfilled for upward of a year and some technical posts for five years.[7]

The best opportunities for recruitment now lie in the two extremes—those persons who have already reached retirement and those not yet embarked upon a career. With the growing realization that technical assistance is here to stay—at least for the foreseeable future—serious attention is being turned to the "junior" or "associate" expert. The Netherlands and a few other countries have made junior experts available—at the government's expense—to the United Nations Expanded Program of Technical Assistance, and similar action is under consideration by other countries. The United States has embarked upon a major "associate" expert program in its Peace Corps.

The possibilities of a career service in technical assistance are also being explored. The United Nations expanded program and the International Bank for Reconstruction and Development are now both developing modest career services of this type. The advantages of such a service are manifest, but there are also limitations: Some types of expertise are needed only intermittently, and some require frequent contact with evolving professional knowledge. However, the potential further availability of even the expert seconded for a single mission can be enhanced by keeping him informed of the evolution of a project he was involved in or of projects growing out of his particular task, through the medium of a newsletter, for example, or by correspondence between the expert and his counterparts.

Another approach to recruitment problems which is receiving increasing attention is the use of consultant and other business firms. The firms have available their own teams of seasoned experts and are in a position to provide planning and backstopping services. Although such firms are not suitable for all types of projects or where there is a potential conflict of interest, they have a useful place and one that is likely to grow.

In addition to increasing the total supply of experts, it is important to use them with maximum efficiency. At the Rome conference, it was suggested that greater use be made of regional experts, that is, one expert serving three or four countries in rotation. After several months in country A, the expert would move on to country B, and so on. At the end of perhaps a year, he would return to country A and complete the circuit again. During his absence from any given country, the work could be carried on by technicians or possibly by junior experts. This scheme has the advantage of permitting periodic check-ups of work in progress. It poses real problems, however, for experts who are accompanied by their families. A second suggestion emanating from the Rome conference, applying to the United Nations, is the use of regional economic commission personnel to help in defining the job and in filling the post while the expert is being recruited.

The most efficient allocation of currently available experts is clearly of prime significance. Competitive anarchy is finding fewer and fewer adherents. National committees have been established in a number of European countries to channel requests and locate, screen, and propose candidates. In many cases, these serve both bilateral and multilateral agencies. In Sweden, for example, there is a "central body for information, planning, cooperation, execution and control of all matters related to Swedish assistance to the underdeveloped countries."[8] A central roster of presumptive experts will be maintained and kept up to date. A public information officer provides information about expert assignments.

At the Rome conference, the hope was expressed that such committees might be developed in other countries, since they appeared to produce better and more consistent results than any other existing method of locating, screening, and proposing candidates for overseas assignments. Such committees should have at their disposal adequately trained and experienced staffs, and an effective recruitment network organized on a functional basis. They should generate, through the use of all national and regional media, a climate favorable to recruitment and promote the adoption of national legislation and formal agreements designed to facilitate the release of personnel for assignments abroad, the protection of their promotion, pension, and social security entitlements during the period of their absence, and their reinstatement, on their return, in positions not less favorable than they could have reasonably expected if they had remained at home. The committees should maintain a roster of candidates whose suitability has been carefully determined. Finally, they should promote the further training of technically qualified younger personnel and facilitate arrangements for foreign language tuition for candidates otherwise considered suitable for foreign assignments.

The employing agencies, for their part, should provide a job description clearly setting out the nature, level, and duration of the assignment, and the final date for the receipt of candidatures; the actual tasks to be performed; environmental factors; the availability of technical services and equipment on the spot; information on terms and conditions of service; the criteria to be applied in recruitment; and such background information as a serious and busy candidate is believed to need to be persuaded of the worthwhileness of the assignment. In addition, they should make available full information on the status of each post for which recruitment had been requested, including notice of postponements, modifications, or cancellations, and estimates of future requirements.[9] It was also urged at the Rome conference that employing agencies make known their reasons for rejecting proposed candidates so that the committees could establish meaningful selection criteria. Even where an agency uses other recruitment channels, it should at least keep the national committees informed of its activities.

The existence of good channels of recruitment, however, does not automatically imply a flow of candidates. The charm of overseas service often lessens in the face of practical considerations. International organizations, particularly, are at a disadvantage in providing attractive offers. Salaries tend to be under the market price in some countries, equivalent salaries are not always paid for equivalent posts even in the same country, and hardship post allowances are extremely difficult to establish on any meaningful basis for international personnel. What may be a hardship post for a national of country A may not be for one from country B, and vice versa. Furthermore, "the U.N. agencies are generally so worried about their administrative costs that they can seldom give the expert the necessary supporting services."[10]

Another handicap is the restraint placed upon them by the nature of their relationships with host countries. Many business concerns seal off their employees in compounds with all the conveniences to which they are accustomed and more, but special privileges granted to an international official, such as duty-free imports, are immediately resented. Even the salary differential between expert and counterpart can be a source of friction.

Moreover, many employers, particularly business and academic institutions, are reluctant to submit to the administrative inconvenience incurred in seconding personnel. To some extent this attitude can be modified by educational campaigns; chambers of commerce can be particularly helpful. The experience gained from a field mission may give an individual new insights and contacts that will redound to the advantage of the employer. This has been increasingly recognized by governments and has been an added factor in predisposing them to look favorably on technical assistance missions. The French Government, for example, now guarantees the expert an equivalent post upon return and the retention of all seniority and promotion rights; similar provisions are incorporated in a draft law under discussion in the Italian Parliament. Even in some of the less developed countries, where there is a desperate shortage of personnel, the short-run sacrifice is seen as a long-term gain on condition that the return of the expert within a reasonable period of time is guaranteed. There is an urgent need for a similar attitude in business and academic circles. An inquiry conducted among some 200 persons in England elicited the fact that the main reason for refusing technical assistance missions was the fear of prejudicing career prospects at home.

One important factor influencing both prospective candidates and employers is the time lag between the first interview and the dispatch of the expert, which may be a year or more. If the expert doesn't withdraw in disgust, both he and his employer are subjected to considerable inconvenience. A royal committee, charged with studying administrative arrangements in Sweden relating to technical assistance, proposed that a candidate should receive a definite reply regarding his eventual appointment within one month from the date of his application. If the day is to come "when technicians and specialists as well as administrators will take absences of a few years on technical assistance missions during their professional careers as a matter of course,"[11] both host governments and employment agencies will have to tighten up their administrative procedures.

The availability of candidates is obviously a prerequisite for recruitment, but this is only the beginning of the story. The recruiter must know what he is looking for. The international official, at least, does not. He is presented with a job description that sometimes conceals more than it reveals and may be quite irrelevant.

All too rarely are requests for technical assistance designed as implementation of a coherent development plan. As a result, the job description has been known to refer to an idea that has vanished by the time the expert arrives, to a plan conceived by a donor without reference to local needs and desires, or to a project that cannot be carried out because it was poorly conceived. Frequently, it is not even clear whether the expert is to design a project, set it in motion, or diagnose problems in an already functioning operation. Each of these calls for a different type of experience, different qualities of mind and personality. Still less information is available on the responsibilities of the expert and the milieu within which he is expected to operate. Is he to execute, to advise, or to train? With what level of officials will he be working? What is their background and training? Will his contacts be wide or narrow? What facilities and material resources are available? What are the expectations of the host government, as regards both the expert himself and the objective of the project? The recruiter needs this information to find his man, and the candidate needs it to decide whether in fact he himself thinks he is fit for the job in question. At the Rome conference, it was also pointed out that the "qualifications" listed by international organizations are frequently couched in terms relevant only to particular countries, and it was urged that a list be established of equivalent degrees or diplomas in the various educational systems.

But the job description is only a tool. How it is used depends on the nature of the recruiting and selection process. Unfortunately, the effort to develop a rational system is continually diverted by a deep-seated belief inherent in most human beings, although not in well-trained recruiters. "I can tell at a glance whether he is a good man or not" is the mark of this sixth sense. Compounding the problem is the technician's insistence that he be the final arbiter, in total disregard of the basic tenet that no man can be accepted as a technician without being accepted as a man. The recruiting services are low man on the totem pole, used for intractable or uninteresting problems.

Many large businesses long ago realized that recruitment and selection require highly specialized skills, that such skills must be adequately compensated and that services carrying out these functions must be located high in the hierarchy so that they can command authority and know in advance the needs they will be called upon to fill. Businesses have learned that a fairly high investment in recruitment and selection is far less costly than the failures and fumblings that otherwise are bound to result.

One of the recurrent themes of the Rome conference was the necessity of strengthening the recruiting services and giving them adequate funds to do the job, including travel allowances to interview candidates and their families, ascertain needs, and perhaps assist in developing the job descriptions. The role of the technician should be advisory, not decisive, it was maintained, and the host government should be involved, in some appropriate fashion, in the selection process so that its interests and wishes may be accurately reflected.

"There is a growing tendency to favor methods which involve extensive checking of personal and professional references, detailed confidential inquiries and the building up of comprehensive documentation on the antecedents of individual candidates prior to the arrangement of a series of interviews, each of which is intended to ascertain a particular aspect of the candidate's personal or professional suitability."[12] The more that is known about a candidate, the greater is the probability that his future behavior can be predicted with reasonable accuracy. As in the case of the French Training Centre for International Technical Cooperation Experts, the knowledge available to the selector is significantly increased. One of the interviewing techniques that has found favor is the numerical weighting of the selection criteria attaching to a particular post. Each interviewer rates the individual item and totals his score. The individual scores are consolidated and any glaring discrepancies discussed before making a decision. The perfection of such techniques, however, must wait for further research and, as far as international agencies are concerned, for the translation of tested methods into forms suitable for multinational selection.

The Rome conference did not attempt to follow the well-trodden path and describe the qualities of the ideal man. Certain needs, however, were stressed and certain questions raised. A representative of a less developed country remarked pungently, "We do not need a book but someone who understands our local problems." Emphasis was laid on the importance of the expert's conviction of the validity of the project and his acceptance of both host government objectives and employing agency. The expert cannot change the philosophy of either, and if he is not in sympathy, he will merely frustrate himself, his employer, and the host government. The expert must be able to express himself clearly and simply, and work himself out of a job by developing a cadre of enthusiastic and trained counterparts. Questions were raised about the facile assumption that because an expert had done well in one country, he would, *ipso facto*, do so in another. Questions were also raised about too close identification with host country nationals lest the expert lose his objectivity and his ability to achieve results. Questions were raised about the importance of language qualifications and the types of situation where these are a crucial factor. Another question that needs further investigation is the influence of different milieu upon the success of an expert. There seems to be some evidence that people from small towns, who may never have seen a foreigner, do better than the more cosmopolitan urbanite. Finally, on a more philosophical level, there is a question that pervades the whole operation of technical assistance. How can one avoid "turning a good Chinese into a bad Westerner?"

Training

There is general acceptance of the fact that a technical assistance expert serving overseas needs more in his luggage than his professional training. Although the objective has been described as the task of making the individual "more creative in a world of different values," there is no clear definition of who should be trained, where, and how.

Obviously, any expert needs to know about the agency employing him. He needs to know its principles and objectives, its character and personality. He has to know how it works administratively: what authority will be delegated to him, what support he can expect, what channels of communication and reporting he will be expected to use. It should go without saying that, before he is hired, he should know in full detail all the conditions of service and should be given a sober, realistic picture of his mission.

How much does the expert need to know about the particular country in which he will be working, and about its language? What does he need to know about the process of fostering change and about the human relations aspect of his mission, and what *can* he be taught? These are all questions that have stimulated much debate and discussion and that are still in a highly unscientific stage of conclusion.

It seems clear that all experts need some training. Even a "sheep expert deals not only with sheep but also with the owner and the shepherd." And the mission chief—that exalted being—is not born to his role. He is the keystone of the project; his knowledge and leadership can tip the scale toward success or failure. He too must be trained, although special training devices may be required. This has been recognized, at least in principle, in the United States, where an intensive nine-month training program has recently been recommended for senior AID personnel.

While it seems clear that all experts need some training, they are not the only ones involved. The expert may have a wife and children. The failure of the family to understand and adjust has probably induced more failures than any other single factor. This is why businesses increasingly include the wives in the training programs.

The third element in the picture is the counterpart, who shares equally with the expert responsibility for the achievement of the objective. It was suggested at the Rome conference that appropriate aspects of training be conducted jointly for experts and counterparts.

In most agencies, governmental and intergovernmental, there is a curious blind spot. What the eye of headquarters does not see, does not exist. It does see—with pain—the time and money spent on training an expert before departure. The guilty conscience of the bureaucrat does not see the far greater expenditure of time and money spent in undirected on-the-job learning in the field.

It has been suggested that all personnel would probably benefit from six months to a year of training, but this is clearly utopian, particularly for experts going out for a year or less. For technicians, the feasible range lies somewhere between two weeks and two months. In this period, they are supposed to learn about their new employer; familiarize themselves with technical assistance in general, understand why it exists, how it operates, and what a technical assistance program really is; learn how their project originated, what results it is expected to yield, and what program it fits into; glean the essentials regarding the culture and economy and the political, administrative, and value systems of the host country, and acquire a knowledge of the typical situations and conditions they will face and an understanding of their role as instruments of social change operating in an advisory capacity. Even these basic ingredients tend to get squeezed out in the press of departure. The following description of a United States expert could be duplicated in many other capitals:

> The recruit who probably has spent many months waiting for security clearance, not knowing whether to sublease his home, ask for a leave, prepare his family for an overseas move, or otherwise do or not do the thousand and one things of normal living while he is being investigated and before getting the firm appointment which, at the last minute, could not fail to come because of program

changes, suddenly finds himself rushed to Washington with or without his family, a recruited technical assistant. Once there and on the federal payroll, Washington is most anxious and somewhat impatient to send him to the country of his assignment, which, of course, has been awaiting his arrival for six to fifteen months. At best, therefore, he is offered a brief noncompulsory "training" period lasting two to four weeks, during which time he is also expected to familiarize himself with his new project and agency, learn about and visit other related Washington agencies, finish taking his shots, arrange for his and the family's transportation, acquire passports and otherwise manage himself and his family. . . .[13]

In the international agencies, the training period ranges from none, except for administrative details, to a few days. The World Health Organization is the only United Nations agency that has developed some systematic training. As a first step toward a more satisfactory situation, the General Conference of UNESCO decided in 1960 to establish a briefing center for international experts near Paris. Courses last for two and a half days and cover the following points:

The United Nations: its political aspects, economic and social activities, autonomous services, regional commissions, the specialized agencies.

Technical assistance: historical background, principles, modalities of action, organization, procedure, evaluation.

The role of the expert in the United Nations and in technical assistance.

The phenomenon of underdevelopment: its characteristics by countries or groups of countries, its economic and social implications.

The expert's adjustment to the country in which he is to work, most common problems, requisite personal qualifications.

The expert's professional problems, possible weaknesses in the project, counterparts, study grants, teamwork, delays.

On the national level there are, here and there, a few examples of similar post-entry training courses. Oversea Service in England, a private institution, runs a three-to-five-day post-entry course for experts recruited by various public and private agencies. In addition to background information on the area or areas to which the experts are going and the problems of adjustment, considerable attention is devoted to such practical questions as clothing, living conditions, and health precautions.

The training requirements for a high-level administrator or policy advisor are obviously more exacting than for a technician, and the gap between need and fulfillment is even greater. For such individuals, the necessary training period has been estimated at three months, and the range of subject matter to be included covers such questions as processes of induced change and the rate of change requisite for political acceptance; effects of such factors as natural resources, traditions, values, and moral systems on development tasks; the balance between planning and execution within the limits of available resources; principles and practices of capital formation; institution building; cross-cultural understanding and communication; and political systems, social philosophies, and ideologies.

One of the unresolved questions is that of language training. There is a general belief that the expert is more successful and more readily acceptable if he knows the local language. Yet it is manifestly impossible in pre-entry training to teach all the languages that may be required. Africa alone has some 1,200 languages. For practical reasons, it is equally impossible, as a general rule, to devote adequate time to language training in a post-entry course. Obviously, in many cases a knowledge of the four vehicular languages—English, French, Spanish, and Arabic—would be sufficient and would certainly facilitate the learning of additional languages, but there are still too many exceptions for this to be a solution, even if it were feasible. There is a "language laboratory" in Paris working on this problem, and experiments on accelerated training have been conducted in Leiden and Hamburg, but so far there are no established techniques that can be relied upon.

Another and very difficult aspect of training is that relating to attitudinal change and psychological preparedness. To what extent are attitudes susceptible of modification by training and how can this be achieved? Two studies conducted in the United States in recent years concluded that it is not possible to change an individual's value system; it is possible, however, to develop more empathy for the environment and to create new insights.[14]

This can be achieved most successfully in small groups, the interaction of the members being itself an important aspect of the educational process. There are also advantages to a multidisciplinary group, so that specialists have an opportunity to transcend their own field of specialization and understand something of the multifaceted complexity of the task on which they are engaged.

In other aspects, however, some degree of homogeneity is probably desirable. From the UNESCO experience, it would appear that too great disparity is a disadvantage and that "as soon as two languages have to be used, any discussion is more or less inhibited."[15] Some people believe that groups should be composed of nationals of one country and participants selected according to the nature of the employing agency—industry, government, and so forth. It is argued that under such conditions much freer discussion is possible. Whether this advantage outweighs the broadening and stimulating effects of an interdisciplinary group is something that needs further research.

There is much that we do not know about the optimum composition of a group, the possibilities of profitable interaction, and the use of returned experts or other experienced personnel. What purposes can be achieved by informational brochures and bibliographies? What should they include? When should they be given to the expert? What is the role of films and other visual materials as an adjunct to training? It was suggested at the Rome conference that there was need for clearing-house services to permit a better exchange of training material. There should also be developed, it was believed, "field laboratories" and pilot projects in which research would be carried on and in which apprentices and newly arrived employees could take part as an aspect of field training.

Responsibility for training should not devolve upon one pair of shoulders. It should be shared. The home country has a responsibility for seeing that its potential experts receive the basic general training upon which specialized orientation can be built in a relatively brief period of time. There are two aspects to this foundation work. The first involves a general understanding of other societies and cultures in both their historical and their dynamic aspects and of the processes of social change. This is a function of the formal academic institutions. In Sweden, a royal committee has suggested that the various university authorities be asked to consider the special problem of the underdeveloped countries in the planning of curricula; the study of the public administration systems of other countries will be included in the program of a proposed administrative staff college. In the United States, there is an important developing relationship between professional schools and foreign area programs in some universities. The Cornell College of Agriculture is specializing in research and training on agricultural development in Latin America and the Philippines, in which it is assisted by the foreign area programs. There is graduate training for both Americans and foreign students requiring research in the field under direction of Cornell professors. The attempt is to study not only the technical aspects of agriculture, but also the psychology and cultural motivations of peasant farmers, in order to discover how to introduce changes more successfully. The universities must also bear a primary responsibility for "developing theories to explain these far-reaching phenomena, research programs to test theory against relevant experience, and a body of professional knowledge and practice which can form the nucleus of educational programs to prepare those who will participate in overseas operations."[16]

The second aspect of home-country training is more directly concerned with the processes of economic development and the kind of knowledge regarding technical assistance that the expert will need. One of the best examples of this type of training is that provided by the French Training Centre for International Technical Cooperation Experts, established in 1957 by the Ministry of Foreign Affairs. Since it is designed to train those capable of becoming technical assistance experts, candidates are rigorously screened and only those with the requisite experience and competence are accepted. The average age is forty. Two courses are held yearly; there are 100–150 candidates, of whom about a quarter are selected. One annual session is geared to those active in professional occupations in the Paris region, with most lectures and seminars held out of working hours. The course of some thirteen hours a week lasts three months. The second session is an intensive one-month course of about forty hours a week. Both courses include information about the various regions of the world, with emphasis on traditional and cultural patterns in certain countries; problems of economic and social growth; the mobilization of human resources; the structure, procedures, and machinery of technical assistance, both bilateral and multilateral; and problems of financing economic development. Courses are structured to bring out the relationships that exist in developing countries between the expert's field of specialization and other areas, and to throw light on the psychological and material difficulties involved in the adaptation of the expert to a developing country and to the human and material requirements for economic development.

The experience of this center, of a special course recently inaugurated in The Netherlands for future experts, of courses under the auspices of the Società Italiana per l'Organizzazione Internazionale in Italy, and of the Deutsche Stiftung für Entwicklungsländer in Germany, indicates a surprisingly enthusiastic response to such training facilities. They inevitably tend, however, to attract certain categories of experts—civil servants, economists, industrialists, teachers, and only rarely the extra-specialized expert or the practitioner, since these become experts fortuitously rather than by intent.

Responsibility for an understanding of and knowledge about the employing agency must rest with the headquarters of that agency. It and the recruiting service must brief the expert fully in the nature of his tasks, the history and background of the project. Such briefing should be factual and congruent, not "glossing over the project's weak points and hinting at desired rather than actual prospects." At the Rome conference, emphasis was laid on the importance of a briefing officer who can direct and supervise the expert's activities, thereby sparing him "many useless visits and long waits in corridors and a thousand other sources of irritation and confusion." Such training presumably can and should be supplemented in the field, in the case of United Nations organizations by the regional economic commissions or regional offices, and by the resident representatives.

It is also the responsibility of the employing agency to see that the expert knows about the processes, functions, and purposes of technical assistance and has some understanding of social change and of the attitudinal and behavioral requirements that will be made upon him. It is not necessarily the function of the employing agency to conduct such training. In fact, a good case could be made for centralizing this aspect under appropriate auspices. Operating agencies are seldom materially equipped to become teaching institutions, and, in the case of the international organizations, the flow of experts is too small and erratic to warrant individual training facilities.

Another aspect of training for which the employing agency should assume responsibility is retraining and refresher courses for long-term experts. In many fields of specialization, expertise diminishes fairly rapidly if the technician is cut off from his professional contacts. Thus, provision must be made for periods of study in which the expert can catch up on new professional knowledge and on the improved application and adaptation of existing knowledge to conditions in developing countries. The generalist needs to broaden his horizons from time to time, compare notes with others in similar positions, and gain new insights. The reluctance of governments to make funds available for such training has already taken its toll, and loss of expertise among many specialists has become a matter of serious concern.

As far as education regarding the particular country of assignment is concerned, it would seem appropriate that a large share of responsibility should fall upon the host country. In the first place, the country has a manifest self-interest in creating an understanding of its mores and problems and is certainly in the best position to do so. In the second place, the host country may be less impatient at the expert's wasting his time, if it is providing the education. In the third place, the expert is more psychologically receptive when he is actually in the field with the evidence under his eyes. Although no studies have been made, it is generally felt that the best period for field indoctrination is after the second month. By this time, the expert has begun to realize what he doesn't know, what he wants to know, and what he needs to know.

Iran now has its own training program for United Nations experts to introduce them to the cultural and social aspects of an Islamic country. Nigeria is hoping to establish a similar program. The pilot project in this area and the most ambitious to date is that of the Delhi Training and Orientation Centre, established in 1954 with a grant from the Ford Foundation. Six to seven sessions of two weeks' duration are held every nine months, and wives and adult children are included. There is a library of 10,000 volumes dealing exclusively with India. Courses cover geography, history, culture, Islam, urbanization, Hindu way of life, social structure, administrative structures, agricultural problems, handicrafts, community development, the role of foreign experts in India, the Indian constitution, economic planning, education, political parties, and so forth. In addition to lectures and discussion periods, participants are shown films, visit an Indian village, and are served an Indian meal with Indian etiquette.

Presumably such centers could be established only in the large countries, but small countries might band together and establish a regional center. A university would appear to provide the most acceptable auspices, with its resources supplemented possibly by lecturers from United Nations regional economic commissions.

All over the world, in countries exporting technical assistance and in those importing it, efforts are being made to find some answer to the problem of training, but information is still lacking upon which sound foundations can be laid. Some of the existing confusion arises from the effort to make up in the relatively brief period after recruitment for inadequacies in the previous educational backround. The result is a grandiose curriculum calling for years of study. To fit the Procrustean time bed, subjects have to be covered in such generalities as to be relatively meaningless.

Until a generation of experts can be given in their formal education the requisite basic orientation and knowledge, the employing agency should, however reluctantly, accept the fact that its experts are going to fall below the ideal and concentrate on those aspects of training that can be meaningfully instilled within the allotted time. This will require field research in cooperation with experts and with host governments—preferably by some independent authority—on the types of knowledge and attitudes that make for success. It will require research units in donor agencies to capture their experience and make it available to the researcher. Upon the findings of such investigation, it should be possible to determine what can and must be taught and the minimum periods that must be devoted to such training. It should also be possible to indicate areas of emphasis appropriate for academic institutions and the respective educational roles that might be played by employing agencies, host governments, and others.

NOTES

1. Milton J. Esman, *Needed: An Education and Research Base to Support America's Expanded Commitments Overseas* (Pittsburgh: University of Pittsburgh Press, 1961), p. 8.

2. *Ibid.*, p. 7.

3. André Chafanel, Report (in French) prepared for the Conference on Recruitment, Selection, and Training of Technical Assistance Personnel (Rome, 1962, mimeographed), p. 2.

4. Robert E. Asher, "In Conclusion," *Development of the Emerging Countries: An Agenda for Research* (Washington, D.C.: The Brookings Institution, February, 1962), p. 215.

5. Esman, *loc. cit.*

6. M. A. El-Shafie, *General Observations and Comments Pertaining to the Problem of Recruitment and Selection*, Report prepared for the Conference on Recruitment, Selection, and Training of Technical Assistance Personnel (handwritten), p. 3.

7. Overseas Service, *An Enquiry into the Recruitment in the United Kingdom of Personnel for Posts in the Developing Countries* (London: Oversea Service, January, 1962), p. 2.

8. *Den Svenska Utvecklingshjaelpen Expertrekrytering och stipendiamottagning* (with a review in English: *Swedish Technical Assistance Expert and Fellowship Problems*), Statens Offentliga Utredningar 1961:50 (Stockholm: Emil Kihlstroems Tryckeri Aktiebolag, June, 1961), p. 69.

9. See Gordon Menzies, *The Recruitment and Selection of Personnel for Overseas Assignments*, Working Paper No. 2, prepared for the Conference on Recruitment, Selection, and Training of Technical Assistance Personnel (mimeographed), pp. 7–10.

10. *Den Svenska Utvecklingshjaelpen*, p. 72.

11. Sylvain Lourié, *Note d'Information sur certains problèmes du recrutement des experts, pour des missions de coopération technique internationale*, prepared for the Conference on Recruitment, Selection, and Training of Technical Assistance Personnel (mimeographed), p. 6.

12. Menzies, *op. cit.*, p. 2.

13. Frank N. and Helen G. Trager, "Exporting and Training Experts," *The Review of Politics*, XXIV, No. 1 (January, 1962), p. 95.

14. See Philip E. Jacob, *Changing Values in College* (New York: Harper and Brothers, 1957) and Edward D. Eddy, Jr., *The College Influence on Student Character* (Washington, D.C.: American Council on Education, 1958).

15. Henrie Laurentie, *Post-Entry Expert Briefing (a) as Undertaken by UNESCO and (b) as Considered as a Basic Problem of Technical Assistance*, Working Paper No. 1, prepared for the Conference on Recruitment, Selection, and Training of Technical Assistance Personnel, p. 5.

16. Esman, *loc. cit.*

MATERIALS AVAILABLE AT THE CONFERENCE

U. S. Department of State, Agency for International Development, *A Ten Point Training Program: Report of the Task Force on Training and Orientation for A.I.D.* (Washington, D.C.: October, 1961).

Franco Casadio, *Pre-Entry Expert Briefing*, Working Paper No. 3, prepared for the Conference on Recruitment, Selection, and Training of Technical Assistance Personnel.

Carnegie Endowment for International Peace, *Report of the Proceedings of the Plenary Session of the Conference on Recruitment, Selection, and Training of Technical Assistance Personnel*, Rome, February 16, 1962 (New York: April, 1962).

P. Juvigny, *Training Centre for International Cooperation Experts* (Paris: Fondation Nationale des Sciences Politiques, April, 1962).

United Kingdom, *Recruitment of the Administrative Class of the Home Civil Service and the Senior Branch of the Foreign Service*, Statement of Government Policy and Report by the Civil Service Commission, Cmnd. 232 (London: H.M.S.O., July, 1957).

Maurice Domergue, *Technical Assistance, Definition and Aims, Ways and*

Means, Conditions and Limits, Problems of Development series (Paris: Organization for Economic Co-operation and Development, November, 1961).

Hans J. Morgenthau, *Preface to a Political Theory of Foreign Aid* (Chicago: Public Affairs Conference Center, University of Chicago, 1962).

John Montgomery, "Crossing the Cultural Bars: An Approach to the Training of American Technicians for Overseas Assignments," *World Politics,* XIII, No. 4 (July, 1961), pp. 544–560.

16. THE ECONOMIC DEVELOPMENT INSTITUTE OF THE WORLD BANK

JOHN H. ADLER

The Economic Development Institute (EDI) of the International Bank for Reconstruction and Development is among the oldest, if not the oldest, of the institutions that have set themselves the task of providing training in the field of economic development.

The first course of the EDI started in January, 1956, but its inception goes back to at least 1951. By that time, the Bank had become aware of the need for improving the efficiency of the economic management of underdeveloped countries. From its contact with governments and government agencies, it had learned that the processes of policy formulation were imperfect and in need of improvement. It had also come to the conclusion that comprehensive programs of economic development, which would focus primarily on capital expenditures in the public sector and, more generally, in the field of economic overhead facilities, were essential if governments were to play an effective and constructive role in promoting economic development. It had realized that the scope and effectiveness of its lending activities would depend to a considerable extent on improvements in the formulation of economic policies and in the preparation of programs and projects the Bank might be asked to finance.

The Bank had already started a modest technical assistance program of its own, which consisted mainly in organizing survey missions to prepare broadly conceived development programs. But it recognized that advice and technical assistance from abroad would meet only a small part of the needs for improvement and that it would be necessary to provide technical competence and appreciation of basic economic concepts in the countries themselves if these difficulties were to be overcome. In the summer of 1951, it joined forces with the Economic Commission for Latin America (ECLA) to sponsor a seminar on the preparation of a development program. The seminar lasted ten days and was attended by seventeen participants from eleven Latin American countries and from the staff of ECLA, with observers from a number of other international organizations.

After this first experiment, the Bank concluded that it would be necessary to approach the problem of inadequate economic management on a systematic and sustained basis, and preparations for providing training began. Once a decision to establish a new institution was made, two basic issues had to be resolved. One was to whom training should be offered; the other, whether it would be desirable for the Bank to organize its own institution rather than make arrangements with a university to provide training in the subjects the Bank thought essential components of a training program.

On the first question, the decision was to aim at the officials of government departments, development corporations, central banks, and similar institutions that were directly concerned with, and responsible for, the formulation of policy and for carrying out policy decisions. By aiming at the top-level officials, the impact of the training to be offered would be more immediate and make itself felt sooner than if the training were to be offered to a younger group in less important posts, or if it were to be restricted to trained economists only.

The decision on the first question also determined the decision on the second question. It was felt—as it turned out, rightly so—that senior officials would be reluctant to "go back to school," but could presumably be persuaded to spend some time at an institution associated with the Bank. Another factor in favor of the decision to establish an institution at or near the Bank was the conviction that the staff of the institution could be kept small and that it would be able to draw on the (frequently unrecorded) experience of the Bank and on the Bank's professional staff.

In the summer of 1954, the Bank invited Professor A. K. Cairncross of the University of Glasgow to come to Washington to advise on the establishment of an institute. Professor Cairncross (now Economic Adviser to the Government of the United Kingdom), after an intensive survey, during which he interviewed many members of the Bank staff and consulted with members of the faculties of several universities, submitted a report recommending the setting up of an institute by the Bank. Professor Cairncross subsequently was appointed the first director of the Institute. In

January, 1957, he was succeeded by Mr. Michael L. Hoffman who remained in charge of the Institute until the end of 1961, when he was appointed director of the Bank's Development Advisory Service. For the first three years of its operations, the Institute received substantial financial support from both the Rockefeller Foundation and the Ford Foundation.

Institute Objectives

Although Mr. Cairncross' report recommending the establishment of the Institute stressed that the Institute should be permitted to experiment and learn from its own experience, and although a number of important changes both in the curriculum and the administration of the Institute have been made, the basic objectives of the Institute have not been changed. To the contrary: The experience of the Institute makes us believe that the choice of its objectives was correct. The chief purpose of the Institute remains to present to senior officials of underdeveloped countries general economic propositions that are relevant to their work, and to bring before them the experience of other countries to serve as a basis of comparison and evaluation of their own experience.

Or, to use a somewhat hackneyed phrase: to help senior officials to discharge better their present jobs or jobs to which they might be promoted in the future. This implies that they must be persuaded to accept some ideas that are new to them, to discard some convictions acquired from their own experience—because experience is not necessarily and certainly not always the best teacher —and, above all, to learn to look beyond the limits of their immediate assignment and to see their tasks in the broader perspective of their government's general economic policies.

Selection of Participants

The first prerequisite for the success of the Institute is the selection of participants. The process of selection is rather elaborate.

In a letter signed by the president, the Bank asks the governments of its member countries to submit nominations of government officials, or officials of central banks, development agencies, or state economic enterprises. Nominations are not restricted to any particular part of government, or to any rank or age group. No specific level of education is required; formal training in economics is not a prerequisite for admission. Knowledge of English is, of course, necessary. The chief requirement is that the persons nominated must be concerned in their jobs with matters of economic policy or be responsible for carrying out policies related to economic development. Thus, the only common denominator of all participants is rather extensive experience in government service or in an agency in the public sector.

The nominations, which are requested five to six months before the beginning of the course, are scrutinized by an Admissions Committee, which is made up of a vice president of the Bank, several department heads, and the director of the Institute. In the selection of participants, the committee is chiefly guided by the qualifications of the nominees: their experience, their closeness to the development process, the importance of the department or agency they work for, their prospects for advancement.

The nomination imposes certain obligations on the nominating government. It must give the nominee a leave of absence with pay for the duration of the course. It must commit itself to assign the nominee after his return from the EDI course to a post of responsibility similar to the post held before leaving or advance him to a higher position. And it must pay a "tuition" of $1,500 to the Institute for each participant. The reason for charging a fee for admission to the EDI course is to assure that the nomination has been acted on by responsible authority. The charge is not levied for budgetary reasons. The contributions cover but a small fraction—in some years as little as 10 per cent—of the operating cost of the Institute.

Despite these conditions, the number of nominations normally exceeds the number of persons accepted by a wide margin, thus enabling the Admissions Committee to apply consistently high standards in the selection of participants, and to disregard, as decisive factors, such considerations as proper regional balance or the desire to see as many countries as possible represented among the participants. The Institute's experience seems to indicate that a selection process based on the nominees' qualifications alone leads at the same time to a fair country distribution and, as a second by-product, a fair representation of various fields of interest and professional specialization.

It has been the policy of the Institute from the outset to limit the number of participants to approximately twenty. The usefulness of this limitation has been borne out by the experience of the Institute. In one year, when twenty-four participants attended the course, the seminar discussions became distinctly more cumbersome and fewer participants took part in them than in other years.

Length of Course

In the preparation of the Institute, and throughout its operation over the last seven years, much attention has been given to the question of the proper duration of the course. Somehow, two conflicting objectives had to be compromised.

The purpose of the EDI on the one hand is to familiarize the participants, who have, on the average, little or no formal training in economics, with some basic principles of economics relevant to their work. With innumerable factors bearing on economic development and development policy, the range of what is relevant is obviously very wide, extending perhaps even beyond the limits of economics proper into such neighboring disciplines as public administration, sociology, and social psychology. From that point of view the conclusion is inevitable that at least a year of training and retraining, and preferably more, would be required to cover the field with reasonable thoroughness.

There is, on the other hand, the fact that the time a senior official can be absent from his post is limited. It is limited by the unwillingness of the authorities to spare him for long, by the participant's own reluctance to be away from his desk—and his normal family surrounding—for a long period, and by the adverse effects of a prolonged absence on the participant's familiarity with current problems, and, therefore, his immediate usefulness. There is likely to be an inverse relation between the availability of top personnel and the length of the course; the longer the course, the more difficult it is to attract key officials to the EDI.

There are other factors that have to be taken into account. One of them is the high cost of bringing the participants—at the Bank's expense—to the Institute. The cost of travel is the same, irrespective of the length of the course. Similarly, the staff requirements of the Institute are not directly, and certainly not proportionately, related to the length of the course. In other words, the marginal cost of an additional month is lower than the average cost per participant. This is an inducement for extending rather than contracting the length of the course.

Another reason for having a longer course is the Washington

climate, which is good in the autumn and in the spring, but can be rather trying in the winter months, particularly for participants from tropical countries, and is generally considered unpleasant in midsummer—for participants from all parts of the world. A longer run also makes it possible to undertake field trips under favorable weather conditions.

All these considerations have led to a compromise solution of having the course extend over six months, usually from October to March. As far as one can determine from experience, the length of the course has not prevented governments or public agencies from sending high officials to the EDI. But most participants who were asked to express their views about the EDI were emphatic in their assertions that the course should not last longer than six months. Several of them expressed the view that the course could be made shorter.

It has become fairly clear that the chief motive of most of those participants who wanted to have a shorter course was their desire to return to their families; after four months or so of separation, they were lonesome. In order to meet this problem—and its adverse effects on the work of the participants—the Bank will, from now on, bear the transportation cost of the wives of participants in the "regular" course (but not in shorter, special courses).

The Curriculum

The preceding account of the composition of the group attending the Institute and of the reasons for limiting the course to six months is essential as a background for an appraisal of the curriculum and of the methods of instruction. The issues are simple enough: What body of knowledge can be transmitted in the course of six months to a group of mature public officials who have little or no formal training in economics, come from widely different cultural backgrounds, with different institutional settings, and have but one thing in common, namely, years of experience in public service in assignments concerned with economic development? And what is the best method of transmitting that knowledge?

The solution to the first problem depends largely on what is considered relevant knowledge about the process of economic development. If persons professionally concerned with economic development have learned anything about their subject in the last ten or fifteen years, it has been that economic development is a highly complex process with many facets, only some of which are economic and amenable to economic policy measures.

It is not enough to limit one's attention to matters economic, to supply and demand, and saving and investment. And it is even less appropriate to define narrowly the economic subject matter of development and deal with such topics as programming and project analysis, without considering the framework of general economic policies and of institutional and administrative arrangements within which the programs and the projects are to take shape. And there is finally the basic difficulty of taking account, in the analysis of development problems, of the divergence in the social, cultural, and political setting of the various countries, and still coming up with meaningful and valid generalizations. (This is not the right context for a discussion of this issue, which goes to the heart of the meaning of general propositions in economics. But I should like to affirm my convictions that meaningful and valid generalizations that are relevant for an understanding of the development process and can serve as a basis for policy advice are possible and are essential if "development economics" is to have any normative content.)

Thus, the practical problem of devising a curriculum for a group like the participants of the EDI is how to avoid an *embarras des richesses*, not how to think up subjects to fill empty boxes in a schedule. There is the danger that the curriculum takes on the appearance of a *smörgasbord*—a little bit of everything—or, even worse, that the appreciation of the complexity of the development process becomes so overwhelming as to leave little more than the notion that "everything depends on everything else"—the complete negation of the possibility of systematic exposition.

It is not for me to say whether the curriculum of the EDI solves the problems and avoids the pitfalls I just flagged. But I think it may be taken as an indication that we are on the right track, that the curriculum we have developed at the EDI is, after seven years of modifications and adjustments, still essentially the same as the curriculum of the first course. On the basis of the comments of the participants and the suggestions of the Institute's advisory committee (five professors of economics, eminent both as economists and teachers), a large number of changes have been made every year. These modifications notwithstanding, the make-up of the curriculum has remained substantially unaltered.

The table below presents the curriculum prepared for the Institute's eighth course (October, 1962–March, 1963). It should be noted that the nine seminars (composed of seventy-eight "regular" sessions) are not offered in straight sequence, but overlap.

The first seminar is an attempt to establish a common basis of what a Washington economist once referred to as "the economics that matters"—which is simple but not easy. It covers in essence the allocation of resources through the price mechanism and through consumption, saving, and investment decisions. In other words, it tries to provide in a limited number of sessions an explanation of the functioning of an economy. It also deals with measures to improve the growth performance of an economy by means of a development program.

Two examples taken from Seminar 1 should be sufficient to explain the essential (and limited) objectives of the EDI course. Only two sessions are devoted to national and financial accounts. It is, of course, impossible to teach the elements of a system of national accounts in two sessions. But it is possible, we believe, to give to the participants in two sessions an appreciation of the meaning of national accounting concepts and the uses to which national accounts can be put in the formulation of economic policies. Similarly, the session on inter-industrial relations is clearly inadequate for a full understanding of the techniques of input-output analysis. But it is sufficient to explain the purposes of an input-output table and to bring out the importance of the demand for intermediate goods.

The seminar on historical aspects of development constitutes an attempt to familiarize the participants with the history of economic growth of countries that are now advanced and to provide them with factual information about the growth performance in other countries and in other parts of the world, against which they can evaluate the growth performance of their own countries.

The purpose of Seminars 3 and 4 is to provide an introduction to the tools of economic policy, while Seminar 5 is concerned in part with analytical concepts and in part with problems of policy.

The second portion of the course (Seminars 6 to 9) is devoted to a discussion of sector problems and the preparation and evaluation of projects. In these seminars, the Institute draws heavily on the experience of the Bank, on Bank documents, and, above all, on members of the Bank's professional staff who present, sometimes alone and sometimes in teams (consisting usually of a desk officer, an economist, an engineer, and a lawyer) specific case studies.

DRAFT CURRICULUM FOR EIGHTH COURSE

(October, 1962–March, 1963)

SEMINAR 1: ECONOMIC POLICY AND DEVELOPMENT
- Session 1: The Process of Economic Growth I
- 2: The Process of Economic Growth II
- 3: The Process of Economic Growth III
- 4: National and Financial Accounts I
- 5: National and Financial Accounts II
- 6: The Multiplier Process
- 7: Economic Statistics—Concepts, Methods and Uses
- 8: The Objectives and Limitations of Programming
- 9: Formulating a Development Program
- 10: Choice and Economic Growth
- 11: Inter-Industry Relations (Input-Output Analysis)
- 12: Planning Machinery

Related Special Sessions
The Measurement of Economic Change
Growth Theory and Growth Models
Development Strategy

SEMINAR 2: HISTORICAL ASPECTS OF DEVELOPMENT
- Session 1: Recent World Economic Growth
- 2: Recent Economic Growth—Africa
- 3: Recent Economic Growth—Asia
- 4: Japanese Growth
- 5: Recent Economic Growth—Latin America
- 6: U. S. Growth
- 7: Growth of the Soviet Economy

Related Special Sessions
Prospects for United States Economic Growth
Italian Growth Experience

SEMINAR 3: FISCAL POLICY AND PUBLIC FINANCE
- Session 1: Basic Considerations in Public Finance
- 2: Fiscal Surpluses and Deficits
- 3: Programming and the Capital Budget
- 4: Problems of Taxation and Tax Reforms I
- 5: Problems of Taxation and Tax Reforms II
- 6: Pricing Policies of Public Enterprises
- 7: Problems of Tax Administration

Related Special Sessions
The Taxation of Foreign Investment

Seminar 4: Monetary Policy

Session 1: The Role of Monetary Policy in Economic Growth
      2: Organization and Function of Central Bank
      3: Control of Money Supply
      4: Economics of Stabilization
      5: Development Banks
      6: A Case Study of Inflation—Chile

Related Special Sessions
The Problem of International Liquidity
Institutions of Financial Markets
The Policy Functions of the Federal Reserve System

Seminar 5: International Trade and Finance

Session 1: The Balance of Payments Mechanism
      2: The Balance of Payments and Economic Development
      3: The Management of the Balance of Payments
      4: Commodity Projections: Problems and Methods
      5: The Future of Coffee and Copper—Two Case Studies
      6: Measures to Stabilize Export Proceeds
      7: International Capital Movements
      8: External Development Assistance
      9: Public Policies Toward Private Foreign Investment

Related Special Sessions
Policies and Operations of the IBRD
International Financing of Industrial Investment (IFC)
The Operations of the International Monetary Fund
The Role of GATT
The Pattern of World Trade
The European Common Market and Primary Producers
United States Foreign Aid

Seminar 6: Agriculture

Session 1: The Role of Agriculture in Economic Development
      2: Irrigation
      3: Research Extension and Demonstration in Agriculture
      4: Agricultural Credit
      5: Agricultural Marketing
      6: Land Reform
      7: Problems in Agricultural Programming
  8, 9, and 10: Case Studies of Agricultural Development

Seminar 7: Industry

Session 1: The Role of Industry in Economic Development
      2: Public Policies and Industrial Development
      3: Extractive Industries
      4: The Pulp and Paper Industry
      5: The Textiles Industries
      6: The Steel Industry
      7: Electric Power I

8: Electric Power II
9: The Role of Transportation in Economic Development
Related Special Sessions
Industrial Management
The Role of Labor Unions

SEMINAR 8: SOCIAL FACTORS IN DEVELOPMENT
Session 1: The International Transmission of Skills
2: Investment in Education
3: The Population Problem
4: Urbanization and Housing
5: Manpower Problems

SEMINAR 9: PROJECT APPRAISAL
Session 1: Practical Problems of Project Preparation and Appraisal
2: Project Evaluation I
3: Project Evaluation II
Case
Studies 4: Agriculture—Irrigation (Roseires)
5: Agriculture—Livestock Project (Chile or Uruguay)
6: Industry—Steel (Japan)
7: Industry—Cement (Peru)
8: Industry—Pulp and Paper (Chile)
9: Power (Volta, Ghana)
10: Transportation—Port (Israel)
11: Transportation—Roads (Ecuador)
12: Transportation—Railroads (Nigeria)
13: Multipurpose Project (Dez, Iran)

Methods of Instruction

Like the curriculum, the methods of instruction have to be adapted to the characteristics of the group to be trained. Participants at the EDI are not scholars or graduate students. Even those among them who have had substantial professional education have been out of school for many years and are no longer used to studying. Moreover, several members of the group usually have some difficulty in the use of the English language.

But the chief problem is not one of study habits or the knowledge of the language of instruction. It is rather, I believe, the reluctance to accept new ideas and views different from the participant's own. This is, I presume, a problem common to all "mid-career" training courses. Persons who by the standards of their own group have been successful in their careers are not open-minded in the way a graduate student eager to increase his knowledge is open-minded. The participants of the Institute have to be shown that they still can learn something and that what is presented to them is important for them to know. Yet, at the same time, they have to be encouraged to present their own views and to share their own experiences with the rest of the group. This is because the more they can be persuaded to participate in the discussion, the easier it becomes to avoid the impression of school sessions and classroom discipline, to which their reaction is bound to be negative.

The same problem has another aspect. Because many of the participants have some doubt that there is anything that they can learn, they are likely to be reluctant to cope with assignments that are difficult or take a long time; conversely, they are also likely to become impatient if the intellectual fare prepared for them is too light. Therefore, both the level of the teaching material prepared for them and the methods of instruction are of paramount importance if the course is to be successful.

The EDI makes use of a variety of means of instruction. As indicated before, it relies chiefly on seminar discussions. But it also invites guest speakers to give lectures (or at times to conduct seminars). It makes use of a group discussion device which we call (with a bow to the Staff College at Henley) "syndicates." It arranges several field trips to visit various industrial and agricultural installations and financial institutions in the United States and one trip to an area of major development activity abroad. As a recent innovation, it asks each participant to prepare a research paper on a subject related to his work. And it encourages the participants to pursue the study of subjects of individual special interest.

Seminars are held as a rule every morning for a period of three to three and a half hours, interrupted by a coffee break. The participants receive, usually a week in advance, a weekly schedule of seminars, together with reading assignments and an "outline." The outlines are a novel device which we have developed and find exceedingly useful. We have outlines prepared for most of the seminars offered by the EDI staff. An outline is a written exposition of the seminar subject which runs in length anywhere from three to twenty-five pages. It is a combination of a précis of the subject and a glossary in which technical concepts are explained. Several of the outlines (which, incidentally, are revised almost every year) take the place of reading assignments; but in most instances, the participants are expected to read both the outline and the reading assignment.

The outlines fulfill several important functions. They assure us that all participants by the time they come to the seminar have a minimum common background of knowledge. (It has been our experience that the participants almost without exception read the outlines with some care even if they fail to read the reading assignments.) They also make it possible for the person conducting the seminar to omit in his presentation some parts of the topic and to concentrate and elaborate on others. This makes for a generally livelier presentation and also makes it possible to limit it to less than an hour, leaving up to two hours for a general discussion of the subject. If at the end of the seminar it appears that the participants, or at least some of them, would like to continue the discussion, arrangements are made for a formal or informal resumption, usually in the afternoon. Informal discussion groups are also encouraged to deal with topics of special interest to a small number of participants.

Syndicates are provided in the curriculum three or four times during the course. For the syndicates, the participants are usually divided into three groups, and the same assignment is given to all of them. The groups are asked to act as a committee or a consultative body to advise on a particular policy issue, such as the fiscal treatment of foreign investment or the advisability of establishing an investment bank. The groups, each of which has a chairman and a secretary, are asked to prepare a short report on the subject assigned to them. The reports are then circulated to the other groups, which in turn prepare a number of questions about them. Finally, a formal meeting attended by all groups is held in which the questions raised are discussed. The syndicate exercises usually last two and one-half or three days. The participants have been virtually unanimous in their opinions that the syndicates are a useful device of instruction and training. Many of them have suggested that more syndicate exercises be provided in the curriculum.

The purpose of the field trips is twofold. The main objective is to show the participants what industrial and agricultural installations in the United States look like, how the financial institutions of New York operate, and (in the case of the trips outside the United States) what the practical problems associated with development efforts are in an underdeveloped country or area. A second purpose is to break the routine of daily seminars and lectures and to bring the participants closer to each other and to the staff of the Institute.

In recent years, the "industrial" field trips have taken the participants to Pittsburgh, Detroit, and a partly industrial and partly agricultural area in Pennsylvania. On the trips, the participants are taken to industrial and agricultural installations, and arrangements are made for meetings with business executives and public officials who discuss with them such topics as marketing problems, labor relations, social services for workers, and municipal affairs.

The "financial" field trip takes the participants to New York, where they visit financial institutions such as the Federal Reserve Bank, a commercial bank, the Stock Exchange, and a life insurance company. Officials of the various institutions speak to the group about their work and the functions of the various institutions. The group also usually visits the Secretariat of the United Nations, which arranges lectures on its research activities.

The field trip abroad, which normally lasts two weeks, is designed to bring the participants into contact with the officials directly concerned with development policies and with enterprises and activities related to development. These field trips have taken the participants to Mexico, southern Italy, and Jamaica.

In the last course, the participants were asked to prepare a research paper dealing with some aspect of their own work or some subject close to their professional interest. A considerable number of the participants considered this assignment as an intellectual challenge and devoted much time and effort to the preparation of a paper. There were, however, several participants who considered the request to prepare a paper as an imposition and tried to discharge this assignment with as little effort as possible.

The volume of work the routine of the Institute requires, together with a fair amount of social activity, leaves not much time for additional individual work. Nevertheless, each year several participants have contacted various U.S. Government agencies or the International Monetary Fund to learn more about specialized subjects or activities close to their immediate fields of interest. Some participants have extended their stay in Washington, or elsewhere in the U.S., to seek further specialized training on subjects of immediate professional concern to them, such as monetary research or national accounts.

The Institute does not give tests to determine the accomplishments of the participants and does not confer degrees. At the end of the course, the participants receive a certificate attesting to the fact that they have participated in an EDI course and making them Fellows of the Institute. We try to maintain contact with the Fellows by correspondence and ask occasionally for their help in nominating and evaluating candidates for the course. Because of the Bank's activities in its member countries, these contacts are rather well maintained. Several of the Fellows regularly attend the Bank's annual meetings as Governors, or Alternate Governors, or as members of their country's delegation. There are now 143 Fellows in 50 countries.

The EDI Staff

In addition to the Institute director, the "academic" staff of the Institute consists of three full-time (or almost full-time) instructors, who take charge of the seminar work, prepare or revise the outlines, organize the syndicates, and supervise the preparation of the papers of participants. They also are available for special tutorial duties, if participants want to pursue certain subjects in greater depth than the seminar work permits.

The small staff of the Institute would, of course, be inadequate if it were not for the support the professional staff of the International Bank provides. As indicated before, a considerable number of seminars are conducted by members of the Bank staff, either alone or in teams, and for the presentation of case studies, in particular, the Institute depends almost entirely on Bank staff. It also invites economists from universities and other institutions who have been interested in economic development or related subjects to come to the Institute for a series of guest lectures.

Special Courses

This account of the activities of the EDI would be incomplete if I did not add a few words about the special courses that have recently been added on an experimental basis. It will depend on the experience gained from them whether they will become a permanent part of the Institute's activities.

In the summer of 1962, the Institute offered a special ten-week course, in French, for officials from countries of French expression. The purpose of the course was to make the facilities of the Institute available to countries that do not have officials whose knowledge of the English language is adequate to follow the regular course. The short duration of the course reflects the belief that in many countries of French expression the shortage of senior officials is so acute that it would be virtually impossible to spare them for a period as long as six months. The response to the invitations to nominate officials to the French course was large, despite the fact that the Bank has not yet established close working relations with many of the countries. The Institute received 38 nominations from 16 countries and accepted 18 applicants from 13 countries, exceeding the limit of 15 participants which it had set itself as a target.

The curriculum for the French course is a compressed and somewhat modified version of the curriculum of the regular course. Because of the small number of sessions that can be held in a ten-week period, many subjects we would consider indispensable for the regular course had to be omitted. It is inevitable that the course is correspondingly less effective than the regular course. The participants have indicated that they also felt that the curriculum should be expanded. At the same time, however, they expressed the view that it would be virtually impossible to send officials to attend the course for a period of six months. Because of the unexpectedly large demand for the course, it was decided to offer the course again in 1963, and, in response to the views of the participants of the first course, to extend it to at least twelve weeks. This permitted a more thorough discussion of some of the subjects of particular interest to the participants, though not the inclusion of more subjects in the curriculum.

Another special course, given for the first time in the spring of 1963, entirely limited in its coverage to the preparation and appraisal of development projects, and was, therefore, an example of a specialized rather than a general training activity. The purpose of this course was to provide training to officials of public works departments, planning agencies, budget offices, and state economic enterprises in a subject in which the International Bank has acquired much experience, probably more than any other institution. Some of the teaching material we were preparing for the course was used also to improve the project appraisal seminar of the regular course.

Publications and Libraries

The publication of studies related to the field of economic development is an extension of the activities of the Institute which, in a sense, is a direct consequence of its main purpose of providing instruction. Several of the studies have had their origin in seminar outlines. The following studies have been published by the Johns Hopkins Press (Baltimore, Maryland): *Development Banks* by William Diamond, *Design of Development* by Jan Tinbergen, *Planning in Morocco* by Albert Waterston, and *Planning in Yugoslavia* by Albert Waterston. Other studies on planning are in preparation. It is intended that some of the teaching material contained in the outlines will be published as "primers" on various aspects of economic development.

Many of the Fellows of the Institute have indicated that in their countries the extension of knowledge of development problems is limited by the difficulty of having access to books and articles pertaining to economic development. The Institute has taken the initiative in helping to remedy this situation by assembling a small library of selected reading and source materials on economic development and making it available, free of charge, to government departments, public agencies, and universities in underdeveloped countries. More than 100 libraries have been distributed. A library consisting of French texts covered the same subjects as the English library is in preparation, and the first steps have been taken to assemble a Spanish library. For the first two of these library projects, the Institute received financial support from the Rockefeller Foundation.

Postscript

Let me conclude by offering a few remarks about what the Institute's experience suggests with respect to development training programs in general.

The first generalization that I believe emerges from the particular experience of the EDI is that there is no such thing as a set of "right" constituents of a training program. What constitutes a right program depends very much on the audience the program is to serve. It is the composition of the group to be trained that determines what the right input mixture is and what are the factors limiting the freedom of action of the teaching staff.

A second general conclusion I think emerges from the history of the EDI is that the success of a training program depends to a large extent also on the method of instruction and on the general treatment accorded the participants. The ability to convey ideas in simple (and, if possible, nontechnical) terms and to keep the interest in a subject going for a prolonged period of time are just as important as the composition of the curriculum. This is particularly true in a program for adult participants who are taken out of their normal environment.

I should like to add a third and final general observation, which does not directly follow from the preceding account of the EDI but is only implied in the discussion of the curriculum. I, for one, have come to the conclusion that the urgent need for training for economic growth in underdeveloped countries is not met by teaching advanced techniques of economic analysis. It seems more appropriate to try to assure that the participants acquire a firm grasp of basic principles. Moreover, it is important to emphasize that the formulation of policies based on rational principles helps to solve only a small, though admittedly important, part of the problem. It is equally necessary to stress the administrative and institutional aspects of the process of development and to impress the participants with the importance of such uninspired and old-fashioned notions as good engineering, good accounting, and good management.

17. NEW SKILLS FOR NEW SOCIETIES

PAUL BERNICK

ORT has been accumulating experience in vocational education for the past eighty years. This article explores the applicability of that experience to the problems of manpower training in underdeveloped countries.

The work in ORT is vocational training in its broadest sense—not only trade schools, but a great variety of training activities that suit the particular problems of Jews in different parts of the world. The initials ORT are derived from the original Russian words *Obshestvo Remeslenovo i Zemedelcheskovo Trouda* (*Society for the Propagation of Skills and Handicrafts and Agriculture*) translated into English as "Organization for Rehabilitation through Training." ORT is not sectarian, in the sense that it has no religious standards of admission, but it is denominational in the sense that it exists primarily to serve Jews and that its funds are derived primarily from Jewish sources.

In several ways the experience of ORT is exceptional and not automatically translatable to other situations. For example, everywhere but in Israel its concern is with one segment of a people, a minority group. Only in Israel is the experience somewhat comparable to the kind of general national problem that would be encountered in establishing a vocational program for an underdeveloped country.

Secondly, ORT is a voluntary agency working in a field that is customarily a function of government.

Then, too, ORT is an international organization. It works in nineteen countries. This brings into play a whole series of special problems. There is, for example, the problem of teacher recruitment. The teacher shortage is an almost universal problem. That is particularly the case with instructors in vocational subjects, who if they are competent can almost always earn more in industry than in the school. The situation is further complicated in that so much ORT activity during the past decade has been in Israel, North Africa, and Iran, areas notably deficient in precisely this type of qualified personnel. ORT has therefore established an international teachers' training institute in Switzerland, which over the years has served to provide a substantial portion of the teaching staff of ORT trade schools in the economically under-developed areas.

Finally, ORT is a vocational training program with social welfare aspects. In-school feeding, distribution of clothing, payment of "bourses" are integral to training among the particular people in whom it is interested. These services are essential prerequisites to enable many to attend, such is the poverty of many students. The range of concern is not limited to youth, but also applies to their parents and their communities. ORT is also concerned with refugees, displaced persons, and other people in need—people who do not normally come within the purview of vocational education.

The Need for Vocational Education

Vocational education is one of the oldest kinds of education. The Eskimo who takes his son out in a kayak to hunt for walrus is engaging in vocational education. So was the American Indian teaching his son to ride a horse. The common features of this type of transmittal of vocational knowledge are immediate apprehension, learning through direct performance of the act, and perfection through frequent repetition.

A second type of vocational education is apprenticeship. Generally, this occurs in handicraft societies. The apprentice lives and works in the same place with his master. He learns simultaneously not only his craft, but also its commercial aspect, its social meaning, and all the set attitudes that go with it.

These two methods have their obvious advantages. The trouble with them is that they are obsolete. They are no longer applicable where modern industry intrudes.

The trade school is the distinctive product of an industrialized and mechanized economy. It reflects a change from handicrafts to mechanized manufacture, from hand and animal power to electrical power, and from the use of hand tools to a totally new set of work skills. In short, the whole content of labor and the work process have been altered. While skill in general has become less important in the modern factory, specialization has become more important. Much of vocational education concerns itself with this rather limited area of modern industrial life—specialization.

The trade school is, therefore, of fairly recent vintage as schools go. Probably the earliest of the modern trade schools goes back no farther than the middle of the eighteenth century, to Germany and France. In reality, the trade school as we know it today is a product of the last fifty to seventy-five years.

In the United States, vocational education often has a derogatory connotation. It is hardly a secret that the New York trade schools, for instance, are regarded as the dumping ground of the educational system. While the term "trade school" describes an institution which may be physically similar in New York and in Casablanca, it bears no resemblance to the status implied in the two localities.

In Morocco or Iran, a boy attending a vocational high school is training to become part of a new elite, with specialized skills that assure him of a secure future. Far from being reduced or stratified to a low level in society, he is mounting an escalator that is elevating him to a totally new status. This relates equally to Burma, India, and other countries entering the stage of industrialization.

The Time Difference

Even this meager review helps to make clear the difference between the role of vocational education in our Western society and in underdeveloped countries. Just as the Industrial Revolution proceeded by stages over a period of 150 years, trade schools had a parallel evolutionary development. For most of recent economic history, acquisition of skills has taken place on the job, within the factory.

But the whole problem of economic development in Asia and Africa is a matter of time. These are nations in a hurry. They make their economic plans by three or five or seven year intervals, not by the century. They can't wait, for example, for a labor force to emerge gradually in the wake of industry. They have an immediate problem of shortage of skills. Even before they have industry in a large-scale factory sense, whole segments of the traditional economy have been dismantled by the impact of imported goods. Whole new mechanisms of a modern state have been installed in transport, communication, and government. In the former handicraft sectors, the same operation has often been converted to machine work.

Morocco and Tunisia have achieved political independence only in the last three years. Of course, these countries do not thereby revert to where they were before the coming of the French. A considerable modern physical structure has been introduced. To realize this, one has only to land at an airport or walk through the completely "European" avenues of Casablanca, with its tall, ultramodern hotels and commercial buildings. Since independence, tens of thousands of French have left. Many of them were in the telegraph and postal system; others were in the railroad repair yards; some were plumbers, electricians, welders, aircraft engine mechanics. They were employed in maintaining aspects of modern technology that are outside the realm of industry as such. They belong to what the economists call the "infrastructure," the foundation elements that must be in place before considerable industrialization can occur. Graduates of ORT schools in these countries have taken the place of some of the French who left.

In other words, even before industrialization per se, the underdeveloped country is in need of technical skills, and usually not the kind of semi-production or production skills of a relatively low order that will be necessary later, but precisely the more advanced, basic skills. This is where the trade school occupies a strategic place, because it makes possible a concentrated effort for creating this basic elite, or skilled cadre, around which other work elements can form with time and development.

Disruption of Traditional Society

We in ORT have been working in Morocco, Tunisia, Algeria, and Iran for about a dozen years. These are all predominantly what we designate as underdeveloped countries. Long stagnant, traditional societies, still based on handicraft production, retain their hold in these areas. But they are societies in transition, moving away from their traditional elements, shaken up by the intrusion of money economy, factory-made goods, and all the other disturbing forces that a modern economy sets in motion when it intrudes on an economy free of the industrial way of life.

Jews there have probably been more seriously affected by modern trends than their Moslem compatriots. The movement toward urbanization has affected the Jew more radically. Furthermore, the high degree of Jewish concentration in a few cities exposes him more readily to modern influences. Educational facilities on a considerable scale have been available to Jews for a long time, so that the mental soil has been made more receptive to change. For many Jewish youth, the traditional path has been foreclosed by the fact that they know something of the modern world. Large numbers of Jews in these areas have been beggars, itinerant peddlers, shoemakers, and tinkers. But for youth, even with a modicum of modern schooling, this life becomes untenable.

It is in just this kind of fluid and ambivalent situation, somewhere between the old and the new, that the trade school can be a revolutionizing catalyst, helping a generation of young people to break out of the traditional mold.

Resistance to Trade Schools

On the other hand, we met with considerable resistance when our schools were first opened. It was difficult to get students. It was not customary, for example, for fourteen-year-olds still to be going to school. Children became breadwinners at the age of ten or twelve. Families are large, and the income of the children is essential to making ends meet. There was, therefore, substantial reality in the resistance of the parents to releasing their children from earning over a period of several years.

This resistance was overcome by stages. The first stage was to offer substitutes for what the children would have earned—financial doles as inducements. At a later stage, the success of the earlier graduates has served as example. We found particularly effective the training of teachers selected from among indigenous youth.

One of the problems in underdeveloped countries is where to find the teachers for the new schools. They cannot be taken out of industry, because industry doesn't exist. What we did was to bring the best of our graduates to the teacher training college we established in Switzerland. We gave them two years of teacher education, followed by a year of work in Swiss factories and practice teaching in Swiss schools. These young men, upon their return to Iran or Morocco or Tunisia, made a powerful impression on the youth of the community. They became symbols of what was possible.

Transformation of Attitudes

These are some of the more general social attitudes that affect the attraction of students to the schools. More complex is the character of the educative process as such. The locus of the trade school lies at the center of a triangle of pressures—midway between the emergence of a new educational system, the beginnings of an industrial economy, and the transformation of traditional society. These three constitute a triangle of forces that shape vocational education.

The new element that vocational schools signify is the linking of work with thought, and thought with the consistent propagation of new personal and social attitudes. A great deal of generalized knowledge based on mathematics and science is essential to modern occupations. This implies good working literacy and general acceptance of an underlying premise of the material world that is different from what exists in most traditional societies.

Most important is the regrooving of mental and emotional processes. The traditional society is highly stratified. Status tends to be fixed by origin. Social mobility is slight. This tends to dampen energies, repress ambition, and contribute to the slow pace of life. We have found this in our own ORT experience in North Africa and Iran. It is true of India today, and it was true of our own western culture all through the Middle Ages.

The "laziness" we find in underdeveloped countries is often an expression of this heavy weight of the past. The rhythm of life tends to be repetitive and changeless, akin to the cycle of nature. Undernourishment, malnourishment, and disease further erode the output of physical energy. We have found in our trade schools in Casablanca or Tunis or Marakesh or Tehran or Shiraz that proper feeding and medical care are not simply desirable; they are indispensable to awakening the body and mind to a sufficiently active level of functioning so that the youth can absorb learning.

The Scale of Values

In such tradition-bound societies, manual work is far down the scale of values. The values exemplified by the upper classes are not associated with energetic activism, but rather with leisure, luxury, idleness. Improvement of one's station in life is measured by the decrease in the amount of work performed.

Going to school, getting an education, is regarded as an opportunity to advance out of the lower classes whose misfortune it is to labor physically. Certainly no one goes to school to learn to work. The trade school is an alien concept that cuts across the natural grain. Much more than its academic counterpart, the vocational training center is a rupture with the past, a revolution in accepted aspiration. For implicit in the acceptance of manual work as a positive value is a whole syndrome of new attitudes.

Time, for example, has a different connotation in our society than in previous ones. Time as a measure of work and as a discipline is a distinctly modern concept. The youth learning to operate a machine must acquire a different body rhythm than what he is accustomed to. He must learn to coordinate with the external stimulus of the motor rather than the internal biological stimulus to which he is accustomed.

He must accept alienation—that is, he must learn to work, not according to his natural instincts or senses, but according to a blueprint prepared by someone else.

He has to acquire a totally new appreciation of precision. Metal machining, for example, is customarily performed to a tolerance of one one-thousandth, and sometimes one ten-thousandth, of an inch. These are not uncommon precision standards. They are generally expected of a student in a machine shop course. But they demand a sense of spatial and arithmetic refinement that are new to a boy in an underdeveloped country.

He must acquire habits of personal hygiene and work cleanliness. Some of these are related to simple job safety.

The heart of the process of vocational education in our ORT schools in North Africa and Iran is the inner transformation of the student. The problem is compounded by environmental handicaps of poverty, large families, miserably overcrowded homes, lack of water and light, chronic diseases, and all the other deleterious features of such a society. Yet it is done. We find that after the first year the youngster makes enormous strides very quickly.

This is one of the most hopeful portents. It has great implications for the tempo of change that is possible in underdeveloped societies. It is impossible to assess the price paid for this in terms of psychological and emotional dislocations and in family conflict. But to go through one of the big air bases south of Casablanca and see our graduates, who are simultaneously graduates from our course in aviation mechanics and from the ghetto, climbing over the engines of jet planes is to see in a flash the infinite adaptability of the human being. The fact is that the hold of the old society has been loosened. All the pull of ambition is toward the new.

This sets up powerful drives which enable the youngster to overcome quite speedily the drag of his heritage.

First Steps

In some respects, vocational education starts as a clean slate on which anything can be written. The problem is what to teach and for how long and who shall be trained. How do you decide what trades to put into a curriculum where the lead does not come from society? In this respect, our experience in Israel is relevant.

In the Mandatory period, the dominant Jewish concern was with pioneering in agriculture. During the first decade of statehood, the priority of farming was reinforced by the need quickly to settle large numbers of immigrants and to produce the food with which to feed them. The ideal situation would have been to make an industrial survey to ascertain manpower requirements. But there was little or no industry, and thus no mirror to reflect the need.

It became the function of the trade schools to anticipate what would be needed in the future, to create the labor force that could work in the industries that would subsequently come into being. In turn, the emergence of these skills became one of the conditions that made possible the establishment of industry.

The whole picture was complicated by the influx of one million immigrants, which tripled the population. Few of the newcomers brought any skills with them. But all sorts of curious situations developed. For example, Israel acquired a large number of doctors. But there were very few laboratory technicians. The result is that Israel today has more doctors per capita than any country in the world, but too few technicians who can make a blood or urine analysis. We therefore established an institute for the training of laboratory assistants.

There is a general guide, however. Experience indicates that certain skills are basic to modern technology. Among these are, for example, welding, motor mechanics, automobile mechanics, electrical installation and repair, the various metal and machine trades. The common denominator of all these is that they apply to a cross-section of industries rather than to any single one. They therefore become the basic vocational content of the trade school.

Different Skill Levels

Still, this does not tell us anything about the level of skill. For example, motor mechanics in any underdeveloped country, as we found in Israel, is a completely different trade than in the U.S.A. In the latter, it is usually enough to know how to fill the tank with gas, put oil in the engine, and replace prepackaged parts units. In Israel, it is something quite different. For while the country depends very heavily on motorized transport and equipment of all sorts, it imports most of its motors. Spare parts are rare. The youngster has to be taught to salvage parts that go bad or to manufacture a substitute part as needed. This implies a different, higher degree of skill than is needed in the American economy.

It is apparent that the onset of industrialization does not automatically bring with it all the apparatus of a modern economy. In fact, there is always lopsidedness and imbalance, which the nature of the training provided must take into account. Yet, despite these imbalances, the emerging economy does not recapitulate all the stages of the Industrial Revolution up to automation. On the contrary, it would be impossible for a new machine factory in Ghana to acquire a seventy- or eighty-year-old lathe. It has to start off with an up-to-date, high-powered, high-precision machine. That is the only kind available. In other words, these countries leap immediately into the most up-to-date stage in many fields.

We have found this to be the rule in Israel's economic development. We have therefore had to tailor our curriculum according to advanced processes. Thus, developments in Europe and North America have resulted in the emergence of a new kind of worker who is generally designated as "technician." He is somewhere between the engineer and the skilled man. Now, we have found a great demand for technicians in Israel. We are beginning to find a similar demand in Morocco. In other words, the necessity for postsecondary vocational education follows swiftly on the heels of the trade high schools.

Danger of a Single-Level Approach

The technicians' institutes exemplify one of the dilemmas of vocational education, as we conduct it in ORT, that would probably be faced in an underdeveloped country. Once reluctance to attend the trade school is overcome, there is a flood of applicants. At our school in Tel Aviv, we have just completed registration for next fall's first-year classes. There were roughly five times as many applicants as places available. The inevitable tendency is to raise admission standards and to select only the best pupils. This reacts on the teachers and on the schools and results in general upgrading, which is very satisfactory to all concerned. The other side of the coin is that lack of adequate facilities, which forces up standards, turns into an elimination procedure what should be working to bring the maximum number of qualifying youth within the scope of this type of education. For a welfare agency such as ours, this is a heartbreaking problem. Yet it arises naturally. It is a product of success, of having good schools, of making a real impression on the community, and of improved standards all around.

But what about those others, the less well educated and otherwise less endowed? In short, precisely those who are in greatest need of vocational training, since they must depend on manual work for a livelihood. The fact is that mechanization reduces the amount and the degree of skill for most workers and, at the same time, creates a need for specialists. Yet large numbers have to be brought within the scope of industrial work. The technician and specialist is part of the new industrial elite. He is at the heart of economic progress insofar as it depends on available personnel. What about the larger number who cannot possibly make this grade?

The result is a constant search for alternative educational forms to overcome this dilemma by setting up a kind of multi-track, multi-level approach. For example, a few years ago we introduced what is called the "Sandwich Plan" in Israel. It was borrowed from European experience. Two groups were enrolled simultaneously. One group was sent off to a factory for three months. The other went to the school. At the end of three months, they changed places. We have developed a modern type of apprenticeship program. Last year we introduced in Tel Aviv something called "guided apprenticeship," a one-year, intensive course preparatory to work on the job. These approaches are tentative, experimental. The search goes on.

The Academic Content

One of the other results of being able to raise the standards of the vocational school is the tendency to increase the length of the course along with the upgrading in the status of the school. The two-year school becomes a three-year school, the three-year school becomes a four-year school, the four-year school becomes a five-year school.

The increase in educational longevity serves to further exclude students from impoverished backgrounds. Furthermore, the tendency is to equate the quality of the school with its academic level. Thus, the stretchout in the schooling period tends to be filled with a rising proportion of academic and general subjects. Parents and students demand that the school provide them with the status of an academic diploma and not only with a vocational diploma.

Probably since the first trade school was established, there has been a large difference of opinion as to the relative weight that ought to be assigned in the curriculum to academic and to vocational subjects. It is one of those questions that has no right or wrong. It depends on a whole set of variables, at least some of which are entirely subjective.

The problem is that the fourteen-to-eighteen-year-old is not only in training to be a worker, but is being educated for life. The ideal would be to integrate the two aspects. But integration is one of those overworked words that as happy connotations while no one knows exactly what it means. Perhaps it is not the curriculum that needs to be integrated, but the student. That is, if his education can be a continuum instead of a series of unrelated compartments, if work and life and leisure and reading and culture and civic responsibilities can be part of each other, then each will reinforce the others. This is not only a social ideal, it can work.

In a number of our schools, especially in North Africa, a spirit of adventure pervades the atmosphere, and the boys and girls and their teachers sometimes seem to have a sense of personal and collective mission. This should be a general possibility in under-developed countries. At least this approach has a place in the kind of trade school that has meaning in such new societies. In most of these countries, nationalism is a powerful generative force that can infuse a constructive elan within an educational context.

This brings me to my last point. The boy of fourteen who enrolls in a trade school today will still be working in the year 2000. What can the school do to prepare him for this?

Obviously, the world, his world, will be far different then. Of course, this is a problem in the U.S.A. and everywhere. But it is particularly acute in Morocco, in Israel, in India—countries where the environment does not adequately firm up, by a daily immersion in technology, that which is acquired in the vocational school. One method proposed is periodic retraining. But this is obviously not satisfactory.

The only answer seems to lie—and this is likewise an unsatisfactory and, at best, partial solution—in the level of general education. For it is general education and general knowledge of science, of mathematics, and of technological processes that introduces the element of adaptability. The literacy and culture of a society is a basic determinant of how vocational education will be used and adapted to changing conditions. Vocational education is not, therefore, a device that can carry the whole burden of occupational transformation, isolated from other social factors. But it is a real lever with which to raise the level of economic activity of people in transitional societies. It can go far to produce the basic technical staff at the skilled worker and technician level on which economic progress can proceed.

FIVE

THE EDUCATIONAL CHALLENGE

18. ENSKILLING PEOPLE

ALBERT AND ROSALIND LEPAWSKY

THERE is grave concern in knowledgeable circles today about the outcome of the international technical assistance effort. Though national income is increasing in underdeveloped countries, few have so far experienced that sustained economic "takeoff" that differentiates underdeveloped from developing societies. Improvements in social welfare and health programs are reducing mortality rates, but the accelerated growth of population prevents per capita income from rising. On the governmental side, although the underdeveloped nations are clearly improving their bargaining power in international politics, they are not stabilizing fast enough domestically to grasp the reins of state as their cultural cohesion slackens.

In short, despite all the current accelerated efforts to assist the emerging nations, there is a distinct possibility that internal distress may continue to plague them, that international aid may bog down, and that the elaborate technical assistance program we have built up may be left nibbling away at the edges of a chronic underdevelopment that continues to threaten world tranquillity. More than ever, therefore, we are now compelled to examine our existing aid efforts critically and to discover more effective alternatives for the future. Otherwise, the public and politicians in all countries may lose heart over what is still a popular, but as yet unproven, world crusade.

In the urgent search for relevant solutions, one of our past failures is now becoming apparent. We have done too little and have been too slow in helping to train technicians, prepare professionals, educate officials, and teach the people of the underdeveloped countries how to organize their own resources and build up their institutions.

We may, in fact, be at a major turning point in technical aid policy-making. Those in the developed countries can, if they wish, continue to lend money abroad, encourage foreign agricultural productivity, stimulate construction of dams and utilities, survey unexploited natural resources, ship prefabricated industrial plants, help plan entire economies, and send teams of technical experts to conduct all these activities. But unless the people in the newly developing nations learn to man their own enterprises and manage their own affairs, the development process will die as soon as outside aid is withdrawn. Consequently, international training and education for human resources development is a crucial component of the entire technical assistance process.

This is not the first time that disadvantaged men have sought guidance where the lamps of experience burned brightest. But now, for the first time in history, the more developed nations have agreed to take the initiative and to accept the responsibility for raising the technical standards and the educational level of the rest of mankind. And if we proceed with due deliberation in the field of international training, the really startling phenomenon of our day may turn out to be not the scientific advances of superpowers obsessed with space exploration, but rather the upsurge of technologically trained masses in the underdeveloped lands.

Role of Training in the Development Process

Training and teaching of some sort has been part of international technical assistance programs from the outset. This accounts for the rise, as part of almost all aid programs, binational as well as multinational, of the system of assigning senior "counterparts," junior "trainees," advanced "fellows," and students of all types for education and training in the various technical skills and professional tasks that confront their developing societies. Yet even where proportionately most weight has been given to training, that is, in the United Nations aid programs, including the work of the Special Fund and the Specialized Agencies, training now consumes less than one-fourth of total technical assistance expenditures.

The panel of experts who formulated the Expanded Program of Technical Assistance as early as 1949 had foreseen the importance of training. Referring to "the gap between the most and the least developed countries" as "one of the most significant and alarming aspects of our contemporary society," they pointed out that "it has tended to become progressively wider in recent decades; for the most advanced countries, by reason of their progress, have an important advantage over the retarded ones. Their higher levels of output and better economic organization make it easier to accumulate capital for further development and to direct it into productive channels. The existence of highly developed and differentiated industry and agriculture automatically provides the best kind of training facilities for managers, technicians, and skilled workers, and each technological advance helps to stimulate further inventions."

According to this discerning analysis, therefore, the two main requirements for sustained development are an accumulation of capital and a reservoir of trained skill and labor. Traditionally, there were three basic factors of economic productivity and development—capital, labor, and land; and, notwithstanding our "capitalistic" orientation today as we interpret the classical literature, the labor or skill factor was originally emphasized. "The Division of Labor" was the first chapter of Adam Smith's *Wealth of Nations*, and its very first sentence refers to "the productive powers of labor" and "the skill, dexterity, and judgment with which it is anywhere directed or applied." Today, most of the newer countries are fairly well endowed with land or natural resources as a factor of production, but they suffer from a lack of the other two essential factors, namely, skilled labor and capital resources.

Which of these should be given greater emphasis? Without downgrading the importance of development capital, which is, of course, vital, the answer may be found in the decisive fact that a developing nation's capacity to absorb capital is often limited by its supply of technical skill and managerial talent. That is why a crucial kind of aid for most newer nations is technical and vocational education, scientific and managerial training, and the broadening of human talent generally. To use a phrase coined by Abu Bakar Abdalla Hamid, one of our United Nations Fellows from the Sudan (and Inspector of Traffic in the Khartoum Police Force), the solution lies in "enskilling people."

The objectives of training are twofold: first, fulfilling the vocational needs of the trainee; second, promoting his country's development plans. Both help to augment the status of the new skill-groups, resembling the former middle classes of the advanced nations. In countries that incline toward the economies of collectivism, where the freedom to amass private property is necessarily restricted, trained skill imparts a special sense of personal possession in lieu of property. It is axiomatic that in a world of competing philosophies the form of development that counts most is that of men and women who, individually and collectively, are capable of navigating the tumultuous seas of a world in flux.

So far as the status of the individual is concerned, international training represents a great paradox. World organizations like the United Nations are supposed to deal primarily with independent nations or member states, and especially to keep the peace among them. Although this strategic function of the United Nations is now undergoing a severe test, its other major function, that of ameliorating the social and economic circumstances of the newer member states, is being moderately well handled. But with respect to the comparatively unforeseen phase, that of training and educating member-states' individual citizens themselves—a function that represents action not upon nations, but rather upon their individual subjects—there is even more progress and greater hope. It will be a strange but gratifying reversal of world history to discover that education, one of the latest responsibilities assumed by the nation-state, is becoming a primary function of the emerging world order.

Within the underdeveloped countries themselves, training is one of the most acceptable forms of international aid. Although their governments are quick to request technical assistance, when the time comes for them to carry out the concrete recommendations made by international experts, they often react as human beings generally do toward gratuitous advice. Even the least developed countries tend to treat foreign counsel cavalierly, unless they actually pay for it or can be made to feel that they are initiating the proposed change themselves. This reluctance does not, however, apply to the teaching or training services offered from the outside. On the contrary, international training is one of the most popular forms of technical assistance.

So far as the actual impact upon development goes, training performs the constructive purpose of distributing technique and talent widely among all levels of government, business enterprise, and social organization. It thus helps to spread responsibility, decentralize power, and broaden opportunity within the newer nations. The stimulating impact upon productivity and policy-making that results from such a widespread build-up of trained talent is invaluable to the sustained development of a rising society.

Development Planning and Manpower Investment

If training is to become the backbone of international development, we must face up to the prospect of having to spend much more of our technical assistance funds for this purpose. In terms of ultimate costs and consequences, training might conceivably displace the more expensive grants and gifts that characterize other forms of technical aid.

The actual substitution of skills for dollars in the developmental planning and domestic budgeting of the newer countries was proposed by Professor Eugene Staley of Stanford Research Institute at the 1960 Seminar on "Training of personnel from developing countries under international technical assistance programs," conducted in Vancouver, Canada, by the Regional Training Center for United Nations Fellows. Professor Staley suggested that instead of undertaking, let us say, a $10,000,000 capital investment plan, a developing country might consider adopting a 10,000 "trained-man" program. Like a financial budget, this manpower budget could then be broken down into the required categories of trained skill.

Already, United Nations officials have worked out other "manpower investment" standards that might, with further refinement, help budget and plan required training facilities, both internally and internationally. In the field of public health, for example, there is a preferred ratio of doctors per 10,000 population. Although WHO has not yet agreed upon an accepted norm for the developing countries, FAO has worked out a global requirement of 200,000 professional foresters, compared with only 40,000 now available. The FAO standard is based on the ratio of one professional forester per 10,000 hectares (25,000 acres) of forest land. Similar calculations can be applied to the whole range of personnel in whose training the underdeveloped societies must invest liberally. United Nations Special Fund director Paul Hoffman reported to his governing council in May, 1961, that the developing countries now urgently need to train a total of 1,000,000 top-level administrators, professional personnel, business executives, middle-level administrators, and supervisory personnel.

But training in relation to international technical assistance must also include a solid educational base on which to build the required skills of a developing society. That a balanced system of education and training for all levels of talent and skill is essential has been demonstrated in the Congo crisis.

The plight of the Congo was not caused by economic shortages of natural resources or capital funds. This heartland of Africa had plenty of cultivable land, rich forests, varied climates, and ample power sources; and the influx of foreign capital had helped it to become one of the world's leading producers of the strategic metals and minerals copper, cobalt, and uranium. The Congo's main trouble, it might be cogently argued, was social, tribal, and political instability, aggravated by the premature withdrawal of Belgian control. It so happens, however, that the Congolese themselves did not choose to recognize colonial rule as a stable form of government. The Belgians had given them considerable training and experience at the clerical and vocational level, but they had been deprived of the prime requirement—trained leadership to conduct the government, manage the economy, and administer the public services.

Realizing that their own trained talent was their principal need, the new government in the Congo at one stage established a caretaker cabinet of young intellectuals under the revealing title of "College of High Commissioners." Most of the commissioners were recent graduates of Lovanium University, occupying an impressive campus on the edge of Leopoldville. This six-year-old institution possessed such extraordinary facilities as Africa's only nuclear research reactor and a 400-bed clinic. Yet the status of the Congolese High Commissioner for Health was still that of a medical student.

Poor programming and improper timing had thus robbed the new university of its chance to be of maximum service to the young republic in its time of crucial need. But even had higher education been properly planned, the total training problem would still have been a stupendous one. This was amply demonstrated by the harsh experiences of both Robert Gardiner of Ghana, the United Nations public administration consultant in the Congo, and Derek Singer, who headed the United States training program there. (See *International Development Review*, III, No. 2 [June, 1961].)

Selecting Priorities for Subject Matter

The main question recurs, "Education for what and training of precisely what kind?" Admittedly, developing countries need a well-rounded system of primary, secondary, university, vocational, and professional education. But if training is to spark the technical assistance process, preference and priority will have to be given to selected skill-groups. Although the precise choice of training priorities will vary with national needs, all developing societies have to fill certain broad categories of personnel: technicians and technologists, managers and administrators, teachers and trainers.

An adequate supply of vocationally trained technicians and scientifically educated technologists is difficult enough to attain in advanced countries, as the elaborate American want-ad pages reveal at times of even lax employment. Continuing technological unemployment accounts for the fact that one of the main provisions of the recent depressed area legislation in the United States is grants for vocational retraining of displaced personnel.

For similar reasons, a properly proportioned system of vocational and scientific training is a special need of the underdeveloped countries. In some, there is already a surplus of generally trained college graduates without jobs, and worse still, a shortage of specialized training institutions that they can attend. Egypt, for example, now has a greater proportion of university students than England, but her unemployment problem is most severe among her educated classes, and she lacks both vocationally and professionally trained people of various kinds. Israel, on the other hand, with her highly educated refugees, has a surplus of doctors and scientific researchers, but a shortage of laboratory technicians.

In fulfilling such training needs, international technical assistance administrators have already accepted the fact that the reputed technological primitivism of underdeveloped people is a myth. Insofar as the supposedly butter-fingered native technicians may be concerned, the situation may actually be the reverse. Not only are mechanics in underdeveloped countries comparatively eager learners and capable workers, but their skills are sometimes more varied and adaptable because they must often fabricate parts and improvise gadgets instead of having access to well-stocked supply rooms full of standard replacements. Similarly, it is now clear that people in the developing societies are entirely capable of learning to master the complexities of business management and the responsibilities of the administrative state.

That training for managerial and administrative expertise is essential for economic and social development, however, has only recently been fully realized.

In a revealing memoir about the business stage of his public career, interrupted by the outbreak of World War I, Herbert Hoover reported: "I had our principal offices in San Francisco, New York, London, Paris, Melbourne, Rangoon, and St. Petersburg. We were a management engineering group directing many mining and metallurgical enterprises with railway and shipping adjuncts; our forte was doctoring of backward enterprises by use of the American technological and administrative methods. At one time or another we had been so engaged in eighteen countries."

By contrast, it is apparent today that one of the most fruitful forms of international development is the bolstering of governmental agencies and administrative authorities in underdeveloped countries, rather than concentrating on their sagging enterprises and failing firms that happen to solicit American management skills. After all, these countries are achieving independence in a changed historical setting, in which proficient public servants often play a larger role than the skilled managers of the private economy. Perhaps what the currently developing nations may need most in this regard is a common form of administrative training for the leaders of both their economic enterprises and their government agencies, especially those dealing with development policy and economic planning.

Meanwhile, the profound wish of the developing countries is for mature and responsible politicians and public administrators. Not all the underdeveloped countries draw a fine line between skilled political leaders and trained civil servants. But they are as distinctly aware as we of the need to eliminate politics from administration. Some even look skeptically on the inscription on Ghanaian President Nkrumah's famous statue in Accra, which reads, "Seek ye first the political kingdom, and everything else shall be added unto you." The young Nigerian diplomat P. C. Asiodu has urged rather "a crash program for training in both the process of policy making and the organization of administrative services."

International and Indigenous Training

Just how to provide the teaching experience required for the training function remains a major international challenge. At present, the developed countries are themselves suffering from serious educational defects, and their existing training facilities are taxed to the limit. Export of teachers to the underdeveloped countries and influx of students from these countries merely intensify an already world-wide educational crisis.

In the United States, some 65,000 persons from abroad, classified as scholars, students, participants, exchangees, or trainees, are accommodated annually in universities, colleges, technical institutes, or specially organized training courses. In addition, hundreds of VIP's and other visitors of all kinds clog, but also charm, the crowded calendars of our busiest and best business executives, professors, scientists, and public officials, in a continuing search for up-to-date practices and techniques of their various trades and professions. The bulk of these visitors and trainees come from underdeveloped countries, but so important a role does international training now play that many come from the developed countries as well.

About 50,000 of the foreign trainees in the United States are enrolled at educational institutions, generally as regular undergraduates, but often as graduate, professional, or special students of engineering, agriculture, medicine, science, and other basic subjects. The remainder represents a variety of key personnel, already basically educated, but on leave from their technical or junior positions or from middle or higher executive posts of the civil services or of economic enterprises in their developing countries. For their rising responsibilities at home, these people are being quickly but comprehensively trained in on-the-job, in-service field work and other carefully tailored courses offered in American governmental agencies, industrial plants, scientific laboratories, and business firms.

The annual number of foreign trainees in Great Britain is approximately the same as in the U.S.A. and the number handled by other British Commonwealth countries under the Colombo Plan is mounting steadily. In the combined countries of Western Europe other than Britain, the number of foreign trainees now actually exceeds the American figure. Russia currently accommodates about one-fourth of the American total, inclusive of the new Soviet Friendship University's first annual contingent of 500 foreign students. About one-half of the Soviet's foreign trainees have been coming from China. And China, at her own crowded institutions, has now assumed the task of training students from some of the neutralist as well as the Communist countries.

These competitive maneuvers of both friend and foe in the realm of international training might, with proper provocation, shift the scene of the hot and cold wars from the battlefield to the college campus.

But overshadowing even this interesting international trend is the growth of on-the-spot training within the underdeveloped countries themselves. Educational institutions and training institutes in the newer countries are developing more rapidly, conform to higher standards, and apply sounder teaching methods than is generally appreciated. Indigenous training now compares favorably with international training for another reason: It is usually more in tune with the native culture, more relevant to development needs, and more productive of the skills required in the emerging countries.

Although foreign educational institutions will continue to beckon, the developing nations will be carrying more of their own training load sooner than anticipated. The rise of indigenous training helps explain why, despite the continuing demand for international training generally, there seems to be a declining number of United Nations fellowship applications from some countries in certain fields. The decline may also be explained by the fact that promising personnel are so few in the developing countries that they cannot be spared for educational leave abroad. Perhaps, therefore, we shall have to evolve more quickly forms of training that will permit the developing nations simultaneously to retain their best talent and to train them on the spot.

One rich source of indigenous teaching talent is the growing crop of recently returned trainees. Upon re-entering their assigned duties, the most qualified of them sometimes undertake to transmit their newly acquired knowledge to subordinates and colleagues. Although more might be accomplished if they were also taught teaching methods along with their substantive subjects, returned trainees are often effective teachers because they know how to fit the shoe. One Indian cabinet minister was so convinced of this that he decided to disapprove all applications for educational leave unless trainees agreed to undertake substantial teaching duties upon their return.

Helpful though this multiplier factor may be, there is a more promising trend in international training today. This is the feedback from the trained talent of one underdeveloped country to another. Under United Nations technical assistance, about one-fourth of the trainees are now assigned for training to other "underdeveloped" lands, because there they encounter some of the best and most convenient training facilities. Trainees in specific fields are now beginning to gravitate to Brazil in Latin America, Egypt in North Africa, and the Philippines in the Asia region. Developing Israel maintains an active and popular service of international training and technical assistance of her own. Even for the most sophisticated technical studies, such as social statistics or econometrics, international training administrators often prefer to assign trainees to countries like India, whose newer institutions and experts now excel in teaching and research in these fields.

In the future, developed countries may be expected to limit most of their efforts to the higher level technological courses, "refresher" training for professionals, postgraduate education, and the training of advanced researchers and university teachers. Meanwhile, we are at an intermediate stage, during which the universities of the developed countries are helping the newer institutions to establish their own professional schools, modernize their academic departments, and train their new faculties. These comprehensive technical assistance services to higher education in the developing countries are provided, under the United States aid system, through government-financed university-to-university contracts, which last year numbered 104 and involved over 57 American institutions. The much earlier European version of this university-to-university device included the grant of privilege to "colonial" universities that met the required academic standards to award "external degrees" of the "mother" university.

The Benefit Works Both Ways

It is now, however, the developed countries themselves that are beginning to benefit in an extraordinary way from international training. Some 2,000 faculty members from American universities, including Fulbright professors, work or study overseas annually. This outflow of American scholars is beginning to balance the inflow of foreign scholars. Moreover, professors from the developing countries are increasingly being assigned as faculty in the developed countries. They now embellish the lecture platforms and seminar rooms of many American and European institutions and are frequently the cream of the crop. Reciprocally, teachers and trainers in the developed countries, confronted by some of the most able students and eager trainees underdeveloped countries can send, are compelled to distill their own knowledge and clarify their ideas as never before. (See Robert Solo in the *International Development Review*, III, No. 1 [February, 1961].) Thus, from this international network of training and teaching, there is emerging an enriched store of intelligence for a changing world in which the distinction between developed and underdeveloped nations is beginning to dissolve.

19. EDUCATION: KEY ISSUES FOR POLICY MAKERS

F. F. HILL

SINCE Point Four began and "development" became an international objective, both donors and receivers of aid have begun a kind of sobering up. There is now more or less widespread recognition of the following lessons from the experience of international aid programs to date:

1. There is no political substitute for social and economic progress. Joining SEATO or CENTO, subscribing to Arab nationalism, deploring imperialism or Communism, appealing to this or that bloc, nationalizing everything—all have been tried or proposed in one part or another of each of the three major less-developed regions of the world—South and Southeast Asia, the Middle East and Africa, and Latin America and the Caribbean area. Yet the basic economic and social problems of these regions remain to be solved.

2. Big physical projects, such as dams, power plants, and steel mills, do not themselves ensure development. The fate of Nuri's regime in Iraq, with its emphasis on delayed returns from long-range projects and its failure to include and activate the mass of the people, has not gone unnoticed in other Near Eastern countries. Even where heavy reliance on such projects as the Aswan Dam in Egypt and steel mills in India continues, there is a new effort to anticipate the human and managerial problems that will follow the completion of such projects.

3. Money alone is not enough to ensure development. The oil-rich countries of the Near East and Venezuela and countries receiving large amounts of foreign aid, such as Korea, Laos, and Vietnam, still face key development problems.

4. Centralized planning and financing are not enough to ensure development. Even where there are considerable central revenues, as in Iran, and centralized planning, as in Pakistan, India, and

Egypt, there is an increased interest in eliciting a more widespread self-help effort from provincial and local governments and the people themselves.

5. Industrialization is only a part of the development process. The first tendency, as in Burma, to neglect agriculture and the rural sector in favor of rapid industrialization is being modified as countries recognize the continuing economic, social, and political importance of the agricultural sector of their economies.

6. Quantitative expansion of present institutions is not enough to ensure development. For example, doubling the size of existing universities may simply mean producing more poorly educated and alienated students and inducing greater frustration in more professors. Improved or new educational institutions and programs are needed.

7. Man does not live by bread alone. The traditional values of existing cultures frequently were regarded in the first days of technical assistance principally as obstacles to development. The contribution of these factors to the coherence, dignity, and independence of societies in the newly independent countries was not sufficiently understood and appreciated. They are now widely recognized.

The lesson of the postwar period is that development stands or falls with the improvement of human and institutional competence. Trained men and women in effective institutional settings, although not the only prerequisite to development, are the key to progress and the essential condition of useful assistance from the outside. The development of a country's human resources is basic to the effective, balanced development of its natural resources.

But how are men and women to be trained? How are their inherent capacities to be developed?

Let me offer a few hypotheses:

1. In modern societies, formal education provides the most important single means of developing people.
2. It is in the long-term economic and political interests of the economically developed countries of the free world to help less developed countries establish effective educational systems of their own.
3. The objective of assistance programs in education should be to help recipient countries develop institutions that fit both their pocketbooks and their needs. This often means insti-

tutions and programs that differ in important respects from those of the donor countries, because of differences in historical background, stage of economic development, and present ability to support a high-cost system of education.

4. Institutions in developing countries should be staffed as quickly as possible by their own personnel, who should assume responsibility for the operation and continued development of the educational system.

If these assumptions are correct, what are some of the problems that confront both the less developed countries and those seeking to assist them in their efforts to establish educational systems suited to their needs?

Every newly independent country, whether it be the American colonies in 1783 or the Congo in 1960, is determined to manage its own affairs. Among other things, this means staffing government, the educational system, business, and industry with its own people as quickly as possible. Africanization of the civil service, of educational institutions, and of business and industry is the cry in every newly independent African country. The Congolese, the Nigerians, and the Senegalese did not take over from the Belgians, the British, and the French so that expatriates from former colonial powers could continue to hold most of the top jobs. They are determined, understandably, to make their own decisions and their own mistakes. Political leaders who advocate a gradualist policy of Africanization are likely to find themselves out of tune and out of office. So it was, too, in the newly independent countries of South and Southeast Asia and the Middle East after World War II.

But while countries such as India and Pakistan were relatively well-off with respect to trained manpower, most of the emerging countries today are as desperately short of men and women adequately prepared to plan and administer the difficult process of modernization as they are short of financial resources to meet their developmental needs, including the need for educational facilities. In this situation, how does a country decide the best use of its resources?

Who Gets Educated First?

From the standpoint of the need for different kinds of trained manpower for development, what should be the dimensions of the educational pyramid in a particular less developed country by, say, 1970? How broad the base in terms of numbers attending elementary schools, the middle in terms of numbers attending secondary schools, and the capstone in terms of numbers attending colleges, universities, and graduate schools? What provision should be made for vocational training, for technical education at the subprofessional level, and for professional education, including graduate study? Should any effort be made in adult education?

Take elementary education. Since in most less-developed countries large numbers of children do not yet have access to elementary schools, the political pressure for more educational facilities at this level is often very great. In at least one African country, a successful political campaign was waged on a platform of making elementary education available to all takers. The winning candidate later discovered to his chagrin that the necessary resources simply were not available to enable him to fulfill his campaign pledge, much less meet the demand for education at other levels.

Dr. Arthur Lewis, a distinguished economist and former deputy director of the United Nations Special Fund, makes a strong case for turning out relatively large numbers of secondary-school graduates in developing economies. Dr. Lewis argues that it is this "middle group" that provides the indispensable human resource base for development. There is much to be said for this view. Certainly most persons who drop out of school after four to six years of what is often rather poor elementary education lack the training necessary to perform many jobs in an economy based on the application of science and technology. Furthermore, a high-school education is prerequisite to many kinds of in-service training and technical education that provide the "middle-level" personnel with specialized knowledge and skills so essential in modern business, industry, and government.

How much of the educational budget of an economically less developed country should be devoted to higher education? Except, perhaps, in the case of a few very small countries, most of the less developed countries' college graduates will have to be trained at home. There are not going to be enough places in the colleges, universities, and professional schools of the more highly developed countries to meet the needs of less developed countries for college-trained manpower.

What about vocational training? To what extent can and should a developing country with limited resources for education rely upon apprenticeship training to teach skills such as the building trades, woodworking, and metal working rather than establish training schools for this purpose?

What about education at the subprofessional level—that is, two or three years beyond high school—in such fields as agriculture and engineering technology? The United States has turned out from 6,000 to 10,000 college graduates in agriculture each year since 1920. Few less developed countries can hope to reach this level on a proportionate basis for decades, despite the urgent need to increase agricultural production. Perhaps the answer, especially in the early years, is to train more persons at the subprofessional level—persons the Latin Americans refer to as *expertos*.

The same kind of question arises in connection with training in engineering technology. Graduates of Pakistan's polytechnic institutes, in which students get first-rate training for three years beyond high school and learn to work with their hands as well as their heads, are currently starting at salaries comparable to those received by newly graduated engineers. This is a measure of the demand for this type of personnel at this stage in Pakistan's industrial development. Prior to the establishment of the polytechnics, Pakistan had a good supply of engineers, a surplus of unskilled labor, but little in between. Pakistanis, in common with the people of most less developed countries, learn mechanical skills quite easily, so there was no serious problem at the skilled-labor level. What was needed was more persons at the subforeman and foreman levels—men who not only understand the principles on which a diesel engine works, but can repair one and show others how to do so.

In an effort to introduce a degree of rationality into decisions that otherwise would result solely from the interplay of conflicting forces, increasing use has been made in recent years of manpower studies. These undertake to estimate a country's manpower requirements for a period of five to ten years in the future—requirements for school teachers, clerks, shop foremen, engineers, doctors, and lawyers. Such estimates can never be more than approximations to be revised at intervals, since it is not possible to forecast with precision the manner in which a particular economy will develop and the resulting needs for trained manpower in various categories at different times. Furthermore, decisions concerning educational and training programs, like other decisions of government, have to take into account financial and political feasibility as well as economic and social desirability. Still, manpower studies provide a useful basis for educational planning. They represent an important advance over the common alternative of leaving the size and nature of the educational budget solely to the play of political forces operating in a highly centralized system.

What Kind of Curricula?

If for years or even decades to come, most of the people in a less developed country can look forward to no more than four to six years of elementary education, how much vocational bias, if any, should there be in the curriculum? Under such circumstances, should a country stick to the teaching of reading, writing, and arithmetic at the elementary level, or, if it is a preponderately agricultural country and likely to remain so, should it undertake to introduce elementary agriculture and rural handicrafts into the curriculum?

Sixty years or more ago, Dr. Liberty Hyde Bailey, the distinguished first dean of the New York State College of Agriculture at Cornell, had this to say: "The district school cannot teach agriculture any more than it can teach law or engineering or any other profession or trade, but it can interest the child in nature and rural problems and thereby fasten its sympathies to the country. The child will teach the parent."

Dean Bailey's answer to the question posed was that agriculture as an applied science could not be taught in the district school. He believed, however, that children could and should be encouraged to develop a love of nature. This, he reasoned, would both add to the pleasure of living in the country and encourage direct observation, a habit of great value to the farmer. "The person who actually knows a pussy willow," he said, "will know how to become acquainted with a potato bug."

In addition to his great abilities as scientist, teacher, author, and public speaker, Dean Bailey was a man of action and a gifted administrator. He undertook, at the turn of the century, to organize and introduce nature study into the grade schools of New York State, at times in the face of strong opposition. His biographer states that "by 1903, nearly 3,000 grade-school teachers were receiving nature study guidance by correspondence; nearly 30,000 children were raising plants in school gardens."

It is possible that lessons learned from Dean Bailey's experiment might be helpful to the economically less developed countries of today, striving to make a limited amount of money provide an education of maximum usefulness to large numbers of rural children.

A country that expects to develop an economy based upon the application of science and technology to production must have a substantial number of people who have obtained a good foundation in mathematics and science at the secondary level. How does a country organize to teach mathematics and science at the secondary level when it does not begin to have enough well-trained teachers or laboratory equipment to meet its needs? Should it concentrate its available resources in a few secondary schools that specialize in the teaching of science and mathematics and, by competitive examinations or other means, select a limited number of students from all over the country to attend? This, of course, means dormitories and dining facilities, which add to expense.

If a country decides to establish secondary schools that specialize in the teaching of science and mathematics, what does it do about these subjects in the case of students who do not attend such schools? Is it possible to develop and staff science courses at the secondary level that will give the non-science student some understanding of the nature, methods, and principles of science and the contributions it can make to improved levels of living? I do not underestimate the difficulties of such an undertaking. But what are the alternatives?

What kind of training should a less developed country with limited resources for education concentrate upon in a field such as engineering? Should it undertake to establish curricula in civil, mechanical, electrical, chemical, and all of the other engineering specialties? Or should it establish a basic course in the engineering sciences, perhaps complete the training of civil and mechanical engineers, which are likely to be needed in large numbers in the early years of a country's development, and send its students abroad to complete their training in other fields of engineering?

Training Better Teachers

A major problem in every less developed country is the training of teachers. Many teachers at the elementary and secondary levels are poorly prepared, with limited schooling, themselves poorly taught, and with little training in teaching methods. Since they cannot be spared for extended periods of further training, heavy reliance must be placed upon short-term in-service training courses. As in the United States, teachers' salaries are usually low in relation to other vocations, with the result that persons who have a high-school or college education are attracted to government, business, and industry. This is particularly serious in countries where there are relatively few trained persons.

Perhaps it will be necessary to device new institutional arrangements to help solve the problem of providing better teachers. Pakistan, for example, has established extension centers in secondary education, one in East Pakistan and one in West Pakistan. Some twenty secondary schools in each region are affiliated with each of the two major centers. Each of the twenty schools functions as a center for all of the secondary schools in its territory. This arrangement provides two-way communication between secondary teachers throughout the country and educational specialists at the teacher-training centers, much as the county agent system links farmers and colleges of agriculture in the United States. Short courses, workshops, and seminars are held, problems are discussed and experience exchanged in an effort to improve both course content and teaching at the secondary level. Perhaps the Pakistan idea could be used to advantage in other less developed countries.

What are the possibilities of television, radio, and teaching machines as partial substitutes for teachers? While some experimental work has been done, we do not yet have reliable answers. It is important at this stage neither to overestimate nor to underestimate possibilities in this direction, but to keep experimenting in an effort to apply technology to the instructional problem.

How Can the United States Help?

A country's educational system must develop as the country develops. Many parts of the United States were economically underdeveloped not so long ago and had educational facilities no better than those in many of the less developed countries today. Many teachers had little schooling themselves and little or no preparation for teaching. The equipment consisted of desks, a blackboard, slates for the pupils, and a few books. As late as 1890, there were only some 2,500 public schools in the United States.

When the Oklahoma Agricultural and Mechanical College opened in 1891, not a single applicant for admission was qualified to undertake college work. Forty-five students were enrolled in a preparatory course. Not until after the turn of the century was it possible for the majority of land-grant colleges and universities to require a high-school certificate for admission.

The development of a national educational system is a continuing, evolutionary process. Every country must start from where it is and move ahead as best it can, taking into account its historical background, its needs, and its resources. Since countries differ in these respects, it follows that their educational systems will differ.

How can we help today's less developed countries meet their educational problems?

First, United States dollars, although needed and useful, will not solve their problems. There are not and never will be enough of them. In 1949, the year in which aid to Europe under the Marshall Plan was greatest, it constituted less than 3 per cent of the gross national product of the recipient countries. The hard fact is that every country has to provide the major part of the resources required for its development, including resources for education.

Second, the United States cannot possibly provide enough teachers to begin to meet the needs of even those countries in which the shortage is most acute. We are short of teachers at home.

Third, the backgrounds, the stages of economic development, and the financial and trained-manpower resources of the countries we are trying to assist are quite different from our own. The educational system best suited to their needs, and to their pocketbooks, is likely to differ in many respects from ours. Substituting a current American model for a former French or British model is not likely to be the solution.

The recipe for the successful development of educational institutions and systems at home or abroad is to bring together persons with constructive ideas and the necessary resources to carry them out. We can help in a modest way for a short time with financial resources, although such assistance will never be large in relation to total needs; nor is financial help likely to be our most important contribution. We ought to make every effort to find able, inventive, and dedicated people with experience in education, who have the ability to analyze situations with which they are not familiar and help devise appropriate means of meeting them. Such people are hard to find and difficult to spare for overseas service, but we should make the effort.

We in the United States can help. In the last analysis, the kind of job we do will depend upon the kind of people we get to do it.

20. PITFALLS AND PRIORITIES IN EDUCATION

DON ADAMS

THERE appear to be two particularly dangerous pitfalls in the attempts of the developing nations to realize the full potential of education. One pitfall to which many visiting American educational advisors, and a few native educators who have spent a lengthy period of study in America, are particularly prone is the unconscious act of subtracting the underdeveloped educational system from their image of the American educational system and measuring progress by the reduction of the difference. The second pitfall, common to a few visiting American educational advisors and to many of the native educators, is mistaking renovation of the educational status quo for the creation of new dynamic educational patterns.

Both of these pitfalls are conspicuously present for those who make decisions regarding primary, secondary, and higher education in the developing areas. The propensity of American educators working overseas to be overly anxious at times about "democratizing" the curriculum, promoting coeducation, and introducing local control are cases in point. On the other hand, professional educators in the underdeveloped countries sometimes expect to have, as well as to eat, their educational cake. Vocational schools, while increasing in number, often remain in imitation of academic schools rather than becoming truly vocational. University spokesmen argue that their institutions could offer leadership in development but at the same time foster, both in program and general institutional climate, the traditional-gentleman complex. Furthermore, the entire educational ladder often remains encased in a series of examinations that test the cheapest kind of education and

EDITOR'S NOTE: Notes corresponding to reference numbers in the text will be found at the end of the chapter.

render impotent internal curricular or methodological innovations. Considering the modern demands on schools, these types of policies remind one of John Dewey's statement that education at times "becomes the art of taking advantage of the helplessness of the young."

The basic educational problem of the underdeveloped nations is to create, imitate, or borrow and adapt an educational system that will (1) produce skills required for specific technical, professional, and administrative development tasks; and (2) assist other societal institutions in producing such social and personal values and attitudes as tend to be the preconditions or accompaniments of development.

Only in recent years has much attention been given to the role of education as a contributor to the whole process of economic and social development. Historically, educators and statesmen in both advanced and underdeveloped countries have declared that the goal of education, particularly school education, should be that of perpetuating the cultural heritage or transmitting the good life. In fact, nations have historically been suspicious if their schools attempted to do more.

Moreover, the history of the extension of educational opportunity in the developed countries does not present a satisfying picture to most underdeveloped societies. In the West, it was only after long centuries of advanced culture and many decades of industrial development that the nations of Europe believed they could afford to give more than a minimum of education to any sizeable proportion of their populations. People of the underdeveloped countries expect much more dynamic progress than this. Thus the dilemma presents itself. Underdeveloped nations must learn educational techniques from nations that expect less proportionate returns from education than they do.

Literacy and Primary Education

The bush school and initiation ceremonies of tribal societies which train for livelihood, procreation, and warfare cannot meet the educational needs of a developing nation. Literacy may not be an essential part of the training for traditional agricultural and handicraft pursuits, which can be learned by apprenticeship or imitation, but it becomes increasingly necessary in an industrializing and urbanizing society. Trial-and-error procedures are too wasteful or too dangerous; the illiterate is an inefficient producer and consumer. Irrespective of the personal joys accrued from reading and figuring, in the factory or business there are rules to be followed, accounts kept, plans and blueprints interpreted. Moreover, a close correlation exists between literacy and media participation—frequently referred to as a "multiplier" in the development process.

Many media depend for maximum efficiency on a literate audience. People do not want the material fruits or the personal standards and styles of modern society if they do not know that these exist. Some economic historians, for example, impute much of the Japanese economic growth during the early part of the Meiji period to the universal primary education that allowed a powerful state to communicate its goals easily.

A rather dramatic relationship exists between literacy and many economic criteria of development, and, indeed, literacy is often used as a measure of the socio-economic advancement of a nation. Coefficients of correlation of well over .80 have been found between literacy and industrialization—where the latter is measured by the proportion of gainfully employed males in non-agricultural pursuits. Striking also is the fact that, in 1957, no country with a per capita income of less than $300 (U.S.) had a literacy rate of over 40 per cent. Looked at from another point of view, only three areas (Puerto Rico, Uruguay, and Venezuela) could be found where the per capita income was over $500 (U.S.) and the literacy below 90 per cent. Interestingly, however, little correlation between literacy and per capita income appears to exist in the 30–70 per cent literacy spread, for both "poor" and "middle-income" countries are represented therein.[1]

Despite the evidence of the demands of development on literacy and the correlation between literacy and a nation's wealth, advocates of compulsory education and mass literacy programs usually argue from a humanitarian or political perspective. Common phrases such as "education is the birthright of all people" and "primary education is the foundation of political democracy" are frequently present in educational literature. While the latter claim is rendered suspect by both historical illustration and contemporary observation, the former as a widely accepted human right is nearly above attack. The timing is of utmost importance, however, and it might be argued that a postponement of the fulfillment of this birthright by some people in order to pay for the accomplishment of other economic tasks might, in final analysis, hasten total satisfaction of the principle.

But crucial questions remain unanswered. How much does a few years of primary education or a few months of literacy education alter the attitudes of its recipient? Does the primary school make the child more empathic or imbue him with the scientific-secular and achievement attitudes seemingly prerequisite to development? If the child is the bearer of divinity, as the great American educator Francis W. Parker suggested, and "the fruit of all the past and the seed of all the future," then the challenge to primary schools is of the utmost significance.

Studies of the contributions of schools in producing the desired attitudes and motivations offer results quite disturbing. Psychological theory and research indicate that the crucial age period for the development of attitudes may lie between the ages of five and ten. This being true, it might be assumed that if the school during the early years stressed attitudes and standards appropriate to development, such training would have profound effect on the children's later life. The few fragmentary empirical studies that have been made, however, do not bear this out. McClelland, reporting a comparative study of Arab children who had attended a "western-style" nursery school with a group that had not, concluded that tests showed but a slight difference in the felt need for achievement among members of the two groups. Though the western-style school emphasized "approval of projects well done" and "some standards of cleanliness and group play," these influences were not of a lasting nature.[2]

Research at higher educational levels, reported by the same author, gave essentially the same results. Studies in the United States frequently attest to the minimal influence of schools in attitude formation. It is probably safe to conclude that American educators, for reasons of oratory or in justification of budgets, have overstated the direct social and psychological contributions of formal schooling. (Even John Dewey argued that direct instruction and exhortation could not in themselves bring about changes in "mind and character.") The educational planner, then, is safer when justifying expenditures on literacy and primary education, at least as these programs are typically conducted, on grounds other than making the children less conservative, more democratic, or even more development-motivated.

More substantial arguments can be given for the significance of the reading and other skills acquired, the improved opportunities for communication, or the increased personal enjoyment. Literacy is particularly cogent in the Lerner chain of increased literacy→increased communication→increased empathy which not only leads in the direction of development, but makes easier the personal adjustment from old to new styles of living.[3] Another argument for extensive primary education—an argument with both democratic and economic dimensions—is that the base of the educational pyramid should be kept broad to increase the probability of identifying educable talent.

Secondary and Higher Education

In the last few years, economic planners and, to a lesser extent, professional educators have come to recognize an increased role for secondary and higher education in the development process. The myriad of middle-level vocational, administrative, teaching (for lower grades), and entrepreneurial skills needed in the early, or at least during the "take-off," period of development cannot be produced at the primary level.

Let us look at the high-priority developmental functions demanded of secondary and higher education under four headings: (1) manpower, (2) teacher education, (3) program diversity and flexibility, and (4) research.

1. One criterion for determining educational priorities which has economic appeal is manpower needs. As part of long-range economic planning, nations in the last few years have begun to classify and project into the future their manpower requirements. Once occupational classifications have been established and equated to educational classifications, the translation to projected school enrollments can be made. Left unsaid, of course, by all mathematical approaches to enrollment patterns are the number and kind of a nation's educational needs other than manpower.

2. The need for teachers is likely to persist from the very early stages of development onward. Harbison, in considering the high-level manpower needs of Nigeria from 1960 to 1970, estimated that nearly one-fourth of the 31,200 needed were teachers.[4]

But a high priority for teacher education may be warranted not only for manpower reasons, but because of the central position assumed by teachers in the educational process. Teachers, often the most highly educated group in the community, can, if properly equipped by personality and training, be the seed corn of educational and possibly even community development. One viewer, in what appears to be an overstatement, suggests an even greater role, "Teachers are to education and economic development as machines-to-make-machines (machine tools) are to plants and production."[5]

3. Although it is not possible here to analyze in any detail the contribution of courses of study to economic or social growth, one general principle has emerged. Because of inaccuracies of manpower predictions and the general vicissitudes of development, educational programs must be characterized by diversity and flexibility. Broadening the curriculum of the secondary schools and universities to include modern content in the social and natural sciences is, of course, essential. Experiments at the secondary level of relating school activities more closely to community needs, when such experiments are tied to a well-planned national effort, may bring satisfactory results. Relating the school more closely to production—but avoiding the extreme of creating a school-cum-factory, as in China—offers possibilities as yet unexplored in most nations. The lowering of traditionally defined standards of achievement has caused many such promising experiments to be discarded prematurely.

Intimately affecting the scope and nature of the university program is the concept of the intellectual's role in society. In the West, economic development until the twentieth century owed little to the contributions of intellectuals.[6] The technological innovators and industrial managers as a group were not highly educated. University graduates entered the professions or administration, but with rare exception avoided commercial and industrial pursuits. In contrast to this early western pattern, the most enthusiastic support for modernization and industrialization in the underdeveloped areas is coming from the new elite, the recent university graduates.

Yet there is substantial evidence that their effectiveness as leaders in the development process leaves much to be desired. In the absence in most underdeveloped countries of the innovating craftsman and the risk-taking entrepreneur, the enlightened intellectual has many roles to play. In actuality, however, the most talented of the new intellectual elite often become administrators or politicians or enter the traditional professions. As in the western experience, the best have found commercial and industrial possibilities distasteful—although most recently the vision of great profit seems to be breaking down this reluctance. As interest in these possibilities is developed, by state-introduced financial incentives or otherwise, universities must alter their programs accordingly.

4. At present, nearly all the research on the problems of economic, social, or educational development is being conducted by persons from the universities of the highly advanced nations. While this is not surprising, the danger is apparent. It can be too easily concluded that the requisites for maintaining a high level of development and the preconditions for achieving it are the same. Equally dangerous is the possibile conclusion that the preconditions for development of the now advanced nations are the same for those nations currently classified as underdeveloped. To avoid such suspect assumptions, not only should more of the necessary research be carried out in the underdeveloped areas, but more should also be undertaken by persons native to the area.

In the field of education, studies of various levels of sophistication could be undertaken with the technical assistance of foreign scholars at universities or research institutes. More needs to be known about the social and economic background of those who attend schools in the underdeveloped countries. In addition, the real rather than the supposed attitudes, aptitudes, and interests of students need to be learned. At a more sophisticated level, applied research in the problems of culture change (and social planning?) might lead to a better design for fitting the school into the dynamics of community development. Research in educational technology, as the term is broadly defined, might result not only in new gimmicks and personnel arrangements that enable schools to do old things better, but might unleash educational potential as yet untapped. The Communist nations, for example, attempt to utilize educational power to the fullest by coordinating the efforts of the school, family, peer group, and state in ideological and economic development. One need not accept the Communist ideology to promote better coordination of all institutions toward national, economic, or social ends.

Educational Priorities and Levels of Development

What should be the educational priorities at various developmental levels? As suggested at several points, professional educators are, quite naturally, prone to overestimate the contributions of schooling to development—particularly to the requisite social and psychological conditions. This does not mean that the development of "human resources" is relatively unimportant. On the contrary, the capacity of a population to absorb and apply knowledge is the key to social as well as economic growth. It is quite possible, for example, since the capacity to produce wealth lies in the people of a country, that substantial economic progress can be made without formation of new physical capital.[7]

Nor does suspicion of the school's ability in the underdeveloped setting to form attitudes and values suggest that the schools should be merely storehouses of knowledge and skills. What is indicated is that for maximum results the schools' efforts must be integrated with the efforts of other behavior-changing institutions—the family, state, and church. Mass media in particular have a potential as yet hardly realized in the formation of the standards, values, and attitudes—the style of living—necessary in the development process. It may be that a truly goal-centered educational system with a development-centered curriculum utilizing more efficient methodology could make the school a much more dynamic instrument for behavior change. McClelland, for example, in his psychological view of economic development, has suggested that *group play, group extracurricular activities,* and *group educational projects* (because all of these increase "other-directedness") have potential developmental rewards.[8]

As several students of culture change have pointed out, traditional modes of behavior are often *best* swept away and new ones implanted by an ideological fervor such as Communism or nationalism. But that schools, as has sometimes been suggested, could be the prime progenitor of such a movement seems highly unlikely. Whether they should be, even if they could, is highly questionable.

If the analysis undertaken in this paper is correct, the first educational priority is not, as is often suggested, universal primary education. An educational scheme along the following lines would seem more in keeping with the demands of development.

1. For those areas where illiteracy is very high, say over 85 per cent, and only a tiny elite has gained an understanding and respect for the modern world (i.e., certain parts of tropical Africa and the Near East, and the mountain countries of South Central Asia), adult education, primary education, and teacher education should have a high priority in development plans. Furthermore,

the educational responsibilities of all public and private administrative, business, welfare, and protective agencies should be stressed.

An initial educational goal might be 50 per cent of each age group in primary school, 10 per cent in secondary school, and 1 per cent in institutions of higher education. During the early stages of progress toward this first goal, elaborate technical assistance in the form of expensive facilities or elaborate long-range planning is probably unwarranted. However, efforts of foreign "experts" in assisting native educators in the development of data-gathering services, curriculum planning, and building of an appropriate educational technology can be rewarding.

2. Nations that already have a well established governmental structure, have fostered substantial literacy (say over 30 per cent), and possess a minimum supply of vocational and administrative personnel have reached a stage where our first "pyramid" would prove inadequate. By this time, a second educational goal should have been shaped that envisions universal primary education, at least 20 per cent receiving secondary education and 2 per cent higher education. Perhaps half of those beyond the primary school should be studying courses that are partly vocational or technical. The crucial role of post-primary education is shown by the fact that many developing countries are at the same time faced with surpluses of unskilled labor and shortages of highly skilled manpower. Both of these problems are related to an underinvestment in certain types of secondary and higher education.

Nations en route to this second goal—most of the Asian and Latin American countries—are able to absorb large-scale technical assistance. Manpower studies are of great value at this level, and their results provide one criterion for educational priorities. The need for teachers remains crucial.

3. A third educational goal could be hypothesized for those that had attained the second "pyramid" described above. The new goal would point toward the expansion of secondary and higher educational opportunities—the amount of such expansion depending on (1) new manpower needs, which in turn are related to the design of the economy, and (2) the importance the nation places on the consumption aspects of education.

The Need to Test Hypotheses

Much of what has been stated or quoted above about the economic, social, and educational conditions of development is still subject to much conjecture. Certain generalized models of economic development and of social change have been suggested in the past few years, but the place of formal education in these models is rarely identified. Moreover, the models themselves may be suspect, built as they often are on empirical or speculative analyses of culture change in the West. There remains a need, not only for a theoretical model suggesting the general interaction of education and the development process, but also models—as well as empirical studies—relating to specific societies. It is even conceivable that one day some underdeveloped nation and its developed benefactor will be bold enough to attempt a sizeable controlled "social experiment" to test hypotheses regarding the interaction of education and other variables that appear prerequisite to development.

NOTES

1. Statistics taken from Norton Ginsburg, *Atlas of Economic Development* (Chicago: University of Chicago Press, 1961).

2. David McClelland, *The Achieving Society* (New York: D. Van Nostrand Company, 1961), pp. 415–16.

3. Daniel Lerner, *The Traditional Society* (Glencoe, Ill.: The Free Press, 1958). See especially Chapter II.

4. *Investment in Education*, The Report of the Commission on Post School Certificate and Higher Education in Nigeria (Federal Ministry of Nigeria, 1960), p. 61.

5. William J. Platt, *Toward Strategies of Education* (Menlo Park, California: Stanford Research Institute, International Industrial Development Center, 1962), p. 27.

6. Edward A. Shils, "The Intellectuals: Public Opinion and Economic Development," *Economic Development and Cultural Change*, VI, No. 1 (October, 1957), 55–62.

7. A further discussion of this is available in a paper by Hans W. Singer, "Education and Economic Development," found in *Final Report: Conference of African States on the Development of Education in Africa* (Addis Ababa: UNESCO, May, 1961), pp. 107–11.

8. McClellan, *op. cit.*, p. 401.

21. AN ALTERNATIVE APPROACH TO MASS EDUCATION

ROBERT BRITTAIN

IT is now generally agreed that developing countries need to build quickly country-wide systems of primary and secondary education, including systematic literacy instruction and follow-up education for adults. Many countries have recently set up long-range programs, but unfortunately these all entail the building of systems modeled, in physical plant and in the disposition of manpower, on those already existing in the industrialized countries. To do this, they must erect thousands of expensive school buildings, equip them with educational materials of all kinds, provide annual budgets for the maintenance of this plant, and above all, staff it with a host of well-trained teachers, each working at any one time with a maximum of thirty or forty pupils.

But the developing countries are all plagued with extreme shortages both of qualified teachers and of development funds. Furthermore, this conventional system, even after it may be established and functioning, will still have two serious shortcomings: (1) the inability of thousands of children to attend, either because of geographical isolation or because, in order to help support themselves, they must work during normal school hours; and (2) the fact that conventional schools can normally do little or nothing about the great problem of adult illiteracy, or adult lack of training and education beyond the primary level.

It would be possible, however, to organize and use the educational resources *at present available in the developing countries themselves* in a way that would make these obstacles less serious and these shortcomings less crippling. Several recent developments in educational practice, which have been individually tested and have proved their worth in Italy, the United Kingdom, the United States, and elsewhere, could be modified and combined into a system with which developing countries, using the trained teachers

251

they already have, could achieve more than they can with a conventional system. And I think they could do it at less cost, more quickly, and without any significant loss in efficiency or any lowering of educational standards.

At the outset, it should be said that in the following proposals there are no suggestions about *what* is to be taught. That is the province of the education authorities in the countries themselves. All we are attempting is to show how certain thoroughly tested, twentieth-century tools and methods can be used to solve a twentieth-century problem.

The proposed system combines three modern pedagogical practices that have proved their worth individually, though they have not been brought together heretofore in precisely this way: the *television broadcast*, the *correspondence-school method*, and something of the *tutorial system*. Each of these requires some initial explanation.

Many educators shy away from any mention of television because they think of it only as a "visual aid" or special "enrichment" program—in other words, as an expensive adjunct to ordinary classroom teaching. Although such use is widely made of television, for most of the developing countries it would be an extravagant luxury. There are even graver objections to the use of television as a medium for disseminating imported programmed material. Neither of these is here proposed. What is suggested is the use of the television broadcast *simply as the means of enabling any number of students to attend simultaneously the daily classroom lesson given by an expert local teacher*. It is a device already widely used: in Stratford-on-Avon, one physics teacher teaches simultaneously, through television screens, in seven high schools; classes in some sixty communities in South Carolina are at present being taught successfully in this way by one teacher in each subject; and the Italian Telescuola conducts classes in literacy and in primary, secondary, and vocational subjects through the television screen, using one teacher to teach hundreds of students in dozens of communities simultaneously.

Correspondence-school methods are suggested to handle the written work of students and to provide for a close relationship between student and teacher. The result would be an arrangement very like the tutorial system now used extensively in many of the best universities of the world, in which the student is taught both by the professor whom he hears lecture and by the tutor with whom he works directly.

How can these elements be combined into an effective system of education? And what would be the advantages, for a rapidly developing country, of such an organization of their educational resources?

Essentials of a New Approach

The first requirement is the setting up of *one central headquarters school*, in which courses would be offered covering the entire curriculum from literacy training through primary education, secondary education, and vocational training. In this school, *each course would be taught by one highly skilled teacher* (ideally, the best teacher of that subject in the country at present) in a series of carefully prepared classroom lessons. He might have before him in the classroom as he worked an actual group of students, as is done in Stratford. Whether he did or not, each lesson would be given as a television broadcast.

This broadcast would be received by whatever number of television receivers the authorities decide upon (either by wireless or through a closed-circuit system), each receiver being set up, not in an expensive, elaborately equipped school building, but in a *community viewing center*. This provision is extremely important if the system is to be useful in most developing countries, where the need for community development programs in isolated villages is a fundamental concern.

The work of the teacher in charge of each course could thus be brought directly into any number of "classrooms," and he would quickly become a familiar figure to any number of viewers. His presentation of ideas and materials would be enhanced by all the usual television advantages of close-ups, camera mobility, etc. Since his work would be going out to dozens or scores of viewing centers, the authorities could afford to supply him with maps, charts, and every other kind of visual aid, which would be prohibitively costly if they had to equip individual teachers in separate classrooms. Thus, the actual lessons presented could be far more effective than any each separate village could hope to have if it had to rely on its own local school.

The expert television teacher would be assisted at headquarters by a group of *reader-teachers*, drawn from the next-best level of professional teachers already in the country and trained in correspondence-school methods. It has been demonstrated that one such reader-teacher can handle effectively the written work of from 300 to 400 students, the number varying slightly from subject to subject. These reader-teachers would correspond to the tutors in a university tutorial system, though their skillful help would be given to a far larger number of students. The Italian Telescuola uses regularly employed teachers in city schools on a part-time, after-hours basis, each handling the work of only about 75 television students. This cannot be recommended: A good reader-teacher deserves a full-time job, and his correspondence students deserve his entire attention. Furthermore, the reader-teacher would be the most direct and personal link between the student and headquarters. He ought to be able, at least once each term, to visit the viewing center or centers whose papers he is handling, and interview his students personally.

Finally, each viewing center should be staffed by *one monitor*, who would keep enrollment and attendance records. He would also collect written work from students and forward it to the reader-teachers at headquarters, receive it back, and return it to the students. If this monitor had no training whatever as a teacher, he could still perform the necessary duties of monitor as long as he could read, write, and keep simple records. If he had any training (a village primary teacher, for example), he could discuss the lessons with students as far as his competence permitted, answer questions, write to headquarters on behalf of the group, and generally help students to a fuller understanding. But the ideal monitor might well be a young teacher-in-training, assigned to the job for a given period as part of the requirement for his certificate as a teacher. Such teacher-trainees would gain valuable experience, not only in doing the routine mechanical work that is part of all teachers' duties, but most importantly in being able to observe daily the classroom techniques of the best teachers in the country.

What Advantages Would This System Offer?

The first and most obvious advantage is that such an arrangement would make the fullest possible use of the extremely limited supply of trained teachers. Although the top level of the teaching profession in a country might be relatively small, each of its most expert teachers could teach effectively several hundred, or several thousand, students instead of the usual thirty or forty. It could make maximum use of the larger, though still limited, group of teachers who have somewhat less training and skill, by enabling them as reader-teachers to work with 300 or 400 students apiece. Furthermore—and I think this is of considerable importance— each of these teachers would be teaching one subject, the one he knows best; he would not be trying to handle all the various subjects that are studied in a given grade, as happens in most conventional school systems, or all that are taught at all levels as was done in the old-fashioned one-room schoolhouse. The students would have, for each subject and at each level, the help of the best-qualified group of teachers of that subject in the country.

If trainees were used as monitors while they were still studying for their certificates, the country would not only be making good use of their talents, but would be giving them at the same time valuable training, both in observation and in many elements of practice-teaching. But it should be remembered that the monitor's job does not require pedagogical training; there is no shortage of untrained manpower anywhere, and some of it could well be started on the road to greater self-development in such work.

One of the big advantages, it seems to me, would be a great saving in the time required to build a broad base of citizens with a secondary education. Television teaching is efficient: It has been reliably estimated, for example, that a half-hour television lesson, even when not followed by written work and a teacher's comment on that work, gives the equivalent educational result of from one to two hours in a conventional classroom. Since the number who can be taught simultaneously is limited only by the number of receivers the government is willing to buy, no child or adult need be told he must wait until there is room for him in a conventional school. And since educational broadcasting hours can be adjusted to the work schedule of communities, and particularly to the seasonal requirements of agriculture, the educational development of the whole country need not be retarded by the inability of many people to take part.

The savings in money should be obvious, particularly in a country where the most costly part of such a program (the initial investment in setting up a television broadcasting service) has already been made, as it has in many countries with the most grave educational problems. Whatever might be spent on teachers' salaries and on teaching materials would yield a greater return in educational development, because it would be used by more people. The cost of each community viewing center would be principally the salary of the monitor and the provision and servicing of the television receiver. This would total considerably less than the equipping and staffing, with both teachers and caretakers, of a conventional school building to do a comparable job.

And the value to the community would be greater. Since these viewing centers would be open during educational broadcasting hours to the entire community, and not merely to children, they could provide an environment in which adults would feel that it was quite natural for them to study whatever subjects they were ready for. The encouragement and the opportunity to go on with education after having become literate, for example, would be constantly there, in a way it can never be in a conventional school designed for children only. Since the viewing center would be the natural repository for all supplied textbooks, it could just as naturally become the nucleus for a community library of books for general reading. There is no pedagogical reason why the receiver should not be used at least occasionally for programs outside the school curriculum. The screen could be a window on the world, through which the whole community could derive pleasure as well as knowledge, and the opportunity of sharing both with their neighbors.

No one should suggest that any developing country relax its efforts to train more and better teachers, to give them more effective teaching aids, to widen and strengthen the curriculum, and in general to work toward building as comprehensive a system of education as possible, with the highest academic standards. But to do it by trying to build a conventional system means throwing away the talents and potential production of at least a generation of untrained adults; it also means offering some educational opportunity, for many years, to only a fraction of the youths. Women and girls, working boys, farming families, people in isolated communities generally, and even masses in city slums will simply have to wait indefinitely. It is just not possible to offer them good conventional schools, and it will not be possible for many years.

A television-correspondence school, on the other hand, could bring the services of the best teachers in the country to these people now. The whole people could move forward at the same speed as the fortunate children who live in cities where good schools and good teachers may already exist. In Italy and the United States, the performance of students taught by means of television is almost exactly the same as that of those who are taught the same subjects in full-time conventional schools. In Stratford-on-Avon, students who receive instruction in physics *from* the television screen have consistently done better in examinations than those who sit in the classroom *with* the television teacher.

By comparison with what can be hoped for in hundreds of villages which cannot possibly, for a number of years, be all staffed with highly skilled teachers and all equipped with good educational materials, I believe the results would be even more favorable in the developing world.

SIX

TOWARD
BETTER
HEALTH

22. NEW DIRECTIONS FOR PUBLIC HEALTH

ABEL WOLMAN

ABOUT a half-century ago, Dr. Biggs of New York coined the happy phrase that "Public Health Is Purchasable." The public health worker has rested upon this appealing and convincing aphorism as his principal guide to action. In the United States, with at least high material resources, accompanied increasingly by a matching public health conscience, the guide was and is reasonable and effective. Here, competition for money among functional requirements is ever present, but certainly less acute and stringent than in many other countries.

The place that health activity should take is reasonably assured. Services are theoretically at least in balance, even though not yet fully meeting all requirements in perfect mathematical adjustment. Appraisals will continue in order to make the best use of increasing funds. Such evaluation should be a necessary daily task of health officer, medical practitioner, nurse, and engineer.

This relatively happy application of the Biggs formula, however, encounters difficulty when one moves into the international field, in general, and into less developed countries, in particular. There we increasingly find severely limited national resources of both manpower and money and stressful competition for even those limited resources. In the social revolution in which we now live, it is not only bread that man demands, but good health, transport, industry, power, houses, schools, and recreation. And he is unwilling to wait for these amenities when they are provided at much too leisurely a pace.

The implications for the health worker in this new arena of competition are manifest. The scene confronting him is well exemplified, with a minimum of statistical boredom, in the following excerpts from a comment early in 1961 by Dr. Mani, Director of the WHO regional office in New Delhi. With minor adjustments, the observations are equally applicable to millions of people elsewhere.

His comments, quoted from *World Health*, January–February, 1961, are:

> The health problems of South East Asia are as vast as our region itself, which must support 560 million people, about 80 per cent of whom live on the land. India alone has half a million villages. Merely to put one simple sanitary well with a small hand pump into each of these villages would cost 70 million dollars. This is three and a half times what WHO will spend on its work throughout the world during 1961.
>
> In spite of facts like these, despite competing calls on slender resources, and despite the crippling shortage of trained workers, the governments of this region can be proud of the health progress that has been made in recent years against such heavy odds. But they, and we of the South East Asia Office of WHO, must measure successes always against what remains to be done. For instance, we can tell ourselves, with some pride, that about 256 million people in our region are protected against malaria by insecticide spraying. But we know that this is little more than half the number who live in malarious places. In the whole of this great region there were in 1959 only 40 reported cases of typhus and not a single death from the disease. But in the same year two countries yielded a total of 22,600 cholera cases, resulting in almost 6,000 deaths. The diagnosed number of leprosy cases in five regional countries is around 380,000. But at the back of all our planning is the knowledge that careful estimates put the actual number at more than two million.

The Need for "Illumination of Choices"

Whether one likes it or not, public health work is being and will be subjected to tests for justification. If these are not made by the health worker, then they will be made, certainly and reasonably enough, by the political statesman, the economist, the sociologist, or the anthropologist. The primary question is a simple one: does health work pay? and its corollary, in what coinage?

The issue may be met in two ways—by sheer resentment at the insult of asking whether peoples' lives should be saved, or by testing present and prospective action by such criteria as may be conjured up or conscientiously developed. Historically, the prevention of disease and the promotion of health have been considered both "necessary and good." After all, what is a country but a collection of people, for whom one desires a higher standard of living? What more valuable resource can a country develop than its human one? These rhetorical questions undoubtedly satisfy the idealist, the humanitarian, even the politician—until one reaches the poverty-stricken minister of finance.

He who is responsible for the distribution of money lives in a world of scarcity, regardless of social or political ideology. He is daily confronted with the necessity for making choice and giving priority. In his search for the "illumination of choices" (so apt a phrase of Eugene R. Black's, in *The Diplomacy of Economic Development*) he turns to, among others, the health officer.

The professional follower of Aesculapius and Hygeia, once he has recovered his equilibrium, rushes to the humanitarian justification of saving lives per se. He invokes the modern image of that great Christian Dr. Schweitzer, bearing the torch of humanity for all to see.

Or he equates lives saved or debilitation rescued into the coin of the realm, by less than convincing dollars, yen, or rupees, while the countries are already overwhelmed with surplus mouths to feed.

In self-defense, he also falls back on the social significance of disease reduction and the creation of self-respecting vital citizens.

As to the impact of his efforts upon the economic progress of his country, hitherto he has contented himself with the generalization that a healthy people make a healthy nation—and, axiomatically, a healthy nation makes a prosperous nation. Pushed to this final wall of economic pursuit, he wishes some benevolent goddess would exorcise the pursuing economic devil.

The arguments here presented and gravely oversimplified will not be sufficient in their strength and perhaps even in their validity to stand the necessary tests for the "illumination of choices." Competition for money, people, and time will increasingly press for new appraisals in the health field. Not the least of these pressures is already coming from people throughout the world who feel strongly that the promised land to be sighted in 1990 is too far away. The health worker, never a peddler of panaceas, does have the obligation, however, of confronting himself with a new and pressing world in which his budget dollar must be stretched over the areas of greatest promise and potential. The political, emotional, and leisurely devotion to functions of least dividends cannot and must not be eliminated, but it must be realistically evaluated, probably reduced, and certainly reoriented. Essentially, reappraisal does mean a recognition that public health work as now practiced will not remain so sacred that it cannot be questioned or assessed.

Western policy and practice may or may not be valuable guides for undeveloped countries. Close scrutiny for adaptation is obviously required. It is surprising, however, that long-tested principles and practices evolved in the western world have been so often ignored by western workers because they have erroneously assumed that such practices are "culture-bound" only to the United States, as Henry C. Bush pointed out in the INTERNATIONAL DEVELOPMENT REVIEW of October, 1960.

The lesson, hitherto emphasized by some cultural anthropologists, that indigenous cultures should be respected and hence untouched has been too well learned by our exported western professional. As a matter of fact, almost every modern precept of public health activity requires a cultural change. Even the introduction of the lowly privy requires significant change in ancient habit and custom. In change, intelligently adjusted to the national soil, lies the future hope of real public health progress. Fortunately, experience is teaching us that change does occur with surprising rapidity of acceptance.

The status quo, culturally, politically, and economically, need not be sustained in the field of health. What reorientations in public health planning and practice should emerge in the immediate future? These might well be in some contrast, at least, with the past, so as to produce more significant values more rapidly in each country.

One of the prime objectives of the world statesman today is to raise the standard of living of each country to a level of modern decency. Many routes need to be traveled to accomplish this. Time, in these days, cannot be too long in building and strengthening such routes. In what way does or can the health worker facilitate this aim? The facile offer to provide healthy people, of all ages, everywhere and for every purpose, falls by the weight of its own generalization. Neither money, time, nor personnel are anywhere visible for many decades to come to accomplish all these objectives simultaneously. Again, whether he likes it or not, he must choose to avoid "devauling the public health dollar" (to borrow another phrase from Mr. Black). Some of these adjustments in choice are discussed here.

The Appraisal of Public Health Necessities

Where a country has all diseases—or as one wise doctor expressed it, "You name it, and we have it!"—some may consider it a waste of time to choose among them. In reality, in such a case, selection is a necessity, not a luxury. Without selection, men and money resources will be dissipated.

Although many examples of conscious choice may certainly be listed, many more are at hand where program is more amoeboid than specifically oriented. Repetition of historically fixed policy is simpler than, but not synonymous with, selection.

If criticism forces stock-taking, then it should be welcomed. It is surprising how few truly systematic health surveys have been carried out in the world as prerequisites to continuing action. (See Karl Evang's *Health Service, Society and Medicine* [New York: Oxford University Press, 1960.])

The Rural Fixation

In almost every country, the tacit policy has been to focus the use of scarce public health forces upon the village. An intriguing essay might be written upon the definitions of village, for it varies from country to country. It appears to have little relation to density or geometry of living. In some countries, it was once legally defined as concentrations of people numbering less than 5,000. Later, this figure was raised to 10,000 to make such groups eligible for central public works grants.

In many so-called villages, the density of living is as high as in the Pittsburgh metropolitan area. Perhaps the only common denominators of such population groups are their vast number, their agricultural pursuits, and their great geographical scatter and often equally great inaccessibility to centers of government. The most significant feature is the emotional devotion in every country to the "rural problem"—a compound of nostalgic heritage and political sensitivity.

It is discussed here primarily because this focus on the rural, to the literal exclusion of the urban, is still emphasized in the present era of unprecedented urbanization and industrialization throughout the world. The choice of the rural battleground for disease prevention is a choice of the most difficult possible logistics. It runs contrary to all precedent of public health history in assuming that sanitary practices move from the farm to the city. The choice of using the public health dollar for the minimum return could not have been more aptly made.

Does this mean that one can ignore the rural peoples? It certainly does not! But, within the framework of scarcity of men and money, the urban area offers the greatest return in reduction of disease per unit of energy and ultimately the greatest source of inspiration to the village. Such urban emphasis is long in arrears. It should not exclude the rural, but it should not be overshadowed by it—as has been the case in many countries.

The wide use of the general term "rural" deserves a detailed scrutiny when public health or any other strategy is being planned. The professional geographer perhaps has a greater awareness than the health officer of the wide variation in density of living in rural areas, even in a single province or state. The classification "rural" conceals vast differences in environmental influences, all of which are essential determinants of public health policy.

Professor Ahmad of the University of Ranchi, India, makes this view abundantly clear in a recent paper on "The Rural Population of Bihar." The distinction is marked between high degree of rural crowding and sparse living, with density categories running from under 300 to over 1500 per square mile. The higher figures approach or exceed those of many metropolitan areas in the United States. The salient question is whether the health officer ever teams up with the geographer.

The Inevitable Restriction by Centralism

One of the major restraints upon public health services lies in the deadening hand of central government. Here, I speak not of political or ideological aspects of centralism, but primarily of the almost universal concentration of sources of money, policy, and management in the capitals of great and small countries. The historical bases for such central responsibility are clear—and they served their purposes well in the evolution of society.

Today, the central government is increasingly burdened by the multiplication of local requirements. Twenty-five years ago the central government was responsible for four or five functions at most. Today, in one typical advancing country, this number now exceeds thirty.

Rehabilitation of local autonomy and responsibility is particularly essential in health work, if for no other reason than that central government resources are rapidly becoming scarcer and scarcer. The public health claim on them runs increasingly into competition with other functions, many of which do not lend themselves too easily to local decision, finance, and effectuation.

The latent strength of local support is surprisingly great, if intelligently tapped and persistently nurtured. Excellent examples of such potentials are beginning to appear in some countries—for example, India and parts of South America. The health officer's awareness of these opportunities is perhaps the key to his future success. It is more than an easy aphorism that local initiative thrives upon encouragement and recognition.

The Evaluation of Economic Impact

One of the most difficult tasks now confronting the international worker is to assay the effect of his activities upon the economic advance of a country or a region. Standards and criteria for such appraisals are difficult to come by, whether in education, health, or agricultural pursuits. That economic impact must remain a significant element in programs, however, should be reasonably self-evident.

Resistance to measuring health work in particular by its assumed or real influence upon the economy of a society stems, of course, from man's continued insistence upon saving lives and strengthening people as a just measure of the general dignity of man. It is not incompatible with human dignity, however, to measure accomplishment in a less than utopian world, in part by the raising of living standards.

Difficult as this area of inquiry may be, adventures into it, in the immediate future, will proceed apace. Measurements will evolve, relative values will emerge, and public health practice will be oriented in part to enhancing the total productivity of society.

A necessary consequence will undoubtedly be the development of more imaginative and ingenious devices for the financing of public health programs. Many of these lag or fall by the wayside because their self-supporting and self-generating fiscal features have remained static for a century. Their failures are not always due to limited local resources. Often the latter are untapped.

Influence Upon the Structure of Government.

A word must be added on the significant values a health officer may contribute to the strengthening of the socio-political organization of a country. This is possible, however, only if he is aware that the mechanisms at his command can and should be used to stimulate local consciousness and responsibility. The federal or state health officer, for example, who uses the grant-in-aid only as a gracious political largesse, misses the subtle opportunity of using this same device to stimulate local growth, to elevate standards of performance, and to entice local financial resources into increasing support for health services.

The creation of voluntary or official mechanisms can result from an imaginative health officer's awareness of the significance of permanent social organization. Unfortunately, examples of such influences upon government are not many. They must be multiplied, because without them public health progress unfortunately will be too slow.

Patterson, an astute observer of the Latin American scene, phrases the situation well when he says the provinces "must cut the umbilical cord to the nation's capital."

23. MORTALITY RATES AND ECONOMIC DEVELOPMENT

HARALD FREDERIKSEN, M.D.

THE death rate in Ceylon declined from 19.8 to 14.0 per 1,000, or 29 per cent, in the year 1946–47. Being most abrupt, this decline in the death rate has given rise to postulations that advances in public health techniques permit significant reductions in the death rate, independently of economic development. Thus, the application of public health measures would increase the rate of population growth and thereby reduce the per capita income, assuming that the birth rate remains constant and economic development lags. Frequently cited,[1-5] such postulations may have been accepted as descriptive of the relationship between health and economic development in underdeveloped areas. However, these hypothetical determinants and consequences of mortality trends in Ceylon are not confirmed by the sequence of events.

It was once accepted that control of malaria, through the application of insecticides, was primarily responsible for the postwar reduction in the death rate in Ceylon. This conclusion is not confirmed by the findings that the most precipitous decline in mortality had preceded large-scale application of insecticides and that the decline in mortality in the malarious area and the unprotected, nonmalarious area of the island had been about the same.[6] Indeed, the net demographic effect of malaria control, which has made a major part of the island habitable, may be a reduction in population pressure.

The death rate of Ceylon has displayed a long-term downtrend, despite a step-by-step improvement in the reporting of deaths. The downtrend was interrupted in 1935, when a disastrous drought resulted in a sharp rise in mortality. A semilogarithmic plot of the

EDITOR'S NOTE: Notes corresponding to reference numbers in the text will be found at the end of the chapter.

death rates for the quarters of the years since the great drought in 1935 through 1957 indicates a constant rate of decline in the quarterly death rates, with a wartime interruption of the down-trend and a postwar return to the prewar downtrend. It seems the wartime rise in mortality, rather than the postwar decline, may have been the notable event.

The wartime rise in mortality suggests that circumstances arising from the war may have exacerbated one of the major public health problems. Malnutrition and malaria have been ranked as the two foremost health problems in Ceylon. Having ruled out malaria control as the primary cause of the postwar decline in mortality, the level of nutrition was examined for fluctuations that may have influenced the death rate to rise during the war and return to the long-term downtrend following the war.

It was found that the wartime rise from 1943 to 1946 and the postwar decline in the death rate were associated with the development and alleviation of a wartime food deficit. The timing and extent of the deficit are indicated by the wartime decline in food imports, which represented the principal source of food for Ceylon. The existence of reserves might have delayed any significant effects of the decline in food imports in 1942 until 1943. Following the war, food imports rose and by 1947 exceeded the prewar level. The extent of wartime malnutrition and postwar recovery is indicated by the significant increase in weights of school children—boys and girls at all age levels from six to eighteen years—between 1945 and 1950.

Although extraordinary events, such as drought or war, have been accompanied by marked deviations from the long-term trend of the death rates, attempts to isolate and measure the effects of specific causes of death or specific measures of survival on the trend of the death rates may be futile or fallacious, at least until the reporting of specific causes of death and indices of economic development provide more specific, accurate, complete, and comparable data. Since data are lacking to exclude the effects of all other factors, the precise or even relative importance of the wartime food shortage as a cause of death cannot be conclusively established. Nevertheless, the available data support consideration of malnutrition as a factor in the wartime rise in the death rate.

The relationship between mortality trends and level of living, at least in the phase of transition in Ceylon, may be indicated by a comparison of the trend of mortality and the per capita allocation of gross national product for personal consumption at constant prices. Although comparable data are lacking for the war years, it is evident that personal consumption and mortality rates have displayed an inverse association, as shown in the accompanying table.

MORTALITY AND ECONOMIC INDICES, CEYLON, 1938 AND 1947–57

Year	Mortality		Per capita indices at constant prices (1938)*					
	Rate per 1,000	Index	Personal consumption	Government expenditures		Remittances abroad	Gross capital formation	Gross national product
				Health	Other			
1938	21.0	100	100	100	100	100	100	100
1947	14.0	67	146	99	113	46	110	120
1948	13.0	62	141	130	113	51	137	129
1949	12.4	59	146	140	123	46	213	132
1950	12.4	59	149	141	125	59	225	148
1951	12.7	60	191	143	108	67	372	183
1952	11.8	56	200	171	121	67	400	175
1053	10.7	51	187	172	133	46	351	167
1954	10.2	49	173	175	131	46	309	173
1955	10.8	51	187	173	135	56	378	188
1956	9.8	47	178	186	164	57	412	180
1957	10.1	48	185	198	162	49	393	173

* Based on the cost of living index.

SOURCES: Statistical Abstracts of Ceylon and Reports of the Registrar General on Vital Statics, Ceylon.

Improvements in the whole range of economic indices were more or less concurrent with the decline in the death rate. Comparisons of the direction and timing of changes in economic indices in the table suggest sectors that have been leading or lagging in the transition. Thus, in 1947, when the death rate had returned from a wartime peak to the previous downtrend, per capita consumption at constant prices had risen sharply above the level of 1938, whereas per capita health expenditures had remained at the level of 1938. In subsequent years, per capita health expenditures and personal consumption rose concurrently with the decline in the death rate. Moreover, as remittances abroad were curtailed, the rate of capital formation was increased to a remarkable extent. Capital formation at the rate of 12 and 13 per cent of the gross national product, such as occurred in five of the seven years 1951–57 inclusive, exceeds the rate of investment in most underdeveloped countries and compares favorably with that in Europe.

If the sequence of events in Ceylon had demonstrated that economic development is no longer a prerequisite for a decline in the death rate, it might have seemed plausible to postulate that modern public health measures would tend to reduce per capital income as well as mortality, with the possible inference that per capita income would rise with a rise in mortality. But the postulation of such consequences of mortality trends is not confirmed by the experience of Ceylon, where a decline in mortality has been associated with development of the economy and rise in the level of living.

The question remains whether a decline in the birth rate will follow the rise in the level of living and the decline in the death rate, or whether there will be a fundamental difference in the interaction of economic and demographic transition in Ceylon and the West. In the course of western civilization, a decline in mortality has been observed as a concomitant of the rise in per capita income and as a precursor of the decline in the birth rate.[1,2,4,5] There have been some doubts whether a similar relationship between the death rates and birth rates will be observed in underdeveloped areas, where postwar reductions in mortality had been considered to be exclusively or largely the result of specific public health measures and quite independent of economic development.[4,5]

The birth rate of Ceylon has declined from a postwar peak of 39.8 to 35.8 per 1,000 population in 1958, when the districts of Ceylon displayed considerable variation in the level of the birth rates. In 1958, the birth rates in the districts ranged from 53.6 to 25.4.

Data for the twenty-one districts of Ceylon suggest a relationship between the level of the death rates and the subsequent level of the birth rates. Comparison of the death rates in 1938 and the birth rates in 1958 demonstrates a remarkable correlation. Low death rates or conditions underlying low death rates merit consideration as contributory factors, if not as prerequisites, for low birth rates.

At this time, the districts of Ceylon with the lowest birth rates are characterized by the greatest density of population or urbanization, the highest literacy rates, and the highest mean age of females at marriage, as well as the lowest death rates. Reductions in the birth rate may be experienced in all districts of Ceylon as the factors underlying the lower birth rates in some of the districts are extended island-wide.

The associations between economic and demographic indices suggest cause-and-effect relationships. However, postulation of the precise nature or direction of the causal relationships may tend to be an oversimplification of a complex process of interaction between multiple causes and multiple effects. Improvement in one index of economic or demographic transition may tend to be associated with improvement in all indices through a process of concurrent and cumulative causation. Thus, economic and demographic transition may tend to be parts of an integral system in which arbitrary indices of welfare and well-being may be mere aspects of one underlying reality.

NOTES

1. *The Determinants and Consequences of Population Trends*, Population Studies No. 17 (New York: United Nations, 1953).

2. E. E. Hagen, "Population and Economic Growth," *American Economic Review*, June, 1959, pp. 310–27.

3. "World-wide War on Malaria," Population Bulletin, Population Reference Bureau (Washington, D.C.: March, 1958).

4. A. J. Coale and E. M. Hoover, *Population Growth and Economic Development in Low Income Countries* (Princeton: Princeton University Press, 1958).

5. F. Osborn, "This Crowded World," Public Affairs Pamphlet No. 306 (New York: Public Affairs Committee, 1960).

6. H. Frederiksen, "Malaria Control and Population Pressure in Ceylon," Public Health Rep. 75, October, 1960, pp. 865–68.

SEVEN

AGRICULTURE AND INDUSTRY

24. ESSENTIALS OF LAND REFORM

ROBERT W. HUDGENS

IN no way is oversimplification more often manifested than in plans for redistribution of land. This arises from a mistaken concept of the nature of agrarian reform. The plain facts are that we are dealing with social revolution of broad proportions, that we can guide that social revolution into quiet waters only by placing under it a firm economic base, and that the base must be firm in all its parts. The job cannot be done in unrelated segments or by the half measures to which oversimplification inevitably leads.

True agrarian reform lies not in the revolutionary redistribution of land, but in the evolutionary process by which people find security on the land. It involves not merely the cravings of land-hungry people, but the whole complex problem of rural insecurity. We are concerned, therefore, with agrarian reform as a process of advancing rural security. In most countries, the term "agrarian reform" already has the connotation of rural security. In all the proposed legislation now pending in Latin America, the two appear to be synonymous.

Redistribution of land will be necessary in many areas, but it is not the main emphasis. In most of Latin America, for example, the chief unresolved factor is not the availability of land; there is enough unused and underused land to feed a realistic program of agrarian reform for the next decade.

In my opinion, there are at least four factors that must be resolved in each country before it is clear whether, how, or to what extent land is to be redistributed.

The chief unresolved factor is how to introduce capital into the process. The only way to provide capital prior to capital accumulation is through credit. And the only safe way to introduce credit to farmers who lack managerial ability is in combination with "managerial" assistance, that is to say, with technical assistance. Credit adequate for rural development has special characteristics, and it is a doubtful assumption that bankers instinctively understand them. One of the most interesting phenomena in the world of finance is how bankers appear to consider rural credit as abnormal commercial credit instead of normal rural credit.

Credit to support agrarian reform must be based on productive potential and not limited to a margin of security. Rural credit consists of credit not merely for production, but also for the services on which the farmer depends. None of these must be left to chance, for the farmer's success often depends less on his own efforts than on services over which he has no control.

The second unresolved factor is how to apply subsidy to support the initial stages of agrarian reform. In a broad rural security program, there are certain things that a country must do for itself and certain others with which it will need help. Similarly, there are certain things that a farmer must do for himself and certain things that must be done for him if he is to succeed. Those things that farmers or nations cannot do for themselves must be subsidized, and the effective application of this subsidy is not softness in an otherwise sound approach, but realism in what will otherwise be failure.

The capital being channeled into rural areas over the next decade must have its own built-in social concept, and that concept must encompass land-people adjustment. The key to the concept is the philosophy under which subsidy is applied to promote social justice in economic development. Let me explain what I mean.

In terms of rural security and promotion of rural development, the U.S.A. Farm Security Administration was one of the biggest agrarian reform programs ever undertaken prior to World War II. It was built entirely around a specialized system of credit and the the realistic use of subsidy in the form of technical assistance and community services and facilities.

FSA had a special interest in the social aspects of rural security. The idea of subsidy in rural development was not new, but FSA changed its form somewhat and made it available to a new group.

In 1939, on one of my field trips as Associate Administrator of FSA, I visited in succession Taylor County, Wisconsin, and Green County, Georgia. I remember one case in each that is typical of one of the basic causes of rural insecurity and of the cruel form of subsidy that forces one family's sacrifice for another family's success.

In Taylor County, a young farmer with a family had agreed to buy from the lumber company 50 acres of cut-over land, with 5 acres cleared and a log house. He was to get it rent-free for the first three-years, and at the end of the third year, he was to make his first payment of $150. During that time, he could farm rent-free all the land he could clear of stumps and brush.

At the time of my visit, the end of the third year had arrived, but the farmer had cleared only 19 acres and could not raise the $150. When I asked him about the future, he said, "I have made another deal with another lumber company for 50 acres, only it already has 20 acres cleared." The agricultural agent later said that the same process would probably be repeated—the young farmer would clear another 20 acres that would still not be enough for an economic unit.

In Green County, a young farmer told me he was doing very well because he had bought his farm for the unpaid debt of the previous owner, who had started by buying the larger unpaid debt of the prior owner. The agricultural agent explained that this farmer had been subsidized by two previous bankruptcies and would undoubtedly succeed.

I reckon from my fourteen years' observations with FSA that 80 per cent of the farms of the United States were partially subsidized in this manner—two bankruptcies, and frequently two families ruined, before the third succeeded. Except where there was irrigation, in the vast majority of those cases the bondholders' investment also was lost and went into the subsidy.

In FSA, we undertook to learn what would be required for the *first* family to succeed, and our findings furnish the basis for budgeting agrarian reform for practically any Latin American country. In any country, serious attempts at agrarian reform must begin with the question, "How much will be required in credit and subsidy for the *first* families to stick?"

Let me list the five services and facilities that stand at the top of the list: *Security of tenure*, either ownership or long-term lease, either directly or through an operating cooperative. *Land ready to be farmed*, that is, already cleared. *Credit that fits the farmer's needs*, in terms both of type of credit and of technical assistance. *Roads, access to market, schools*, and other community facilities. The latter may be acquired gradually, but the point is that they cannot be financed by the income from the small farms. *An agricultural extension service* to promote general improvement of the country's agriculture, including research and market promotion.

— Subsidy both to the farmer for his deficit needs and to the country for its general program is merely delayed payment for raw materials and agricultural products brought out at bargain prices to subsidize industrial development elsewhere. There is a corollary to the law of cause and effect which should say that if raw materials and bargain-priced agricultural products are taken from a colonial area and an equal amount of capital in some form is not put back, then the *people* will come out or the whole place will explode.

Let us identify the immediate needs that must be met from outside. The greatest need is a dependable source of credit from regional or international credit agencies *earmarked for rural development*. The next great need that must be imported is technical assistance to credit institutions, so that they in turn can provide technical assistance to farmers. An arrangement, practicable from every point of view, would be for regional banks, such as the Inter-American Development Bank, to provide technical assistance to local banks and to rediscount loans made by local banks to farmers and processors of agricultural products.

The third essential factor in a land reform program is to discover an appropriate method of compensating landowners for land taken up in agrarian reform—which is another way of saying, to establish a method of converting lifeless capital now invested in underused land into more productive enterprises. This is not a matter of helping out the landlord, but of converting capital into a more dynamic form for use elsewhere in the economy. Underused land represents billions of dollars of stagnant capital that ought to be reinvested in some form faster than can be done by agricultural production.

All the Latin American countries now considering agrarian reform are trying to arrive at some realistic method of financing land purchase, and most of them are contemplating the use of bond issues for this purpose. Unfortunately, there has been no organized attempt by any of the international agencies to arrive at a plan that might serve as the typical pattern or as the starting point for each country's consideration. I suggest that a realistic scheme should include payments to be made partly in cash and partly in bonds due at regular intervals of, say, five, ten, and fifteen years. I suggest that central banks in countries having land reform programs form a pool participated in by the Inter-American Development Bank to support at least partial negotiability of these bonds on a regional basis so that the bonds might be exchanged for capital stock of industrial enterprises. When that is done and credit for production and for expanding small units is available, then credit for land purchase on a larger scale will have to be made available.

Finally, the fourth and overriding factor still unresolved in most countries is how to administer agrarian reform so that no essential service is left to chance—that is, so that all essential services are subordinate to the main objective.

Too often, the agrarian institute controls only the distribution of land, and credit is left to the whims of the bankers. Agrarian reform programs are more often sabotaged by the so-called orthodoxy of the credit system than by the lack of available land. Too often, new settlers and their produce are left stranded by unconcerned planning of roads and markets.

The guiding principles of sound administration are clear:

1. Control of land distribution and control of credit must be under the same authority. Invasion of new lands, unguided by sound family selection and technical planning and unsupported by credit, will produce only failure.

2. These must be closely coordinated with control of the subsidy for roads, clinics, and other facilities.

3. The operation must be sound from a technical point of view; that is, the technical staff must be competent, for security on the land is rooted literally in the soundness of the farming operation.

4. Within these guiding principles, administrative procedure must be flexible. A common error is to write into agrarian legislation details of procedure that should properly be left to the judgment of technicians and administrators. Each successful agrarian reform program with which I am familiar has properly changed in pattern as it progressed. The unsuccessful programs are often explainable by overdetailed planning.

Rural security is not something that planners can take or leave. A noted economist, speaking of rural development, recently said: "Hopes for development and for capital on which to grow will not materialize unless they improve their agricultural performance. There is no country now making progress that is not doing so."

This is another way of saying that the nations of the world now struggling with poverty and its dire fruits, with social revolution and threats of violence, are paying the penalty of having squandered the human and natural resources of their rural areas and having failed to create a function for unused and underused land and for their restless and underemployed people.

25. *MODERN SMALL INDUSTRY*

EUGENE STALEY

LARGE factories are a characteristic feature of a modern industrial economy, but they are not the whole of it. Not all manufacturing is more economical on a large than on a small scale, even in countries where markets are wide and industrial technology most advanced. In the United States, more than 90 per cent of the manufacturing establishments have fewer than 100 employees. These relatively small factories employ 26 per cent of all manufacturing employees and produce 22 per cent of the total value added by manufacture. In Japan, nearly 60 per cent of manufacturing employment is in establishments with fewer than 100 employees.

Development planners in most newly industrializing countries have paid too little attention to the benefits to be gained by helping existing small industry to modernize and by stimulating the growth of new, modern small industry. Often the attitude is that small-scale manufacturing is an inevitably backward and lagging part of the economy, perhaps to be aided for social reasons and in a rather defensive or protective spirit, but not to be regarded as a promising opportunity for development. A latent resource has thus been overlooked and neglected.

Lately, however, many countries have shown interest in developing a modern type of small industry. Among the countries that the United Nations classes as "underdeveloped," India has by all odds the largest, most comprehensive, and the best planned program. Japan, at a further stage of industrialization, has evolved a wide array of measures. The United States has an active Small Business Administration, which supplements many aids provided through other public institutions and through the private business system. The Scandinavian countries, the Netherlands, Germany, the United Kingdom, France, and other European countries have adopted a variety of measures with different emphases, sometimes

283

focusing on the financial needs of small manufacturing units, sometimes on technological and managerial training and productivity improvement, sometimes on product design and marketing. In Puerto Rico, there is a very active industrial development program, and a large proportion of the enterprises assisted under it are small units. A number of Latin American countries—Mexico, Brazil, Colombia, and others—have special banking institutions designed to stimulate small industry, and also industrial development centers and productivity centers. Pakistan, the Philippines, and the Federation of Malaya are experimenting with techniques of small-industry promotion. Nor is attention to small industry confined to countries that favor private enterprise. Reports from mainland China indicate much emphasis on a nation-wide continuing campaign to establish and improve small, local manufacturing plants.

Types and Role in Development

One obstacle to clear thinking about the role of small industry in industrial development is the confusion over use of terms. To some, "small-scale" in manufacturing means establishments with fewer than 10 persons. To others, it means establishments having up to 500 or, for some purposes in some industries, 1,000 employees. In our program of small-industry development research at the Stanford Research Institute, we usually mean by "small industry" manufacturing establishments with fewer than 100 employees. We prefer, however, to think in terms of certain functional characteristics of small industry: relatively little specialization in management ("one-man" management); lack of access to capital through the organized securities market; no special bargaining strength in buying or selling in a major market; and often, though not always, a relatively close integration with the local community, through local ownership and management and dependence on nearby markets and sources of supply.

These characteristics give small industry certain disadvantages and certain special needs for types of advice and aid that are not so much needed by large manufacturing firms. They also confer some advantages, chief of which is flexibility. The close personal contact that "one-man" management makes possible between the top manager and production workers, customers, suppliers, and owners, can, if the manager is good, be a source of strength. This characteristic goes far to explain why, and in what kinds of manufacturing, modern small industry can compete successfully.

It is essential to distinguish a number of types of small industry, for these different types have very different prospects as a country transforms itself from a traditional preindustrial into a modern industrial economy.

One important distinction is that between traditional small industry and modern small industry—the latter defined as manufacturing units in which reasonably good application is made of the best science and technology currently available—it is *modern* small industry, or movement toward it, that holds promise for newly developing countries.

It is also important to distinguish between household industry, artisan industry, and small factories. Household industry is manufacturing carried on in or near the home, mainly by family labor. It is sometimes called cottage industry, although more properly this term might be reserved for rural household industry. This oldest form of manufacturing is still important in many countries striving to modernize, and undoubtedly it will continue to exist for a long time. But I believe that the long-term trend in developing economies will be for household industry to disappear, save for a few special functions. Among these are part-time supplementation of the income of farmers or mountain dwellers, as in Sweden and Switzerland; providing work for the handicapped; special types of handicraft; and leisure activities of an artistic or quasi-hobby sort. But for purposes of regular production of manufactured goods, the place of household industry in a modernized economy is and should be limited, for it is an inefficient method of production and is subject to social abuses that are practically impossible to control, such as low rates of pay, long hours, and child labor. Newly industrializing countries will do well to regard their household industries as a temporary form, to be supplanted over the long run by geographically decentralized small factories, artisan workshops located outside the home, and large factories.

Artisan industry is manufacturing carried on in workshops by craftsmen working singly or with a few hired helpers or apprentices and without extensive division of labor. The potters, weavers, blacksmiths, shoemakers, bakers, and other ancient crafts are examples of "old line" artisan industry. As an economy moves toward modern industrialism, the outlook for artisan-type activity is, on the whole, rather favorable. "New line" artisan activities arise with modern industry and modern technology. They may not involve manufacturing as such, but rather provision of services, as in automobile and truck maintenance, repair and servicing of radios and other electrical equipment, and photographic work. The rise of these new branches has belied predictions that were common a half-century ago, in the then industrializing countries of Europe, that factory competition would lead to the disappearance of the craftsman. The highly industrialized, modern economies of today seem, on the contrary, to be using increasing numbers of new types of craftsmen who supplement rather than compete with factory goods.

The long-term problem of the newly industrializing countries would therefore seem to be to help their artisans to adjust themselves to new functions. Village blacksmiths must learn to install and repair irrigation pumps and diesel engines, skilled weavers to concentrate on designs and qualities not readily reproducible by machine, shoemakers to turn to shoe repairing. Not all the old-line craftsmen will be able to make such adjustments, however; many of them, or their sons, must be guided into entirely new occupations (for example, as mechanics or electricians) for which the demand will rise as development proceeds.

The small factory is distinguished from artisan industry by its greater division of labor and the consequent need for planning and coordination. The manager, rather than the craftsman, becomes the central figure.

How can a small factory, lacking a staff of specialists and with limited access to capital, compete against large, highly organized, highly capitalized firms? The answer is that, while many small factories can and do compete successfully, others do not compete directly with large factories, but rather serve as a complement to them. Here are four ways in which the small factory can manage to coexist successfully with large industry:

1. It can outcompete large industry, in well-chosen products, in certain circumstances. The well-known economies of scale are much more important in blast furnaces and cement kilns than in the making of furniture or garments or machine tools. Bricks and tiles can be produced more economically in relatively small, local establishments than in a great central factory that would incur high shipping costs. Small manufacturing establishments have an advantage in meeting highly specialized or individualized demands or in catering to a small-volume market or one requiring frequent

quick adjustments because of style changes or for other reasons. Where labor and social laws are applied more stringently to large than to small plants, as is often the case, especially in newly industrializing countries, this may be a factor, whether or not a desirable one, in the competitive ability of small plants.

2. The small factory can "fill the cracks" between the large-volume, standardized outputs of large industry. Near Madras, India, I visited the thatched-roof factory of Rapid Cycles, a small firm with about 30 workers. Two years later, when I visited again, employment had grown to 100 workers and there was an excellent new building with modern equipment. Yet only a few miles away was the very large plant of T.I. Cycles, Ltd., manufacturing bicycles with the collaboration of a well-known British firm. How could the small enterprise compete so successfully? It was not, in fact, competing directly. Instead of the standard-size bicycle, it was producing a junior size, also tricycles and tricycle-mounted delivery carts. The proprietor said he had no difficulty selling all he could produce.

3. The small factory can produce components and supplies for large industry. One of the reasons for the efficiency of industry in the United States is that large plants integrate their production with the production of hundreds or even thousands of other plants, both large and small. The Ford Motor Company in a recent year purchased from an estimated 20,000 different suppliers, the United States Steel Corporation from 50,000, and the Eastman Kodak Company from 3,500. A large part of Japanese small industry produces on subcontract for large industry.

4. The small factory can initiate new products and sometimes grow with growth of the market for such products. Henry Ford and other pioneer automobile manufacturers started on a very small scale. The electronics industry today is bursting with small firms, as well as large ones, hopefully exploiting new ideas. In countries where industrial diversification is at an early stage, small-scale manufacturers may find opportunities in introducing products that are new to the country, though not necessarily new in the world.

Benefits of a Modern Small-Industry Sector

The policy implications of the preceding analysis may now be summed up.

First, development leaders in countries striving to accelerate the rate of industrial advancement will do well to give attention to the constructive possibilities in modernization and growth of the small-industry sector. A country will have the most productive industrial structure when it has an interwoven combination of large and small units, the place of each determined on the basis of economic efficiency.

Secondly, as a country moves through the transitional stage from a traditional toward a modern economy, the outlook is for household industry to be *replaced*, for artisan industry to be *transformed*, and for the small but modern factory to be *developed*.

Thirdly, in encouraging development of small factories, careful selection of suitable products and situations is essential. The suitability of a given product for small-scale manufacture will vary from country to country, from one part to another of the same country, and from time to time as the country develops. Provision for continuing analysis of specific technical and economic factors is therefore advisable in small-industry development programs.

Even in highly industrialized economies, small industry continues to play a significant and valuable role. In newly industrializing economies, the contribution of a vigorous, modernized small-industry sector, if such a sector is encouraged to develop, can be relatively even more important. The size of the market for nearly all kinds of manufactured goods is smaller. Markets are more broken up into relatively isolated sub-markets because of the comparatively inadequate development of transportation and communication. Also, there is likely to be a scarcity of people experienced in managing large operations, and among the workers, the habits of industrialized discipline necessary for the success of large-scale factories are likely to be less well established.

Industrializing countries that devise ways to encourage the modernization and growth of their small-industry sectors can thereby tap resources of capital, of entrepreneurship and managerial talent, and of labor that would otherwise not be effectively available. Perhaps the most important of these resources is entrepreneurship. An active, modern, small-industry sector should function as a seedbed of entrepreneurship, out of which will spring latent talent for organization and management, which may, in some cases, graduate into medium-scale and large industry.

Small industrial units may play a useful role in new regional development, industrial decentralization, and growth of rural or small-town industry. Vigorous growth of small industry can help to build a more truly competitive and less monopoly-ridden private sector, and this in turn reduces the burden on the government of having to regulate and watch the private sector in detail. There are sociological and political advantages in encouraging small modern industry, namely, the growth of a middle class of independent, smaller-scale businessmen. This is a desirable balancing element in a society that values democratic self-rule.

Designing a Small-Industry Development Program

Suppose that the responsible officials of a country in the course of development want to initiate a program to encourage modernization and growth of small industry, or perhaps to supplement and integrate a number of more or less uncoordinated measures already under way, so as to achieve a revitalized small-industry program. Three guidelines can be suggested.

1. The program should not be modeled directly on that of any other country. Basic conditions affecting small-industry opportunities and needs vary considerably from country to country, as do government policies, the accepted roles of the public and private sectors of the economy and relationships between them, administrative traditions and capacities, and the existence of public or private organizations capable of carrying out development programs. Hence, each country requires a program tailor-made in general approach and in details to fit its own situation. Suggestive ideas from many countries should, however, be sought; some of these may be taken over, but always with appropriate adaptations. The annotated bibliography and the directory of organizations listed in the references that follow this article will be helpful in this connection.

2. A small-industry development program should be reasonably comprehensive. Usually, it does little good merely to set up an institution charged with making capital and credit more readily available to industry without, for example, doing anything to improve techniques of production and management. An action program, to be effective, must simultaneously push outward on a considerable number of limiting factors. Which factors are most strategic in the circumstances of a particular country must be determined by preliminary study. Usually the limiting factors so revealed will be multiple, and the action program will need to be

a broad, integrated one, so that each kind of assistance reinforces the other kinds and is reinforced by them. Also, the need to provide for the following services or functions should be considered, and the relative urgency and feasibility of the necessary action should be evaluated:

A favorable environment for industrial growth
Advisory services and managerial training services
Industrial research services
Measures to improve small-industry financing
Common-facility service centers
Industrial estates
Marketing aids
Contracts and assistance by large firms
Government purchases
Quality control systems
Improved procurement of materials and equipment
Consolidation and cooperatives
Mutual self-help through industrial associations

3. Responsibility for developing and coordinating the small-industry program should be placed in one administrative agency, whose head should be granted the authority and budget to enable him to elicit the cooperation of other organizations. Preferably, this agency should be charged solely with the task of promoting the development of small (or small and medium-scale) industry. If this is not practicable (and it may not be in a small country, especially where administrative and technical personnel are in short supply), the responsibility for small-industry development should at least be given organizational expression in a special division of a broader development agency. Small industry has problems and needs that are somewhat different from those of large industry. Also, where an administrative agency is charged with advancing industry of all sizes, the problems of small industry are likely to be neglected.

The initial program, if it is at all extensive, should include a built-in provision for staff training, especially a regular system of in-service training by means of seminars, conferences, and occasional study tours abroad. There should also be built-in provision for periodical, or even continuous, evaluation of the program as a whole and of its principal methods and activities. These provisions will facilitate correction of mistakes, which will surely be made, and will help to improve and expand the program as it proves its worth.

References

THE following studies on small-industry development are products of a research program carried on at the International Industrial Development Center of Stanford Research Institute, assisted by a grant from the Ford Foundation. The purpose of the research program, which is closely coordinated with practical field work in cooperation with development agencies in newly industrializing countries, is to clarify the role of small industry in economic development and to identify the most effective methods of fostering modernization and growth in the small-industry sector.

BOOKS (available from the publishers indicated)

Small Industry—An International Annotated Bibliography, Marian Crites Alexander-Frutschi, compiler (Glencoe, Illinois: The Free Press, 1960), 218 pp., $6.00.

Small Industry Development Organizations—A Worldwide Directory, Donald R. Liggett, compiler (Glencoe, Illinois: The Free Press, 1959), 137 pp., $10.00.

Managers for Small Industry—An International Study, Joseph E. Stepanek (Glencoe, Illinois: The Free Press, 1960), 245 pp., $6.00.

Small Industry Advisory Services—An International Study, Joseph E. Stepanek (Glencoe, Illinois: The Free Press, 1960), 193 pp., $6.00.

Industrial Estates—Tool for Industrialization, William Bredo (Glencoe, Illinois: The Free Press, 1960), 240 pp., $6.00.

Aiding Small Industry through Government Purchases, Kennard Weddell (Menlo Park, California: International Industrial Development Center, Stanford Research Institute, 1960), 51 pp., $3.00.

Industrial Entrepreneurship in Madras State, India, James J. Berna (Bombay, India: The Asia Publishing House, 1960), 240 pp., Rs. 18.00. (Also available from their New York office, 119 West 57 St., New York 19, at U.S. $6.00; or from their London office, 447 Strand, London, W.C.2, at 45s.)

Economic Research for Small Industry: India's Experience, S. Nanjundan, E. Robison, and E. Staley (Bombay, India: The Asia Publishing House, 1961).

PAPERS (available free on request from the International Industrial Development Center, Stanford Research Institute, Menlo Park, California, U.S.A.)

"Small Industry Development," Eugene Staley, 1958, 26 pp.

"Notes on Small Industry and Handicraft Development in Mainland China, 1952–1958," 1958, 55 pp.

"Rural Industrialization for Agricultural Development," William Bredo, 1959, 21 pp.

"A Means of Assisting Small Mining Operations," George V. Mueller, 1959, 12 pp.

"Small Industry in Economic Development of Contemporary Countries," Stanislaw Wloszczowski, 1960, 61 pp.

The Center has in preparation an international comparative study on the problems and methods of financing small industry, a manual on communications in industrial extension work, and a general treatise on "Modern Small and Medium Industry for Newly Industrializing Countries."

EIGHT

COMMUNITY DEVELOPMENT

26. HENS THAT LAID GOLDEN EGGS

WILLIAM C. SMITH

MARGARET MEAD has remarked that in technical aid programs and in administration among newly emerging peoples, the anthropologist has become the symbol of conservatism and pessimism, "the specialist who states that most changes seen as desirable by the technician, the economist, or the administrator, will be very difficult, practically impossible, or, if practicable, destructive."[1] The reason is not far to seek: The literature on applied anthropology overflows with accounts of unsuccessful programs of directed culture change.

In this paper, we are concerned with the circumstances of a successful technical aid project, analyzing the reasons for success and assessing the consequences of change.

Since 1952, UNESCO's CREFAL (Centro Regional de Educación Fundamental para la América Latina) has carried out community development work in twenty-one Tarascan Indian and *mestizo* villages in the Lake Pátzcuaro area, 250 miles west of

EDITOR'S NOTE: Notes corresponding to reference numbers in the text will be found at the end of the chapter.

AUTHOR'S NOTE: *The fieldwork for this report was carried out during the summers of 1959 and 1960 under the direction of Professor George M. Foster (Department of Anthropology, University of California), as part of a four-year program supported by a National Science Foundation grant dealing with the comparative study of culture change in several Mexican communities. My expenses were partially covered by a National Institute of Mental Health supplementary grant, and as Professor Foster's research assistant, I received additional funds from the University of California Research Committee.*

One of the most pleasurable aspects of fieldwork in the Pátzcuaro area was the opportunity for association with the staff and students of CREFAL. I am particularly indebted to Professor Lucas Ortíz, Director of CREFAL, Dr. Anibal Buitrón, Assistant Director, and Dr. Gabriel Ospina, Director of Research, whose encouragement and generous assistance made this study possible.

Names of persons in the report are fictitious.

Mexico City. Students come from most Latin American countries to receive eighteen months' training, which includes participation in the planning and execution of development programs. One aspect of this work has been the attempted introduction of small-scale commercial chicken farming. In the small Lake Pátzcuaro island community of La Pacanda, this program has been remarkably successful, while in most nearby villages it has met with only slight enthusiasm. The people of La Pacanda have learned that chickens indeed "lay golden eggs."

When students and technicians from CREFAL first came to La Pacanda, they found a small Indian community of fishermen and farmers who met their overtures with polite suspicion and silent uncertainty. During the following two years, various groups of workers from CREFAL continued to visit the island, trying to gain the confidence of the local people and, with little success, to arouse interest in programs of home improvement, public health, and chicken farming.

Then, in 1954, three men agreed to accept twenty-five pullets each, to be raised according to CREFAL's instructions. When the chickens started laying, CREFAL arranged to pick up the eggs and market them, crediting the income against the cost of production and providing a small profit for the farmers. The following year, these three men were sufficiently pleased with the results to accept loans covering the purchase of equipment and the building of chicken houses, and each received from CREFAL about 135 pullets. Veterinary care, weekly allowances of feed, and financial and technical supervision were also provided. In 1956, two more La Pacanda men arranged loans, built chicken houses, and so became involved in CREFAL's program. The next year, seven more loans were set up; in 1958, the number jumped by twelve and, in 1960, by twelve more. Now more than half of the sixty-five families in La Pacanda are raising chickens under CREFAL's program, and many more have applied for loans.

Acceptance of such a loan is regarded by the farmer and his family as a major commitment; success in chicken farming has come to be regarded as a major achievement. CREFAL's administrators and technicians consider La Pacanda to be their most successful experiment in community development, and changes taking place in La Pacanda are noted and commented upon by local people throughout the Pátzcuaro area.

Why have the people of La Pacanda responded so enthusiastically to CREFAL's chicken farming program? Before attempting to answer this question, we must briefly consider certain ecological, social, and economic characteristics of La Pacanda's traditional culture.

To begin with, the geographical fact that La Pacanda is an island community is important; the area of land available for cultivation is severely limited, although in the surrounding lake several species of fish abound. La Pacanda's agricultural productive capacity is so limited that under optimum conditions only enough maize can be grown to meet about one-third of the annual requirement of the population. This means that twice as much maize must be imported as is produced by the community. Similar conditions often prevail in Mexican peasant communities, and agriculture frequently is supplemented by herding of livestock or by craft specialization such the production of pottery, woolen materials, hats, or furniture. But the island of La Pacanda lacks the natural resources required for such craft production and has far too little area for the commercial raising of livestock. Fishing, in short, is the primary response of the people of La Pacanda to their ecological demographic situation.

The fishing technology of the Pátzcuaro area involves use of two main types of nets and of flat-bottomed dugout canoes of several sizes.[2] Small fish are taken in a fine-mesh gill net, which is staked out along the shore and can be tended by one man or by his wife and children. Use of this technique is limited to certain months of the year and often results in a very small catch. Larger fish are taken in mid-lake or in weed beds along the shore with a large seine operated by four persons, usually adult men, working in one canoe. Frequently these four are related, consanguinally or affinitively (by marriage), in which case the catch may be divided equally. More often, the owner of a canoe and seine hires other men to help him, paying them a wage or a share of the catch. The slight income that fishing provides is indicated by the fact that a man who owns his own canoe and fishes with his own sons can just manage financially when fishing is good. When it is poor, there is no margin of profit; often there is no income above what is urgently needed for food. The traditional economy of fishing and farming reflects a delicate balance between technology, population, and conditions of the natural environment. Even a small change in either of the latter factors could be expected to upset the balance, which, once disturbed, could be re-established only by population reduction or by modification of technology and economic organization.

Lake Pátzcuaro has subsurface outlets, and its level fluctuates somewhat, independently of the annual amount of rainfall. For many years, the surface level of the lake fell steadily, and as this happened, fishing declined. Early in the 1950's, with the possibilities of farming and craft specialization so limited, it became apparent to the islanders, that something must be done. Some of the men went away in search of jobs, but most were reluctant to do so. When CREFAL tried to initiate its chicken farming program, the island people responded with uncertainty and distrust; but finally, in 1954, the first three men agreed somewhat desperately to take part in the program on a trial basis. Thus, in the initial acceptance of the proposed economic change, one of the principal motivational factors was the recognition by these individuals that something was needed to supplement the traditional fishing-farming economy.

What were the personal characteristics of these first three chicken farmers? What life experiences had they had that led them to see in CREFAL's proposed innovation a possible solution to their problems? Full answers to these questions would require psychological data not yet available; but much is suggested by the economic and social positions they held in the community.

When CREFAL's technicians first came to La Pacanda, Eduardo was one of the community's most influential members. He was wealthy, by local standards; he had successfully held the offices of *jefe de tenencia* (the chief political position) and *secretario*, both of which demand above-average education and tact; and as *carguero* (the local term for a religious major-domo), he had fulfilled important ritual obligations by helping to organize and financially support community religious activities. Having worked for several months as a *bracero* (seasonal farm laborer) in the western United States, Eduardo also enjoyed a reputation for sophistication in dealing with outsiders.

Unlike Eduardo, both Roberto and Pepe were poor, uninfluential men; they owned no property, had held no community offices, and had made no outstanding contributions to local religious life. But like Eduardo, they both had the prestige that comes from successful contact with the outside world. Pepe had worked in the United States of America as a *bracero*; he spoke superior Spanish, and by local standards was well read. Roberto, with the assistance of a former schoolmaster, had attended an agricultural school in Morelia, the state capital, for a year; later, he had served for three years in the Mexican national army, during which he was away from the village almost continuously.

Thus, of these first innovators, only one had the traditional type of prestige that is based on comparative wealth and successful participation in local religious and political activities. But all three had the prestige that comes from a reputation for successful dealings wtih outsiders. They had traveled and worked away from La Pacanda, and because of this their opinions about the outside world carried more than average weight with their neighbors. When they decided to have a go at CREFAL's chicken farming scheme, they were putting at stake their reputations for superior sophistication. While the first two years of the program did not bring notable financial success, neither did they bring failure; and because of this, the sound judgment of the first three innovators was confirmed in the eyes of their neighbors. Several more young men became interested in the program, not only because of the possible financial return, but also because of the prestige that they now saw could be gained through association with CREFAL.

CREFAL representatives, in turn, recognized the possibility of making La Pacanda a showcase in community development. More and more time went into the details of planning for an expansion of the program, and technical experts visited the island several times a week. Thus, there was a degree of supervision and help frequently lacking in developmental programs. No chicken farmer went for long with an unanswered question; the teachers were there almost constantly to show the way. This meant that from the standpoint of the islanders, opportunities for learning were optimum. Constant supervision and technical aid, instead of a few lectures and an occasional demonstration, were very important factors in the acceptance of chicken farming.

The importance of supervised credit, made available through the Banco Nacional de Comercio Exterior de México and administered by CREFAL, can hardly be overestimated.[3] The villager was required to invest his time and labor in the construction of a suitable chicken house and in care of his flock, but loans were extended to cover all costs of materials, equipment, pullets, feed, and veterinary care. Without such financial support, no one in La Pacanda could have participated in the program. Wise management of each chicken farmer's account has helped to assure the prompt repayment of loans and the re-investment of profit.

Moreover, the program, as designed by CREFAL specialists, fitted well with traditional economic and social patterns. As in other parts of rural Mexico, the bilateral nuclear family is the basic social and economic unit, and broad cooperative mechanisms are minimal. Land is owned by individuals, the single farmer tends his fields, and most fishing is carried out by a small entrepreneur or a small family group. Recognizing this fact, CREFAL's specialists made no attempt to sell chicken raising as a cooperative village enterprise. They dealt with individuals as heads of households, as independent economic units. Loans were made to individuals, instruction was given to individuals, chicken houses were constructed by individuals, and the care of each flock was entrusted to a nuclear family. Each participant was given a separate credit account at CREFAL. All this meant that innovation could be decided by single persons; group decisions, always hard to achieve in Mexico, were of no importance. Had CREFAL attempted to sell chicken farming as a cooperative enterprise, failure probably would have ensued.

CREFAL's program was also well designed in that it did not conflict with the traditional division of labor in fishing and farming. In these activities, by far the largest share of work is done by men, who would find it hard to accept an increased work load. By contrast, women and girls make little direct contribution to this work. But the requirements of chicken raising are such that they can do many of the chores, thus substantially increasing their economic contribution and raising the total productive potential of the family.

By 1958, the increased economic potential of the family that added chicken raising to the traditional activities of fishing and farming was clearly demonstrated. Those well established in the program had succeeded in repaying their initial loans, enlarging their chicken houses, and buying new supplies of chicken feed and medicine. They began to improve their homes by cementing the floors, whitewashing the walls, and building larger, cleaner kitchens. Now, almost all families wanted aid; during the next two years, CREFAL tripled the number of chicken houses in La Pacanda and received applications for still more.

In the beginning, the success of CREFAL's chicken farming program was due to the fact that three La Pacanda men saw in it a possible solution to their precarious economic and ecological situation. Once initiated, the program expanded because it was well designed and had adequate economic and technological support from CREFAL, because it was initially accepted by men of prestige in the community and was subsequently seen by others as a means of achieving higher status, and because its economic advantages finally became apparent to all.

We can now turn to a corollary question: What will the economic and social consequences of this program be for the people of La Pacanda? An innovation of this magnitude, accepted by so many people, is certain to restructure traditional culture in many ways. Some of the results—a majority, we hope—will be beneficial, but it is likely that some disruption and disorganization will occur as the traditional positions of people are altered by newly acquired wealth and prestige.

In a general way, these consequences can be forecast without much difficulty:

With increasing dependence upon chicken raising as an adjunct to the traditional practices of fishing and farming, there is certain to come increasing involvement in the regional and national economic systems of Mexico. Eggs produced in La Pacanda are marketed in Mexico City; thus, the islanders are entering the national market on a scale heretofore undreamed of. This offers real advantages, but it also holds dangers; to a far greater extent than before, families will be at the mercy of shifting prices, which go down as well as up. Greater participation in national life also seems inevitable, because La Pacandans now make use of credit, are learning about interest and bank accounts, and are developing a series of commercial contacts they previously did not need. Their aspirations are rising, and ultimately they may seek to gratify them through increased political activity.

Traditional economic and social differences on the island have been slight. But with increased financial opportunities, some families will be more successful than others, and increased wealth differences probably will lead to increased social differences. With modification of traditional forms of social interaction, there will probably be changes in the value orientations in terms of which interaction is validated, and of the ceremonial behavior through which value orientation is expressed.

More concretely, some of the consequences of change can be

seen by considering briefly what chicken farming has meant to the three individuals who first accepted the innovation.

Eduardo, it will be remembered, was a man of comparative wealth, with the prestige of successful participation in local religious and political life. Through CREFAL's chicken farming program, he increased his economic advantage and his reputation for sophistication in dealing with outsiders. In the community's relationship to CREFAL, he saw further opportunity for personal aggrandizement. He participated as a free agent, not as a community leader. When CREFAL instituted a cooperative store, Eduardo became its clerk and proceeded to use its stock and its finances for his own purposes. When CREFAL helped to provide a motor launch for community use, Eduardo became launch-driver and used the launch for personal transportation. Community resentment grew; finally, at the village's annual election, Eduardo was removed from his positions of authority. Now he takes no part in the religious fiesta cycle nor holds political office. With increasing isolation from community life have come increasing alienation from community goals and values and increasing orientation to the outside world. Eduardo seeks more and more to identify himself with prestigious outsiders; and his neighbors say that it would be better were he to leave La Pacanda and go elsewhere to live.

Both Roberto and Pepe, on the other hand, were lacking in wealth and influence.

By taking part successfully in the chicken farming program, Roberto gained a leading role in representing the community to CREFAL. His superior education and experience outside the village prepared him for such a role; and he succeeded in validating his new position by appropriate participation in religious activities and by service in the offices of *jefe* and *secretario*. But as his prominence in community affairs increased, his responsibilities increased as well. CREFAL's technicians relied upon him more and more as their main go-between in La Pacanda. His relatives began to expect him to use his influence with CREFAL to gain special favors for them; and as the productive possibilities of chicken farming became apparent, they demanded from him increased financial support in family crises. When, in 1959 and 1960, CREFAL tripled its activities in La Pacanda, Roberto's commitments to both the community and CREFAL increased until he had little time for his personal affairs. He now had acquired land, but could not farm it, nor was he able to continue fishing. When CREFAL offered to pay him a substantial wage for coming to live at its headquarters and learn some of the finer points of chicken raising, he accepted eagerly. Closer association with CREFAL has increased his prestige in La Pacanda still further, but may eventually result in alienating him from the values of local community life.

Pepe's initial gains were primarily economic; with the income from chicken farming, he built new henhouses and bought more pullets; obtaining additional loans from CREFAL, he continued to increase his flocks. He invested in a corn-grinding machine with a gasoline engine, and from the service thus performed for village women, he realizes a small but steady profit. He became a small-scale entrepreneur, purchasing fish at wholesale prices on the island and reselling them in nearby market towns. He bought new fishing equipment and built a new house for his family. Economic success opened new opportunities for participation in local civic and religious activities. He successfully held the offices of *secretario*, *jefe*, and *carguero*, and he continues to take a leading role in sacred and secular affairs. He helped obtain the loans that paid for La Pacanda's cooperatively owned motor launch, and now he is working for a second launch and is exploring the possibility of obtaining electrical power for the island. He hopes to better the education of children in La Pacanda, and insists that Tarascan-speaking islanders must improve their command of Spanish if they are to deal effectively with outsiders. He is committed to these and other progressive ventures, and upon their success his own prestige will continue to depend.

The roles through which the local peasant community is related to the larger society of which it forms a part are always of crucial importance. Januslike, the incumbent of such a role faces in two directions, toward the community and toward the outside world;[4] his performance is probably never entirely free from strain and uncertainty. As conditions change and relationships to the outside world are altered, the individuals occupying such positions are among the first to be affected. If relationships alter rapidly or drastically, these persons may be faced with a painful dilemma. Should they maintain their roles as institutionally defined or modify them in order to deal with changing conditions? If they choose the latter alternative, they may be accused of violating tradition; if they choose the former, they run the risk of demonstrating their incompetence. In either case, they may lose the prestige they have already gained or hoped to gain through successful role-performance. Often, they choose not to act at all; or else, renouncing their community responsibility, they may seek their own personal advantage, their own security and prestige, in manipulation of changing circumstances. Eduardo chose the latter course, but the community rejected his bid for power without responsibility.

In the situation where established community leaders choose not to act, a further ambiguity arises. Individuals may appear who lack wealth and the influence of traditional leadership roles, but who have prestige based upon a reputation for worldliness and sophistication through prior successful dealings with outsiders. Such individuals, like Pepe and Roberto, may temporarily supplant traditional leaders as mediators between community and larger society, and so introduce and facilitate the acceptance of innovations consonant with the new relations to the outside world. In doing so, they stand to gain in influence. But to maintain this newfound status, they frequently must validate it by appropriation of traditional leadership roles and by ceremonial behavior in terms of traditional values. Committed to both the traditional roles they have taken over and to the new forms of relationship they have helped to introduce, they may find these conflicting interests more than they can successfully manage. On the other hand, they may be able to consolidate the two, thus to some degree expanding and redefining the roles themselves and perhaps altering the value orientations by which role behavior is validated. There is evidence of the former situation, I believe, in Roberto's attempt to insulate himself from the demands of the community; and of the latter, something may be seen in Pepe's campaigns for transforming the life of La Pacanda. For the individual, the consequences of economic and technological change have been conflicts of value orientation and of role definition; for the community, such conflicts appear to be part of the process whereby closer relationship to the larger society is achieved.

NOTES

1. "Applied Anthropology, 1955," in *Some Uses of Anthropology, Theoretical and Applied* (Washington, D.C.: The Anthropological Society of Washington, 1956), p. 98.

2. George M. Foster, *Empire's Children: The People of Tzintzuntzan* (Washington, D.C.: Smithsonian Institution, Institute of Social Anthropology, Publication No. 6, 1948), pp. 101–12.

3. Anibal Buitrón, "El Desarrollo de la Comunidad en la Teoría y en la Práctica," *America indigena*, 1961, pp. 141–50.

4. Compare Robert Redfield, *Peasant Society and Culture* (Chicago: University of Chicago Press, 1956), pp. 43–44; Julian A. Pitt-Rivers, *The People of the Sierra* (Chicago: University of Chicago Press, 1954), pp. 32–33; Eric Wolf, "Aspects of Group Relations in a Complex Society," *American Anthropologist*, 1956, 58, 1065–78.

27. INDIA'S COMMUNITY DEVELOPMENT PROGRAM: CRITIQUE AND SUGGESTIONS

OM P. TANGRI

THE Community Development Program in India, which has now been in operation for over eight years, was initiated in a time of unprecedented economic, social, and political troubles. Opinions and ideologies differed as to solutions. Exclusive reliance on any one of the traditional approaches was considered neither safe nor practicable in a nascent democracy. The program of community development was evolved as an alternative to either totalitarian or capitalistic methods of social change. It has been somewhat controversial for some time, but in recent years, certain opponents have gone so far as to question its basic philosophy and declare it an expensive luxury, purely for ornament and contributing "but little to agricultural expansion." (See, for example, *Hindustan Times*, "White Elephant," July 27, 1960, and "Money to Jam," March 5, 1960.)

The author of this article disagrees with such criticisms as these and appreciates the merits of the program. Its achievements, however, will not be discussed here, since they have been amply treated elsewhere in the professional literature. (For example, United Nations, Bureau of Social Affairs, *Community Development and Economic Development, A Study of the Contribution of Rural Community Programmes to National Economic Development in Asia and the Far East*, Part I, July 25, 1960, Table 2, p. 26. Unpublished preliminary draft.) The purpose of the article is to point up certain important shortcomings that have tended to minimize the effectiveness of the program, and to suggest ways

AUTHOR'S NOTE: I am indebted to Professors Murray R. Benedict, David J. Allee, and Paul S. Taylor of the University of California for making very helpful suggestions and bringing several issues to the fore in their comments on an earlier draft of this discussion.

of overcoming them in light of basic economic theory in production and marketing. Some of these shortcomings have been pointed out by other writers, but they are included here because they have not had effective remedial action.

1. Community Development has not made adequate progress in getting the farmer to adopt new and improved techniques. Farmers are loathe to change their habits for a variety of reasons. For example, in India, farmers operating on a small scale frequently hire only one worker. They pay him a specific amount per day because of legal requirements or tradition. In such cases, they may be unwilling to adopt new machinery or techniques, since their total wage bill will remain the same even though the number of daily hours of labor is less. While changing laws is beyond the direct scope of Community Development, changing traditions is not. Farmers are also unwilling to use new techniques, improved seeds, fertilizers, etc., because of inadequate credit facilities. Here it would seem that the Community Development Program might do more than it has done to ease the credit situation. Another difficulty is that the farmer is in many instances not convinced that the new techniques are better. Such shortcomings as selection of poor demonstration plots and inadequate informational activities frequently leave him unconvinced of the merit of the new ways. Last in a series of examples that might be increased manyfold is a lack of adequate storage and transportation facilities, which keeps the farmer from adopting new production methods. (See Food and Agriculture Organization, *Preliminary Report of the Survey of the Fertilizer Economy of the Asia and Far East Region*, Rome, July, 1960, p. 4.) All this accounts for the continuance of subsistence farming and the lack of diversification and noticeable shifts in the crop pattern.

2. Community Development has in some cases failed to make good use of opportunities available to it. For example, in the second plan period, according to V. T. Krishnamachari, Deputy Chairman of the Planning Commission, enough water to cultivate 3.5 million acres was available from completed large dams. This water was not used because engineers failed to provide convenient outlets from canals to villages, and villagers failed to construct field channels because they lacked persuasion and advice. If Community Development did not know of this opportunity, its lines of communication to other agencies are badly in need of repair. If it did, and still missed the opportunity, the problem is more

serious. Unless this can be remedied, India has lost the use of 3.5 million acres of irrigated land, 35 thousand field channels, and the employment opportunities of constructing the channels. The figures assume that a field channel approximately one mile long is needed for every 100 acres.

3. The village-level worker, the main link between the people and the government, is greatly overworked. He is assigned five villages with some 3,000–4,000 persons. As against this heavy responsibility, he receives a meager salary of Rs. 80–100 (around $20) a month. The low salary and the large number of villages under his care no doubt reflect the inadequate resources of the Indian government; but since the village-level worker's job is so important, this may not be the best place to economize.

4. From several U.N. reports and other sources, it appears that the staff of the Community Development Program has not paid enough attention to the task of minimizing violent seasonal price fluctuations in Indian agriculture. Basic production theory tells us that such fluctuations make sound and rational economic decisions very difficult. Minimizing them should therefore be high on the list of priorities in the agricultural program. To be sure, overcoming this difficulty is a task beyond the powers of the Community Development Program itself, but some improvements could be made locally, and local efforts would be helpful in bringing the problem into focus nationally.

5. The administration of the program is cumbersome, confusing, and all too frequently apathetic. Even worse, many of the practices of the administrators invalidate the philosophical ideas on which Community Development is based. (This complaint was stressed in a recent study by S. C. Dube, *India's Changing Villages* [Ithaca: Cornell University Press, 1958].)

Most of the deputy commissioners, who have the responsibility for community development in their districts, "continue to regard Law and Order and Revenue functions as their major duties," as Scarlett Trent says in "Community Development Administration —An Evaluation" (*The Economic Weekly*, X, Nos. 26, 27, and 28 [July, 1958] p. 889). Few take "an active interest in their new development responsibilities." Thus the major developmental function still rests with the district planning officer. If he is not a specialist, or is junior by length of service and salary and must supervise the work of specialists of senior status, complaints and troubles arise.

All too frequently, the village-level worker must act in accordance with targets set by his superiors, but with little opportunity to advise them about the felt needs of his villages. This is a definite weakness of administration, because it tends to leave the villagers cold and unresponsive to projects assigned top priority by the Community Development organization as a whole.

The people's association with the officials in the program, through nonofficial members of their village serving on the committees, is also difficult to achieve. The nonofficial members are usually the village elite. They tend to prefer to agree with the official members, since they wish to keep their positions on the committee and in the village intact.

Suggestions

Credit: Community Development needs to do more research and to step up its efforts to improve the credit-worthiness of the farmer by providing security for certain approved loans, and to improve the flow of savings from cities to villages and from within financial institutions in the villages to the farmers. One possible way to achieve this may be to introduce a credit supervisory system in collaboration with the cooperative and other credit institutions that are designed to provide credit on reasonable terms.

Income: More projects should be designed to reduce underemployment, to increase the farmer's capacity to store products, and to provide supplementary sources of income. Projects such as reclamation of land, construction of field channels, storage, warehousing, and buildings for cooperatives and schools might be profitably undertaken in the idle season to achieve these objectives.

Finance: The Ministry of Community Development or the Ministry of Agriculture, or both, should look into the possibility of using goods or funds derived from P.L. 480 shipments to finance some of the projects mentioned or others that might be appropriate. In the idle and even partly busy season, payment of wages in kind or cash might enhance people's incentives to contribute their labor to projects of general benefit. The use of P.L. 480 funds might be of particular help to the large class of landless agricultural labor.

Small-scale industry: Industrialization is an important goal of Indian economic planning. To achieve a smooth and orderly transition from the present heavily agricultural to the projected more industrialized economy, Community Development should conduct research on the following problems:

1. At the manufacturing level, what type of small-scale industries will best facilitate the process of industrial change without increasing costs to the economy through subsidies? The nature of such industries should be determined not entirely on the basis of doctrinaire philosophy, but on the dynamics of the projected forces of demand and supply. The choice does not have to be entirely between the extremes of Ambar Charkha and giant mills. As Japan's early economic development shows, appropriate technologies can be designed in such a way as to aid in setting up efficient small- and medium-scale factories.

2. At the processing level, what kind of plants can be set up in villages? Can they be integrated with manufacturing plants in the urban areas? Many of the bulky products like cotton, groundnuts, and coconuts are still being carried in raw form to the city plants on slow bullock carts plying unsurfaced roads. For these products, it might be possible to establish plants in close proximity to agricultural producing areas. This would mean reduced transportation costs to the farmer and possibly lower prices to the consumer. In addition, encouragement of such industries would provide additional avenues of employment and income to the village populations and thus reduce pressure on the already crowded urban centers.

3. Should such industries be financed by the national government, by foreign governments under programs like P.L. 480, or by international agencies?

Marketing arrangements: Long chains of intermediaries between farmer and buyer still exist in most of the rural economy, even in areas where Community Development has been in operation. Where possible, Community Development must reduce the middleman's charges, which at present severely cut into the farmer's share of the price. To do this, Community Development will need to work more closely with the marketing cooperatives in an effort to improve the economic efficiency of marketing operations.

Administration: Suggesting administrative improvements is a subject by itself and too vast to go into in this paper. Certain points, however, may be suggested for consideration. Since several evaluation reports have expressed serious dissatisfaction with the administration of the program, and since $840 million has already been earmarked for the Ministry of Community Development in the proposed Third Five-Year Plan, the Planning Commission should objectively review the conditions and considerations that necessitated enlargement of the then Community Development administration agency into a full-fledged ministry and should appoint an independent body to make a thorough inquiry into the present administrative machinery. The Planning Commission should then decide whether the present Community Development Ministry should be abolished, merged, modified, or retained as it is.

Even if the present ministry is retained, administrative changes should be made to improve the operations of the village-level worker, the district officers, and others. The Community Development Ministry should also make every effort to utilize the research staffs and technical assistance already available in the ministries of Agriculture, Education, and Health, and other agencies in carrying out their present program and the research program outlined here. Every effort should be made to keep from proliferating and duplicating research departments, since this tends to become an empire-building process.

In Conclusion

The philosophy of the program is sound insofar as it seeks to initiate economic growth in Indian agriculture through qualitative changes in human beings, brought about through democratic principles of self-help, incentives, and response.

That it has failed to achieve its goals as fast as anticipated is a result of difference of opinions about objectives, the absence of conditions that the program had taken for granted, and some defects in administrative arrangements.

Since Community Development expects to operate through improved human beings, and since human beings operate it, it is doubtless unfair to expect quick miracles. Continued usefulness of the program, however, requires an attitude conducive to examining faults as well as merits. So far, Community Development seems more often than not to have been in the position of either receiving extravagant plaudits or suffering unduly, like the person who cries, "When I am right, no one remembers; when I am wrong, no one forgets."

28. *COOPERATIVE* vs. *COMMUNE*

HENRY W. FAIRCHILD and SHAMSUL HAQ

COMILLA is a small city of about 50,000 people. It is situated about 100 miles north of Chittagong, the chief port of East Pakistan, and about 60 miles southeast of Dacca, the capital. It lies on the Gumti River on the alluvial plain that comprises most of East Pakistan, just 4 miles to the west of the Pakistan border between the Tripura State of India and East Pakistan.

Comilla is the central service center for a region covering several hundred square miles. Before the partition of India into India and Pakistan, Comilla was intimately tied to the economy of much of Hill Tippera, as Tripura State was then called. It also provided a market for the products of the hills—thatching grass, bamboo, pineapples, firewood, and other products.

All along the border area, an integrated economy had developed between the plains on the one hand, now in Pakistan, and the hills on the other, now in India. In every village along the edge of the hills, but situated on the plains (now Pakistan), there were persons, mostly landless laborers, who made their living going to the hills to cut *shan* grass for thatching material or to gather firewood. This was their only livelihood. They brought these materials to the delta villages to sell. Likewise, many farmers owned land in the hills which they used as a source of pasture for their cattle and goats. Many of the hill residents owned paddy land on the delta from which they obtained their rice and vegetables.

Following partition, passage across the border was stopped. Much of the supply of thatching grass and bamboo was cut off. Much of the rice supply was stopped from entering the hills. The integrated economy was severed. Many people suffered as a result and still suffer today.

The population of Comilla *thana* (roughly equivalent to prefecture, or county) is high. Although the census of 1961 has not yet been totaled, it is believed that the rural areas of the *thana* have more than 1,500 persons per square mile. There are about 400 villages in the area. Most of the villages are cultivators' villages. There are, however, weavers' villages, potters' villages, and other kinds of villages where crafts are practiced and are often the sole source of income.

The economy of the development area, then, is dominated by agriculture. In turn, the agriculture is dominated by paddy culture. Three paddy crops a year are grown on a small part of the land, two crops are grown on a considerable part. One crop, *amon* paddy, is grown on probably 90 per cent of the cultivated land of the area. (Paddy is rough unpolished rice. *Amon* is autumn rice, *boro* is winter rice, *aus* is summer rice.) Comilla *thana* produces vegetables, fruit, and a little jute. It is not, however, an important jute area. As in other areas, cattle population is high. Goats and poultry are common. There are a few sheep and ducks.

The natural hazards to agriculture are the monsoon flood and the winter drought. From June through August, much of Comilla *thana* is flooded, often severely so. This often floods out the *aus* paddy and sometimes even kills the *amon*. From December through March, however, the land is dry and hard. Bullocks cannot plough it. There is no rain to sustain the crop. Other natural calamities, such as cyclones, tornadoes, and hail storms, occur, but they are sporadic.

The social and economic problems are the problems of most of East Pakistan. Farms are small and fragmented, people are deeply in debt. Interest rates on borrowed money are prohibitive. The people are illiterate. Agricultural methods are traditional. There are too many mouths to feed. There is too much unemployment. All the problems associated with the tradition-bound feudalistic society and overpopulation are found here. Transportation is one of the major problems.

A Village Case Study

South Rampur is an all-Muslim village of 500 persons. It is located along an intermittent drainage channel which splits the alluvial plain. The plain is the dominant feature of the landscape —the plain with its little water channels, but without permanent rivers. It is this plain that shapes the destiny of the village. The plain is almost dead level, varying from 15 to 18 feet above the

Bay of Bengal level. During high tide, the plain is sometimes even below sea level. Thus, when the waters rush from the hills to the east and west, they are caught on the pan-like plain. Prior to 1960, which was a fortunate year, the farmers of South Rampur had lost all their paddy crops for five years in a row.

The village is composed of 90 families living in 14 kinship neighborhoods. Each neighborhood is situated around a tank, a pond or hole for water.

The most striking fact about the village is that it has increased from about 150 persons to 500 in about 100 years, according to the old residents of the village. These same old people stated that in the same period there had been only a little expansion in total cultivated land. They said that there had been considerable increase in double cropping, but no other major change in the agriculture. The number of fields had doubled in the past 60 years.

South Rampur now is farming about 240 acres of cropland. Even allowing for a slightly smaller acreage 100 years ago, each present inhabitant has only about one-third as much land now as his ancestors had then. Present acreage per person is only one-half acre. The present average size of farm is 2.68 acres.

These small farms, lying as they are in a flood-prone area, have not been able to keep up with the task that was cut out for them. It has been necessary for practically every farmer in South Rampur to borrow from local money-lenders. From figures collected by the authors, it is estimated that the average family in this village owes more than Rs. 1,000. At the locally prevailing interest rates of two *maunds* of polished rice for each Rs. 100 loan, most farmers owe 20 *maunds* of rice a year just as interest payments. (A *maund* is 82.28 pounds or 37.64 kilograms.) This is more than half their total rice production.

The major crop of the village is *amon* paddy, but in recent years, even this has been flooded out. In good years, however, it may yield about 20 *maunds* per acre. *Aus* paddy is sown on about half the land, but frequently it, too, floods out.

This will suffice to indicate the poverty and problems that confront the villagers and to suggest the basis for the feelings of frustration and hopelessness that have characterized this area. In April, 1961, this village was ravaged by a local tornado and then again in May by the general cyclone. More than two-thirds of its buildings were blown down. Such are the hard facts of life in South Rampur. It was in this atmosphere of constant hardship and frustration that the Pakistan Academy for Village Development began working to organize a village cooperative. South Rampur is now considered one of the best of the cooperatives in the Academy's program.

A Typical Family

Ali Ahmed (the name is fictitious) is a farmer in South Rampur, the same village where he, his father, his grandfather, and his great-grandfather were born. Ali Ahmed is married to a woman from a neighboring village. Although Ali Ahmed is only thirty-five years old and his wife twenty-five, they have been married for thirteen years and have had a total of eight children. Only three of these children are living now. Their oldest son is ten, their daughter is five, and their youngest son is four. Mr. Ahmed's mother, aged about sixty, lives with them. His father is dead.

The Ahmeds are considered to be middle-class villagers by their neighbors. They live in a neighborhood in the village consisting of six houses. Two of these houses are occupied by Mr. Ahmed's brothers. He is the eldest brother. The other three houses are occupied by an uncle and two first cousins.

The Ahmeds own just over two acres of cultivated land, distributed in six plots over the southern part of the village area. Their largest field is just under a half-acre in size. It is also their best field, because it produces two crops of rice almost every year. Mr. Ahmed works all his own land himself with the help of his son.

The Ahmeds own a house in a cluster of six other houses arranged around a rectangular courtyard. It, plus the tiny kitchen garden, the cowshed area, and the tank, is jointly owned with the families in the neighborhood. The Ahmeds own five or six banana trees and two papaya trees and co-own two mango trees.

Their house is comprised of three buildings and is better than those of Mr. Ahmed's two brothers. The main house is built of sun-dried brick plastered inside and out with mud. The floor is tamped clay. The roof is bamboo covered with thatching grass. The house is 12 by 24 feet in size and is divided into two rooms. Mr. Ahmed is more fortunate than most of his neighbors because his house has a parlor. It is of the same construction as the main house. It is 12 by 18 feet in size and has one room. This room has a bed, a table, and two chairs in it. The main house also has one bed and a table. The third building is the kitchen. It is made of bamboo with a thatched roof. It is 8 by 10 feet in size and is situated immediately behind the main house.

Ali Ahmed owns one bullock of a pair he bought three years ago. One of them died last year. He has three goats, six hens, and three ducks. He used to own a dairy cow, but she died two years ago.

Ninety per cent of his farmland, or just under two acres, is devoted to paddy. In a good year, Mr. Ahmed will get a total of forty-five *maunds* of paddy or about thirty *maunds* of polished rice. In addition to rice, he grows peppers, eggplant, sweet potatoes, bananas, papaya, and several other kinds of local fruits. He sometimes grows tomatoes. Last year, he grew a few white potatoes.

Neither Mr. nor Mrs. Ahmed is literate. Their eldest son went to *madrassa* school for two years, but is not literate. There is no school in their village. They have only meager possessions, but they do not have the need for many. Mrs. Ahmed has not made the trip to Comilla in ten years, even though it is only five miles distant. Mr. Ahmed has a pair of sandals, although he seldom wears them.

The Ahmeds are deeply in debt, as are all their neighbors. They owe 900 rupees. This they borrowed over the past seven years. They have been unable to repay the loans because of poor crops. More than 500 rupees of this debt was used to purchase four bullocks, three of which are now dead. When they took these loans, in three difficult years, they had to deed to their money-lenders .05 acres of land for each Rs. 100 they borrowed. This means that, although they work two acres of land, almost one half acre (0.45) of this really belongs to their money-lenders. When they repay their debts, if they ever can, this land will be returned to their ownership. Meanwhile, however, they work the land. Last year, the interest on this debt amounted to 18 *maunds* of polished rice, more than half their total production.

Mr. Ahmed worries about his sons and their future. He knows that even if he can hang on to his two acres of land, this will not be enough to divide and feed his sons' two families. Furthermore, he may have more sons. He complains that things are much worse now than when he was a boy. His grandfather owned five acres of land and four bullocks and had two sons. His grandmother owned gold ornaments. He blames his troubles on the population growth. Whereas his village now has 500 people, even when he was a little boy it had only half as many. He needs another bullock, but does not like to borrow more money, because he can barely pay the interest on his loan now. He fears that he may lose his land as many of his neighbors have. If this should happen, he would be ruined. But when asked what he and his sons will do, his reply was "Allah will provide," because he is a God-fearing and pious man.

Anyone who knows the village situation in East Pakistan, and in Comilla district in particular, knows that Ali Ahmed's case is slightly better than the average. The average family has only 1.7 acres of cultivated land. The average family does not own a bullock. The average man is even more deeply in debt in proportion to his resources than is Ali Ahmed.

Such, then, is the plight of many Ali Ahmeds in the Comilla area. He is poorer than his father was. He is illiterate, and it appears that his children must remain illiterate also. He owns only one bullock, whereas his grandfather owned four. He has less than half the land his grandfather held. He is head over heels in debt, on which he pays half his total farm production in interest. He is at the mercy of the wind, the flood, and the drought. There is a black future ahead and little that can be done about it. This is what Ali Ahmed and all his neighbors believe.

On the other hand, Ali Ahmed's nation, Pakistan, expects many things of him in the future. The Second Five-Year Plan expects him to increase his food production by 14 per cent between 1960–65. It expects him to pay more taxes and become a market for more industrial goods. Can this be done? Here lies the problem.

Thinking the Problem Through

When the Second Five-Year Plan was published, it said, "A disappointing feature of implementation of the plan [the first plan] was the failure in the key sector of agriculture. The highest priority is attached [in the second plan] to increasing agricultural production." The cure for the problem was widely recognized. It was a matter of devising and implementing a new kind of social organization to match the new kind of technology that must be introduced to increase national production. But the big question was, and still is: What kind of new organization will it be? Within intellectual circles, the arguments raged. Some maintained that

Japan had the answer in rural areas with her state-supervised co-operative system. Others argued, "No, China has the real answer in the communes." Still others thought that the proper system was the cooperative system of Yugoslavia. There were many suggestions, but it was obvious that no one knew the answer for East Pakistan.

At the Comilla Academy, various schemes were studied and discussed. Between August, 1959, and January, 1960, many villages in the Comilla area were visited, and many village groups were interviewed to get their opinions. The Academy Director, Mr. Akhter Hameed Khan, who had spent more than twenty years working with the problem in East Pakistan, felt that the answers were not known. He believed that scientific experimentation would be required to discover a workable pattern.

He believed that the most effective way to find suitable institutions for carrying out economic development was through the use of a small pilot area. Here, economic development ideas could be tested in an intensive fashion under conditions that prevailed in most of the nation's villages. By January, 1960, the Director had received permission to use the Comilla development area as a laboratory in rural development. The Academy was ready to move.

In the words of Akhter Hameed:

> We think that we are now in a position to initiate an experiment in agricultural and economic development which may be very significant. Briefly, the chief objective of this experiment would be to promote the formation of small cooperative groups of farmers who would adopt improved methods, implements, and machines. The small group cooperative will aim to become self-sustained. The members would learn to save and collect their own capital and invest it in better farming. A cooperative group would overcome handicaps of small holdings. It would be possible for members to use implements and machines which they could not own individually, and, on this basis, it may be possible to build a bigger structure of cooperative credit and marketing.

In another note on small-scale mechanization Akhter Hameed Khan said:

> Agricultural production can be greatly increased and farmers can become intensely interested in improved methods and techniques. Their traditional apathy disappears as soon as they are convinced of the possibility of larger incomes.

Improved implements and small machines can be used as the chief means of arousing their interest and showing them the prospect of immediate gain. The use of machines can ensure increased production. For instance, a power pump will enable the farmers to have *rabi* crops in lands which are now lying fallow. The use of a tractor will enable them to plough dry soil, which is too hard for their bullocks, and thus ensure timely sowing and better yields.

The majority of the farmers in this area, as in many parts of East Pakistan, have very small holdings and it is not possible for them to buy these implements and operate them economically on an individual basis. Therefore, a good alternative is a cooperative pool of machines and implements for a number of families whose total land would form an economic unit ranging from 20 or 30 acres to 100 acres.

After numerous discussions in many villages we find that farming families are willing to come together to form such cooperative groups. Though there is little possibility of consolidation of holdings, the families would willingly join to buy the implements and let them on hire among themselves.

The improved implements and the machines can thus become the nucleus of a cooperative group. The prospect of immediate gain will induce the members to save and make sacrifices in order to build up their own working capital. Thus the idea of profitable investment in farming will grow and displace the old idea of investment in only buying land. An important psychological and social development would be that the use of machines will interest the educated boys, who are at present unwilling to work on the land. Moreover, the prosperous farmer who at present does not work with his own hands will be drawn closer into the operation. The laborers will also become more skilled.

Developing a Working Plan

Any large potential for production increase must lie in the land currently being cultivated. This potential is large indeed. The first way in which farm production can be increased is by putting the land in crops during the months of December through March. At present most of the land of the *thana* is idle during this period for lack of sufficient water. In many areas of the *thana*, there are available water sources which could be used for winter irrigation. The Gumti River, which crosses the area from east to west, is a ready source of irrigation water. In addition to this, each village in the *thana* has several tanks that contain water. There are several permanent water channels scattered over the area and a great number of intermittent channels. While the ground water potential is not known, it must be large. Tube-wells could undoubtedly be used to supplement the surface supply.

The winter is the best crop season at Comilla. Technically, on the alluvial soil of the East Pakistan delta area, under good management—including winter irrigation and the ordinary farm practices of Japan or Italy—it would be possible for more production to be gleaned from the land during the winter period than is now obtained during the rest of the year.

The second method of increasing agricultural production is to obtain higher yields on the land during the conventional farming season from April through November. Since the greatest single hazard to agriculture is the monsoon flood, which occurs from June through September, the simplest technical solution to this problem is to leave the land idle during this period and concentrate the cropping during the remaining eight months of the year. This could be accomplished only by having irrigation facilities available. In actual practice, it would work out that two sure crops would be produced and the third would be planted in the hope of getting a crop during the monsoon season.

With this adjustment in the cropping pattern, and with the introduction of improved varieties of seed, properly balanced fertilizer of the correct amount, improved tillage and weed control, certain and controlled irrigation, proper pest and disease control measures, and improved harvesting and storage techniques, crop production could be doubled or tripled in the Comilla area. Similarly, there is no technical reason why livestock production could not be increased.

The major stumbling block to increasing agricultural production is the present lack of proper social, economic, and administrative organization.

Based upon long experience of working in the local villages around Comilla, the Director of the Academy drew up the first tentative plan for a cooperative pilot project. The outline was given as follows:

(1) The Academy would sponsor a central cooperative. (2) The central cooperative would have sets of improved implements and machines like power pumps, small tractors, etc. (3) It would undertake the demonstration of these implements in various villages and run training courses for the farmers. (4) On receiving requests from farming families, it would help in the organization

of small cooperative groups, who would buy the implements on a hire-purchase basis. (5) The central cooperative would carry on an intensive educational program stressing the need for saving and investment in farming and the learning of better methods for increasing production and the income of the members. (6) If the habit of cooperation grows, the members would learn to do their buying and selling jointly, as well as the planning of crops.

Mr. Shamsul Haq, a special officer for cooperatives with more than twenty-one years of cooperative organizing experience, was deputed to the Academy in March, 1960. However, even before he arrived, the Director of the Academy and Mr. Nurul Haq had already organized a few local village cooperative groups. In April, 1960, the services of Mr. A. K. M. Wajihullah, the Assistant Registrar of Cooperatives for East Pakistan, were obtained for a short time as a consultant.

Mr. Wajihullah spelled out the scheme. He recommended that the Academy first appoint some cooperative extension agents to carry out a program of education and joint action among the people of the *thana*. He suggested that these extension agents should be enlightened farmers "who are primarily interested in their own development and are also interested in their neighbors by virtue of their social position and standing among the people in respect to integrity." He suggested that the Academy should train these agents in cottage industry methods, agricultural extension methods, and cooperative organization methods. The Cooperative Special Officer at the Academy should train and supervise them. The agents should organize the village people into beginning cooperative groups and give them not less than three months' attention each.

When a particular group had acquired the necessary grounding for working together, an organizer should be appointed from among the group. The organizer should then become the liaison man between the Academy and the group and replace the extension agent. Eventually, the society should be taught to save and to work together, and it should become registered.

The consultant recommended that three kinds of primary societies should be organized—agricultural credit and service cooperatives, industrial credit and service cooperatives, and commercial credit and service cooperatives.

Mr. Wajihullah recommended that a central federation should

be formed separately from the Comilla Central Cooperative Bank, which he stated "can hardly serve this purpose. . . . There should be a Thana Central Society with multiple objectives as a federation of all the different types of primary units that will come into being under the pilot project." He recommended that the Central Society should supply credit, distribute supplies, provide services (such as fertilizers, seeds, etc.), market products, provide cooperative education, help with cooperative organization, and, provide for various kinds of member training.

The organization created to conduct research work in the Development Area was a committee of the faculty of the Academy called the Central Extension Committee. This committee was organized in February, 1960.

In terms of working with village groups, Mr. Nurul Haq, Instructor in Rural Business Management at the Academy, worked with the non-agricultural groups. Mr. Shamsul Haq, special officer for cooperatives, worked with all the twenty-one agricultural village groups.

Organizing the Groups

The Academy began its organizational task by appointing extension agents, who were leading farmers of the villages from which they came. They were paid a small amount to cover transportation to come to the Academy for training in extension methods and group organization. They were given some training in improved methods of agriculture. Their task was to go among the villagers of their locality and try to organize some groups interested in cooperative action. Even though these extension agents were not highly enlightened or highly trained people, they were interested and willing. This apparently was what was required because they did get groups together. Following the formation of a group, the special officer for cooperatives met with the group.

Mr. Shamsul Haq, the special officer for cooperatives, has stated that he went about organizing a cooperative group in the following manner.

If he became convinced that the group was a genuine one, truly interested in working together, and if it was large and homogeneous enough to develop into a viable social group, then he proceeded to state the conditions under which the Academy would work with them. The group must:

1. Organize into a formal group and elect officers. Later it would have to become a registered society.

2. Agree to hold regular weekly meetings and to make it compulsory for members to attend. Records were to be kept of these meetings.

3. Agree to save money in a regular fashion. They would save regular small weekly amounts, which would be deposited in individual accounts with the society and recorded in individual passbooks. The entire amount would be deposited in a joint account in the Central Cooperative Bank. At harvest time, they would agree to make in-kind savings in larger amounts.

4. Agree to select a trusted and intelligent man from their midst and send him as their organizer twice a week to attend regular meetings at the Academy. The organizer would collect and carry their savings to the Academy meeting and deposit them at the Academy. He would bring back useful information he had learned and teach it to the group. During the first year, the organizer would be paid a small allowance from the Academy, after which the group would agree to take over this cost.

5. Agree to keep good accounts and to appoint a man to keep them. They would have to agree to let him be trained at the Academy and to pay him for his services.

6. Agree to do joint planning to improve their business, to engage in joint efforts such as the joint use of a power water pump or tractor, the joint purchase of seeds, and the joint taking of loans. In other words, they would have to give some of the privileges of acting as individuals and accept some of the burdens of acting as a group.

7. Agree to the joint use of supervised credit based on the farm or village production plan.

8. Agree to adopt improved agricultural practices and accept training in improved skills. They would have to agree to use improved machines.

9. Agree to join later in a cooperative federation for securing credit, purchasing and marketing services, and educational materials.

10. Agree to engage in long periods of discussion where all members of the society were present and thus to prevent government of the cooperative by the Managing Committee only, as had been the practice of so many societies in the past in East Pakistan.

It can be seen that many of the principles of sound group organization are included in the list. Mr. Haq believes that only through understanding, development of group loyalty, and the receiving of some real economic benefits from belonging to the group can these village groups survive.

Since the pilot experiment began, fifty-six organizers' meetings were held at the Academy up to June 1, 1961. Average attendance at these meetings was 95 per cent of the organizers.

A summary list of topics discussed in the course of the year-and-one-half period includes: cooperative principle and practice; improved method of cultivation; credit—supervised on pre-planning by the group; capital formation by savings; joint use of agricultural implements; joint storage of water; joint planning; formation of bullock groups; services through mutual aid team; conduct of meeting and accounts keeping; village plan; marketing of agricultural produce.

Besides the formal training carried on at the Academy, much informal learning took place.

In about sixteen months of working with various organizers, some of these men have developed into splendid teachers and group leaders. Others have failed completely. One or two have failed their trust by stealing money. They were caught and had to be relieved of their duties with considerable embarrassment.

If there is any single feature that serves best to distinguish the Academy's pilot cooperative experiment from the half-century of cooperative effort that has been made in East Bengal, it is the village cooperative meeting. Here is the agenda of a typical meeting of a good village cooperative society: (1) supply of water to the members by power pump, (2) increasing the rate of cash savings deposit, (3) in-kind deposit during harvest time, (4) payment to the co-villager employed as power pump driver, (5) selection of members for giving training in power pump, tractor, and spraying operations, (6) planning for future production, (7) miscellaneous.

Omitting further details at this point, it is sufficient to say that the Academy has tried to introduce the idea of compulsory weekly meetings where all of the members can discuss their common problems. It has tried to introduce the idea of talking over, in session after session, the actions individuals must perform for their cooperative and the things they have a right to expect from their group. It has tried to get the group members to talk about the problems they can do something about rather than about things beyond their control or ideas not concerned with village group economic action. At this writing, it can be said that the objectives originally set by the Academy are being pretty largely met.

Individual and Group Savings

One of the aims of the pilot cooperative experiment was to get villagers to save some of the capital they normally accumulate over and above their usual consumption requirements, excluding interest paid to the money lender.

At present, the money lender serves as a dependable kind of village bank. If a villager has land, the money lender will provide him the bullock he needs and will purchase his seed and fertilizer. For this service for the period of one year, the money lender charges two *maunds* of polished rice valued at about Rs. 60 for each Rs. 100 he lends the villager.

Because the money lender normally gets paid, it is incorrect to say that farmers cannot accumulate capital over and above consumption needs. It is correct to say, however, that under the present lending system they cannot save capital of their own from the accumulation in excess of their consumption requirements.

As a specific example, it was found that in South Rampur village thirty-eight farmers were indebted in the amount of Rs. 54,000 to the money lenders. The interest on this debt amounted to 1,080 *maunds* of polished rice, or more than half their total rice production. The fact that this amount of interest had been paid in years past indicated the villagers' ability to accumulate capital above their consumption requirements. The fact that they had to pay this capital as interest indicated their inability to save for themselves.

Suppose that this group of cultivators could somehow have accumulated Rs. 54,000 of their own, or could have borrowed it at a low rate of interest, then the difference between what they had previously paid the money lender (1,080 *maunds*) and what they would have to pay now could be saved.

It was upon this kind of argument that the individual savings program was based. It was emphasized that for every Rs. 10 that a villager did not have to borrow from the money lender, but which he could save for himself, there would be a savings of Rs. 6 in interest which he would not have to pay to the money lender next year.

Although this is logical reasoning, it was not the reason that the savings program became a success in the pilot area. The reason for its success was that one credit institution, the money lender, was replaced by an equally disciplined savings system, that provided by the cooperative group.

Twin slogans were adopted: "No village is too poor to save," and individually, "No villager is too poor to save." The authors believe that these mottoes would have made virtually no impact at all except that they became a part of the ritual of the village cooperative meeting. Saving became a goal to be met, a sacrifice that must be made; and the motto was repeated by the members sitting in the hearing and judgment of their peers.

Case after case shows that many farmers were skeptical at first, and in many societies they still are. But after the initial campaign by the Special Officer of Cooperatives and the Director of the Academy, small savings began to accumulate, one anna at a time, occasionally a rupee. In a short time, a society had 100 rupees, then 200, and then a discovery was made.

This discovery was that group savings brought economic power. Societies found that they could use their savings to secure a loan from the Cooperative Bank. The savings served as the collateral for the loan. A lesson was learned: Group action brings group benefits. Enough of the leading members of the various groups realized this to provide a force over the rest of the members who perhaps were passive or reluctant savers.

The mechanism of saving became the weekly cooperative meeting in the village. There in the open meeting, it became a regular feature to collect the savings. This the village organizer did. After the savings had been collected, the organizer stood up and in open meeting read the name of the member and the amount he had saved. This reading out loud served two purposes. First, it brought group approval of the savers and group disapproval of non-savers. Second, it assured the membership of the honesty of the organizer and of the accuracy of the records, because in an illiterate group the spoken record is the only record that can be checked by all the members.

For keeping records of savings, each member was given an individual passbook by the cooperative. In this passbook the organizer recorded each deposit. The passbook also recorded loans or other financial transactions between the member and the cooperative.

After the savings had been collected in a village, the organizer carried the money to the Academy when he attended the next regular organizers' meeting. There, he deposited the money with a clerk and received a receipt. The Academy clerk then carried this money for the village society to the Central Cooperative Bank, where the money was deposited and a bank receipt was obtained. A copy of this receipt was then given to the village organizer. He returned the receipt to the village. In this way, the villagers were assured that their money was in safe keeping.

Thus, systematic savings were introduced to villagers who have never saved systematically before. The record of accomplishment in savings in eighteen months is impressive—Rs. 30,000 in 25 village cooperatives.

In a country where there are two money systems, cash and rice, the savings in kind must not be overlooked. In East Pakistan, it is the custom to store paddy at home following harvest. Later, as the need for cash arises, the paddy is husked, polished, and sold in the local market. Most debts are paid in kind.

With this in mind, a drive was begun by the cooperative committee of the Academy before the *amon* paddy harvest in December, 1960, to attain in-kind savings by the societies. The goal set was a high one. The members were asked to pledge one-fourth of their harvest as in-kind savings. By this means, all the farmers' societies but one pledged paddy. The twenty-one participating groups pledged a total of 2,680 *maunds* of paddy.

At the time of this writing (June, 1961), although the main season for selling the stocks is during July–September, the twenty-one participating societies had deposited a total of Rs. 7,090 resulting from the sale of 530 *maunds* of paddy. This amount of money represented an amount equal to 28 per cent of the regular weekly cash savings.

Joint Planning and Supervised Credit

From the beginning, the Academy encouraged groups to think about their problems both as individuals and as a group. When they had finished talking about their problems, they were encouraged to work out solutions and have these solutions written down. These solutions worked out jointly were called group plans.

It cannot be claimed that these early efforts were very sophisticated. Nevertheless, they represented analytical efforts by groups not used to making an analysis of their own economic affairs. For this reason, these plans are significant. They represent a real outgrowth of education rather than something handed down to the group by an outsider.

Of the twenty-five village groups, fourteen have developed such plans. It is estimated by the Academy specialists working with the groups that have written plans that about 30 per cent have plans that represent the work of all members of the group. The remaining 70 per cent unfortunately represent mostly the work of the organizer and the managing committee. This is an area that will require much more education.

Unfortunately, most loan-making in the past in East Pakistan had not been based upon a farmer's ability to pay from production, or even been made for productive purposes. If a farmer had land or gold he could use as collateral for a loan, the loan was given. It was as simple as that. Villagers are used to this system. Thus, the idea that a loan should be made for productive purposes only, and based on the ability of that production to pay for the loan plus the interest, is a novel and foreign idea. It may not only be foreign—it may appear to be a little silly to village people. Thus, the introduction of supervised credit breaks sharply with the past. Farmers cannot understand why, if they have land to mortgage, they should not be given a loan from cooperative loan funds even if it is for a daughter's wedding rather than for the purchase of fertilizer.

There is another barrier in East Pakistan to sound loan-making. For years, farmers have been able to get things from the government if they went through the proper form or said the proper words. Thus, if they met and put some peoples' names down on a piece of paper that was given the proper label, the government in East Pakistan in many cases provided them with money for one thing or another. In this way, the people learned that it was the form one followed rather than the action one took that counted. This system bred advocates and self-interested touts rather than village leaders interested in the general welfare.

Realizing, then, that the process of supervised credit will be fully accepted only after several years of education and experience by the great bulk of the members, the Academy went to work.

Each group that wanted a loan—and all of them did—was told that it would have to sit down in meeting after meeting and work out a production plan based upon the realities in the village. Thereafter, based upon the ability to repay out of production, a loan might be given.

The Special Officer for Cooperatives at the Academy used the loan as a club over the societies to get certain essential things done. If members did not save in a regular fashion, they were denied loans. If they did not attend meetings, if they did not make realistic plans, or if they did not make in-kind savings, the loan was denied. To believe that it is possible to educate villagers in East Pakistan with words alone, and without using sanctions, is merely to be ignorant of reality. Thus, the Academy used the spoken word and the sanction. Gradually, some societies are learning what supervised credit is and are becoming strong advocates of the idea. It will require years of experience by the villagers themselves before the idea will be fully accepted in the community.

The money in a loan account could be withdrawn only by action of the general meeting, and then only if it was in accordance with the group plan. In many cases, this was an ideal rather than a reality. In general, however, the purposes of the plans were adhered to. But again, this is an area requiring a great deal of future work.

Regarding loan repayments, the pilot project has not yet been operating for a long enough period to record much experience. It is believed, however, that there will be no real difficulty in recovering loans. A great deal of care has been taken to make the loans not too large. They are within the repayment ability of the groups. With this in mind, plus the fact that the groups themselves realize the advantage of getting future loans, it is anticipated that the loans will be repaid in full.

Member Education and Joint Action

In general, there are three types of member education that were carried on in the pilot experiment. The first was specialized technical education, such as accountant and organizer training. The second was general member education, concerned with the cooperative and how it could serve the members. The third was improved methods and skills education. This type was given to specific interest groups in some cases; in others, the entire membership was trained.

For teaching improved skills and methods, the Academy employed special training classes ranging from beekeeping and poultry raising to family planning. There were conferences for wheat growers, for potato growers, and for people who raise silkworms.

The Academy published picture stories and Bengali booklets covering a variety of improved agricultural methods. There were spraying demonstrations and demonstrations in the use of the Japanese method of paddy cultivation. Demonstrations were made of fish culture.

A major problem locally in cooperative member education is the inability of three-quarters of the cooperative members to read. This placed a greater responsibility on the cooperative officers to see that booklets and pamphlets were read aloud in the villages. The program of increasing literacy will have to be enhanced in the future and is the fundamental building block in a complete educational program.

The power water pump provided a great stimulation to production and income in the villages where it was used.

The major limitations to the use of the pump were resource-wise and organizational. The chief limitation in resources was the lack of readily available water for pumping.

In East Pakistan, where fields are so small and farmers so many, the technically simple task of building a small water canal across a quarter-mile of level alluvial plain is a major organizational accomplishment. It may cross the fields of twenty separate owners. Even a rich man could not afford to purchase the easements and rights-of-way that would be required to irrigate his distant plots. Thus, the only solution is one in which all the owners come together and agree that the canals can be built across their lands. This is what the village cooperatives accomplished. Not only did they agree to the building of canals upon their lands, but they all did the building themselves.

The introduction of the power water pump early in 1960 was the first experience the Academy had with the introduction of the machine to the East Bengal village.

The first problem with the pumps came with the Agriculture Department's pump operators. They did not want to live in the villages. Neither did the villagers want them. The operators ran away from the job. They deliberately broke the pumps down so they could go on leave. Something had to be done. The Director of the Academy felt that if village boys could be trained to operate the pumps these difficulties would vanish. Under this new arrangement the village cooperative had to pay its own pump operator. Immediately after the installation of these resident operators, hours of pump operation went up and breakdown time went down.

The second problem became the servicing and maintenance of pumps. It was found that this could best be done by a central servicing agency at the Academy with the use of a roving mechanic who visited the villages on a bicycle.

Experience has already shown that it will require many years of useful functioning before an individual village cooperative society will be able to buy and run its own pump. Therefore, the conclusion has been drawn that, if an individual village society wants a pump, it should contribute, or loan, money to a central association equal to the value of about 1½ pumps. In this way, the central association or federation can own a sufficient number of pumps and spare parts to guarantee that the individual village will have a functioning pump continuously for the period of the dry season.

Another experience coming out of the use of the pump is the need for medium- and long-term loans in rural areas. Until they become available, there will be only limited action on projects of this kind.

In April, 1960, the Academy obtained two Ferguson 35-horsepower wheel-type tractors as a demonstration unit from the Agriculture Department. It also obtained one British hand-type Rotovator. Later, the Academy received three Japanese Satoh hand tillers. All these tractors were put to work in the villages.

Most of the conclusions regarding the use of the pump apply also to the tractors. It will be many years before villagers (or village groups) can or should own tractors. In the meantime, the machines should be owned and serviced by a central association, probably at *thana* headquarters.

It was obvious that rental of tractors to widely scattered farmers with widely scattered fields was uneconomic. Instead, the Academy began renting tractors to groups that could provide several days of work in a single village.

In practice, the fragmentation of holdings was not as insuperable an obstacle to small-farm mechanization as it is commonly pictured in the newspapers and around the conference table. Of much greater importance in East Pakistan is the problem of using the tractor effectively throughout the entire year. The tractor works well in the winter and spring months, perhaps until May. But it does not appear to be of much use from May through September. The land is too wet and muddy. The tractor is always getting stuck in the mud. Until this problem is solved, farmers will still need

bullocks to work land for *amon* paddy. With regard to tillage instruments and practices, the farmers using tractors in 1960–61
around Comilla liked the tractor. It was cheaper than renting
bullocks and it did a better job. The machine selected for tillage
with the tractor was not the plough, but the disc harrow. It was
less expensive than ploughing and still it did a better job than bullocks.

Concluding the tractor discussion, it appears that the machine
is economic, is liked by farmers, and is here to stay. It is much too
early to try to evaluate the economics of tractor operations in the
village situation here because no one really knows how to use the
tractor economically as yet. In the next three or four years, accurate estimates can be given of the costs.

Other forms of joint action were introduced into the villages. In
Monsasan, for example, mutual assistance work teams were organized. These are simply groups of farmers who trade farm work,
such as weeding. There is nothing startling in the idea, except that
it is new in the Comilla area. Much more of an innovation is the
collective agricultural operation. The Kamalapur society, for instance, has rented three acres of land and is working it jointly as a
group project. Any profits from the operation will be deposited to
the credit of the Cooperative Society.

The Amratali Weavers' Cooperative is purchasing cotton yarn
jointly. The Kashinathpur-Balarampur Rickshaw Pullers' Association has saved money and has purchased ten rickshaws for its
members. Members of the Comilla Vegetable Growers' Association have imported vegetable seeds jointly. Several cooperatives
have gone together to jointly purchase bamboo and thatching
grass following a recent typhoon.

Out of the joint use of the tractor and pump and the joint use
of other equipment, several villages are forming what are called
"bullock groups." These groups simply agree that they will use
each others' bullocks according to some plan. It is significant
because it has not been done before. This may make it possible
to stretch the work of a few bullocks over a larger area.

Many other forms of joint action have been tried in the villages
so far. The significant omission to date has been the failure of villagers to try to pool their land. Though much discussion has taken
place, there does not appear to be any trend toward this at the
present time. Farmers themselves feel that there is no need when
they can pool their other resources so easily.

Progress Since June, 1961

Work has broadened greatly since last June. There are now almost sixty primary cooperative societies. The Central Federation is established and is working to serve the villages. It has its own staff and facilities. Twenty Massey-Ferguson tractors are being rented to the villagers to disc-harrow their land. Twenty-three diesel-powered pumps are irrigating winter paddy, white potatoes, sugar cane, and vegetables.

Recently, the Pakistan Government has approved a five-year program to spread the organization of primary cooperatives to all the villages of Comilla *thana*. The Ford Foundation is helping on this. The first year's program is proceeding well. The money, materials, and people are being organized for this big push over the next four years. It is expected that 300 to 400 primary cooperatives will be formed.

Other groups are looking for guidance from this project to spread the idea to other *thanas* of East Pakistan. The World Bank, through its Pakistan representative, has shown interest.

Within the existing village cooperatives, the work is both widening and deepening. Gradually but surely, a sense of social cohesion is developing among the other groups. They are presenting a united front against the money lender's desire to collect intolerable rates of interest. They are cooperating jointly on many kinds of village and local community projects.

Institutional development continues. The cooperative bank is replacing the money lender. Joint marketing of paddy has been introduced for the first time. There are several thousand bushels of paddy in joint storage in cooperative warehouses in the villages and at the Academy. The vegetable growers are marketing their produce cooperatively.

Leadership and skill is growing. The continuous training program at the Academy is building new pools of skill in the *thana*. There are now several dozen tractor drivers and pump operators. Hundreds of farmers know how to use the hand sprayer. The leaders who two years ago were untried and unsure now are beginning to speak in firmer tones, with greater self-assurance. The organizers are developing managing ability.

Capital is growing in the villages. Several new grain warehouses have been built. Some wells have been sunk. More fertilizer is being used. Farmers are accumulating more capital in joint savings accounts. They are beginning to put more investment in present land holdings rather than trying to buy more land as has been the past pattern. Productive rather than exploitative fish culture is being undertaken in several villages.

All these things are resulting in and from the true beginnings of a movement. The people of Comilla *thana* are beginning to teach the lessons they have learned to their neighbors. A recent visitor to the Academy from more than a hundred miles away summed it all up. He compared his village with the villages in the pilot project area.

"My village is poor," he said. "These villages are poor. The bullocks in my village are sickly and thin. These bullocks are sickly and thin. Yet there is a difference here. It is in the spirit of the people."

29. MOBILIZING VILLAGE LEADERSHIP

AKHTER HAMEED KHAN
and A. K. M. MOHSEN

THE Kotwali *thana*, a 100-square-mile area, is for the Comilla Academy a testing ground for several experiments. First is the five-year plan for the development of village cooperatives and introduction of supervised credit, use of machines, and joint marketing. Second, the Kotwali Thana Council is run as an experimental model to find an efficient pattern of rural administration. In addition, there are school projects and work with youth groups and with women. Extensive records are kept, and the results are analyzed to enhance our understanding of rural problems and to help us discover better methods.

Pilot Public Works Program

In September, 1961, a Planning Commission official asked the director of the Academy whether it was possible to organize a public works program in the villages to increase employment and income, and whether the workers would accept wheat in part payment of their wages. Receiving affirmative responses, he suggested that Public Law 480 funds and surplus wheat might be used for rural development. The director welcomed this proposal because during the previous two years no other fact had become more obvious than that the two main obstacles to agricultural prosperity were the recurring risk of monsoon floods and the absence of winter irrigation. By putting the large and idle village labor force to work, these obstacles could be removed. A rural public works program would bring a double boon: supplementary income for distressed farmers and increased agricultural production.

Many kinds of development works are needed in the long-neglected countryside, including roads, bridges, culverts, schools, houses, ponds. But measures of water control, including a network

of drainage channels, with properly designed embankments, regulators, and sluice gates, claim an evident priority. Roads are next
in importance and, with skillful planning, can become an integral
part of the water control system. Good drainage and irrigation is
the first and most essential step in the direction of agricultural
development, and though the fact is generally admitted, surprisingly little is done to assure that this step is taken. Enormous
damage is caused every year by choked channels and unregulated
excess of water or by drought. Yet thousands of sturdy farmers sit
idle and unemployed during the dry months when they might be
mobilized to solve the problem.

The Academy director agreed to organize a pilot rural public
works project in the Kotwali *thana*.* There were several questions
and doubts that could be resolved not by arguments, but only by
actual work:

1. What kinds of public works can be started easily in rural
   areas?
2. What should be the organizational and administrative
   agency to best execute such rural public works?
3. What should be the role of Union Councils?
4. Is the requisite technical competence available?
5. Is it possible to mobilize village laborers extensively and in
   sufficiently large numbers to carry out such works?
6. Will they accept wheat or other foodstuffs as wages?
7. How much will local farmers contribute voluntarily in labor,
   land, or money to the support of such works?
8. What would be the economic benefits of such a works program and to whom?

Close contact with union councils and village cooperatives over
the past two years has given the Academy staff certain insights
that enabled them to make the following assumptions regarding
these questions:

1. Public works to develop a comprehensive system of drainage,
irrigation, and communications can usefully be carried on for
several years in Kotwali *thana*. Such works can be started quickly
and easily.

EDITOR'S NOTE: Approximate U.S.A. equivalents of administrative units
referred to in the text are: union = township; *thana* = county; circle = 2–4
thanas; district = state; division = region.

2. The most effective and least expensive organizational and administrative agency would be the Thana Council and its constituent members, the Union Councils. The circle officer, as the representative of the civil administration and as secretary of the Thana Council, should be the executive chief.

3. The role of the Union Councils is central and vital. They should prepare the schemes in consultation with the villagers themselves, organize the work (employ labor, disburse wages, keep accounts, ensure correct specifications, etc.), and undertake subsequent maintenance.

4. The Union Councils and village leaders can supervise earth work competently. Farmers are very knowledgeable about local drainage. Small schemes prepared by them are generally sound. Engineering assistance, however, is needed in the case of large projects.

5. Large numbers of laborers can be employed from approximately November to May under the supervision of Union Councils on extensively scattered projects.

6. The laborers will accept wheat in part payment of their wages.

7. Local contributions in land, labor, and money would be forthcoming for projects designed and carried out by the local people for their own benefit.

8. Rural public works would relieve distress caused by unemployment; increase agricultural production; build the much needed development infrastructure of drainage, irrigation, and communication; create managerial and technical skills; strengthen local governmental bodies and enable them to raise more taxes.

Preparation of a Plan

The director of the Academy placed the rural public works proposal before the Kotwali Thana Council. Early in 1961, this council had located its headquarters at the Academy, and the Union Council members began to be trained in program planning and organizational leadership. This project provided an opportunity to test their ability. They might provide a model for the province if they could organize the work in Kotwali *thana*. The following procedure was adopted:

Union Council chairmen called meetings of the members and explained the proposal. The members, in their turn, held meetings in their wards and invited suggestions for local schemes of drainage and irrigation:

The members' local project proposals were then discussed and consolidated by the Union Councils, and the Union Council projects were consolidated and approved by the Thana Council.

The consolidated plan was then forwarded by the circle officer to the irrigation engineer of the provincial Water and Power Development Authority (WAPDA) for technical scrutiny. Some of the projects were modified according to his suggestions.

After technical processing and revision, the plan was written on the appropriate Planning Commission form and, after approval by the deputy commissioner and the district council, was submitted to the provincial government's Agriculture Department, which had funds available for small irrigation schemes.

The proposal was first discussed in the Thana Council in October, 1961. By November, the consolidated *thana* plan was ready and all other formalities were completed. The official sanction was received before the end of December.

The Union Councils planned twenty-one drainage and irrigation projects, mainly re-excavations of existing channels that had been choked by encroachments and silt. It was estimated that more than 8,000,000 cubic feet of earth would be removed from 37 miles of these channels at a cost of Rs 150,000. Forty-five thousand rupees were estimated as local contribution. The rate of compensation for earth work was estimated at 18 rupees per 1,000 cubic feet.

Two Union Councils planned five projects for prevention of flooding of a 12-square mile low tract by reconstructing 12 miles of embankments and dykes, and by building one sluice gate and ten water flow regulators. Here, removal of 5,000,000 cubic feet of earth was estimated to cost Rs 81,000, while the masonry work was valued at Rs 97,000. Public contribution to the extent of Rs 23,000 was expected. The totals were impressive: 13,000,000 cubic feet of earth, 49 miles of channels and embankments. The works were widespread and far-flung over the 100 square miles of the Kotwali *thana*. Yet the government was requested to contribute only Rs 258,000, of which half was to be in cash, the other half in wheat.

The Revised Plan and Actual Work

The plan had to be revised, and it was fortunate that the revision could be done promptly. Planning at the village level is far from perfect, hence rigid adherence to initial plans may be fatal. A flexible approach, which allows corrections to be made in the light of experience, is much safer and wiser. Six projects had to be abandoned because of lack of interest or violent controversies among the local residents. The original plans for sluice gates and regulators were found to be too ambitious. Further study of the volume of water involved and other data was necessary, so much of the work was postponed till next year.

Since the work is still going on in some projects as this is written (June 15, 1962), final figures cannot yet be given. Out of the original 24 projects, 16 have been completed, 6 have been dropped, and work is in progress in 2. Out of 7 new projects, 3 have been completed and work is continuing in 4.

Nearly 8,000,000 cubic feet of earth have been removed at a total cost of about Rs 150,000, the average cost per 1,000 cubic feet being Rs 14. More work remains to be done, but out of the total government grant of Rs 258,000, only Rs 146,000 have been spent so far, including the expenditures on regulators. Workers came from 195 villages, and their total labor days to date exceed 45,000. About 4,000 *maunds* of wheat flour were paid in wages (1 *maund* = 82.28 lbs. or 37.64 kgs.).

It is now possible to answer the questions raised at the beginning of this report and to examine the validity of the assumptions described. The facts and figures speak for themselves:

1. A comprehensive program of public works was designed and carried out within the short period of six months.
2. The Thana Council and the Union Councils proved themselves remarkably efficient in planning and executing the project.
3. The Union Councils mobilized and supervised the laborers much better and more cheaply than private contractors would ordinarily do.
4. The village leaders' own skills in earth work and their ability to follow the engineers' instructions were fully demonstrated.

5. Employment was provided to a substantial number of laborers at widely scattered localities in the *thana*.
6. The laborers accepted half their wages in wheat.
7. Public contributions, except in the form of gifts of land and clerical and supervisory services, were hard to obtain. Our insistence on realizing them led some to attempt subterfuge and dishonest manipulation of accounts, as described later.
8. The public works carried out by the Union Councils with the help of local leaders aroused much enthusiasm. Foundations were laid for a good drainage system. To a certain extent, flood risk in the area was reduced. Managerial skill was created, and the position of the Union Councils was greatly strengthened.*

Organization and Administration

How was the plan implemented? How was it administered? What were the guiding principles? How were the local leaders trained? What sorts of difficulties were encountered and how were they overcome? All these topics are thoroughly treated in the full monograph report, of which this article is a summary. Here, only some salient features are presented. The administrative setup was as follows:

The circle officer, who was also the secretary of the Thana Council, was both the drawing and disbursing officer and the chief supervisor.

Each Union Council established a committee for every individual local project. If a project extended over a rather wide area, it was subdivided into convenient sections, and each section was

* For further research and analysis of any administrative or economic aspect of the project, the following records are available: (a) the plans prepared at the village, union, *thana*, and district levels; (b) proceedings of the Union Councils and the Thana Councils; (c) circulars, instructions, forms, etc., issued by the circle officer; (d) the training courses prepared and conducted for Union Council members; (e) diaries of the circle officer and the training officer concerned with the project; (f) diaries of the supervisors and the *thana* council workers; (g) muster rolls and accounts; (h) the project engineer's report, blueprints, and training courses; (i) the training officer's report; (j) data on laborers collected by the agricultural economics section of the Academy; (k) visual records of the operations, including 200 feet of documentary black and white film and many photographs.

A cordial invitation to utilize this exceptional collection of research materials is extended to any investigator who may be interested.

entrusted to its own committee. The Union Council member representing the ward in which the project was located was appointed chairman of the committee, and he chose influential local leaders to help him employ and supervise the laborers.

For technical advice, the circle officer and the project committees depended on the subdivisional irrigation engineer of the WAPDA and the American Peace Corps volunteer engineer posted at the Academy. Private surveyors were engaged for a few days as required.

The Kotwali Thana Council was fortunate to have some staff available to assist in the project—a supervisor and twelve workers. They had been engaged in training the Union Council members in program planning, budgeting, and coordination. First, they assisted the members in planning the projects, then they checked earth measurements and payment of wages.

As the funds were sanctioned by the Agriculture Department, the *thana* agriculture officer and some of the union assistants were also involved in supervision and checking.

The training officer of the Academy, who is an experienced member of the East Pakistan Civil Service and a Village Aid veteran, was the guiding spirit of the pilot project throughout— the planner, advisor, trainer, and recorder. He is the author of the full monograph report on the project and is also writing a rural public works manual. Later, he will be responsible for training the other circle officers, if the government decides to have them trained at the Academy, for conducting similar works in other *thanas*. Help and advice were given by the director of the Academy as circumstances required.

The financial and supervisory procedures were streamlined for speedy execution.

In the first place, it was decided not to engage any contractors for doing simple earth work. Tenders were invited, however, for masonry work on gates and regulators. But the margin of profit permitted was so unattractive to the contractors that no tenders were submitted, and ultimately even the masonry work, like the earth work, was done under the direct supervision of the project committees and the Peace Corps engineer. Successful elimination of the exorbitant middleman—the ubiquitous contractor—has resulted in both very speedy execution of the projects and remarkably frugal costs.

Every project committee was allowed to take an initial advance of money and wheat estimated to be sufficient to defray the wages required for one week's work. A bond was signed jointly by the chairman of the project committee and the chairman of the Union Council holding themselves responsible for proper use of the funds. After being given the initial advance, the project committee was reimbursed only when the receipted muster rolls were produced and after the amount of work performed had been certified by the supervisors.

Funds were withdrawn from the treasury by the circle officer as required and disbursed to the project committees. There was no hitch or delay.

Engineering Advice and Supervision

Doubts are most frequently expressed about the technical soundness of earth work not directed by engineers and contractors. Obviously, such doubts are misplaced in the case of simple operations, such as removal of silt from old water channels or the construction of village roads. But sound engineering advice is essential before digging new channels or obstructing or diverting the flow of existing channels. Above all, a master plan for drainage, irrigation, and communications for the whole *thana* should be designed only after a thorough survey by qualified engineers. Unfortunately, there is no precedent for such localized but comprehensive planning. In fact, the engineers are so preoccupied with either routine work or with big individual projects that none of them has cared to focus his attention on the fundamental problems of a single *thana*. But clearly enough the union plan and the *thana* plan are the bases of development. The Kotwali project is the beginning of a comprehensive plan for this *thana*. Both the Peace Corps engineer and the WAPDA engineer will observe the next monsoon flood and then design roads, channels, embankments, and regulators accordingly. Further surveys and further earth work may well be necessary during the next three or four years, as the problem is neither simple nor small, and it would be childish to expect a quick solution.

The first year's plan, as already stated, was scrutinized and revised by the two engineers. Actual work was also supervised, largely by the Peace Corps engineer. He also trained the Thana Council workers and the project committee members. He made the blueprints for the water flow regulators, and when the contractors refused to submit tenders, he engaged skilled masons, called them to the Academy, and built a model of the regulators for their instruction. He cautioned against placing the sluice gates and too many regulators this year without the benefit of full data, and consequently the plan was revised. His skillful and accurate measurement of earth work soon put an end to all attempts at cheating.

Training and Difficulties

The central idea of the pilot project was faith in the ability of Union Council members to undertake responsibilities that had never before been given to them: to carry out cheaply and quickly a public works program that cannot be carried out by engineers and contractors except at great cost and with inordinate delays.

Much depended on the training imparted to the members. First, a change of attitude was required. The traditional image of the councilor was that of an advocate, a spokesman, or a petitioner. The new role was that of an organizer, a planner and supervisor. Instead of writing petitions or making speeches, the member was expected to mobilize local labor and actively direct the solution of a problem. Secondly, the skills for performing the new tasks had to be taught and taught quickly. Several training camps were therefore held. All members of one council were called to the Academy at a time, and the principles of program planning and of coordination and group work were explained. When the project committees were formed, their chairmen and secretaries were trained in measurement of earth work, in keeping accounts and muster rolls, and in the use of wheat.

That so much work was done with such speed and so few breakdowns proves without doubt that a vast reservoir of true leadership exists in the villages, waiting only to be tapped. And the quick response also proves the importance of persistent training. A manual is therefore now being written at the Academy that will explain the methods of organizing public works and the principles of training local leaders as executive agents.

Though much work was done in the relatively short period of four months, some difficulties were encountered, which are here described very briefly; details will be found in the full report. Similar difficulties, it is feared, will be met in other places if such projects are undertaken.

As this was the first lesson in assumption of responsibility by local leaders, a great deal of imperfection need not cause much surprise. It was found that some of the schemes were drawn up carelessly and without consulting the villagers. Some members depended mainly on guesswork. Others could not resolve local conflicts; they were not persuasive or influential enough. A few had vested interests in certain encroachments and secretly sabotaged a project or two. Others were slow to learn the importance of punctuality and accuracy in the keeping of accounts. But on the whole, initial lack of skill or interest was soon remedied, and the majority of project chairmen and secretaries became good workers. Many of them displayed extraordinary ability. There is no substitute for learning by doing. These projects have created a numerous body of managers in the nooks and corners of Comilla *thana* who are now ready to undertake bigger tasks.

The worst obstacle at the initial stage was the tradition of corruptness. Government officers are assumed by the public to be dishonest; hence, public work conducted by them is considered a fair opportunity for graft. Well-informed village leaders are willing to participate in dishonest dealings and are not much troubled by pangs of conscience in defrauding the government or the public. Test relief operations, Village Aid community works, and small irrigation schemes have not been completely free from such taint. And often the Union Councils' earth work has been inflated to the disadvantage of the taxpayer.

The Kotwali *thana* public works were at first considered by the villagers to be similar in kind to what has gone before and goes on everywhere. Strict checking of measurements, verification of payments to laborers, and inspection visits by the overseers all came as a surprise to the village people. Even more surprising to them were the suspension of work at the least sign of fraud and the firm announcement that work would be done honestly or not at all. Meetings of Academy personnel with laborers in the villages and on the work sites had a most wholesome influence, as did also a lot of plain speaking to the assembled chairmen of Union Councils and the project committees. Though various fraudulent practices as well as the counter steps are described in detail in the full report, it may not be too optimistic to state that the crisis caused by a corrupt tradition was overcome by strenuous efforts to impose rigorous standards of honesty, and that after the first difficult month the work proceeded with acceptable integrity. Whether similar strenuous efforts would invariably be made in other areas it is impossible now to say. But strenuous efforts would undoubtedly be needed to establish a reasonable standard of integrity in the execution of such projects.

Public Contribution

One main source of fraud was the so-called public contribution. The evaluation reports of the Indian Community Development Program have pointed out that in many cases the "local share" is purely fictitious. The estimates of costs are inflated, thus allowing the work to be completed by means of government funds alone, while the manipulated accounts give fraudulent credit to the locality's spirit of sacrifice and participation. There are good reasons to believe that similar fictitious contributions are not uncommon in Pakistan. In the very first fortnight of this project, it was discovered that the old trick was well known to the Union Councils of Kotwali *thana*. Misleading attempts were made to show public contributions in either of two ways. (1) Cost estimates in the plan contained a labor rate of Rs 18 per 1,000 cubic feet of earth moved. Project committees were actually paying only 9 or 10 rupees to the laborers, but obtaining a receipt for 18 rupees, thus fulfilling the condition of a 50 per cent public contribution. (2) Sometimes the earth work measurements were inflated—for example, 20,000 cubic feet in place of the 10,000 of actual digging —to make up the public contribution.

The chairmen seemed surprised when both these practices were denounced as cheating and fraud. "How else," they asked innocently, "has the public contribution ever been raised?" They had done it so many times before. But they were firmly advised not to do it now. And the fiction of a public contribution was discontinued. Actually, however, nothing was lost, because even though the laborers were paid at the rate of 10 or 12 rupees the actual cost was much less than the estimated cost.

There was, nevertheless, a genuine contribution in three ways. The laborers accepted very low rates of pay—almost half of what is quoted by the contractors for departmental works. All organizational, supervisory, and clerical work was done by the project committees without remuneration, thus bringing the establishment charge down to almost nothing. All land required for digging, or for new channels or roads or embankments, was donated without any compensation.

Further genuine contributions may be expected after the benefits of the projects have been demonstrated. It is hoped that the Union Councils would in future be able to raise taxes to maintain the drainage, irrigation, and communications works in good condition, and that the farmers would not grudge the expense when they realize that it is incurred for the sake of their own security and prosperity.

Payment in Wheat

Comilla farmers are rice-eaters, hence their resistance against part payment in wheat as an innovation was expected. A lower price of wheat, which was to be the chief incentive, was unfortunately not fixed till the middle of April. Thus, for three months, the project committees had to persuade the laborers to eat wheat flour that cost them 20 rupees while they could easily have bought their favorite rice at 22 rupees—not a very attractive margin. Naturally, there was much grumbling, yet the project committees had sufficient influence to obtain labor at their terms—half wheat, half money. When the price of wheat was reduced to 12 rupees, it became readily acceptable.

There were some minor problems—about the transport and distribution of wheat, shortages due to bulk purchase, and retail supply—but these were easily solved by the ability and good sense of the project committees. In the course of four months, 3,000 *maunds* of wheat worth Rs 60,000 was paid to hundreds of laborers as wages.

Long-Term Plan and Recommendations

The development of a well-designed system of drainage, irrigation, and communication in a 100-square-mile area calls for long-term planning. This can be demonstrated in Kotwali *thana*, and the Union Councils have been advised to prepare a three-year plan in the light of their recent experience. At the end of each year the plan should be revised and extended for another year, till in seven or eight years the entire system would be fully developed. By that time, there should be sufficient skill and increased wealth to maintain this portion of the infrastructure of an agricultural economy.

There are 301 miles of village roads in the *thana*. These roads are generally in bad shape. There are twenty-eight scattered markets. Now the Union Councils are planning to build good roads linking the villages with the markets, the provincial highways, the town, and the three railways stations falling within the *thana*. These roads will not only improve communication and marketing facilities but will also serve as dykes for the low-lying lands. Bridges and culverts will be constructed, with flood gates to control the water. The three-year plans will include re-excavation of the remaining channels; building of old and new link roads, sluice gates and regulators, bridges and culverts; excavation of large ponds for irrigation; and afforestation and erosion control.

These works will provide employment to thousands of distressed farmers and also improve agricultural production to a considerable degree.

The pilot project has resolved many questions for us and clarified the pattern of planning. Though much remains to be learned by the painful process of trial and error, for the present the following recommendations are made with considerable confidence:

A rural public works program of far-reaching significance, both economic and political, is feasible, but it should be suitably phased. Its successful effectuation demands a high standard of integrity and competence on the part of executive officers and intensive training of the village leaders. Sound engineering advice and supervision are also essential. It would be advisable, at the outset, to start the program only in the 50 *thanas* adjacent to district and sub-divisional headquarters. Experienced officers could subsequently be moved to outlying areas, and all 400 *thanas* of East Pakistan may be covered in a period of eight years.

The executive agencies should be the Thana Council and the Union Council, and chief authority should be vested in the *thana* circle officer. A supervisor, an accountant, and an overseer should be provided to the selected Thana Councils as extra staff.

Funds should also be given for training and contingencies. Fifteen thousand rupees at most should be enough to pay the salaries of the extra staff and to cover training and contingent expenditures. Without the extra staff, it would be impossible to train or supervise the council members, and without intensive training and supervision, especially in the first year, the program would end in a fiasco. Therefore, Rs 15,000 should be budgeted as the establishment cost of the public works.

If the government seriously desires the success of rural public works (which can make it immediately and immensely popular), it will have to choose the first group of officers very carefully.

They must possess integrity, energy, and a capacity not only to organize, but also to teach and train Union Council members and other village leaders. The selected officers should be sent for a month to the Academy to study the work in Comilla *thana* and acquaint themselves with its theory and practice. They should come in small groups so that individual attention may be given to each of them. If begun promptly, such training can be completed before next winter. Similar training can also be imparted to the supervisors, accountants, and overseers.

A manual and other materials, which would help the officer in his training of the Union Council members, would be supplied to him at the Academy.

After these officers are trained and placed in charge of their areas, they should assist the Union Councils and the Thana Council in preparing good plans. There must be constant consultations and meetings with the villagers, and the councils should be authorized to revise or amend the plans. Impersonal planning by letters and official directives would lead nowhere or give birth to bogus projects.

The plan for each *thana* should also be phased, the volume of operations gradually increasing with the growth of local managing ability. An investment of one lakh in the first year and two lakhs each in the second, third, and fourth years seems to be a reasonable estimate (1 lakh = 100,000 rupees).

Sound engineering advice must be obtained. By placing the first projects near the district and subdivisional headquarters, the services of WAPDA engineers can be made available most conveniently.

To ensure the success of the program, the officers should not only be selected with care, they should also have an incentive to make it succeed.

30. ACCIÓN COMUNAL *IN COLOMBIA*

E. GORDON ALDERFER

THE State, or Departmento, of Caldas in the Republic of Colombia sits on top of the Andean backbone of the continent. In its intermontane valleys, the biggest share of Colombia's great crop—coffee—is grown. Caldas, like other organized states of the Republic, is divided into a number of *municipios*, a form of local organization somewhere between the county and township of the U.S.A. The core of each *municipio*—that is, its town center—is surrounded by various kinds and sizes of villages, called *veredas*. The structure of government, however, penetrates only as far as the *municipio* level, and, at that, rather haphazardly. Belen de Umbria is such a *municipio* in Caldas and illustrates many of the problems confronting the Republic. Located in the rich coffee highlands, it has nevertheless suffered severely during the twelve to fifteen years of civil strife that nearly disrupted the nation. Its entire population of 28,000 has lived through years of uncertainty, distrust, fear, burnings, and killings. Today Belen de Umbria is at last beginning to rebuild.

This was one of the ports of call of the CARE community development survey team in a rapid-paced survey of what forces of development were at work in Colombian community life, what obstacles those forces faced, and what potentials existed for winning the local battle against violence, dissolution, and poverty. The survey resulted from a shared-cost agreement between CARE and Colombia's National Federation of Coffee Growers, after Richard W. Reuter, CARE's executive director, had explored with President Alberto Lleras Camargo ways to instrument the latter's great hope for rebuilding the local fabric of national life.

David Howie, who came to join the survey task force from his CARE post in Mexico, visited the *municipio* in July. To make the rounds of its *veredas*, he had to travel by horse, since, like hundreds of other Colombian communities, they lacked almost any semblance of access roads. He found that the rebuilding of the area, like pacification, is a slow process. The army still maintained military control of the area, but in this case the army was proving more than a temporary security force. It was lending a hand to help people build for a future.

Guerrilla leaders were still at large here despite the general amnesty declared by the government of President Lleras. Banditry was a problem too, for during the years of chaos, violence and banditry had become virtually a way of life for some who foresaw no future in the status quo. But the great majority preferred building to destruction; they were tired of flames and hatreds, and when Colonel Valencia, who was in charge of the army brigade controlling the area, would visit them and ask what they wanted most, nearly all answered simply "a home." Thus, the military garrison was ordered to start helping the rebuilding process, particularly for the several score of "violence widows," women with children to support whose husbands and close male relatives had been slain in the years of chaos. Local municipal and church authorities pitched in too, and the CARE mission in Colombia provided construction tools and some of those unusual earthen block-making hand presses developed by Centro Interamericano de Vivienda. More than twenty houses were built during the first year, and a number of others are in various stages of planning and completion. One of the *veredas* also built its own school, by developing a work schedule involving each adult in the community. Thus, with a little outside stimulus and some practical material aid, a community is moving from despair to hope.

No matter how often members of the survey team encountered this process, it was always like a thrill of new discovery.

The field survey started on July 11, 1960, and continued operations for three months. The team consisted of three experienced CARE representatives, to which was added the full-time services of the knowledgeable and enthusiastic Dr. Hector Morales, appointed to the survey by the President's Office of Rehabilitation. Professor Richard W. Poston, author of various community studies, who, as CARE's consultant on community development, had just finished a round-the-world survey, also aided the Colombia study.

The team visited about 85 community projects in 14 of the 17 states of Colombia during this period, studied some 30 different agencies operating in Colombia at the commuity level, played a key role in the formation of two community development co-ordinating bodies in the important states of Antioquia and Valle, participated in the work of the newly formed Inter-university Seminar on Colombian Community Development, helped in setting up, through CARE missions, a study tour made by two Colombian representatives to study community development activities in the Philippines, India, Iran, and Israel, and participated in discussions that led to the formation of a new national Division of Community Action in the Ministry of Government. The 100,000-word report that resulted from the survey's work has now been issued, and plans are in the making for its translation and book publication in the Spanish language.

This has been the first survey of its kind to be undertaken anywhere in Latin America. Perhaps nowhere else in Latin America has the ground been so well prepared and the intellectual climate so stimulated for an assault upon the problems of local poverty, illiteracy, and disease at the local community source of national life as here in Colombia. Indeed, the significance of this pioneering inquiry is that its *raison d'être* is embedded in the tumultuous recent history of Colombia.

Only two years ago did this country at the strategic hub of our hemisphere begin to emerge from a tragic period of twelve years of savage civil violence. During this period, some 300,000 people lost their lives; entire communities were destroyed, and many of these, already separated by geographic barriers and an inadequate system of communications, were torn out of the national fabric; thousands of acres of cultivated land were ravished and reverted to a state of wilderness; many millions of dollars' worth of property were wantonly destroyed. A mere semblance of national life was precariously maintained by an increasingly irresponsible dictatorship. The national debt soared to unprecedented heights as a result of ill-conceived and ill-planned national capital investments and the decay of trade and production. Perhaps most serious of all was the decay of civic and local responsibility. After twelve years of savage violence, the roots of collective community responsibility had widely atrophied.

Finally, in 1958, the country recoiled from the brink of further disaster and national disintegration. The two major political groupings, after the dictatorship was replaced by a military junta, re-established a regularly constituted national governing authority, under which there was to be a system of parity in the distribution of federal, departmental, and local offices so that each party would share equally in the task ahead, first under the four-year presidency of one party and then of the other.

The new government under the leadership of President Lleras has had an uphill struggle to reconstitute national authority, pacify dissident elements, control the national debt, establish a better balance of payments, and begin to create facilities for a more meaningful community life with a view toward social and economic justice. Violence in certain sections of the country has not yet ended, but it has been contained in large measure. Enormous strides have been made toward the attainment of an equitable balance of payments and the re-establishment of national credit. But at the level of life of the *campesino* in the rural areas and the propertyless poor who have flocked in increasing numbers to Colombia's cities, the high objectives of the new era have not yet been reached. Although the CARE survey report contains numerous stories of many individual community efforts to establish a more viable and meaningful community life, so far as the nation as a whole is concerned, such efforts appear scattered, limited in outlook, and uncoordinated in plan and execution.

The fact remains, however, that the new Colombia is fervently seeking ways to develop its resources and enrich the lives of its people where the great bulk of its population lives and where development really counts most—the local community. This is the reason why *acción comunal* is a term of wide currency and great hope in Colombia.

Yet this concept of *acción comunal* has been difficult to instrument. First of all, the long period of violence disrupted community life throughout many areas of Colombia and ended in the virtual disappearance of the habit of community cooperation. Secondly, continuing political volatility and factionalism seriously inhibit the process of national cooperation so necessary to community growth.

Moreover, as in many newly developing countries, the structure of civic government is built upon those nineteenth-century French constitutional principles that place the effective force for development at the political and economic apex, rather than at the communal roots of civil life, so that action and responsibility are extremely centralized. In other words, in Colombia there is very little legally constituted structure at the local level to support and carry out a process of development.

These conditions have also tended to aggravate another set of factors inhibiting local development—the uncertainty and insecurity of land tenure, the difficulty and expense of obtaining secure land ownership, and the effects of maldistribution and ineffective use of land. Without effective local legal entities to define boundaries and stabilize land tenure, a centralized government must inevitably find the necessary job of land administration and development a long and troublous one.

Colombia is by no means alone in wrestling with factors that seriously inhibit the improvement of local life. The fact of overriding significance is, however, that its progressive leaders have foreseen that economic health, social justice, and the physical well-being of its people must derive out of a process that begins at the local level. The improvement of national credit, industrialization, the enrichment of its cities will in the end be insufficient to support a nation desperately in need of growth and security, unless these forces for development are supported by a community life that is both progressive and peaceful.

Thus, the aims of the CARE survey were directly related to the most pressing current conditions and needs of the country, with the end objective to mark out the conditions for effective planned community action on a national scale. The survey's specific aims, originated in conversations between Mr. Reuter and President Lleras, included:

Bringing into one report-focus not only the scattered experience of Colombian communities in finding ways to improve their dismally low standards of living and to induce social stability after well over a decade of civil violence, but also the facilities available from both Colombian and international sources for community improvement.

Stimulating a realization that community development is a technique that has a special relevance to the underdeveloped world, and for this purpose seeing that representatives of Colombia witness first-hand, through the auspices of CARE, the advanced community development programs in the Philippines, India, Iran, and Israel.

Defining the kind of training and personnel most suited to the conditions of Colombia upon which the success of a national movement of community development must depend.

Assisting the process of publicizing the concept of community development as a broad-based national movement.

The findings of the survey revealed above all a fact that, surprisingly, even few knowledgeable Colombians seemed to realize —the fact that a national community development movement of significant proportions already existed. The basic concepts of the community development movement—as a collective effort to improve conditions of local life simultaneously on various fronts— has been maturing for at least two years under the leadership of President Lleras. The basic facilities to realize it are available, and both public and private organizational structures and financial resources are being developed to assist.

The *Cafeteros*, for example, are ready to spend 85,000,000 pesos a year for rural social development in coffee-growing areas and for training *socio-tecnicos*, or village workers, to do the job. The federal government's various branches are organized to assist local programs in road building, housing, rural credit, cooperatives, public health, education, and agricultural improvement. Most important of all, the government established in September a Division for Community Action in the Ministry of Government, to serve as a focal point and chief coordinating agency for the national program. International and U.S. agencies are participating on a number of fronts. A regional TVA-type agency like the Cauca Valley Corporation not only extends electric power resources to the countryside, but also carries out local extension services in health, home improvement, and agriculture. A variety of private agencies—Acción Cultural Popular (Radio Sutatenza), the Rockefeller Foundation, the National Apprenticeship Service, Heifer Project, and CARE—have contributed in a very substantial way to the improvement of local life by means (respectively) of rural radio education, agricultural and medical research, vocational training, livestock extension and improvement, and the programming of tools and equipment for direct community use.

There is no question about the availability of substantial resources for the job of rebuilding community life. This may be a surprise to many, even Colombians, who regard this republic as one of the so-called underdeveloped areas. (With an average per capita annual income of only $283, a population that has tripled in the last fifty years, less than half its people able to read or write, prevailingly low public-health standards, rapidly spreading slum areas, and serious disturbances in the public order, the classification of underdevelopment is understandable.) What is lacking —or has been until now—is the coordination of these substantial resources of money, material, and organizational structure for the rebuilding of local life.

The need for effective coordination was perhaps the chief emphasis of the survey's recommendations. Among other things, the report proposed the establishing of a permanent *working* congress of representatives from all major agencies operating at the community level to provide a medium for exchanging information, working out inter-agency means for avoiding wastage and duplication, and sharing knowledge of new technical and social developments that could improve community life.

The role of the government must be paramount in this. Upon that leadership will depend the growth of an increasing confidence and public sense of partnership in government. The scattered efforts of many entities—federal, international, regional, state, private (both non-profit and commercial)—can set the tempo for local development, as they have been doing. But in an explosive situation like Colombia's, explosive politically and economically, the time is short—and scattered, uncorrelated efforts will not lift a nation from the edge of chaos to internal security, progressive growth, and economic and social justice. Besides, continuing the job that way would be unduly expensive, in money, time, and effort.

We cannot help reminding ourselves that *underdevelopment is often a disparity not so much between industrialized and non-industrialized countries as between the widely separated sectors of the rich and the poor within the same country.* Colombia is a not untypical example. An economic and political elite exists as an inheritance traceable all the way back to the imposition of Spanish rule. During the intervening centuries, bloods may have mingled, but the institution of the elite has persisted and hardened. The measured steps to a social order built upon opportunity for all responsible members of the body politic, rather than on a widely distrusted status quo, have not been well learned. The process of learning those steps is not easy, but it is greatly to the credit of the Lleras administration that efforts at national development are being made at the base of the economic pyramid as well as at its apex. Rebuilding the base is essentially what we conceive of as *community* development in the interests of those most desperately in need of opportunity.

To the establishment of a teamwork of resources and a reorientation of the elite toward longer-range national goals and responsibilities must be added another ingredient. Progress at rebuilding the community base of national life will depend in large measure also on administrative aptness. The design of plans and charts for proposed developmental operations—so prolific a habit in newly developing countries—is not enough. The important thing is the ability to translate plans into solid, measurable accomplishments. Perhaps one of the distinguishing characteristics of countries in immature stages of development is the vacuum that seems to exist between plan and action—a curious extension of Parkinson's Law. Plans seem to multiply like rabbits (fortified, indeed, by surveys), but effective action is slow to generate.

One of the disturbing characteristics of Colombian plans studied by the survey was their hierarchical character. In their descriptions of the personnel to be trained to carry out the job of stimulating local development, invariably they were divided into federal, regional, zonal, and local categories. Too frequently the emphasis was placed on the upper brackets. But, assuming a range of local flexibility in the job, no elaborate hierarchy is necessary to support the process, especially in view of the fact that the resources and basic machinery already exist. Community development means beginning at, and in, the community, not in a hierarchical payroll.

In recognition of this principle, the President's Office of Rehabilitation established a limited number of multi-value teams (*equipos polivalentes*) of community workers at a time of dangerous instability in rural areas. Each team was composed of a medical doctor as team leader, two agronomists (one to work with adults, the other to concentrate on youth groups), a nurse, a home improvement worker. Before a team went into local operation, a study was made of the make-up and basic needs of each community it covered.

The polyvalent team was a group of professionals and specialists—but, luckily, they were more than that. They were trained, briefly, to serve above all as members of a community development team, and served in their specialized capacities only within that team context. Because their assignments took them to remoter and more disturbed areas, their double assignment—as community developers and as specialists—proved remarkably successful. Into most of these areas no single development operative or specialist had dared to appear alone for years. But what made the team idea succeed was the quiet, effective way it stimulated the community —even the most dissident elements and guerrilla raiders, in some cases—to learn again how to work together, to discover its basic problems in its own terms, and to set in motion its own resources for improvement.

It would obviously be impossible, however, to apply the poly-valent concept to a really substantial national program that would penetrate the entire country. Involvement of so many professionals would be too expensive, for one thing. For another, with the receding of the violence, the team-type of operation is no longer so widely needed.

What is needed under the present circumstances—and quickly —is the development of a large corps of *promotores del pueblo*. The term is only awkwardly translatable, and, in a sense, it signifies a new set of skills, a new profession. The "promoter's" job does not require advanced academic training, but it does require a training in the application of common sense to community prob-lems, a knowledge of what specialized skills and professional resources should be called on to meet specific community needs and where to find them, a sensitivity to the community as a living organism and not merely as an unlinked chain of economic in-terests. He is not an "extensionist" with a single professional skill, but a community generalist geared to help induce the process of local development. It is, at least from the point of view of the survey, the most important job in Colombia today.

The professional skills for development—in public health, prac-tical education, agronomy, home improvement, local small-scale industry—already exist in some considerable measure in Colom-bia, according to the findings of the survey. They should be used as professional skills, called on as needed. Finding the personnel for training as *promotores* is a different matter, but preliminary searches seem to reveal large numbers of underemployed young people eager for this kind of service to their country. The real test will come in the evolution of an adequate national training pat-tern for the job and the extent to which various operative agencies make use of it.

As a pioneering venture, the survey seemed to us significant for a number of reasons. As the first survey of its kind in Latin America, we felt that CARE was exploring a new potential of development for this part of the world, as messages from both President Lleras and President Lemus of El Salvador indicated. It was significant, too, because it was made in a part of the world where the local community has been traditionally and tragically overshadowed by the central sources of power and wealth.

Also, the survey represented a unique joining of forces between CARE and a major economic, non-governmental agency of another country. The Federacion Nacional de Cafeteros and CARE shared equally the costs of the survey, but the cooperation is more than that. There was much evidence that the progress of the survey had indirect but considerable influence on activities in various parts of the country and on centering attention on the potential for local development. Early in September, for example, the Coffee Federation established a regularly operating department of socio-economic affairs, with the prime object of creating the facilities for a major community development effort throughout coffee-growing areas all over Colombia.

Finally, the survey represented unique evidence of CARE's versatility, and perhaps a new departure which can in the future mean much to deepening CARE's relationships with other peoples. Never before has CARE "programmed ideas, information, and personnel," rather than material, quite so directly. Never before has it entered into the survey kind of operation, except in task forces aimed specifically at establishing a standard CARE program. It was perhaps a daring thing for CARE to undertake. But perhaps it is that quality that makes CARE an unusual symbol of the responsibility and capacity North American peoples feel for partnership with other peoples to face the challenge of "the revolution of rising expectations."

NINE

THE CULTURAL ASPECTS OF DEVELOPMENT

31. THE MONKEY AND THE FISH

DON ADAMS

THERE is an old Oriental story that accurately depicts the plight of an unwary foreign educational adviser: Once upon a time there was a great flood, and involved in this flood were two creatures, a monkey and a fish. The monkey, being agile and experienced, was lucky enough to scramble up a tree and escape the raging waters. As he looked down from his safe perch, he saw the poor fish struggling against the swift current. With the very best of intentions, he reached down and lifted the fish from the water. The result was inevitable.

The educational adviser, unless he is a careful student of his own culture and the culture in which he works, will be acting much like the monkey; and, with the most laudable intentions, he may make decisions equally disastrous. Using Korea as a case in point, I shall describe some of the cultural pitfalls facing an American working in that country. The description will involve examining some of the basic assumptions, or "unconscious canons of choice" as the distinguished anthropologist Ruth Benedict called them, of the Korean people. This analysis will be made in terms of the behavior promoted by such assumptions, in order to indicate how such behavior may appear to be illogical or even unintelligible to a western adviser. Many of the value orientations described here also appear in other East Asian countries where similar cultural roots may be found. Japan and Korea, for example, were both greatly influenced by a variety of cultural forces emanating from China, the most profound of which has been called Confucianism. But sharply contrasting twentieth-century forces of militarism, Communism, and democracy have brought elements of noticeable dissimilarity among Asian countries that make extensive generalizations dangerous.

Time Orientation

The first obvious cultural difference noted by the American in Korea is regarded by some to be an especially important element in differentiating cultures. This is *time orientation*, the perspective with which a nation views the process of time. All peoples must examine problems rooted in the present or past and yet must try to anticipate the future. The differences in the view of time pointed out here are related to the degree of precedence given.

The American, for example, has historically looked with pleasant anticipation toward the future. Tomorrow is expected to be brighter than today, and, with minor exceptions, only things bigger and better can be envisioned for the future. History itself is often viewed as a continuum of progress, with each succeeding generation more advanced than the former. American schools consider that one of their major functions is the examination of the present so that their products may better plan the future.

Contrast this with the Korean culture, which historically has been oriented to the past; where the Good Life has been defined completely in terms of past living; where history has largely been viewed as cyclical, with the future regarded as a mere repetition of some portion of the past; and where innovations in terms of things bigger and better may be disrespectful to one's ancestors. The American technical adviser, geared to "getting things done" and "getting things moving," is often frustrated by situations in which his Korean colleagues appear to be acting too slowly or even stalling. Conversely, the American may by his direct approach appear exceedingly rude to the Korean, who sees no reason to be upset over current ills since the good times of the past are bound to reappear.

Historically, then, Korea has not viewed its institutions as developmental to the same degree as is done in the U.S.A. While not adept at operational thinking, however, Korean students often pursue with skill the more purely academic and aesthetic interests. In so doing, they exhibit characteristics that make the current-and-future-oriented American often seem superficial, even at times crude. Education in this cloistered setting could not be expected to be dynamic or experimental, and until the Japanese introduced colonial-flavored modern education in the twentieth century, the Korean school system was designed only to perpetuate the best of the past in an unaltered form. From ancient times, the prescribed curriculum was the written wisdom of the Chinese sages and constituted what might be called a series of Asian Great Books. From the tender age when he memorized his first Chinese character, until many years later when, if exceptionally able, he might pass the royal examination and become a government official, the curriculum of the scholar was the literature of the past. He studied not only the ideas involved, but the author's phraseology and his technique of calligraphy. As the ancient texts assumed the proportions of canons, he studied to imitate rather than to exceed, to conform rather than to create. Education that was prized was divorced entirely from the social, economic, and scientific problems of the present.

The Man-Nature Orientation

A second cultural difference lies in the relation of man and nature or what might be called *man-nature orientation*. In America, man has increasingly expected to gain mastery over nature and he has watched his wildest expectations come true. Mountains he crossed, tunneled through, or even pulverized. Rivers proved no obstacle to his energy, for these were easily dammed or bridged. In the East Asian culture, man typically has not been so concerned with gaining mastery over his environment as he has been with living in harmony with it. Mountains that might obstruct travel and rivers that might be impassable during certain seasons have not been viewed as merely frustrating inconveniences. Rather, these are historical facts to which man must discipline himself. The challenge lies not in constructing new weapons for mastery, but in developing a higher degree of resignation.

As with time orientation, the traditional view held by Koreans with respect to nature has not contributed to a dynamic educational system. If man does not seek mastery over nature, there is little need for the schools to be concerned with the tools and skills for manipulating the physical universe. Rather, schools should be concerned with developing not the active, but the passive, person, one who seeks to avoid the common, tedious, daily environment by finding and developing problems in a more aesthetic realm. The educated man is the man of contemplation who carries about him at all times an air of peace and tranquillity. His view toward the natural environment is shown in many and diverse ways, but perhaps is best expressed in his works of art, in which he so often chooses as his subject the essential harmoniousness of the universe and avoids portraying the raucous world of change and discord.

This view of man's relation to nature, coupled with his orientation to time, has created what Thorstein Veblen once called "a poverty of wants." Until recent years, little need was felt among the great bulk of the population of Korea for the fruits of an educational system geared to produce the wide variety of skills and understandings needed to revamp and improve the existing mode of life. This does not mean that the less sophisticated people lack educational drive. On the contrary, individual families willingly make tremendous sacrifice to obtain schooling for their children. Yet these same families exert no pressure toward making the school an economically oriented institution capable of teaching functional knowledge. The urgency of keeping up to date, lest history leave you behind or nature overwhelm you, is not present to the same extent in the Korean culture as in the American. The goal of Korean education was, until the recent impact of Western culture, adjustment rather than improvement.

The Power and Status Orientation

A third cultural difference could be called *power and status orientation*. The U.S.A. has been proud of its decentralization of political and educational responsibilities. Under a system where considerable power is exercised at the state and local levels, every citizen becomes a leader, inasmuch as he has the right to share in decision-making. The town meeting, the school board, and all the trappings of direct and representative democracy have been widely eulogized. Because of these opportunities, the American citizen, it has been said, is a more sophisticated voter than his foreign brother, and the American student a more independent learner, as well as a better team man. Obviously, there is more than a little jingoism mixed in these interpretations. Nevertheless, the fact remains that Americans are still committed largely to the belief in shared decision-making.

A power structure has existed in Korea that has equated position with authority, while social custom has further equated authority with validity. This hierarchal structure and manner of decision-making are also reflected in the classroom and in the family. The teacher and the father both occupy positions of ultimate trust, respect, power. Their word is law. The obvious difficulty of using modern educational methods within this framework is readily seen. The school in both fostering cooperation and stressing at the same time reliance on the individual's ability to solve his own problems runs into conflict with family and societal tradition. Moreover, it is difficult to break down the school's authoritarian structure, because of the fear that the teacher may lose the traditional respect felt for him.

The organization and administration of Korean education reflects the power structure found elsewhere in Korean society. Until 1948, and to a gradually modifying degree since then, Korean education has operated within a framework that was highly centralized. Major decisions emanated from the Ministry of Education. Even though opportunities for local control have been provided, they have not been taken advantage of, and lesser educational officials invariably refuse to take responsibility for decisions clearly within their jurisdiction, but prefer the decisions to be made "higher up." The danger, in addition to the perpetuation of authoritarian procedures, is that the bases for determining professional action are largely founded on judgmental evidence as represented by the expressions of a status person rather than on factual evidence.

There are further and widespread educational implications of this lineally organized society. As with individuals in an organization, the schools have a definite order of rank, as do the courses of study within the school. Since academic subjects carry the most prestige, the technical and vocational schools, in attempting to gain recognition, tend to de-emphasize the applied parts of their curriculum. There is so much status value attached to abstract and difficult works that Korean students enjoy being immersed in little understood concepts and often rebel in studying subjects within their comprehension.

Language is another major curriculum problem that is rooted partly in status factors. Although a simple phonetic alphabet, Hangul, had been developed in Korea in the fifteenth century, it had never been widely accepted by scholars. Government officials historically have used a written script based on Chinese characters, which has served to create and perpetuate the gulf between the Korean people and their culture. During the latter part of the Japanese annexation, to further complicate matters, the Koreans were required to use the Japanese language on all occasions. After being freed from colonial status, Korea erased most traces of the Japanese language, and the vernacular was not only re-introduced into the schools, but also increasingly stressed in all literature.

The net result of this complex language situation is that Korea in 1959 finds itself with very little professional literature appropriate for students at the secondary school and college levels. There are few modern technical or professional books written in Chinese, and the children entering school after 1945 have been receiving only limited work with Chinese characters anyway. Most of the books written in Japanese (and all educated Korean adults are fluent in this language) have been destroyed. Moreover, the generation of Koreans now in school have no familiarity with the Japanese language. And at the present time, despite official government urgings, newspapers and most professional periodicals are being made incomprehensible to a major part of the Korean population by the inclusion of a large number of Chinese characters rather than relying on the vernacular. (It is interesting to note that, under Communism, North Korea has made great strides in eliminating the use of Chinese characters, simplifying and refining the pure Korean. It appears that all literature being published in North Korea uses only the simple, practical Hangul script.)

The indirect influences of the West through Japanese colonialism and the direct contacts since 1945 have forced a re-examination of Korean value orientations. The sincere if awkward attempts to industrialize and democratize a nation with a long agrarian and authoritarian heritage have produced a considerable number of inconsistencies within the Korean society. For example, the political party in power one day exalts democratic freedoms, yet on the next may order all students to participate in "spontaneous demonstration" to promote a particular party bias. Police in one section of the country initiate youth clubs to combat delinquency, yet themselves may at times use extremely harsh methods. The government through all avenues of propaganda promotes moral education, yet, as in older times, the bribe may often be the easiest recourse for the Korean citizen who attempts to get action through official channels. Such discrepancies indicate not only policy incongruities and personal confusion, but also identify a major obstacle to a smooth cultural transition. Unity, loyalty, and morality are well defined and practiced in the family, making this an institution long admired in the West, but these qualities are yet to be raised to the societal level.

The Adviser as Catalyst

The role of the foreign educational adviser in this setting is, then, both sensitive and difficult. His own knowledge and skills are to a certain extent culture-bound and unintelligible or incongruous in new surroundings. Yet, it may be precisely his new perspective that is badly needed. The task of technical assistance can obviously not be defined as "teaching them to do it our way." But neither is the counter alternative, "helping them to do what they wish to do better," completely satisfactory. The former runs the danger of technical inapplicability or of cultural resistance, while the latter may involve no substantial progress toward the newer and only partially defined goals. The adviser by his increased technical knowledge sheds light on possible alternatives, but neither through coercion nor through persuasion does he determine the direction of change.

Perhaps the adviser can best be likened to a catalyst. By bringing his knowledge and experience and points of view to the new situation, his role is to speed desirable change. To fulfill this role adequately, the adviser must be a student of the culture and meta-culture. He must establish guidelines that will determine in broad outline educational priorities acceptable to the host nation. He must face up to the enigmatic problem of focusing attention on grassroots education—for example, increasing literacy, helping the farmer to eke out a slightly bigger yield per acre—or striking out on a broad scale to teach the highly developed skills and understandings needed by a nation moving toward industrialization. Since it is extremely difficult or impossible to change a cultural pattern by attacking its isolated parts, he must answer the question whether the establishment of a few model projects can be justified in hopes that their influence will spread.

Korea is a nation in the throes of a rapid but uneven cultural change. While members of the older generation may still cling to the belief that "the scholar should neither shoulder a carrying pole nor lift a basket," young students are beginning to seek the skills requisite for nudging an ancient culture toward new directions. In Korea, as in any developing country, cultural modification depends primarily on the initiative and drive of the people. Through his minor but vital role, the adviser, by participating from the beginning with the people whose lives are being affected, may be able to lessen the traumatic effects of such change.

32. *WHAT UNDERDEVELOPED COUNTRIES DO NOT WANT*

EDWARD T. HALL

On many trips out of the United States, I have talked to people in every major continent. After I got to know them, and they relaxed a bit, or felt that they could trust me, they always had things to say about the Americans. It is this that I would like to discuss.

Today, twenty years after our early technical assistance programs in Latin America, the world has had considerable experience with what we bring. They have learned that technology can be both a boon and a curse. They have also learned that all Americans are not alike. But, by and large, when a lot of Americans arrive, there are a number of patterns that repeat themselves. What I have to say here is not particularly pleasant to contemplate, because we have pride in our way of life. Nevertheless, our way of life, our way of proceeding overseas has an impact that is not always what we would like it to be.

Most of the places where we have foreign missions are rather poor. Their lack of material possessions stands in stark contrast to our own material wealth. The sheer mass of what we bring with us makes the gap between them and ourselves much greater than it need be. Many look at the riches that we bring with us and conclude that we are richer than we are, or that somehow or other we got this wealth by exploiting somebody else.

I have yet to see anyone who could understand our habit of establishing exclusive American colonies overseas which the inhabitants refer to as the "Golden Ghettos." Certainly this sets us apart and gives the impression that we feel that we are better than others. One of the by-products of the way in which we live is that we tend to drive rents upward wherever we move in. This does not endear us to the local inhabitants. Not only that, but we upset the employer-servant relationship by overpaying servants and underdisciplining them. We let our children run wild, particularly our teen-agers. We block the streets with our big cars. Even if we behaved differently, there are times when the sheer number of Americans is overwhelming.

Nobody likes to be looked down upon. Yet there are many things in our behavior—not in what we *say* but in our *behavior*—that indicate in subtle ways that we look down on others. For instance, we tend to ignore, or fail to make, important national and ethnic distinctions; witness the remark, "All Japanese look alike to me." As a matter of fact, all whites look alike to Orientals. To say that everyone looks alike may be permissible at first, but after a person has spent ten or more years in a country, it is ridiculous.

A seemingly small and rather insignificant annoyance has to do with the fact that we often fail to learn the systems of names and naming and the formal patterns of address. These are, admittedly, quite different from our own. Some other languages use honorifics. Now the American does not "go for" the honorific. But at the same time, we don't like it when foreigners become overly familiar with us too soon. To ignore their naming systems and their systems of address is a constant reminder that we do not care enough and that they don't matter enough for us to take the trouble to learn even this first point of contact.

We tend to place knowledge of local customs low on our priority list, not only in the field, but here at home too. A very high official of one of our largest international agencies once explained to me, when I was bewailing the fact that little or no use was made of the knowledge of culture or the people who study culture, the anthropologists, "Out of a list of fifteen priorities, the type of 'know-how' you represent occupies position number twelve. We are working with the top five." Yet this is the "know-how" of getting along with other people.

There are also times when aspects of our own culture improperly or incompletely explained or stressed give the wrong idea. In the United States, subversion is political subversion, but in many parts of the East, subversion is cultural subversion. Our technical changes are not welcome, because they shake the very roots of life. In many countries in Southeast Asia, we seem to represent science, a science that controls nature, molds it, and adapts it. This seems very natural to us. But their view of nature is that man should not attempt to control it, but to discover its secrets. We fail to make clear the situation between our science and our technology.

Actually, our science also emphasizes discovery of the laws of nature so that we can work within them. Very few people realize the importance of the difference between *discovering* and *controlling*—but some of those who live in Southeast Asia do understand.

In the running and planning of our missions, we take the bull by the horns and set up programs we think are needed. All too often, teams of experts arrive without the local nationals being properly prepared. The *form* of local clearance is gone through, but the process is not complete. The impression is left with everyone concerned (and as long as this impression remains, the damage is done) that we are sending people to them whom they have not asked for and do not need. A constant complaint is, "Please, if you Americans could just consult with us a little more on what our needs are."

One of the most serious errors we make is failing to learn the local language. There is no form of impoliteness that carries quite the same implication of rejection as failure to concern oneself with the language of the people. When we fail to learn the local language, we appear to say, in clear tones, "We do not think it is worth the time to learn to communicate with you. You must learn to communicate with us." This says as clearly as it can be stated, "We think we are better than you are."

I recall the wife of one American official in a Far Eastern country who quietly and unobtrusively learned the local language and started speaking it one day at a cocktail party. The diplomatic community fairly buzzed. Our friends in the country were sure that American relations were going to take a turn for the better—that a new day had dawned because an American had learned their language.

For one like myself who spends a good deal of his time out of the country talking to Americans, their rationalizations for not learning the language become somewhat tiresome.

Think for a moment what it would be like if we had, say, ten thousand foreigners, all of the same nationality, living in our midst, none of whom learned our language and who kept themselves isolated from us. Who, furthermore, gave parties, imported their own goods, drove their own brands of automobiles, insisted on using their own law courts, mispronounced our names, couldn't tell us apart, and then made rude and tactless remarks such as, "How much is this in 'real' money?" Yet this is just the way we behave overseas.

Finally, one of the most sensitive of all problems from both points of view has to do with the political tie-in. "We will give you technical aid if you will be on our side against the Communists." There are a great many people in the world who like to take advantage of the things we have to offer. But they don't like the two tied together, one contingent upon the other. They don't like the feeling that they are being bought. Many new nations today are struggling with all of the problems of recent independence. That their independence should tie them to our apron strings is sometimes difficult to accept and does not make for a good relationship.

I know that my comments are not pleasing to many Americans, but as an American I can afford to pass on things to my countrymen that non-Americans have said to me. Somehow we are going to have to learn the lesson that we can no longer afford to "look down" on people, or give the impression that we look down upon them, by our behavior.

I would reiterate that our failure to learn the language and our tendency to keep apart are probably among the most serious errors we make. I do not agree with the remark that "a little language is a dangerous thing." You can never learn a lot of language without learning a little language first. If there is no beginning, one can certainly never finish.

BIBLIOGRAPHY

This brief list has been compiled from the book sections of the INTERNATIONAL DEVELOPMENT REVIEW, from *Selected Readings and Source Materials on Economic Development* (Washington, D.C.: International Bank for Reconstruction and Development, 1962, 66 pp.), and from Saul M. Katz and Frank McGowan, *A Selected List of U.S. Readings on Development* (Washington, D.C.: U.S. Agency for International Development, 1963, 363 pp.). It is limited to recent books and monographs in English.

WHAT IS INTERNATIONAL DEVELOPMENT?

ASHER, ROBERT E., *et al. Development of the Emerging Countries: An Agenda for Research.* Washington, D.C.: The Brookings Institution, 1962. 239 pp.

BAUER, PETER T., and YAMEY, BASIL S. *The Economics of Underdeveloped Countries.* London: James Nisbet & Co.; Cambridge: Cambridge University Press; Chicago: University of Chicago Press, 1957. xiii, 271 pp.

BLACK, EUGENE R. *The Diplomacy of Economic Development.* Cambridge, Mass.: Harvard University Press, 1960. x, 74 pp.

CLARK, COLIN. *The Conditions of Economic Progress.* 3d ed. London: Macmillan & Co.; New York: St Martin's Press, 1957. xv, 720 pp.

HEILBRONER, ROBERT L. *The Great Ascent.* New York: Harper & Row, 1963.

HIGGINS, BENJAMIN. *Economic Development: Principles, Problems, and Policies.* New York: W. W. Norton & Co., 1959. xviii, 803 pp.

HIRSCHMAN, ALBERT O. *The Strategy of Economic Development.* New Haven: Yale University Press, 1958. xiii, 217 pp.

HOFFMAN, PAUL G. *World Without Want.* New York: Harper & Row, 1962. 144 pp.

KINDLEBERGER, CHARLES P. *Economic Development.* New York: The McGraw-Hill Book Co., 1958. xiii, 325 pp.

KUZNETS, SIMON S. *Six Lectures on Economic Growth*. Glencoe, Ill.: The Free Press, 1959. 122 pp.

MEIER, GERALD M., and BALDWIN, ROBERT E. *Economic Development: Theory, History, Policy*. New York: John Wiley & Sons; London: Chapman & Hall, 1957. xix, 588 pp.

MYRDAL, GUNNAR. *Rich Lands and Poor: The Road to World Prosperity*. New York: Harper & Bros., 1957. xx, 168 pp. English edition, *Economic Theory and Underdeveloped Regions*. London: Gerald Duckworth & Co., 1957. 168 pp.

ROSTOW, WALT W. *The Stages of Economic Growth: A Non-Communist Manifesto*. New York: Cambridge University Press, 1960. x, 179 pp.

STALEY, EUGENE. *The Future of Underdeveloped Countries: Political Implications of Economic Development*. Rev. ed. New York: Harper & Row (cloth); Frederick A. Praeger (paper), 1961. xx, 483 pp.

THEOBALD, ROBERT. *The Rich and the Poor*. New York: Clarkson T. Potter, 1961. 196 pp.

United Nations. Department of Economic Affairs. *Measures for the Economic Development of Underdeveloped Countries*. Report by a group of experts appointed by the Secretary-General of the United Nations. New York, 1951. ix, 108 pp. United Nations Publication 1955. II. B.1.

PAYING FOR DEVELOPMENT

ASHER, ROBERT E. *Grants, Loans, and Local Currencies*. Washington, D.C.: The Brookings Institution, 1961. 142 pp.

BASCH, ANTONIN. *The Future of Lending for Foreign Development*. Ann Arbor, Mich.: University of Michigan Center for Research on Economic Development, 1962. 45 pp.

DIAMOND, WILLIAM. *Development Banks*. Baltimore: The Johns Hopkins Press, 1957. xiii, 128 pp.

NURKSE, RAGNAR. *Problems of Capital Formation in Underdeveloped Countries*. New York: Oxford University Press, 1953. 163 pp.

PAAUW, DOUGLAS S. *Financing Economic Development: The Indonesia Case*. Glencoe, Ill., The Free Press, 1960, 474 pp.

PLANNING AND ADMINISTERING DEVELOPMENT

HAYES, SAMUEL PERKINS. *Measuring the Results of Development Projects*. New York: United Nations Educational, Scientific and Cultural Organization, 1959. 100 pp.

LEWIS, JOHN P. *Quiet Crisis in India*. Washington, D.C.: The Brookings Institution, 1963. 336 pp.

SWERDLOW, IRVING (ed.). *Development Administration: Concepts and Problems*. Syracuse: Syracuse University Press, 1963. 162 pp.

TINBERGEN, JAN. *The Design of Development*. Baltimore; The Johns Hopkins Press, 1958. viii, 99 pp.

WALINSKY, LOUIS J. *The Planning and Execution of Economic Development*. New York: The McGraw-Hill Book Co., 1963. 240 pp.

MANPOWER FOR DEVELOPMENT

CLEVELAND, HARLAN, *et al. The Overseas American*. New York: The McGraw-Hill Book Co., 1960. 316 pp.

TORRE, MOTTRAM (ed.). *The Selection of Personnel for International Service*. New York: World Federation of Mental Health, 1963, 161 pp.

THE EDUCATIONAL CHALLENGE

HARBISON, FREDERICK, and MYERS, CHARLES A. *Education, Manpower and Economic Growth*. New York: The McGraw-Hill Book Co., 1963. 244 pp.

PARNES, HERBERT S. (ed.). *Planning Education for Economic and Social Development*. Paris: OECD Mediterranean Regional Project, 1962. 270 pp.

TOWARD BETTER HEALTH

WINSLOW, CHARLES EDWARD AMORY. *The Cost of Sickness and the Price of Health*. Geneva: World Health Organization, 1951. 106 pp.

AGRICULTURE AND INDUSTRY

ACKERMANN, JEAN MARIE. *Communicating Industrial Ideas*. Menlo Park, Calif.: Stanford Research Institute, 1962. 145 pp.

BRYCE, MURRAY D. *Industrial Development: A Guide for Accelerating Economic Growth*. New York: The McGraw-Hill Book Co., 1960. 282 pp.

HEADY, EARL OREL. *Agricultural Policy Under Economic Development*. Ames, Iowa: Iowa State University Press, 1962. 682 pp.

SENIOR, CLARENCE O. *Land Reform and Democracy*. Gainesville, Fla.: University of Florida Press, 1958. xiii, 269 pp.

STEPANEK, JOSEPH E. *Small Industry Advisory Services: An International Study*. Glencoe, Ill.: The Free Press, 1960. xiii, 193 pp.

COMMUNITY DEVELOPMENT

ALLEN, HAROLD B. *Rural Reconstruction in Action: Experience in the Near and Middle East*. Ithaca, N.Y.: Cornell University Press, 1953. xviii, 204 pp.

MAYER, ALBERT, *et al. Pilot Project, India: The Story of Rural Development at Etawah, Uttar Pradesh*. Berkeley: University of California Press, 1959. xxiv, 367 pp.

POSTON, RICHARD W. *Democracy Speaks Many Tongues: Community Development Around the World*. New York, Harper & Row, 1962. 206 pp.

CULTURAL ASPECTS OF DEVELOPMENT

ERASMUS, CHARLES J. *Man Takes Control: Cultural Development and American Aid*. Minneapolis, Minn.: University of Minnesota Press, 1961. 365 pp.

HAGEN, EVERETT EINAR. *On the Theory of Social Change: How Economic Growth Begins*. Homewood, Ill.: Dorsey Press, 1962. 557 pp.

HOSELITZ, BERTHOLD F. *Sociological Aspects of Economic Growth*. Glencoe, Ill.: The Free Press, 1960. vi. 250 pp.

McCLELLAND, DAVID C. *The Achieving Society*. Princeton: D. Van Nostrand Co., 1961. xv, 512 pp.

MEAD, MARGARET (ed.). *Cultural Patterns and Technical Change*. Paris: United Nations Educational, Scientific and Cultural Organization, 1953. 348 pp. A manual prepared by the World Federation for Mental Health.

NAIR, KUSUM. *Blossoms in the Dust: The Human Factor in Indian Development*. New York: Frederick A. Praeger, 1962. 197 pp.

NOTES ON THE CONTRIBUTORS

Membership in SID is indicated by a small circle supra°.

Donald K. Adams° is associate professor of Comparative Education at Syracuse University and director of its Center for Development Education. Previously, he taught comparative education at the George Peabody College for Teachers. In 1957–58, he was consultant in teacher education in Korea under the George Peabody College–ICA contract; in 1954–55, he held a similar post in Korea under the sponsorship of UNKRA and the American Korean Foundation of the Unitarian Service Committee. During 1955–56, he taught at the University of Massachusetts and at Springfield College. He has served with the U.S. Army Air Corps (1941–43) and the U.S. Air Force (1951–52) and is a graduate of the University of New Hampshire (B.S., 1949) and the University of Connecticut (M.A., 1954; Ph.D., 1956). He is co-author of *Patterns of Education in Contemporary Societies* and editor of *Progress in Educational Planning*. Professor Adams was born in North Berwick, Maine, in 1925. (International Development Review: "The Monkey and the Fish," March, 1962; "Pitfalls and Priorities," December, 1962.)

John H. Adler° was appointed director of the World Bank's Economic Development Institute on January 1, 1962. He had been a member of the Bank staff since 1950, as economist (1950–57) and as economic adviser (1957–61). Previously, he had been economist in the Federal Reserve Bank, New York (1947–50); deputy chief, finance division, U.S. War Department, Vienna (1945–47); economist, Board of Governors, Federal Reserve System (1944–45); instructor in economics, Oberlin College (1942–44); and research assistant, Yale Institute of International Studies (1941–42). Born in Tachov, Czechoslovakia, in 1912, Dr. Adler, now a United States citizen, holds the degrees of Dr. juris (University of Prague, 1937), and Ph.D. (Yale, 1946). He is co-author of several books and author of many articles in economic journals. He is currently a member of the Council of

SID. (INTERNATIONAL DEVELOPMENT REVIEW: "The Economic Development Institute of the World Bank," March, 1963.)

E. GORDON ALDERFER,° is executive director of the Estes Center for Research and Education. Currently he is on leave as assistant executive director of CARE, Inc., which he joined in July, 1956. He has planned and directed the program research and development activities of the organization and was a principal architect of CARE self-help programs. He has also carried out various special assignments in behalf of CARE: in 1960, as director of the Encuesta para Acción Comunal, Colombia; in 1961, as director of CARE's partnership program with the U.S. Peace Corps; in 1962, as program officer for an AID research project on the introduction and use of small-scale electric power systems for underdeveloped rural areas; in 1963, as CARE representative at a conference of European nongovernmental agencies engaged in the planning of developmental activities overseas. Mr. Alderfer has been active in SID since 1958 when he helped to found the New York chapter. He became its first president. He is currently an elected member of the SID World Council, a member of its editorial board, and book editor of the INTERNATIONAL DEVELOPMENT REVIEW. He is also a member of the advisory board for the McGraw-Hill Book Company's series in international development. Prior to his service with CARE, Mr. Alderfer was executive assistant to the president of the American Academy of Political and Social Science and director of research for the American Friends Service Committee. He was also involved with a large number of publishing, editing, and historical research enterprises and studies and was a co-founder of Penns Valley Publishers, Inc. He graduated from the University of Pennsylvania in 1941 with Certificates of Distinction and Major Honors. (INTERNATIONAL DEVELOPMENT REVIEW: "*Acción Comunal* in Colombia," February, 1961.)

PAUL I. BERNICK,° executive director of American ORT Federation, has extensive experience and firsthand knowledge of the vocational training activities that are ORT's specialty. He has surveyed and studied ORT vocational schools in Europe, North Africa, and Israel and has participated in many conferences concerned with vocational problems in these areas. He is a member of the Executive Committee of the American Council of Voluntary Agencies in Foreign Service, a vice-chairman of the Council's Technical Assistance Projects Committee and Committee on Africa, and a participant in the Technical Assistance Projects Clearing House. A Chicagoan by birth, Mr. Bernick attended Crane Junior College and the University of Chicago. (INTERNATIONAL DEVELOPMENT REVIEW: "New Skills for New Societies," October, 1960.)

EUGENE R. BLACK has been a director and consultant to the Chase Manhattan Bank, New York, since his retirement on January 1, 1963, as president of the International Bank for Reconstruction and Development. In 1919, he became associated with the Atlanta office of Harris, Forbes Company, New York investment house, and in 1933 was named assistant vice-president of its successor, the Chase Harris Forbes Corporation. Later that year he joined the Chase National Bank, predecessor of Chase Manhattan, as a second vice-president. He was promoted to vice-president in 1937. In 1947, he left to become the United States director of the World Bank. In January, 1949, he returned to Chase and was appointed a senior vice-president and the following July resigned to become president of the World Bank. Mr. Black is a member of the board of directors of various corporations, a trustee and chairman of the Finance Committee of the Ford Foundation, a trustee and president of the American Shakespeare Festival, a trustee and chairman of the Board of the Brookings Institution, and a trustee of the Johns Hopkins and Oglethorpe universities. He is also a special financial consultant to the Secretary-General of the United Nations and was a special adviser to President Kennedy on the supersonic transport program. Mr. Black holds honorary degrees from the University of Chattanooga, Columbia, Oglethorpe, Syracuse, Macalester College, the University of Arkansas, Rutgers, Harvard, Princeton, Yale, Oxford, Hamburg, Northeastern, Tufts, and the University of Sussex. Italy conferred upon him in March, 1963, the order of Cavaliere di Gran Croce dell'Ordine della Repubblica Italiana, highest of the five classes of this order. In April, 1963, he was awarded the insignia of Grand Officer of the French Legion d'Honneur. In 1963, he was also appointed Great Officer of the Order of Oranje-Nassau, a Netherlands honor, and received a decoration from the Republique Islamique de Mauritania. Mr. Black was born in Atlanta, Georgia, in 1898. He holds an A.B. (1918) from the University of Georgia and was elected to Phi Beta Kappa. During World War I, he served in the U.S. Navy. (INTERNATIONAL DEVELOPMENT REVIEW: "So Hopeful a Challenge," October, 1959.)

ROBERT BRITTAIN° is a free-lance writer, at present doing research in London. Educated at Oklahoma University (B.A.) and Princeton University (M.A. and Ph.D.), he taught for a number of years at Queens College in New York, at Columbia University, at Ohio State University, and elsewhere. As a writer and lecturer, he has been much concerned with problems of international development; his principal book in this field, Let There Be Bread, is in print in seven languages. In 1961, Dr. Brittain prepared for the Food and Agriculture Organization a report called "The Role of Education and Training in Agricultural and Economic Development"; in 1963, he was responsible for

Volume II, *Natural Resources*, in the series *Science and Technology for Development*, published by the United Nations and based on the United Nations Conference on Applications of Science and Technology for the Benefit of Less-Developed Areas, held in Geneva in February, 1963. (INTERNATIONAL DEVELOPMENT REVIEW: "An Alternative Approach to Mass Education," December, 1962.)

HENRY C. BUSH° is currently (since August, 1963) adviser to the National Institute of Administration, Office of the President, Republic of Vietnam. Previously, he had been a U.S. AID technician serving as adviser on training with the Ministry of the Interior in Indonesia. He had also worked with the Indonesian Ministry of Home Affairs as a public administration adviser under ICA auspices. Between 1956 and 1959, he served as director of ICA programs for groups of Indonesian local officials at Wayne State University and, in 1958, was adviser on similar programs at that university for groups of Brazilian local officials. In 1951–53, he taught at Hirosaki University, Japan; in 1953–54, at the University of Alabama; in 1954–56, at Hunter College, New York. He has also lived in India (1944–46) and in parts of southwest China (1946). Dr. Bush classifies himself professionally as a teacher of political science specializing in Asia, international relations, and comparative bureaucracies (especially Asian). Born in 1916, he holds A.B., M.A., and Ph.D. degrees from the University of Chicago. He is co-author of *American Government: The Clash of Issues* (Prentice-Hall, 1960), and contributing author to *Modern Society* (Prentice-Hall, 1959, 2d ed.). He co-authored three books on administration and related fields published by the Republic of Indonesia, and was editor of *Background on World Politics*, 1957–59. He has contributed to the Manchester *Guardian*, *Public Opinion Quarterly*, the *Journal of Politics*, and other journals. (INTERNATIONAL DEVELOPMENT REVIEW: "Transplanting Administrative Techniques," October, 1960.)

ANTONIO CARILLO FLORES, Ambassador of Mexico to the U.S.A., has had a crowded career, of which only a few highlights can be given in a brief space. Born in Mexico City in 1909, and graduating in 1929 from the University of Mexico as Dr. of Law, he was professor of law and administration at the University for fifteen years, professor in the National School of Economics for five years, and director of the National School of Jurisprudence for two years. He held various posts in the Federal Justice Administration, was magistrate and founder of the Federal Fiscal Court, and, for the past twenty years, has devoted his time mainly to Mexican financial administration. His duties in this field have included service as a member of the Board of Directors of the Bank of Mexico, director general of credit in the Department of the Treasury, director general of Nacional Financiera (National Finance Corporation), and Secretary of the Treasury. He has been Mexican delegate (and frequently served as chairman) at many economic and financial conferences of inter-American or world scope, including the United Nations, FAO, the Board of Governors of the World Bank and the International Monetary Fund, the Inter-American Economic and Social Council, and the Inter-American Economic Conference. Author of "Economics and the Rights of Man in the Constitution of Mexico," "The Juridical Defense of Private Citizens before the Administration in Mexico," and numerous monographs, Ambassador Carillo Flores has been decorated by the governments of Belgium, France, the Netherlands, Germany, and Italy. (INTERNATIONAL DEVELOPMENT REVIEW: "Unsolved Financing Problems," May, 1960.)

MILTON J. ESMAN° is professor of Public and International Economic Affairs at the University of Pittsburgh Graduate School of Public and International Affairs, where he directs the education and research program in economic and social development, focusing on the less industrialized nations of Asia, Africa, and Latin America. Dr. Esman holds an A.B. in government from Cornell and a Ph.D. in politics from Princeton. During the United States occupation of Japan, he served as civil affairs officer on General MacArthur's headquarters staff in Tokyo, specializing in executive and legislative reorganizational problems. Dr. Esman has conducted research with the United States Civil Service Commission as a program planning officer and with the Johns Hopkins University Operations Research Office. He spent four years as an intelligence research officer in the U.S. Department of State and subsequently headed the Cambodian-Laotian desk (and later the Vietnamese desk) in the Agency for International Development. His last assignment before going to Pittsburgh was that of program officer for the U.S. aid program in Vietnam. (INTERNATIONAL DEVELOPMENT REVIEW: "Institution Building in National Development," December, 1962.)

HENRY W. FAIRCHILD° has until recently been associate professor in the department of natural resources, Michigan State University, East Lansing, and, beginning in 1959, was adviser to the Pakistan Academy for Village Development, Comilla, East Pakistan—a Ford Foundation-sponsored project of the Pakistani Government. In 1954–59, he served in Korea with the International Cooperation Administration as agricultural adviser and, subsequently, as head of agricultural economics activities. Previously, he had taught soil science at Michigan State University and at West Virginia University. Dr. Fairchild was born in 1921. (INTERNATIONAL DEVELOPMENT REVIEW: "Cooperative vs. Commune," March, 1962.)

382 *Notes on the Contributors*

HARALD FREDERIKSEN,° M.D., has been with the U.S. Public Health Service since 1949. He is currently serving as adviser to the National Malaria Eradication Program of the Government of India. In 1959, he was appointed program officer of the Division of International Health after assignments in the U.S.A., United Kingdom, Bolivia, and Iran. As director of the Inter-American Cooperative Health Service in Bolivia, he was instrumental in the eradication of smallpox there. For his service in Iran, he received the Arthur S. Fleming Award (U.S.A.) in 1955. He has published articles in journals of public health and tropical medicine on smallpox, interference between viruses, and the role of health in economic and demographic transition. Born in Cristobal, Panama Canal Zone, in 1924, he received his elementary schooling there and his secondary education in Austria and Denmark. During the war, in an area under German occupation, he was a catalyst for the development of a network of resistance groups. Subsequently arrested by the Gestapo, he was liberated at the end of the war. A graduate of the Medical Faculty of the University of Vienna (M.D., 1948), he completed his internship at the Public Health Service Hospital in New York in 1950. He holds postgraduate degrees from the University of Liverpool (C.P.H., 1951), Harvard University (M.P.H., 1953), Liverpool School of Tropical Medicine (D.T.M. & H., 1954), and the Certification in Public Health by the Board of Preventive Medicine (1956). (INTERNATIONAL DEVELOPMENT REVIEW: "Mortality Rates and Economic Development," March, 1962.)

EDWARD T. HALL is currently professor of anthropology at the Illinois Institute of Technology in Chicago. Born in Webster Groves, Missouri, in 1914, he received his Ph.D. in anthropology at Columbia in 1942. From 1950–55, he served with the U.S. State Department's Point Four Training Program, where he trained technicians for service overseas. He has taught at the University of Denver, Bennington College, the Johns Hopkins School for Advanced International Studies, and the Washington School of Psychiatry. In 1962, he was the Leatherbee Lecturer at the Harvard Business School. In addition to teaching and research, Professor Hall serves as a consultant to business and government agencies with international operations. (INTERNATIONAL DEVELOPMENT REVIEW: "What Underdeveloped Countries Do Not Want," October, 1959.)

GOVE HAMBIDGE,° writer and editor, was with the Food and Agriculture Organization for eleven years, first as director of information and later as North American regional representative; with the United States Department of Agriculture for ten years as editor of the Yearbook of Agriculture and coordinator of research information; a freelance writer for ten years; a Hearst magazine editor for five years; and a publicist and book and magazine editor for ten years. He is the author of *Time to Live, Enchanted Acre, Six Rooms, The Prime of Life, Your Meals and Your Money, New Aims in Education, The Story of FAO,* and numerous magazine articles, radio broadcasts, and reports. Born in Kansas City, Missouri, in 1890, he received his B.A. degree at Columbia University in 1913 and has had a Pulitzer scholarship, a Carnegie Corporation grant, and the Lord & Taylor Design-for-Living award. A founder of SID, he was its first executive secretary and editor of the REVIEW. He is currently editor emeritus.

SHAMSUL HAQ was special officer for village development in the Pakistan Academy for Village Development in Comilla, East Pakistan, from 1960–63. Born in Dacca in 1910, he was graduated from Dacca University in 1933 and served for twenty-one years in the Cooperative Department of the government. In 1954, he entered the East Pakistan civil service and was successively deputy magistrate, circle officer, and trial judge until 1960, when he was selected by the Academy, because of his reputation as an organizer of cooperatives, to spearhead village organization work in the new pilot project. He is the author of many reports and various articles on cooperation. Mr. Haq retired from government service in mid-1963 but has maintained his connection with the Academy and is serving as deputy director of its Central Cooperative Association. (INTERNATIONAL DEVELOPMENT REVIEW: "Cooperative vs. Commune," March, 1962.)

F. F. HILL has been vice-president of the Ford Foundation in charge of the international programs since October, 1955. He was Provost of Cornell University from 1952–55, culminating a long association with that institution, which he first served as an instructor in land economics in 1930–33. United States Government service intervened for seven years, but he returned to Cornell in 1940 as professor of land economics and became head of the Department of Agricultural Economics in 1943. From 1933 to 1940, he was with the U.S. Farm Credit Administration, of which he became governor in 1938. (INTERNATIONAL DEVELOPMENT REVIEW: "Education: Key Issues for Policy Makers," December, 1962.)

JOHN FRED HILLIARD is currently on leave from the Ford Foundation to serve as deputy assistant administrator of the U.S. Agency for International Development. He has been consultant on manpower with the overseas development program of the Ford Foundation since 1959 and also served until recently as the Foundation's representative in the United Arab Republic. Previously, he had been co-chairman of the National Labor-Management Manpower Policy Committee (1957–58), manpower adviser to the government of India (1956–57), manpower adviser to the U.S. ambassador to NATO (1955), deputy assistant director and assistant director of the Office of Defense Mobilization (1953–59), and chief of program development of the Defense Manpower Administration (1950–53). In 1945–47, he was a delegate to the U.N. Conference of International Organizations. Born in Falls County, Texas, in 1911, he holds a B.S. degree from Texas A & M College (1932) and was a postgraduate student there in 1934–35. (INTERNATIONAL DEVELOPMENT REVIEW: "Manpower Planning," March, 1962.)

PAUL G. HOFFMAN° has been managing director of the United Nations Special Fund since 1958. Business executive, corporation trustee, and economic liberal, he is no stranger to public service. He started with the Studebaker Corporation as an automobile salesman in 1911, and by 1935, was president of the company. From 1942 to 1948, he was board chairman of the Committee for Economic Development. In 1948, President Truman appointed him to head the Economic Cooperation Administration (ECA), the first of the U.S. "foreign aid" agencies set up to administer the European Recovery Program—the Marshall Plan. (Its successors were MSA, FOA, ICA, AID.) In 1951–53, Mr. Hoffman was the first president of the Ford Foundation, and, in 1956–57, he was a member of the U.S. delegation to the U.N. He is a director of various corporations, including the Encyclopaedia Brittanica, and of the Fund for the Republic and the Institute for International Order. Born in Chicago, Illinois, in 1891, he holds honorary degrees from the University of California at Los Angeles, Columbia, Harvard, Yale, and other universities. He has received the Freedom House Award as well as numerous other awards. Mr. Hoffman was elected president of SID in 1963.

ROBERT W. HUDGENS,° originator of "supervised credit," retired in 1963 as president of International Development Services, Inc., which he founded in 1953. In 1942–47, he was director of the American International Association for Economic and Social Development. Under Hudgens' direction, AIA's program of technical assistance was established in health, nutrition, agriculture, public administration, credit, and education. In 1934–39, he was director of the southeastern region of the USDA Farm Security Administration and served as associate administrator of FSA in 1939–46. He was a member of the firm of Alester G. Furman Co., investment bankers of Greenville, South Carolina, from 1922 to 1934. In 1933, he became chairman of the Greenville chapter of the American Red Cross. He initiated the rural rehabilitation program that first combined credit and education in the form later known as supervised credit—an institutional device that was extensively used by FSA and has since spread over much of the world.

Mr. Hudgens has been Visiting Lecturer at Syracuse University and Regents Lecturer at the University of California. Born in Laurens, South Carolina, in 1896, he was graduated from The Citadel in 1915. He was a founder of SID, its first president, and chairman of the Interim Commission. (INTERNATIONAL DEVELOPMENT REVIEW: "Essentials of Land Reform," October, 1961.)

HUGH L. KEENLEYSIDE° is co-chairman of the British Columbia Hydro and Power Authority. Previously, he had been chairman of the British Columbia Power Commission and adviser to the government of British Columbia on resource development policies. In 1950–59, he was director-general of the United Nations Technical Assistance Administration and then became U.N. undersecretary for Public Administration, retiring in the same year to return to Canada. Prior to joining the U.N. staff, he had served as deputy minister of Canada's Department of Mines and Resources (and subsequently of the Department of Resources and Development); Canadian ambassador to Mexico; assistant undersecretary of state for External Affairs; and counselor and first secretary of the Department of External Affairs—a post which took him to Tokyo for about eight years of service in Japan. He has served on a number of international councils and commissions, including the Arctic Research Advisory Committee (chairman), the Advisory Committee on Northern Development, and the Advisory Panel on Atomic Energy. A member of many learned and professional societies, a director of the Toronto-Dominion Bank, and a member of the senate of the University of British Columbia, he holds a B.A. degree from that university, M.A. and Ph.D. degrees from Clark University (Massachusetts), and honorary degrees from seven colleges and universities. He was born in Toronto, Ontario, in 1898. Mr. Keenleyside was elected president of SID at its first international conference in 1959. (INTERNATIONAL DEVELOPMENT REVIEW: "Obstacles and Means in International Development," October, 1959.)

AKHTER HAMEED KHAN has been director of the Pakistan Academy for Village Development at Comilla, East Pakistan, since 1958. Previously, he had served as administrator of Village Agricultural and Industrial Development (V-AID) in East Pakistan; as principal of Comilla Victoria College; as a school teacher in Jamia Millia, Delhi; and for several years as a member of the Indian Civil Service. Born in 1915, he has an M.A. degree in English literature from the University of Agra (India) and studied for two years at Cambridge University as a member of the ICS. His special fields of interest are economics, religion, political science, and classical languages. Mr. Khan spent about nine months in the U.S.A. in 1958. He received the 1963 Magsaysay Award for "his inspiring personal commitment of experience and energy to scientific testing and application of a workable formula for rural emancipation among his people." (INTERNATIONAL DEVELOPMENT REVIEW: "Mobilizing Village Leadership," September, 1962.)

ALBERT LEPAWSKY° is professor of political science at the University of California, Berkeley. He has been on intermittent U.N. assignments since 1950 and has carried out assignments for the Agency for International Development. A recent foreign post was that of director of the Regional Training Center for United Nations Fellows at Vancouver, Canada. This project, launched in 1959, was a joint undertaking of the University of British Columbia, the government of Canada, and the United Nations, designed to experiment throughout western Canada and the United States with more effective methods of international training, to help with the recruiting of experts from this region of North America for service abroad, and to conduct international seminars on subjects related to development. Rosalind Lepawsky has worked closely with her husband on the complex training problems involved and has written newspaper articles on Mexican developments. (INTERNATIONAL DEVELOPMENT REVIEW: "Enskilling People," October, 1961.)

RAYMOND F. MIKESELL° is W. E. Miner Professor of Economics and associate director of the Institute of International Studies and Overseas Administration of the University of Oregon. He is also director of the overseas research and training program carried out by the university in cooperation with other universities and with Latin American institutes. The program began in 1960 and is financed by a Ford Foundation grant. Among some thirty special assignments during the past several years, Dr. Mikesell has served as consultant to the U.S. Department of State; member of the Advisory Committee of the U.S. Council, International Chamber of Commerce, and of an advisory committee of the U.S. Senate Interstate and Foreign Commerce Committee. He has been project director of a U.S. Senate Foreign Relations Committee study of Latin American economic development; seminar director of a Ford Foundation regional faculty research seminar; project director of a University of Oregon study of U.S. postwar foreign investment experience, financed by the Ford Foundation; member of the working group on the common market, ECLA; consultant to the Pan American Union; and staff member and consultant of the President's Council of Economic Advisers. Prior to coming to Oregon in 1957, he had been professor of economics in the University of Virginia for eleven years, economist in the U.S. Treasury Department, and Treasury attaché at Cairo. Born in Eaton, Ohio, in 1913, he holds the degrees of B.A. (1935), M.A. (1935), and Ph.D. (1939) from Ohio State University. He is the author of many books, monographs, and articles on economics, especially in the field of development and international trade. (INTERNATIONAL DEVELOPMENT REVIEW: "Possible Approaches to Country-Level Coordination of Lending," June, 1961.)

A. K. M. MOHSEN has been training officer at the Comilla Academy in East Pakistan since 1959, after serving in the same post at Dacca in the Village Agricultural Industrial Development (V-AID) program, which he joined in 1956. Previously, he had been a member of the East Pakistan Civil Service (1949–56) and before independence had served the government of Bengal. Born in 1921, he has an M.A. degree in economics from the University of Dacca. (INTERNATIONAL DEVELOPMENT REVIEW: "Mobilizing Village Leadership," September, 1962.)

TEODORO MOSCOSO° is Director of the Banco de Ponce, Puerto Rico, and a member of the Committee on the Political Status of Puerto Rico. Previously (1961–63), he had been U.S. coordinator of the Alliance for Progress. He was U.S. ambassador to Venezuela (1961); head of Puerto Rico's Economic Development Administration (1950–61); and president of its predecessor, the Puerto Rico Industrial Development Company (1941–50). Thus, he was the first director of Puerto Rico's famous Operation Bootstrap—a post he held continuously for some twenty years. Earlier, he had been Administrator of Housing for Puerto Rico, after serving as head of the Ponce municipal housing authority (for low-income groups), which he joined in 1938. Mr. Moscoso came to public service via his father's drugstore in Ponce, of which he became general manager and, later, head of the Moscoso wholesale drug company. Born in Barcelona, Spain, in 1910 (his parents were U.S. citizens), he attended the Philadelphia College of Pharmacy and the University of Michigan (B.S., 1932).

BRAJ KUMAR NEHRU has been ambassador from India to the U.S.A. since September, 1961. Previously, he was India's commissioner-general for Economic Affairs. A distinguished member of the Indian Civil Service, often described as his country's "roving economic ambassador," Mr. Nehru started his official career upon joining the Indian Civil Service in 1934 as assistant commissioner in the government of the Punjab. In 1939, he was posted at the Union Government's headquarters as undersecretary to the Department of Education, Health, and Lands. Thereafter, he joined the Department of Finance and, after serving in that ministry in different capacities, was appointed secretary to the Department of Economic Affairs in 1957. Earlier, from 1949 to 1954, he was stationed in Washington as executive director of the International Bank for Reconstruction and Development. He also served as minister of the Embassy in Washington. Ambassador Nehru has been connected very closely with the formulation and execution of plans for the economic development of India and simultaneously has been intimately associated with international affairs. He represented India at the Reparations Conference in 1945 and at various Commonwealth Finance Ministers' Conferences. Mr. Nehru also represented India at the U.N. General Assembly from 1949 to 1952 and again in 1960, and at the Bandung Conference of Asian and African States in 1955. He was a member of the United Nations Advisory Committee on Administration and Budgetary Questions from 1951 to 1953 and is at present a member of the U.N. Investments Committee. He was born in Allahabad in 1909, and was educated at the University of Allahabad, the London School of Economics, Oxford's Balliol College, and the Inner Temple, London. (INTERNATIONAL DEVELOPMENT REVIEW: "A Rational Approach to Foreign Assistance," October, 1960.)

MALCOLM D. RIVKIN° is a planning consultant in Boston. A graduate of Harvard and MIT, he was a Fulbright Scholar in the Netherlands in 1953–54 and later was resident planner at Cleveland's University Circle Development Project. He was planning officer of MIT from 1958–60, and became, in 1960, a consultant in regional planning from the Organization for Economic Cooperation and Development to the Turkish Government, a position he held for two years. In 1964 he was appointed an associate in Robert R. Nathan Associates, Washington, D.C. (INTERNATIONAL DEVELOPMENT REVIEW: "Let's Think Small for Development," March, 1963.)

H. W. SINGER° joined the U.N. Secretariat in 1947 and is now principal officer in the Department of Economic and Social Affairs. In 1961, he was chairman of an expert committee, set up by FAO to develop plans for the use of surplus food, which prepared a memorandum called "Development Through Food: A Strategy of Surplus Utilization." He has been attached at various times to the U.N. Economic Commission for Africa in Ethiopia and the Economic Commission for Asia and the Far East in Thailand and has participated in U.N. missions in Brazil, Turkey, and the Philippines, as well as in the recent conference of the International Economic Association in Addis Ababa, where he presented a paper called "Small-Scale Industry in African Economic Development." A British subject, born in 1910, he holds a diploma from Bonn University and a Ph.D. from Cambridge (1936). Dr. Singer is a visiting professor of economics in the graduate faculty of the New School for Social Research, New York, and a faculty associate of Columbia University and has lectured at many universities in various parts of the world. He is author and co-author of a number of books and reports and of many articles in professional journals. (INTERNATIONAL DEVELOPMENT REVIEW: "Use and Abuse of Local Counterpart Funds," October, 1961.)

MENDON W. SMITH is trust officer in the Long Island Trust Co., Garden City, New York. Previously (1952–63), he had held the same post in the First National Bank and Trust Co., Ithaca, New York and (1948–52) was investment analyst in the First National City Bank of New York. Born in Springfield, Massachusetts, in 1925, he is a graduate of Harvard (A.B., 1947) and the Stonier Graduate School of Banking at Rutgers University (1960). He has contributed articles to financial journals and is an avocational student of history, with a special interest in the structure of revolutions and the social, economic, and political action needed to prevent them before they start. (INTERNATIONAL DEVELOPMENT REVIEW: "Recipe for International Investment," October, 1961.)

WILLIAM C. SMITH is acting assistant professor of anthropology, University of California, Davis, and president of the Kroeber Anthropological Association. In 1962, he completed a year's field work in anthropology in Michoacán, Mexico, and taught in the University of California, Berkeley, in the summer of 1963. Born in Monroe, Louisiana, in 1932, he served in the Far East during the Korean War and, after a year of study in Mexico City, entered the University of California, where he received his B.A. degree (Phi Beta Kappa with highest honors) in 1959. He is interested particularly in the application of anthropological method and theory in community and industrial organization. (INTERNATIONAL DEVELOPMENT REVIEW: "Hens That Laid Golden Eggs," October, 1961.)

EUGENE STALEY,° a senior international economist at Stanford Research Institute, is director of basic research in the Institute's International Development Center. In 1955–57, he served in India as consultant on industrial development (in particular, small industry and applied economic research) for the Ford Foundation and the Indian Government. Early in 1960, he revisited that country on a similar mission and in 1963 served as a member of the International Perspective Planning Team on Small Industries. In 1962, he headed a Stanford Research Institute team that helped the Banco Popular and other institutions in Colombia to draw up a small-industry development program; he has also served as a consultant on small-industry development in other countries. Other assignments have included directing a study in 1952 for the Council on Foreign Relations on political implications of economic development; organizing the program for the conference on human values in industrial society (jointly sponsored in 1951 by the Corning Glass Works and the American Council of Learned Societies); and serving as chief economist with the World Bank's mission to Cuba in 1950. Previously, he had been instrumental in forming the World Affairs Council of Northern California (1947) and participated in the research program of Stanford University's Hoover Institution on War, Revolution and Peace. A consultant to the U.S. Budget Bureau in 1941 and an economist in the State Department in 1942, he assisted in the establishment of the U.N. Relief and Rehabilitation Administration, was sent to China by UNRRA, and served as a member of the international secretariat of the U.N. Charter conference at San Francisco. A faculty member of the University of Chicago from 1931 to 1937, he also taught at the Graduate Institute of International Studies in Geneva, the Fletcher School of Law and Diplomacy, and the Johns Hopkins University School of Advanced International Studies. Dr. Staley has a B.A. degree *magna cum laude* from Hastings College (1925), and a Ph.D. from the University of Chicago (1928). He has studied at the Graduate Institute of International Studies in Geneva and other European institutions under a fellowship of the Social Science Research Council. His books include *War and the Private Investor* (1935), *Raw Materials in Peace and War* (1937), *World Economy in Transition* (1939), *Raw Material Problems and Policies* (1946), *World Economic Development* (1944), and *The Future of Underdeveloped Countries* (1954; revised and paperback edition, 1961). His latest book, *Modern Small Industry for Newly Industrializing Countries*, co-authored with Richard Morse, will appear early in 1964. (INTERNATIONAL DEVELOPMENT REVIEW: "Modern Small Industry," June, 1961.)

OM P. TANGRI° was born in Lahore, Pakistan (then India), in 1930. His undergraduate and M.A. work was done at Panjab University (Camp) College in New Delhi, India, and he received his M.A. in Economics in 1956. He did more than two years' research and field work on production, marketing, and resource development problems in certain community development areas in connection with his Master's thesis on the economics of the Bhakra Nangal project, a major multipurpose river valley project in northern India. In 1957, he joined the Giannini Foundation of Agricultural Economics at the University of California, Berkeley, to work for his Ph.D. in agricultural economics, carrying out a year's research on the development potential and limitations of U.S. Public Law 480 in India's agricultural program. Currently, he is an assistant professor in agricultural marketing at the University of Manitoba. (INTERNATIONAL DEVELOPMENT REVIEW: "India's Community Development Program," October, 1961.)

CLARENCE E. THURBER° is associate professor of political science and public administration at Pennsylvania State University. He is also chairman of an interuniversity committee administering the program of Study Fellowships for International Development, supported by the Ford Foundation. Previously, he had been program associate in the Ford Foundation's international training and research program. His earlier experience was in the U.S. Office of Strategic Services, the U.S. Department of State, and the Brookings Institution's international studies group. Born in Nampa, Idaho, in 1921, he took his graduate and undergraduate work at Stanford University, graduating in 1943. (INTERNATIONAL DEVELOPMENT REVIEW: "Training Administrators for Developing Countries," June, 1961.)

VICTOR L. URQUIDI,° born in 1919 and educated at the London School of Economics, was an economist with the Banco de México from 1940 to 1947, with the International Bank for Reconstruction and Development from 1947 to 1949, and with the Secretaría de Hacienda y Crédito Público of Mexico from 1949 to 1951. In 1951, he joined the staff of the United Nations Economic Commission for Latin America, serving as director of its Mexico City office from 1952 to 1958. He is now a consulting economist with the Banco de México and the Secretaría de Hacienda y Crédito Público. He was director of the magazine *El Trimestre Económico* from 1949 to 1958 and is the author of many works, including the widely translated *Trayectoria del mercado común latinoamericano*. (INTERNATIONAL DEVELOPMENT REVIEW: "Legislation for Economic Development in Latin America," March, 1963.)

HENRY A. WALLACE,° editor, author, plant breeder, and agricultural expert, was U.S. Secretary of Agriculture from 1933 to 1940, Vice-President of the U.S.A., 1941–45, Secretary of Commerce, 1945–46, and candidate for President in 1948. From 1910 to 1924, he was associate editor of *Wallace's Farmer* and then served as editor of that paper, and the merged *Wallace's Farmer and Iowa Homestead*, until 1933. He is the author of *Corn and Its Early Fathers* (with Dr. Brown) and *Corn and the Midwestern Farmer*, 1956; *Toward World Peace*, 1948; *Sixty Million Jobs*, 1945; *Democracy Reborn*, 1944; *The Century of the Common Man*, 1943; *The American Choice* and *Price of Freedom*, 1940; *Paths to Plenty*, 1938; *Technology, Corporations, and the General Welfare*, 1937; *Whose Constitution*, 1936; *New Frontiers, Statesmanship and Religion*, and *America Must Choose*, 1934; *Correlation and Machine Calculation*, 1924; *Corn and Corn Growing*, 1923; *Agricultural Prices*, 1920. (INTERNATIONAL DEVELOPMENT REVIEW: "The Most Important Investment," May, 1960.)

ANNE WINSLOW is head of the Research and Publications Department of the Carnegie Endowment for International Peace, and the Endowment's editor-in-chief. She has been associated with the Endowment since 1947. Previously, she had worked with the Commission to Study the Organization of Peace, Group Health Cooperative, Medical Administration Service, and the Frontier Nursing Service. Between 1952 and 1960, Miss Winslow was an officer of the International Conference of Consultative Non-Governmental Organizations, and she is currently a member of the board of directors of the Public Affairs Committee. (INTERNATIONAL DEVELOPMENT REVIEW: "The Technical-Assistance Expert," September, 1962.)

ABEL WOLMAN° is emeritus professor of engineering at the Johns Hopkins University; lecturer and professor at Harvard, Princeton, the University of Chicago, and other universities; and consulting engineer to many U.S. cities and organizations, including Baltimore, Detroit, Jacksonville, Miami, Seattle, the U.S. Public Health Service, the U.S. Army, the U.S. Atomic Energy Commission, the National Research Council, the American Red Cross, the Tennessee Valley Authority, the Pan American Sanitary Bureau, the Association of American Railroads, and the Bethlehem Steel Co. He is a member of the National Academy of Sciences and has been president of the American Waterworks Association and the American Public Health Association. Born in Baltimore in 1892, Dr. Wolman holds the degree of Doctor of Engineering from Johns Hopkins. In 1952, he received the Lasker Award. (INTERNATIONAL DEVELOPMENT REVIEW: "New Directions for Public Health," October, 1961.)

The Society for International Development (SID)*

Originator of the idea of a Society for International Development: ROBERT L. OSHINS.

Volunteer Organizing Committee: January-October, 1957. Ten members.

First Organizing Conference: October 19, 1957, Washington, D.C. Sixty participants.

Interim Commission, set up by the conference to establish SID: *Chairman*: ROBERT W. HUDGENS; *Executive Secretary*: GOVE HAMBIDGE; *Treasurer*: JEROME JACOBSON; *General Counsel*: PHILIP M. GLICK; *Draftsmen of SID Constitution*: PHILIP M. GLICK, MARION CLAWSON; *Incorporators of SID*: ROBERT E. ASHER, PHILIP M. GLICK, MICHAEL L. HOFFMAN; *Date of incorporation*: January, 1958.

Elected Officers of SID, *in order of succession*:

President: ROBERT W. HUDGENS (1958); HUGH L. KEENLEYSIDE (1959); P. S. N. PRASAD (1960); JOSÉ ANTONIO MAYOBRE (1961–62); PAUL G. HOFFMAN (1963–65).

Vice-President: P. S. N. PRASAD; ARTHUR T. MOSHER; HENRY VAN ZILE HYDE; MARION CLAWSON.

Regional Vice-President: *Africa*, ROBERT K. GARDINER; *Asia*, RAMON BINAMIRA; K. S. KRISHNASWAMY; K. B. MADHAVA; *Europe*, EGBERT DE VRIES; *Latin America*, RAUL PREBISCH; FELIPE HERRERA; *North America*, HENRY VAN ZILE HYDE; LUTHER H. EVANS; MICHAEL L. HOFFMAN.

Appointed Officers, *in order of succession*:

Executive Secretary: GOVE HAMBIDGE; ROBERT L. OSHINS; MARION CLAWSON; ANDREW E. RICE.

Assistant Executive Secretary: PASTOR B. SISON.

Treasurer: JEROME JACOBSON; IRVING S. FRIEDMAN.

General Counsel: PHILIP M. GLICK.

Editor: GOVE HAMBIDGE; ANDREW E. RICE.

Editor Emeritus: GOVE HAMBIDGE.

* As of July, 1964.

Governing body: A Council of fifteen elected members. Elected officers of SID are also Council members ex officio.

International conferences: Washington, D.C., 1959, 1960, 1961, 1962. New York, 1963. Washington, 1964.

Chapters: Ankara, Athens, Bogota, Bombay, Boston, Calcutta, Columbia University (Student), Indiana, Israel, Khartoum, Madras, Manila, Michigan, New York, Nigeria, Puerto Rico, Rome, San Francisco Bay Area, Southern California, Switzerland, Washington, D.C.

Journal: The INTERNATIONAL DEVELOPMENT REVIEW (quarterly).

Address: 1346 Connecticut Avenue, N.W., Washington, D.C., 20036, U.S.A.

INDEX